THE

MONEY CULT

THE

MONEY CULT

CAPITALISM, CHRISTIANITY, AND THE UNMAKING
OF THE AMERICAN DREAM

CHRIS LEHMANN

MELVILLE HOUSE
BROOKLYN · LONDON

THE MONEY CULT

Copyright © 2016 by Chris Lehmann
First Melville House Printing: May 2016

Melville House Publishing   8 Blackstock Mews
        46 John Street   and   Islington
    Brooklyn, NY 11201   London N4 2BT

mhpbooks.com   facebook.com/mhpbooks   @melvillehouse

Library of Congress Cataloging-in-Publication Data
Names: Lehmann, Chris, author.
Title: The money cult : capitalism, Christianity, and the unmaking of
    the American dream / Chris Lehmann.
Description: Brooklyn, NY : Melville House, [2016]
Identifiers: LCCN 2016001439| ISBN 9781612195087 (hardback) |
    ISBN 9781612195094 (ebook)
Subjects: LCSH: Capitalism—Religious aspects—Christianity. |
    Capitalism—United States—History. | Christianity—Economic
    aspects—United States—History. | Wealth—Religious
    aspects—Christianity. | Christianity—United States—History. |
    BISAC: HISTORY / United States / General. | BUSINESS &
    ECONOMICS / Economic History. | RELIGION / History.
Classification: LCC BR115.C3 L44 2016 | DDC 261.8/50973—dc23
LC record available at http://lccn.loc.gov/2016001439

Design by Marina Drukman

Printed in the United States of America
1   3   5   7   9   10   8   6   4   2

To Deborah, without whom . . . nothing

In the Middle Ages priests spoke only of the other life; they scarcely worried about proving that a sincere Christian can be a happy man here below. But American preachers constantly come back to earth and only with great trouble can they take their eyes off it . . . It is often difficult to know when listening to them if the principal object of religion is to procure eternal felicity in the other world or well-being in this one.

—ALEXIS DE TOCQUEVILLE

CONTENTS

Introduction

PAY TO PRAY

In the midst of a recent slew of personal trials, I got a hand-addressed letter, in a gray greeting-card envelope. When I glanced at the envelope's Houston postmark, I scoured my memory to think of anyone I knew in that sprawling east-Texas metropolis. Maybe one of the confidants I'd corresponded with during my painful, still-pending divorce had moved? Idly, I opened the envelope expecting to be greeted with some friend's report of a new job, new relationship, or new research sabbatical in the Southwest.

Instead, the greeting card inside bore a simple inscription on its front: the word "hope," in a white reverse-type cursive script, just above a name that, for many Protestant believers in America today, is a virtual synonym for that elusive, serene condition: "Joel Osteen."

Osteen is the beaming, gently drawling prophet of the new millennial prosperity gospel—or the theology of abundance, as he's more decorously given to call it. Sermons from his Houston megachurch, Lakewood—the former Compaq Center, a 16,000-seat sports arena where the Houston Rockets once played—are broadcast to millions of viewers every Sunday. And his core message is that the Christian God is an indulgent, amply rewarding father, doling out unlimited success to his devoted followers. "Why put limits on God?" is a frequent refrain in Osteen's preaching—and it's meant to convey that God, in turn, intends to place no limits on your own worldly success and achievement.

This was very much the message that came appended to my own quasi-personalized greeting card. Beneath a hand-scrawled salutation, the body of the card opened with a scripture quotation, from Proverbs 13:12:

"Hope deferred makes the heart sick, but a dream fulfilled is a tree of life." Osteen then assured me that he and Victoria—his wife and co-minister—"believe with all our hearts that God wants your dream to come true."

To speed God's plan along, the Osteens proposed to recite a personal prayer on my behalf. Perhaps, they said, my dream was "to have a family or . . . see someone in your family healed." Or "maybe it's to have a home or new job. Whatever your dream is," the pitch continued, "you must know God cares and so do we. I've enclosed a small card for you to write your dream on and send back to us. We want to pray for you. We believe in the power of prayer!"

That last exclamation seemed a bit defensive—as though I might doubt the efficacy of the Osteens' own faith in their chosen method. In reality, though, it was the prelude to the main pitch: "As you write down your dream, I am asking you to invest in a dream"—the further expansion of the Osteen ministry. "Your gift will allow people to hear the Gospel, experience the unconditional love of Jesus and discover God's plans for their lives. That's a dream worthy of your best gift." For good measure, my anonymous pen-wielding correspondent in Houston had appended a handwritten note: "Chris, Please give your best gift. The message of hope is making a difference! God bless!"

Sure enough, alongside the blank index card that was to carry my dream (together with my name and my email address) to the Osteen ministry, there was a handsome form that offered a pair of premiums in exchange for my prayer-enabling donation; a contribution of any size would yield an "inspiring 4-message CD/DVD resource" called "With You For You," whereas a gift of more than $125 would net a special leather-bound edition of Osteen's *Hope for Today* Bible. On the reverse side of the form, where you filled in your credit card information, you were nudged further into setting aside monthly donations, to be automatically debited on your card, with a helpful disclaimer explaining that "IRS regulations permit you to deduct contributions in excess of the fair market value of goods received from this ministry. Your full contribution benefits the expansion of Joel Osteen Ministries."

This random fund-raising encounter forms a perfect set piece in what

I've come to call the Money Cult: the frank celebration of wealth as a spiritual virtue in American Protestantism. The Osteen operation, no slouch in divining the soft spot in a marketing appeal, knew that I might be in search of some badly needed life affirmation—and, perhaps, new spiritual support: I had, the month earlier, attended the couple's "Night of Hope" rally in the Washington Nationals' stadium, on an assignment from Salon. com. And it's true that in my own personal distress, I had picked up their cleverly packaged appeal under the vague impression that it might contain, if not a message of hope, then at least a welcome personal missive.

What I got instead was, in many ways, what the core message of popular Protestant faith has boiled down to in post-meltdown America: a contract to pray my way into a better life in exchange for a "best gift" that would ideally be somewhere north of $125—or better yet, a tax-deductible tithing arrangement of indefinite duration. Such appeals are now so common in the materially expansive faith of Protestant culture in America that they pass unremarked; the Osteens send out countless such fund-raising pitches, and our pulpits and bestseller lists abound with a gospel of spiritually self-made success. For the most part, all this glides serenely above the pinched and unyielding conditions of our actual political economy, which now largely confines the spread of prosperity to the already-prosperous. The message of a great deal of Protestant worship in the Osteen era plays a crucial role in mediating this awkward contradiction; why question any of the cartelized and cronyist arrangements that make up the market culture we casually idolize, when it is so self-evidently the handiwork of the Creator? By minting the promise of individual salvation into a precept of economic advancement, today's prophets of prosperity bypass entirely matters of economic justice as they pertain to Christian morality—while also embodying a new gospel of success that conflates material reward and punishment with the eternal, prophetic kind.

Protestant piety in the United States has had an often fulsome, occasionally fraught relationship to the quest for material wealth, but never before has it transacted a vision of spiritually sanctioned prosperity on such a blunt pay-to-play basis on such a vast scale. In the not-so-distant past, Oral Roberts—the most prominent prosperity minister in the postwar era—was treated as a late-night TV punchline for mounting a bald fund-raising pitch around the threat that the Lord would be calling Roberts home if he failed to meet his allotted quota of $8 million to rescue his eponymous Oklahoma-based university from a sea of red ink. Now, however, the link between the personal discipline exacted by one's faith and the promised expansion of one's bottom line is so casually reiterated in the evangelical world that it's become banal. In bestselling tracts such as Osteen's *Become a Better You*, Bruce Wilkinson's *Prayer of Jabez*, T. D. Jakes's *Strength to Stand*—to say nothing of the voluminous back catalog of evangelical success literature, from Bruce Barton's *The Man Nobody Knows* to Og Mandino's *The Greatest Salesman in the World*—true Christian observance is linked directly to individual wealth.

The Growth Gospel

There are countless ways to dismiss the individual spiritual entrepreneurs of the Osteen persuasion. They can be aspiring political power brokers, in the vein of Pat Robertson or the late Jerry Falwell. They can be garden-variety TV hucksters, like Jim and Tammy Faye Bakker. They can be purveyors of healing prayer and off-the-rack success mantras like Benny Hinn or Robert Schuller. Or they can be manic strategists of megachurch expansion, such as Rick Warren. In most of these scenarios, prosperity preachers are mere charlatans and hustlers, and their followers are credulous boobs; like the passing manias for certain social-media trends or mortgage-backed securities, they're taken-for-granted bubble indicators in the nation's marketplace of religious ideas.

But to characterize them like this is to miss the larger theological and practical Protestant embrace of market values—and a good deal of American religious history in the bargain. For one thing, the familiar caricature of the prosperity-minded minister-on-the-make is almost completely an individual character portrait, rather than a critical rendering of the institutional practices and ideas that lend such characters their charisma in the first place. Deriding high-profile preachers as nothing more than hucksters who prey on popular fears and superstitions may satisfy the very broad dictates of left-leaning secular cultural superiority, but it tells us almost nothing about what the *followers* of the new gospels of wealth actually think and believe—let alone how the Money Cult's distinctive gospel influences the culture at large.

These changes turn up most palpably in the numbers on American church growth. Three of the nation's four largest mega-churches ply a prosperity message, and the Mormon Church—which, as we shall see later, is a crucial vanguard faith in the Money Cult—has grown at a staggering pace over the past two decades. By some counts, Mormon congregations increased in size by 30 percent from 1996 to 2008—roughly twice the rate that the overall U.S. population grew at the same time. The most conservative estimates of Mormon Church growth show an annual increase of 18 percent, still rendering it the fastest-growing Christian denomination in the country. The next-highest rate of expansion—14.9 percent—occurred among the Assemblies of God, the denominational home of most Prosperity Gospel congregations. Meanwhile, the "mainline" Protestant churches—Methodists, Congregationalists, Presbyterians, and the like—saw their numbers decline by 12.8 percent, and Catholic congregations declined by 5 percent over the same period.[1]

This sort of steady growth doesn't stem from fly-by-night hucksterism. Rather than serving as gullible marks or on-the-make networkers in search of the main chance, the faithful adherents of the money cult are not that different from believers in other major religious traditions. They count on church sanctioned rituals and rites of passage to lend order to their lives, they look to sacred texts and orations to steady their faith amid the workaday challenges of modern living, and they are inspired by visions of eternal repose in reward for their virtuous conduct—even as they anticipate that the world at large is headed toward a great moment of reckoning for its sins.

It's difficult to disentangle the basic elements of the Money Cult faith from the insinuations of soul-profiteering, and for a simple reason: The Money Cult's modern consolidation coincided with, and in many ways directly fed, the rise of a distinctive secular sensibility within American culture. That development has made it easy for wised-up secular observers to dismiss the sanctification of market values as so much opportunistic claptrap, perpetrated by the oldest sort of con artist. And a corresponding strain of secular dismissal blames the credulous followers of Joel Osteen and his many forebears in our religious past: They are, and always have been, crass worshipers of Mammon, eager to seize on any available spiritual alibi to make the mythologies of American success appear not merely venerable, but sacred and foreordained.

Such shibboleths don't do remote justice to the real inner workings of our prosperity belief. They are too comfortable, too self-distancing, too easy. And most important, they don't offer any account of how Money Cult worship functions as a bona fide brand of faith—how it strives to impose order on the chaos of our inner lives; how it explains the recurrent spiritual mysteries of suffering, grace, and redemption; how it interprets the divine plan of cosmic history; how, in short, it charges believers to envision their materially striving selves as their better spiritual selves. What's more, the casual view of Protestant materialism as a plaything of hucksters, custom-made to shake down rubes and marks, gives us no coherent account of how it came to prominence within our theological history. One mid-twentieth-century journalistic survey of the prosperity faith neatly summed up this cynical and static posture of wised-up scoffing in its title: *God Is a Millionaire*. (Indeed, this title, by *Newsweek* reporter Richard R. Mathison, was originally published under the far more anodyne title *Faiths, Cults and Sects of America*, suggesting that the denunciation of the nation's pious fleecers follows its own sensational sort of market logic.)

In lieu of explaining significant historical and theological movements, the scoffers' narrative offers a plug-and-play account: Once they've choreographed this or that readymade mode of Mammon worship, they either collapse under the weight of their own divinely imbued hubris—in the way that popular modern revivalists always seem to, eventually—or they prosper and flourish according to the crass guidelines of their gospel, building new institutions, congregations, and missions, all cynically profiting from the guileless trust of the striving American masses unto a virtual eternity. In this view of things, no meaningful change in belief ever occurs, no theological ideas enter the picture, and no party to the transaction—hustler or rube—ever learns anything.

This stationary set piece elides just about every truly remarkable development that has radically reconfigured American Protestantism into something rare, strange, and infinitely adaptable to the market-based American culture of the main chance. What sets the Money Cult apart is how closely the *content* of this potent American offshoot of Protestant faith now mirrors so many of the baseline assumptions of consumer capitalism. In this curious vision of a world turned upside down, America's long-standing quest for the purified and restored version of true primitive Christian worship has produced the hulking megachurch and the spectacle-driven piety of the televangelist age. The social ethic of the New Testament—under which the poor were the true heirs to the planet, and early Christians held all property in common—has morphed into the prosperity gospel, which deems worldly success a direct sign of divine favor, and translates the ministry of Jesus into a battery of business stratagems and motivational slogans.

This far-reaching transformation hasn't occurred overnight, of course. Indeed, what makes it difficult to grasp the full sweep of the American Money Cult is that the typical rhythm of Protestant revivalism—with broad-based religious enthusiasm succumbing to backsliding and worldly temptation, eventually spurring a fresh revival that perpetuates the cycle—leaves each generation experiencing its own iteration of the Money Cult. So to appraise the full contours of the Protestant-capitalist alliance in America, we must also take fresh stock of many of the assumptions that have shaped our views of American Protestant history.

We think we know this story; it's the tale of how the "Protestant ethic" gave birth to the capitalist market economy. It begins with the Puritan believers who settled the colonies, and their obsessive quest for any sign of salvation from an unfathomably remote and imperious God, who thought nothing of consigning infants to eternal damnation on grounds of their alleged sinful natures. This intense, high-stakes spiritual anxiety had to find an outlet somewhere, and so, in the famous account of sociologist Max Weber, the Puritans hit upon the idea of a worldly "calling" as the prime testing ground for the individual believer's standing with the frightfully distant Calvinist God. The energies that New England Puritans ploughed into their callings created remarkable wealth. Material gain, weirdly enough, served as the most secure evidence that Puritans had aligned their hearts and souls with an otherwise maddeningly unknowable and immaterial God, who only worked obscurely through human institutions and human history to disclose his will.

These fiercely conflicting realms of mundane prosperity and heavenly assurance might have sowed tremendous confusion among a different kind of believing community: How could one really place one's entire faith in a worldly calling and its gains, when the baubles of wealth were a notorious temptation to pride, covetousness, and other sins? But the Puritans of North America couldn't afford to repudiate the worldly returns on their labor outright. Too much was riding on their fully realized callings, both in terms of the individual soul's disposition toward salvation, and the survival of colonial New England's "errand into the wilderness." So they turned their Yankee ingenuity on the far more ambitious—and unlikely—project of sanctifying the sphere of economic endeavor. The curious compound of self-denial and untrammeled business ambition that Weber called "worldly asceticism" was born—and so, in this account, was the distinctive ethic of modern capitalism. By stressing the steady accumulation of wealth and the vigilant suppression of vice and indulgent display, the Protestant ethic had given the calculating soul of capitalist enterprise a potent new spiritual home.

To clarify the broad contours of the narrative of Puritan decline, it helps to imagine it as a sort of diorama. The first panel might show one of those austere colonial New England chapels where even the display of a cross was held to be an untoward distraction from the high Puritan mission of earnest religious self-inspection; the chapel would be thronged with guilt-ridden pilgrim worshipers desperately seeking any sort of assurance for the future redemption of their sin-ravaged souls. The next panel— designed to illustrate the American colonies' spiritual growing pains as they sought to articulate a new national mission—might feature a bustling waterfront custom house, and perhaps George Whitefield and Jonathan Edwards, revivalists of the First Great Awakening, calling wayward believers, steeped in luxury and frivolities, back to the terrible awareness of sin that precedes a revived sense of God's loving grace. The final piece in this triptych would depict a boomtown bazaar, preferably in the center of one of the port cities feeding a steady stream of commerce into the Erie Canal—the federally subsidized waterway that long symbolized the promise of the rapidly expanding western frontier. Off to the side in this set piece, we might see a clutch of Methodist circuit riders, urging crowds of energetically moaning and singing common folk to shuck off the cold and sterile bonds of Calvinist predestinarian dogma. In this version of the decline narrative, theological forces tend to prefigure social change; raw Jacksonian democrats (and their Methodist keepers) rushed in, as it were, where angels had formerly tread.

From there on out, it was more or less a simple matter of time before the fragmenting logic of market individualism—urged on by the new order of laissez-faire religious competition that took hold after 1833, when Massachusetts became the last state to disestablish its Congregational church—stranded the bewildered, denatured heirs of the Puritan experiment on the farther shores of secular modernity. Thus was the great, soul-corroding process of religious alienation—what Weber famously dubbed "the disenchantment of the world"—unleashed on an unsuspecting republic.

But this familiar story is wrong, in several important ways. For one thing, by focusing so intently on the *origins* of our capitalist spirit, it fails to account for that spirit's distinctive—and not at all secularized—later development. The prolonged state of spiritual discontent that social critics and religious thinkers have long seen overtaking the older religious certainties of the Puritan age never actually came to pass. Instead of market forces briskly doing away with the old Puritan superstitions, a new brand of American faith invaded the New World's burgeoning new market economy.

In retrospect, as we'll see, the Puritans' coming-of-material age was not quite the surprise to the community of visible saints that Weber imagined it would be. To begin with, the Puritans had no monopoly on the stuff of material sanctification. Recent studies have disclosed far wider currents of an upstart gospel of wealth running through the popular folk-religious practices of the colonial era. These traditions placed a great emphasis on the magical properties of certain valuable commodities: the precious metals associated with alchemy, the land-surveying crafts of divining and money-digging, and the healing remedies of domestic folk religion. These rival money faiths coexisted in obvious tension with the orthodox Puritan establishment, but ordinary believers rarely experienced such blunter material beliefs as heretical. Indeed, the devoted Sunday Puritan churchgoer and weekday folk healer or money-digger were often enough the same worshiper; they were certainly neighbors, co-workers, and family relations.

This fund of background beliefs about the hidden, magical properties infusing the material sphere would continue to be in creative and syncretic tension with official Protestantism throughout our religious history. At times it would recede, when spiritual leaders would denounce pride and greed in the backsliding ranks of the faithful, or seek to launch a crusade to extinguish the hateful habits of the unchurched in the nation at large. More often, though, these quasi-pagan money faiths would surge to the forefront of public religion in America, as the market economy's stunning growth rendered prosperity both a sturdy fact and an inarguable blessing of American life.

But because the Protestant conscience couldn't abide the straightforward worship of Mammon, the Money Cult's saving doctrines became bound up with broader American beliefs about the individual self and its cosmic destiny. To bless the American as a divine creation, one first had to identify, and sanctify, the spiritual traits that the market selected for success. This meant not merely the time-honored Weberian virtues of thrift, accumulation, and delayed gratification, but also something more untamed and exotic, and fully imbued with the promise of self-reinvention in the New World. The Money Cult's most fervent adherents, from the first colonial generation forward, were instinctively *Gnostic* believers—that is to say, they preached a highly distilled and militantly individualistic version of the solitary Puritan encounter with the divine.

Throughout Christian history, Gnosticism has had a tangled, much-disputed, and reliably occult legacy stemming from its pagan stirrings in the first century AD. But in the American context, Gnostic faith is nowhere near so forbidding or strange. It is, as we shall see, the venerable American faith in a heroic spiritual individualism—the eternal principle of liberation that survives beneath all of the corrosive encrustations of tradition, habit, and nature. Gnostics historically have viewed the individual soul as a divine spark of cosmic truth that has become tragically marooned in an alien and fallen created world. To rescue this unsullied and inviolate nature, Gnostic believers elevate themselves above the grubby demands of merely social existence, preferring to project their cosmic identities into a drama of redemption beyond history, in which they are reunited with the true, transcendent, and hidden God who authored their heroic destiny.

America's ecstatic communions of spiritual selfhood have gone by several quasi-clinical names, from the Protean Self to the Narcissistic Personality. Such constructs have shed considerable light, but in neglecting the specific religious character of this cultural ailment, they render only a partial diagnosis. Self-infatuation is typically a developmental phase; self-*transcendence* is a spiritual project, and more important, it is the durable American conceit that enables all manner of cultural evasions of unpleasant facts, from the cult of the redeemer nation to the smiling assurances of the prosperity gospel. Refusal to apprehend the expressly religious distortions of the material realm has served as a de facto license for their continuation.

Viewed within this crucial compass of American selfhood, Gnosticism was the logical terminus of the profound spiritual unrest of the New World—but this transformation has been so gradual and familiar in its appearance that it has been hiding in plain sight throughout our religious past. To reclaim its basic coordinates, we need to understand just how distinctive—and how robustly material—the American religious experiment has been from the moment of its inception, and how thoroughly it undergirds our social mythologies, spiritual and secular alike.

Over time, the strange symbiosis of the calculating Puritan conscience and the vernacular worship of the many totems of our unique New World prosperity would become the dominant motif of American religious life. It stretched across traditional denominational boundaries, coursed through the boom-and-bust cycles of religious revival, and stamped itself decisively on the careers of new prophets and religions, from Joseph Smith's Mormonism to Joel Osteen's Pentecostalism.

More broadly, the Money Cult's core dogmas are what feed many of America's popular superstitions about economic life, from the belief that individual merit is the strict and undeviating guarantee of individual wealth, to the myth that Wall Street investment bankers are Promethean "job creators," to the mystical faith that digital commerce will upend all traditional limitations on human enterprise, and indeed, human existence.

The enduring power of the Money Cult is also a key explanation for one of the great mysteries of the so-called modernization thesis that has governed sociological theories of religion since Weber's day: Why has the United States sustained high, and indeed increasing, levels of religious belief amid conditions of rampaging mass secularism in the wider culture? How, in this greatest of all modern capitalist economies, have the most fundamental precepts of Protestant faith remained so stubbornly intact—even thrived—in the face of the same forces that stoked mass unbelief and indifference in other developed Western societies?

The Self-Made Spirit

We can only begin to make sense of the Money Cult's real underpinnings by grasping a central fact of our history: Religion in America was never really secularized; instead, the market was sanctified. With impressively consistent force, the prophets of our Money Cult have transformed the raw materials of capitalist striving into the stuff of transcendent spiritual virtue—and more than that, they've elevated our business republic's most powerful and successful strivers to a higher plane of being.

To cite just one example of this dynamic in action, consider the American economy's great foundational myth of self-made opportunity. This ideal stretches as far back as Benjamin Franklin's intensely market-minded cultivation of scrupulously honest, punctual, and thrifty individual character. But to match up with the reigning currents of economic success as it actually exists—in a distinctly *un*meritorious compound of cartelization, rent-seeking, and workaday political corruption—the faith of the American self-made man has always hinged on a talismanic belief in the rewards of personal virtue. This faith is rooted in the same heterodox tradition that discerned extravagant riches buried beneath the earth's surface or in the path of newly surveyed waterways—with the significant proviso that the bounty of the New World had to be *earned*, from the standpoint of both personal exertion and spiritual election.

The self-made-man myth is also a significant entry in the Money Cult catechism because of its intensive focus on the believer's individual character—and on how seamlessly the most stalwartly spiritual attributes of that character are rewarded in the marketplace. The close connection between Protestant faith and capitalist market expansion has imbued the most intimate conceptions of the American self. For generation after generation, American religious figures have seized upon the canons of self-reinvention lurking behind our great self-made fortunes as the primal stuff of divine favor and grace. As Irvin G. Wyllie notes in his 1954 study of the self-made man, it was common for ambitious ministers in the nineteenth century to compose popular tracts outlining the spiritual path to worldly wealth and distinction; significantly, the first and most influential figures promoting the American gospel of success were also preachers in the nation's Sunday pulpits.

This was, for the time, a natural affinity. The mainly Northeastern and mid-Atlantic preachers of the nineteenth century's prosperity gospel typically led congregations in the industrial and financial centers of the age. Two key pioneers in the genre, John Todd and Theodore Hunt, preached in the Massachusetts towns of Pittsfield and Malden—both booming company towns for the shoe industry. And the best-known divines of the age, Congregationalists Henry Ward Beecher and Lyman Abbott, were both open celebrants of the urban leisure class's largess, as they successively presided over one of the nation's richest congregations, at Brooklyn's Congregational Plymouth Church.[2] Matthew H. Smith nicely distilled the business outlook of nineteenth-century Protestantism by plying a dual vocation as a minister and a boosterish Wall Street journalist. He sagely counseled that future historians of American business would, like him, pull double duty as students of American religion. As to the theological implications of this congruence, Smith, like every other preacher in the Money Cult tradition, was admirably clear in spelling out the Bible's wholesale identity with the canons of capitalist ambition: "Adam was created and placed in the Garden of Eden for business purposes," Smith wrote in 1854 for *Hunt's Merchant Magazine*. "It would have been better for the human race if he had attended closely to the occupation for which he had been made."

Indeed, one of the very first ministerial adherents of the success gospel, the revivalist preacher Thomas P. Hunt, summed up the theological outlook of the many generations of success-minded divines who would follow in his wake, in the title of his 1836 tract, *The Book of Wealth; in Which It Is Proved from the Bible that It Is the Duty of Every Man to Become Rich*. And the most prominent literary apostle of self-made success, boys' book impresario Horatio Alger, began his professional life as a Unitarian minister.

In today's information economy, the self-made gospel is presented in the guise of a sleek and scientific-sounding euphemism: *meritocracy*. The beau ideal of individual merit hasn't weathered any better in our age than it did in Alger's own, the heyday of robber-baron capitalism. Nevertheless, today's meritocrats insist with their own religious fervor that material reward gravitates naturally, by dint of a self-evidently benign spiritual force, to the most deserving, most talented, and best-educated class of achievers, who have stayed faithfully attuned to the market's higher dictates. In other words, the core theology of the achieving self has scarcely shifted from its initial inception down through the bailout-weary routines of our intensively financialized age of crony capitalism.

It's important to fix this point clearly in mind, for the simple reason that the image of the striving American seeker after success is such a durable fixture of our social mythology that we take it entirely for granted. In reality, the self-made man was, unto his innermost parts, a self-made social invention, conjured from the potent forces of Protestant divinity to make the apportionment of worldly reward a metaphysical fact of life, beyond all merely mortal questioning. The self-made man is, in other words, a *talisman*: a token—and increasingly, it seems, a holy relic—of the achieving, high-individualist gospel.

To get a sharper picture of this talisman's ongoing power, just consider the present, uninspiring pass in the saga of self-made success: In strict economic terms, the meritocratic ideal is basically a dead letter. Quasi-socialist Old World welfare states such as Denmark and England now report greater upward socioeconomic mobility than is reported in the free-market, recession-battered United States. Newly matriculated students bearing the name-brand diplomas that were once the passports to continued advancement up the career ladder now find themselves hard-pressed to line up any sort of job in a stagnant, service-driven labor economy—which also means, thanks to the heavy student-loan burden most of them now carry, they're looking at an adulthood largely eaten up by debt peonage.

But almost none of this glum reality penetrates our most popular pulpits, televangelical broadcasts, and megachurches. The message here is an abiding tale of joyous and exciting worldly conquest, as prosperity preachers urge the Money Cult faithful on to one divinely sanctioned pinnacle of wealth after another.

Indeed, in many instances, the apostles of our money faith go ahead and conscript the figure of Jesus himself into the front ranks of the Money Cult—a ploy revived most recently by the redoubtable Catholic culture warrior Bill O'Reilly, whose mammoth bestseller *Killing Jesus* argues that Jesus was crucified for protesting the Roman system of taxation. (In the great tradition of many predecessor prophets of the money faith, O'Reilly has also claimed a divinely inspired vocation for himself: a direct visitation from the Holy Spirit instructing him to write the book.)

Never mind that the moneychangers who Jesus attacked in the temple were, in fact, Jewish officials skimming revenue from Jewish congregants—and that, in his famous "render unto Caesar" pronouncement in Matthew 22, Jesus explicitly steered his followers *against* resisting Roman taxes. No, in the gospel according to the Money Cult, Jesus *must* preach the Tea Party verities of possessive individualism—which is also why this bowdlerized account of the heroic capitalist Jesus will carefully sidestep his admonitions to feed the hungry, heal the sick, and comfort the poor, and certainly *never* include the bit about the camel navigating a needle's eye before a rich man might enter the Kingdom of Heaven.

Much like the practices of alchemy from which it has drawn consistent inspiration, the American Money Cult has effectively transmuted the baser materials of competitive capitalist self-assertion into a kind of saving grace. This is less the theology of the Invisible Hand—Adam Smith's famous, mystic claim that individual profiteering in a market economy conspires to create a far wider set of social virtues—than the far more primal stuff of revelation. In Smith's Enlightenment political philosophy, humans are the unwitting agents of a redemptive scheme that they scarcely can fathom; the Money Cult, very much by contrast, pivots on the individual believer's transforming moment of *self-realization*: the investiture of a successful worldly calling with a great divine imprimatur. As Osteen and scores of his Money Cult forerunners have preached, the great truth of converted faith is that God has meant for you, the believer, to be a conqueror of the material realm. To be successful, in other words, is to realize your true identity and ascend to your divinely appointed destiny. And the market that vouchsafes your success to you is, just as self-evidently, a field of blessed endeavor that the Lord has appointed for the working-out of the individual fates of the faithful.

The Commerce of the Cosmos

Just how this scheme of salvation-through-abundance has gripped many of the leading movements in our Protestant tradition is the subject of this book. There have been, as we shall see, many odd and exotic theological reckonings and revisionist experiments that have given the American Money Cult its own distinctive voice and shape. And by a process of compensation familiar to any student of psychoanalysis, this dream of market deliverance—in which the great divine arbiter of prosperity and ill fortune swoops down to bestow each individual believer with customized earthly rewards reflecting that worshiper's fervid faith and higher spiritual worth—has taken firmer and firmer hold as our corporate economy has become ever more impersonal, corrupt, and impervious to public accountability. Within the logic of the Money Cult, market failure works mainly to increase the pressure on the self to continue conjuring fresh and plausible individual alibis for social calamity. If the fundamental project of spiritual self-reinvention hasn't yielded the expected material returns, then the American believer's solution is always to reinvent him- or herself all the more frenetically.

This is why the Gnostic precepts of the Money Cult have evolved into a dogma that's curiously un-material. Deprived of any model of economic reward in which hard work equates to upward mobility, American believers have rallied to a purely supernatural account of how things work on the worldly plane of enterprise, where labor and capital alike obey the reassuring, though ultimately unfathomable, dictates of a greater divine intelligence. As it turns out, the market gospel of a Joel Osteen is a robust, shape-shifting version of the original Protestant ethic—but it is also one that the nation's Puritan founders would never have recognized.

Which is not to say that America's money faith was entirely a new thing under the sun. Its substance would bear some superficial resemblance to the founding spirit of the Puritan colonies. It would, most crucially, be grounded in the stark sense of individual isolation that Puritans wrested from their harsh doctrines of absolute divine sovereignty over the created world. But where the Puritans had sought, in notably frantic and single-minded fashion, to secure the marooned and sin-stricken individual believer behind a bulwark of institutions—the church, the magistrate, the family, and (finally) the saving notion of a worldly calling—the animating spirit of the Money Cult beckoned believers in another direction entirely. Money Cultists substituted the unquestioned authority of individual experience for the Puritan polity's obsessively cultivated habits of obedience and social deference. Where the old Superego of colonial caste and communion had formerly ruled, the untamed Id of the seeker after a new class of New World spiritual truth would be unloosed into the great American sanctified market.

Much good has come of the restive spirit of rebellion that's infused our Money Cult. It has largely spared America's religious culture the dead hand of established orthodoxy, and has firmly inscribed freedom of conscience as a central article of the country's civic faith. Innovation is an undeniable virtue, in spiritual and economic life alike. But the incorrigibly individualist cast of the Money Cult has also betokened a far broader tilt toward a solitary, unencumbered vision of salvation, selfhood, and social order: the sort of faith tailor-made—paradoxically—for mass allegiance in the consumer marketplace.

And despite the anti-institutional mindset that's driven its growth, the modern Money Cult has founded an impressive battery of institutions devoted to spreading its gospel. The movement's embrace of full-scale market triumphalism in the first decades of the twentieth century occurred, happily enough, just as a new cohort of modern evangelical business moguls were looking to endow bible colleges and parachurch organizations and outfit them with fire-breathing new laissez-faire curricula and policy agendas. Under this tight institutional guidance, the language of worship and the invocations of market favor have merged into a seamless spiritual whole—the unique New World faith dispensation that Alexis de Tocqueville astutely identified a century earlier as he wondered whether the true object of the revived American religion was "to procure eternal felicity in the other world or well-being in this one."

The crucial, formative tradition of American Protestant dissent has become inextricably fused with broader superstitions about the redemption of the self in the spheres of economic and financial reward. Thanks to our frenzied imbuement of market forces with mystical, soul-transforming powers of their own, our spiritual and economic worlds now promiscuously spread their bounty across all previously known formal boundaries of culture, commerce, and faith. After all, as Joel Osteen says, Why put limits on God?

THE

MONEY CULT

1

A FOUNDING FAITH

Strange as it may seem to anyone versed in the money nostrums of today's Protestant scene, the worship of wealth didn't come naturally to the first European settlers of North America. As envisioned by the divines who streamed into the New England colonies in the seventeenth century, their governing spiritual covenant was no free-market Valhalla; rather, it was a cooperative commonwealth, in which rich and poor alike were bound together in mutual spiritual obligation. The first settlers of New England were enjoined not merely to launch the dissenting church anew in a vast and (to them) unknown wilderness, but also to practice new forms of Christian charity—to generously share the bounty of the New World among their fellowship and to hold significant swaths of their property in common.

They found the relevant precedents for such practices in scripture, of course, but also in the charitable conduct of the first Christians—members of the so-called Primitive Church of the first century AD, which would serve as a powerful spiritual ideal for Protestant Americans throughout our history. The Primitive Church occupied pride of place in America's emerging religious life thanks in large part to a host of parallels that the divines of the Puritan age drew between the Primitive Church's first apostles and themselves: Both groups were, in the Puritans' view, breakaway spiritual pioneers defining a new faith at the margins of a corrupt and repressive spiritual regime; both were likewise held to be the bearers of an unadorned, and singularly demanding covenant with God—a compact that, indeed, stretched well back into the histories related in the Hebrew Bible, where the New England Puritans tended to locate a good deal of the patriarchal authority that governed their own churches and townships.

In these ways and scores of others, the New England Puritans imagined themselves to be among the most ardent disciples of the Reformation's quest to restore the ancient rigors of the Christian social ethic, and to revive the individual believer's sense of direct communion with the divine. Indeed, that quest for an intimate yet transcendent social fellowship was how the sojourners into the British colonies came by the name "Puritan" in the first place; it's only in the common modern caricature of the colonial founders that the term has come to signify sexual repression and the obsessive cultivation of personal rectitude. In reality, the Puritan settlement of the New World was animated by a strong social vision of mutual obligation and liberal charity among the parties to the divine covenant adopted as the colonies' founding social compact. How this vision morphed into the sanctified capitalism of our own era is in large part the saga of the Money Cult's ascendance.

But to begin at the beginning: The Puritan dissenters who initially populated the colonies of New England were at once tireless strivers after divine favor and sticklers for political order. At first, this may seem a paradox. As radical Protestants who'd fallen out with the Church of England, they might appear at first blush to be seventeenth-century populists, in the mold of radically dissenting sects back in England such as the Ranters and the Levellers. In the school of religious history that reads the eventual triumph of liberal democracy back into the colonial past, the dissenting founders of Puritan New England were eager to devolve power to the Protestant priesthood of all believers, and to get the colonies' eventual break with the British Empire over with.[3]

In reality, of course, history does not plot itself along such an orderly graph, registering the inevitable arrival of familiar outcome after familiar outcome. If anything, it was the Puritans' falling out with the Anglican Church that turned them into such anxious guardians of their own highly disciplined spiritual order. The Puritans' status as stigmatized dissenters in England rendered the maintenance of political discipline a spiritual duty—and the most vital evidence of that discipline was to be their own freestanding spiritual community in the New World.

Yet for all the Puritans' well-documented rage for public order, they still preached what was, for the age, a radically egalitarian version of the Protestant gospel. For ready confirmation of the leveling social vision of the New England Puritan faith, one need look no further than what is still the best-known sermon in American letters, John Winthrop's "A Modell of Christian Charity." Winthrop's discourse, composed and presumably preached on board the British ship *Arabella,* bound for the Massachusetts Bay Colony in 1630, is best known for bequeathing to posterity the signature image of American exceptionalism: the portrait of the fledgling colony as " a City upon a Hill," inviting the scrutiny of other nations and believers across the globe.

But Winthrop's formulation—and indeed the entirety of his sermon—sparked no great interest among his contemporaries. It's only been the modern scholars of Puritanism who have plotted out a foundational genius in Winthrop's vision; indeed, "A Modell of Christian Charity" wasn't even published during Winthrop's lifetime and went unanthologized in the Christian histories of the eighteenth century as well (unlike, say, the no-less-exceptionalist sermons of Winthrop's far-better-known British contemporary John Cotton). But this was not due to the negligible reach and influence of the Winthrop oration; indeed, since Winthrop was the first governor of the Bay Colony, his words carried special weight for the authority-minded contingent of some 700 settlers who arrived on the *Arabella.* No, the reason that his contemporaries took no special note of Winthrop's pronouncements was that the sermon conveyed convictions already held firmly and widely among the Puritan settlers of the New World. As Winthrop's biographer Francis J. Bremer notes, "Christian Charity was an exposition of the social gospel that had been proclaimed . . . elsewhere in England" among the dissenting Puritan congregations of the early seventeenth century.[4]

The Heavenly City

What were the elements of this social gospel? First, Winthrop sought to lay bare the divine logic that permitted inequality to take root in human societies. Unlike Ronald Reagan—who famously adopted the imagery of

the "City upon a Hill" in his 1984 nomination speech at the Republican National Convention—Winthrop didn't suggest that inequality was
the simple reflection of superior talent finding its natural way to superior
worldly gain. Winthrop argued instead that God sanctioned different economic rewards among humans so that they could see believers of different
stations perform the signal works of justice and mercy that set Christians
apart. God appointed different life outcomes to different people, Winthrop reasoned, so as to instruct them in the varieties of Christian charity
best suited to their social standing. The poor, he preached, must embrace a
benevolent view of their social betters to ensure that they "shall not rise up
against their superiors and shake off their yoke." But the rich will undergo a
reciprocal movement toward greater social compassion, Winthrop argued;
God will "manifest the work of His spirit . . . upon the wicked in moderating and restraining them, so that the rich and the mighty should not eat
up the poor."[5]

God's more fundamental stake in perpetuating social and economic
distinctions, however, was to constitute human society as a single organic
body. At the center of Winthrop's vision of charity in social practice is the
notion of "liberality" in mutual aid for the Puritan settlers—and especially
toward those in acute economic need. Over the familiar objection that
prudent believers need to safeguard their surplus wealth to meet future
rainy-day exigencies, Winthrop directs his listeners to the language of
Scripture, which explicitly grounds the promise of divine reward on the
practice of charity in this world. "He that gives to the poor, lends to the
Lord," Winthrop preached, "and he will repay him even in this life ten or
a hundredfold to him and his."[6]

Winthrop's injunction to liberality in personal charity grows yet more
radical when he weighs the prospect of the Puritan community facing collective peril. Just as the Old Testament had directed lenders to forgive
debts every seventh year—the sabbatarian notion of the "jubilee year" as
expounded in Deuteronomy 15:1–2—so must the new Puritan community
establishing itself in the New World set aside all claims of personal property in the event of an emergency. Recurring to the example set by the
primitive Christian church, Winthrop advocated something that would

cause his self-styled Reaganite acolytes to blanch in horror: a proposal to redistribute the community's wealth on the basis of need. The scriptural basis of Winthrop's argument is so carefully and persuasively demonstrated that it bears quoting at length:

> Hence it was that in the primitive Church they sold all, had all things in common, neither did any man say that which he possessed was his own. Likewise in their return out of the captivity, because the work was great for the restoring of the church and the danger of enemies was common to all, Nehemiah directs the Jews to liberality and readiness in remitting their debts to their brethren, and disposing liberally to such as wanted, and stand not upon [the Hebrews'] own dues which they might have demanded of them. Thus did some of our forefathers in times of persecution in England, and so did many of the faithful of other churches, whereof we keep an honorable remembrance of them; and it is to be observed that both in Scriptures and latter stories of the churches that such as have been most bountiful to the poor saints, especially in those extraordinary times and occasions, God hath left them highly commended to posterity, as Zaccheus, Cornelius, Dorcas, Bishop Hooper, the Cutler of Brussels and divers others. Observe again that the Scripture gives no caution to restrain any from being over liberal this way; but all men to the liberal and cheerful practice hereof by the sweeter promises; as to instance one for many (Isaiah 58:6–9) "Is not this the fast I have chosen to loose the bonds of wickedness, to take off the heavy burdens, to let the oppressed go free and to break every yoke . . . to deal thy bread to the hungry and to bring the poor that wander into thy house, when thou seest the naked to cover them . . . and then shall thy light brake forth as the morning and thy health shall grow speedily, thy righteousness shall go before God, and the glory of the Lord shalt embrace thee; then thou shall call and the Lord shall answer thee," etc.[7]

Much is striking in this passage, but note especially the historical sweep of Winthrop's appeal. He begins with the Primitive Church, proceeds backward in time to the fifth-century-BCE prophet Nehemiah, then fast-forwards into a litany of saints from the biblical and more recent past who have earned divine favor by practicing generosity in "extraordinary times and occasion." Winthrop then seals the case by quoting another Hebrew Bible prophet, Isaiah, to drive home Scripture's clear message: that there shall be "no caution to restrain any from being over liberal in this way."

Winthrop was a lawyer, but in constructing this case, he was not merely appealing to precedent for precedent's sake; rather, he was invoking what, for his audience, was a direct sense of the biblical past's interpenetration into the present. Puritan divines interpreted biblical history as a sequence of "types"—that is to say, as a train of events and characters that served as a universal, living model of spiritual and social relations. (This was the way that the leaders of the colonial errand interpreted the lessons of the Old Testament's Exodus saga: as a direct forerunner of their own spiritual community-in-exile.) In the same vein, the New World mission that Winthrop and the other founding leaders of the Bay Colony were launching flowed directly from the precedents of the biblical past: Like other Protestants, they viewed the surest path to genuine worship as a restoration of the conditions of the Primitive Church, with spiritual authority tied to personal communion with the divine. For a lay preacher like Winthrop, it was a straightforward reading of Christian history to locate this ideal in the annals of saintly martyrdom—and, most pointedly, within the terms of the covenant launching his communion's settlement in the New World.

The strict separation of spiritual and mundane kingdoms was the legacy of St. Augustine's vision of the permanently estranged City of God and City of Man, and Augustine's forceful spiritual account of this divide was what kept the Puritan experiment closely confined within the ranks of the Church's authority. The original founders of the Bay Colony were indeed theocrats, but the chief aim of their theocracy was to insulate the spiritual kingdom of God from the earthly powers of man—not to casually annex the fallen world to an expansive regime of religious-cum-social conquest. "It was reserved for the American Puritans," Sacvan Bercovitch writes, "to give the kingdom of God a local habitation and a name."[8]

Familiar and Constant Practice

As Winthrop presses his argument further, he seeks to demonstrate the ways that the Church, and the Church alone, must cultivate the social habit of charity among the elect. He notes, for example, that it is by force of living out the injunction of loving one's brother on the model of the Scripture, rather than by conventional exhortations to human reason, that true mercy takes hold of the believing soul. Citing the Apostle Paul's dictum that love is the fulfillment of the Old Testament law, Winthrop embarks on a somewhat tortured analogy, one that would later be taken up in a markedly different context by Enlightenment-era Deists seeking to transport God himself off the stage of history. The operation of Christian mercy, Winthrop contends, is like the mechanism that sets off a clock to ring on the hour. "As when we bid one make the clock strike," he writes, "he doth not lay hand on the hammer . . . but sets on work the first mover or main wheel; knowing that will certainly produce the sound which he intends." Likewise, "the way to draw men to the works of mercy, is not by force of Argument from the goodness or the necessity of the work; for though this cause may enforce a rational mind to some present act in mercy, as is frequent in experience, yet it cannot work such a habit in a soul." For that more profound transformation, Winthrop writes, mercy must be made to work like, well, clockwork, i.e., to "prompt on all occasions to produce the same effect, but by framing in these affections of love in the heart which will as naturally bring forth the other, as the cause does effect."[9]

To render this same injunction to charity in more recognizable and intimate terms, Winthrop seizes next on another familiar New Testament image from Paul: the conception of the Church as a body, and of love as the crucial "ligament" permitting the socially disparate parts of the organic whole to move in unity. It is this model of charity, he argues, that makes up the Church's transhistoric progress toward mercy, across the pages of Scripture and into the present Puritan errand:

> The like we shall find in the histories of the church, in all ages; the
> sweet sympathy of affections which was in the members of this body
> one towards another; their cheerfulness in serving and suffering

together; how liberal they were without repining, harborers without grudging, and helpful without reproaching; and all from hence,
because they had fervent love amongst them; which only makes the
practice of mercy constant and easy.

It is in this spirit of liberality that Winthrop urges a dictum for his
band of settlers that sounds scandalous to the market-addled temper of
today's political and religious discourse: In founding an appropriate mode
of government, he writes, "the care of the public must oversway all private
respects." Indeed, in what amounts to a photographic negative of Adam
Smith's later theory of the social benefits created by the "invisible hand" of
the market, Winthrop counsels that even the logic of self-interest dictates
that all members of the Church's body attend to the health of the com-
monweal: "It is a true rule that particular estates cannot subsist in the ruin
of the public."[10]

Winthrop then proceeds to equate this "fervent love" among the
church community with a state of marriage with the divine. The vows that
animate this marriage between the body of the Church and the spirit of
the Lord are extraordinary, mandating a most demanding sort of fidelity
from the believers seeking to practice true charity: "That which the most
in their Churches maintain as a truth in profession only, we must bring
into familiar and constant practice, as in this duty of Love we must love
brotherly without dissimulation, we must love one another with a pure
heart fervently, we must bear each other's burdens." And as was the case
in God's original covenant with Israel, the newly betrothed Puritans must
expect intensive scrutiny from their divine partner: "He hath taken us to
be His after a most strict and peculiar manner, which will make Him more
jealous of our love and obedience." The stakes of honoring the full terms
of the new covenant are therefore tremendous; God will "look to have it
observed in every article," and thus the settlers of the Bay Colony must be
vigilant in their practice of mercy:

if we shall neglect the observation of these Articles which are the
ends we have propounded, and dissembling with our God, shall fail

to embrace this present world and prosecute our carnal intentions, seeking great things for ourselves and our posterity, the Lord shall surely break out in wrath against us, be revenged of such a perjured people, and make us know the price of a breach of such a Covenant.[11]

True covenant observance requires, in other words, total social solidarity. "We must be knit together in this work as one man," Winthrop exhorts. "We must entertain each other in brotherly affection, we must be willing to abridge ourselves of our superfluities for the sake of others' necessities, we must delight in each other, mourn together, labor and suffer together, always having before our eyes our Commission and our Community in the work." Only under these extraordinary conditions of liberality, mercy and solidarity will God's favor become manifest; then, Winthrop prophesies, "we shall see much more of His wisdom, power and truth than we have formerly been acquainted with . . . He shall make us a praise and glory, that men shall say of succeeding plantations: the Lord made it like that of New England."[12] And it is only at the end of this demanding yet exhilarating litany of mutual Christian love, organic social solidarity, and overt wealth redistribution—*we must be willing to abridge ourselves of our superfluities for the sake of others' necessities*—that Winthrop introduces his now-famous walk-on simile, duly transcribed in every modern spiritual account of American exceptionalism: "For we must consider that we shall be as a City upon a Hill." And even here, he reverts instantly not to the rewards of divine favor—he's laid that out in a sparse three sentences in his exhaustive account of the new covenant—but to the dire spiritual consequences of abrogating the new divinely sanctioned marriage accord: "If we shall deal falsely with our God in this work we have undertaken, and so cause Him to withdraw His present help from us, we shall be made a story and a by-word through the world."

Indeed, the phrase "city upon a hill" had its origins in the Bible, as most Puritan expressions did. And in its full scriptural context, the simile is clearly an exhortation to live publicly in charity, rather than to bask in the Lord's preordained favor. In the Sermon on the Mount (Matthew 5:14–16), Jesus preaches that "a city that is set on a hill cannot be hid. Neither do men light a candle and put it under a bushel, but on a candlestick, and it giveth light unto all that are in the house. Let your light so shine before men, that they see your good works, and glorify your Father who is in heaven."

Like those in other themes of Winthrop's oration, this image was a commonplace one among Puritan divines; as Bremer notes, the figure of the city on the hill was used to characterize the dissenting community of Stour Valley in England, where Winthrop had grown up, while British Puritans made regular use of the figure of particularly godly people as individual "lights" reflecting divine works. (Indeed, the same language would come to characterize the first significant schism over revivalism in the New World in the 1740s, when partisans of the first Great Awakening were dubbed "New Lights" and its detractors were known as "Old Lights.")

As Bremer further observes, Winthrop's principal theme of knitting the unequal human parts of Puritan society into a unitary and self-sustaining body of believers was likewise a frequent exhortation among Britain's dissenting clergy. One minister from Winthrop's Stour Valley community, John Knewstub, preached that inequality didn't arise from human social arrangements, but rather inhered in God's broader plan of redemption: "The Lord is the author of the diversity of gifts," and so "the envying of others for their gifts given unto them is indeed to pick a quarrel with the Lord." Still, this vision didn't translate into the social fatalism one might expect from divinely sanctioned gaps in social standing—let alone into the complacency that the wealthy can adopt under the knowledge that their success has unfolded according to a divine plan. As Thomas Carew, another Puritan contemporary of Winthrop's in England, patiently explained, "There hath always been, are, and shall be diversities of estates and degrees in the world, some rich and some poor, and many times it falls out, though not always, that wicked men have a greater portion of outward things than godly men . . . [so] no man can say, 'I am rich, therefore I am loved of God.'"[13]

Winthrop obviously was preaching these subjects to a self-selected community of believers, so it would be misleading to generalize too widely from his premises. He wasn't advocating the principles of social charity for all of humanity—though he did instruct his audience to honor them *toward* outsiders, to the extent that his ethnocentric and racialist outlook permitted. He was not propounding, in other words, a universal socialist brotherhood. But Bremer is certainly correct to characterize Winthrop's sermon as an exemplary Puritan version of the social gospel—and while it is not a programmatic scheme of governance, it nonetheless contrasts strikingly with the evangelical piety of our own day, which preaches wholesale distrust of government (and by extension, any conception of a public sphere), a fatalism about most measures of social reform, and most of all, an instinctive embrace of worldly success as perhaps the surest proof of divine election. The leading lights of today's Protestant faith in America are not merely inclined to endorse the notion that the rich are beloved of God—they are themselves rich, and cite their worldly success as evidence of God's favor.

Of Profits and Prophecy

The history of New England Puritanism is told, for the most part, as a long saga of theological schism and spiritual declension that steadily displaced Winthrop's vision of a righteous theocracy—beginning with Winthrop's own later efforts to purge the Bay Colony of the dissenting piety of Anne Hutchinson, who preached what was known as an "antinomian" theology of free-will conversion, imbuing individual believers with an experiential "inner light" that posed obvious and ominous challenges for Winthrop's view of more rigid, church-based social cohesion for the colonies. Much the same challenge to Puritan authority emerged from the separatist preaching of the great Baptist dissident Roger Williams, who was eventually exiled by Winthrop and his allies to Williams's own breakaway colony of Rhode Island.

But the gradual breakup of the old Puritan consensus is as much a story of economic transformation as a saga of theological infighting—even though historians still aren't much closer to accounting for the true causes of this transformation. Part of the problem, it appears, is that the very basis of Winthrop's settlement was shot through with more than its share of real-world contradictions: The divines founding the Bay Colony were

seeking to launch an alternative spiritual commonwealth at the same time
that they were operating under a royal corporate charter. In other words, in
order to prosper as a Christian community of mutual aid, the colony first
needed to realize healthy net returns for the Crown. Indeed, the colony's
royal charter itself was ratified as the result of a regional trade rivalry,
with one party of conforming Anglican divines first seeking to unseat a
reprobate band of traders in the Western end of the colony. But the settlers
under the initial charter, which stipulated that the community's fishing
rights were to profit the Crown, failed to make a go of it, and the colony
passed into the hands of the nonconforming noblemen allied with Winthrop. A prosperous London lawyer, Winthrop owed his leadership post,
in other words, to the spiritual equivalent of a hostile takeover bid.

And Winthrop, together with his Old World corporate sponsors, well
understood that his own chartered claim to the New England colony could
vanish just as suddenly as the one held by the failed fishing interests who
preceded him. Hence one of Williams's earliest—and least forgivable—
trespasses against the Puritan establishment in New England was to openly
dispute the legitimacy of the Bay Colony charter launching the Winthrop
settlement. Williams charged that the charter should have been returned
to England on the grounds that its signatories had not "compounded with
the natives" of the New World. As Williams later explained, the charter's
"great sin" was its arrogation of real property in the name of Christ: Under
the spurious and worldly provisions of the charter, he complained, "Christian kings (so called) are invested with Right by virtue of their Christiani-
tie, to take and give away the Lands and Countries of other men."[14]

The Puritans' involvement gave a new and earnest spiritual complexion
to the New World experiment, but they were still obliged to honor the terms
of their charter, which directed that one-fifth of the colony's real wealth go to
the Crown. They would also have to meet less-specific, but still substantial,
revenue goals for the corporation's directors, who remained in England and
did not share anything close to the Puritan governors' passion for Christian
charity. In today's financial terms, that meant that the settlers had to show at
least a 20-percent profit in order to meet the basic terms of their land grant.

Fortunately, the English Puritan settlers proved to be masters of enhanced productivity. As Max Weber has famously argued, the Calvinist strain of the Reformation that counted the New England Puritans among its most zealous converts unleashed vast new entrepreneurial energies that shaped the course of Western capitalist development.

Weber baptized Benjamin Franklin, the arch Yankee philosopher of flinty self-help, as the ideal-type of the capitalist spirit—but noted that the famous maxims of unstinting time management and flinty wealth accumulation that Franklin coined in popular tracts such as *Poor Richard's Almanack* and *The Way to Wealth* had been a guiding folkway of the New England colonies long before Poor Richard put quill to parchment. "In order that a manner of life so well adapted to the peculiarities of capitalism . . . should come to dominate others," Weber wrote, "it had to originate somewhere, and not in isolated individuals alone, but as a way of life common to whole groups of men." Thus it was, Weber continued, that "in the country of Benjamin Franklin's birth (Massachusetts) the spirit of capitalism . . . was present before the capitalist order. There were complaints of a peculiarly calculating sort of profit-seeking in New England, as distinguished from other parts of America, as early as 1632."[15]

The Puritans' ironclad devotion to their callings, in other words, ensured that the Bay Colony would prosper. This was no small matter, especially after less spiritually minded settlements, such as the infamous Virginia colony in Jamestown, nearly died out—in that case, because the expedition's leaders brought along more equipment for gold-digging than for the cultivation of crops. But once the New World coaxed forth the twinned defining tensions of the Puritan faith—Winthrop's scriptural communitarianism and Franklin's calculating economic rationality—the collateral psychic confusion would determine the peculiar course of American religious history. For just as Puritans in the New World couldn't help but accumulate wealth as they worked fervidly and indulged in precious few worldly vices, so, too, were they certain to feel guilty—or, as the theological argot of the age had it, convicted—over the scale of their worldly success.

As Weber made clear, the close calibration of personal success in the Puritan world was a spiritually fraught business. Believers needed to prosper enough so that their sense of vocation might be confirmed, but not so much that the pursuit of wealth became an end in itself and the luxuries that multiplied alongside that pursuit turned into a spiritual snare. Hence Richard Baxter—a seventeenth-century Puritan preacher in England whom Weber adopts as the ideal-type of the capitalist spirit's early germination—counseled that "you may labour to be rich for God, though not for the flesh and sin," and worked out a characteristically tortured theological rationale for this dictum:

> If God shows you a way in which you can lawfully get more than in another way (without wrong to your soul or to any other), if you refuse this, and choose the less gainful way, you cross one of the ends of your calling, and you refuse to be God's steward, and to accept His gifts, and use them for Him when he requireth it.[16]

Thus was the common latter-day evangelical notion of the scriptural stewardship of wealth—a de facto charge to maximize profit as a means of glorifying God and honoring his scriptural will—installed as an uneasy founding tenet of the New England Way. Much the same posture of ambivalent achievement characterized Puritan attitudes toward culture. Like worldly luxury, cultural pursuits represented a potentially fatal distraction from the main business of recognizing and celebrating the material blessings of God.

The Puritan quarrel with culture, too, was a fraught business, for the simple reason that the Puritans' suspicions of leisured excess were grounded in close familiarity with the temptations of privilege. The Bay Colony boasted a higher percentage of college graduates than there was in seventeenth-century England, and Puritan divines tended to be among the most educated members of Britain's rising bourgeoisie. Yet non-gainful, leisured activities aroused deep distrust among the visible saints who led Puritan congregations, by the same logic that propelled them to elevate their worldly callings into divinely preordained destinies. They drove away the specter of "joy in life," as Weber called it, with the same grim (and faintly self-hating) efficiency with which they dispatched rivals in the marketplace. In Puritan communities, he writes, the toleration of pleasure in cultural goods . . . always ran up against one characteristic limitation: They must not cost anything. Man is only a trustee of the goods which have come to him through God's grace. He must, like the servant in the parable, give an account of every penny entrusted to him, and it is at least hazardous to spend any of it for a purpose that does not serve the glory of God but only one's own enjoyment.

But this pecuniary logic, Weber observes, goes on to create an intolerable pressure on the inner life of the believer: Stifled under the dual mandate to maximize profit and resist pleasure, the business of Puritan living can breed a kind of existential resentment:

> The idea of a man's duty to his possessions, to which he subordinates himself as an obedient steward, or even an acquisitive machine, bears with a chilling weight on his life. The greater the possession the heavier, if the ascetic attitude toward life stands the test, the feeling of responsibility for them, for holding them undiminished for the glory of God and increasing them by restless effort.[17]

For the modern heirs of the Puritan-bred capitalist order, Weber argues, this burden has grown crushing: The logic of relentless accumulation, shorn of joy in living, has landed the modern soul in the "iron cage" of bureaucracy, awaiting the unlikely prospect of some unimagined new deliverance from on high. "The idea of duty in one's calling prowls about in our lives like the ghost of dead religious beliefs," he glumly observed; "in the field of its highest development, the pursuit of wealth, stripped of its religious and ethical meaning, tends to become associated with purely mundane passions, which often give it the character of sport."[18]

Believers at Bay

The psychic tension that Weber diagnosed at the heart of the Puritan's exertions in the world is crucial for understanding the arc of our economic and religious history; however, the disenchantment that supposedly crowned

the historical evolution of the Protestant spirit of remorseless accumulation was far less secular—in all senses of the word—than he imagined.
In large part, this was because many of the colonists who fell away from
the Puritan tradition had never adhered to it very firmly in the first place.
Indeed, as the historian Jon Butler has noted, the early settlement of the
American colonies was a time of anemic religious observance, particularly
in the Middle and Southern colonies along the Eastern Seaboard. And
even within the centers of Puritan piety in New England, the anxious
accumulative reveries advanced by Calvin and Winthrop succumbed fairly
swiftly to more accommodating modes of worship. The New England religious scene shifted dramatically over the first generation of settlement,
with the sectarian drive toward "doctrinal heterogeneity" gaining as newer
immigrants gravitated to less-austere visions of God and more-forgiving
schemes of salvation. Even as Winthrop exiled the leaders of these heterodox confessions, such as the Baptist Roger Williams and the antinomian
Anne Hutchinson, the New England clergy understood that Winthrop's
ideal model of Christian social unity couldn't withstand a long stream of
banishments: "the clergy avoided direct confrontations on narrower theological issues, or on the larger problem of heterodoxy within the society,"
Butler writes. "Virtually all of Hutchinson's many followers, for example,
remained unmolested, if not uncensored, in Boston."[19]

And when rival forms of worship weren't springing up, the settlements were changing in response to what would be the defining pattern
of cultural commerce in the New World: freshly arrived immigrants, har-
boring very little ambivalence about the spiritual perils of worldly success.
"After 1650 new immigrants joined churches far less frequently than did
earlier settlers," Butler writes:

> That New England's post-1660 immigrants carried fewer links
> to Calvinist congregations in England is not surprising, since the
> English congregations were declining themselves. Although we know
> little about these immigrants, they appear to have been young, sin-
> gle indentured servants not unlike the settlers of the early Chesa-
> peake. Frequently, they worked as seasonal laborers in the expanding

New England countryside and in the older seaport towns of Boston, Salem, and Plymouth. Economic opportunity rather than religion— New England rather than New Zion—attracted them to America. They formed a new, increasingly secular population in an older, highly Calvinistic culture. Together with congregational tribalism and more individualistic settlement patterns, their arrival reshaped lay adherence patterns in seventeenth-century New England communities.[20]

The changed complexion of worship in places like Boston was hard to miss. As late as 1645, census figures showed that nearly 70 percent of the households in the city claimed at least one spouse linked to the main church. But the changed city quickly registered a changed religious profile: "If servants were added to the figures, by 1649, more than 50 percent of Boston's men already stood outside the church," Butler writes "The implication was ominous. As early as 1650 the Boston church was a place for families, especially for those who had arrived first and set the tone of town worship. But servants and new families with weak or peripheral connections to English Puritanism viewed the churches from the outside when they arrived and remained there when they settled."[21]

The immigrants pouring into the Bay Colony were, in a sense, catching up with the spiritual preferences of their neighbors to the south. In Anglican Virginia, for instance, the practice of infant baptism—one of the most basic sacraments of the faith—atrophied dramatically in the latter half of the seventeenth century. In the Charles Parish of York County, records show that between 1649 and 1670, 85.4 percent of infant Caucasians—111 out of 130—were not baptized. And as Butler notes, the trend held during the following decade, even as other nearby Anglican parishes began to launch public congregations.[22] Meanwhile, public worship was so poorly supported in Maryland—founded under a charter held by the Catholic Lord Baltimore, but like all the colonies, heavily Protestant in the makeup of its ordinary citizens—that the colony's ability to retain any institutional identity as a Christian settlement was gravely in doubt. Quakerism prospered briefly in colonial Maryland, but the strongest-held religious conviction of the age appears, ironically enough, to have been anti-Catholicism.

As popular unrest shook up the colonial councils governing the settlement, Lord Baltimore's faith served as a convenient scapegoat for political
rivals seeking to galvanize greater popular support. By 1675, the Anglican
preacher John Yeo was lamenting that "noe care is taken or provision made
for the building up [of] Christians of the Protestant religion" in the Maryland colony—and the baleful results were everywhere to see: "the lord's day
is prophaned, Religion despised, and all notorious vices committed . . . it is
become a Sodom of uncleanness and a Pest house of iniquity."[23]

More Perfect Unions

Of course, just because the institutional churches were coming up short of
their dreams of New World conquest, that didn't mean their citizens held
no religious beliefs whatsoever. In the Middle Colonies and the South,
believers outside the established churches aligned with a broad array of
heterodox sects, mostly found on the fringe of the radical Reformation in
England. These radical faiths, such as Quakerism and Baptism, helped to
open up the Christianizing landscape of the New World for more extreme
brands of Protestant piety, such as the Schwenkfeld, Muggletonian, Sabbatarian, and Immortalist sects. These movements also overlapped in important ways with breakaway mystical and perfectionist communities, such
as the Rogerenes in the Connecticut Valley, the mid-eighteenth-century
Ephrata settlement in Pennsylvania, and the New Israelites in Vermont.

This bewildering welter of sectarian movements was extremely diverse
in terms of doctrine, but they were all part of a significant counter-Puritan
tradition that preached the attainability of spiritual perfection. Most forecast the imminent arrival of the millennium—and preached that among
the spiritual gifts earmarked for humanity during the last phase of human
history was the secret knowledge so long suppressed by corrupt church
establishments: the original saving wisdom that God handed down (as
some sects had it) to Adam in the Garden of Eden.

Such teachings were clearly at odds, in almost every way, with the
Puritan ideal of an organic and hierarchical civil order closely managing the
social conditions by which the collective salvation of the New World was to
be worked out. These early counter-Puritan dissenters, by contrast, eagerly

embraced the anti-Calvinist faith known as *Arminianism*—the view, associated with the seventeenth-century Dutch theologian Jacobus Arminius, that individual experience, and not the inscrutably all-powerful will of God, was to serve as the fundamental scheme of salvation. Anne Hutchinson had given the Puritan leaders of New England a foretaste of the havoc that Arminian teaching could wreak with their dreams of organic civic order—but they could never hope to police orthodoxy across the sprawling expanse of the colonial wilderness. What's more, the doctrines of human perfectibility that gathered under the heretical banner of Arminian faith were clearly attuned to the economic rigors of frontier migration in the New World. Mastery of the material world was an invaluable precondition of the pioneering life, and just as the accumulating logic of the Puritan calling lent itself to the amassing of wealth in colonial port cities and manufacturing centers, so did the insurgent spirit of Arminian rebellion crop up along the western interior of New England and the more rural Middle and southern colonies. There was a reason, after all, that the natural outcome of Winthrop's schism with Roger Williams culminated in Williams's expulsion to an untamed colonial frontier—just as there was a reason that Williams's heterodox Baptism took firm root in the virgin soil of Rhode Island.

There was another, more immediate contradiction evident in the project of enforcing theological orthodoxy in the New World colonies. Even though Arminian belief was a fearful, and widely suppressed, backsliding tendency among early Puritan congregations, all these breakaway Arminian sects could justify their dissenting views by simply citing the original Puritan apostasy from the Church of England. The animating premise of the European settlement of the New World was, after all, a flight from the corruptions of institutional faith; the dissenting radicals in such colonial polities as Rhode Island, the Jersey colonies, and Pennsylvania simply maintained that they were hewing to the Reformation's true spirit by resisting the power plays and idolatries of the state-established faith.

There was one important, if informal, affinity among the colonies' growing cohort of dissenting radicals: a fascination with the spiritualization of matter, by means of such traditions as folk healing, hermeticism, and alchemy. This disposition, too, is easily waved away as inconsequential superstition, right out of the opening act of *Macbeth*—but as scholars such as John L. Brooke have shown, the hermetic obsession with the manipulation and transmutation of worldly materials formed a vital stratum of popular religion in the colonial era. Just as the America we now inhabit is on paper a sober, churchgoing republic of evangelicals who nonetheless throng to the blissed-out New Age counsels of a Deepak Chopra and the spiritualized success nostrums of *The Secret*, so were many colonial Americans exhorted in public to greater levels of churchly piety—and then, when they'd adjourned home, prone to divine for water and buried treasure on their farms, learn their fortunes from the stars, and try to cure their ills with folk medicines.

Such practices have understandably fragmentary records, since they enjoyed neither the institutional nor intellectual support of the colonies' spiritual establishment, but it's nonetheless clear that popular religion in the colonial era was steeped in magic and folk belief, straying into occult traditions such as divination and Gnosticism. It was this motley grouping of heterodox practices that the Puritan leaders of New England famously depicted as witchcraft and viciously sought to stamp out. Not surprisingly, these exercises of civil authority tended to treat the alleged excesses of witchcraft as starkly opposed to the Protestant ethic: In addition to exposing the free-ranging influence of the Devil, witchery was commonly linked to unearned wealth. The infamous witch trials in Salem, for example, were famously preceded by a long series of local "disputing over ministers, churches, taxes, and roads that made a mockery of John Winthrop's sermon aboard the *Arabella*," by fomenting widespread civic discord and bitter theological quarrels, as Butler notes. Butler cites a wide array of scholarship showing how accusations of witchcraft tracked the town's drift away from traditional Puritan values—with occult powers that supposedly seduced believers with offers of "money, silks, fine cloathes, ease from labor" and even outright tenders of houses and land. The charges also bore obvious gender implications, since accused witches typically had accrued "considerable economic power"; as the historian Carol Karlson has shown, "a remarkable number of New England's accused witches had amassed property, usually through their husbands' deaths."[24]

These official charges were of course demented fabrications, as even one of the lead accusers in the Salem case, Cotton Mather, would later confirm. But in one sense, the frenzied pursuers of witchery weren't entirely off the mark in equating the nascent culture of wealth in New England with popular belief in magic. Puritan divines themselves had made startlingly explicit connections between worldly favor and spiritual election. The New England faithful should not let themselves "be possessed with doubts because we are suffered to prosper so much," John Davenport preached in a 1667 Cambridge election sermon. Thanks to the "Mercy of the *New-Covenant*," God's chosen settlers of the New World could expect "Promises of Converting and Sanctifying Grace; and thereto . . . an addition of Promises respecting *Temporal Blessings*." Small wonder, then, that this freshly covenanted corps of believers should enjoy "the Blessings both of the *upper and nether Springs*, the blessings of Time and Eternity."[25]

Preachers such as Davenport were subtly reworking the terms of the covenant envisioned by Winthrop to render his admonitions to demonstrate liberality in charity something of a redundancy amid the self-evident blessings of the "nether Springs" of worldly fortune. The counterposed spheres of public worship and private gain were already collapsing into a single stream of abundant "Temporal Blessings" in affluent communities such as Davenport's Cambridge. In the audacious embrace of the apparently seamless "blessings of Time and Eternity," the careful Augustinian separation of the temporal and eternal cities was casually abolished.

The counter-Puritan communities of spiritual dissent in the American colonies advanced this process one step further, by yoking their faith in human perfectibility to the actual material basis of wealth. In these heterodox communities, practitioners commonly ascribed occult magic properties to money; the operations of the economy, after all, appeared to be driven by irrational, remote forces (a condition that has stubbornly endured amid all matter of modern, and purportedly scientific, innovations in the study of economics), and the overt power of money has always possessed a mystic and talismanic importance. Money itself was the object of various popular magic practices, from the proto-scientific and Gnostic study of alchemy to the folk traditions of divining and money-digging. The scandal of purported witchcraft stemmed at least in part from the sound intuitions of the Puritan elite that its members were rapidly losing control of the social and economic order they had lovingly plotted out as a model for a New Jerusalem.[26]

It's easy to caricature these sub-currents of material transmutation in the colonial past as the overblown esoteric stuff of a Dan Brown novel. In reality, though, the popular theories of alchemy and hermetic cosmology—which held that the raw stuff of matter could be refined into precious metals, and by extension, that the fallen human could proceed, via similar gradations of improvement, into a kind of divinity—took firm root among the dissenting prophets and seers of the New World. As John L. Brooke shows in his groundbreaking study *Refiner's Fire*, the hermetic scheme of redeemed metaphysical matter found its fullest articulation in the cosmology of Mormonism. Many of the radical innovations to Mormon theology that Joseph Smith introduced late in his career align directly with the main themes of hermetic speculation, stretching all the way back to the Renaissance: the notion that the created world exists on a continuum with the divine; the belief that the first man, Adam, was initiated into crucial secrets of the cosmic order, and could well have been a deity in his own right; the belief that the transmutation of metals prefigures, and opens onto, the broader progression of humanity toward the divine; the idea that humans can obtain experiential access to spiritual truths via dreams and visions. What's more, as Brooke has shown, Smith in his youth had direct contacts with practitioners of hermetic popular faith, via kinship networks and encounters with diviners and money-diggers. Indeed, as a young man, Smith worked as a money-digger himself, hiring his services out to landowners in upstate New York who hoped the precocious diviner could ferret out alleged reserves of Indian and pirate treasure that, according to longstanding area folk tradition, lay buried everywhere in the hills of this frontier farm country. It made perfect sense, in the logic of the spiritual-cum-economic faiths of the American interior, that Smith's background in money-digging eventually steered the young prophet toward the purported discovery of the gold plates bearing the updated New World scripture that would come to be known as *The Book of Mormon*.

But that all comes later in the formation of the modern Money Cult. What's crucial here is to note the core, conflicting theological visions that date almost from the moment of the first settlement of New England. On the one hand, the spiritual leaders of New England sought to uphold the communitarian Puritan ideal of a public faith administered by a priesthood of all believers. On the other hand, though, they were hard-pressed to counter the steady undertow of the motley, powerful conviction that ordinary Americans could possess the materials of their own salvation in their own hands.

Such Stuff as Dreams Are Made On

More daunting still was the common intuition among heterodox religious movements in colonial New England that the stuff of salvation was carved into the very landscape. The diviners, money-diggers, and alchemical speculators of the colonial interior were early augurs of the economic exceptionalist creed that fed America's self-image as a truly New World. With the stuff of prosperity so readily tamed and worshiped, it seemed clear to prophets and preachers alike that the British colonies were on track to sidestep the bitter class divisions rooted in the feudal societies of the Old World. And much like today's financial elite, the leaders of colonial New England turned to speculative new financial instruments to ratify their rising sense of economic chosenness.

Many of the currents of the emerging sensibilities of New World wealth were on abundant display in the little remembered episode of the colonial land bank. One of the central champions of this scheme was John Winthrop's eldest son and namesake—who in keeping with Davenport and other later-born New England divines, had brushed aside his father's sober counsel to celebrate the mystic properties of colonial prosperity.

Indeed, John Winthrop Jr. is a remarkable transitional figure in the annals of the Money Cult faith, for whereas he was firmly grounded in the Puritan social gospel by birth, he was also an enthusiastic student of esoteric folk religion. The younger Winthrop possessed one of the largest libraries of alchemical and hermetic works on either side of the Atlantic. And like many adherents of alchemy—whose core beliefs were predicated, after all, on the fungible nature of precious metals—the younger Winthrop was attracted to economic schemes that reflected the shifting character of material wealth. In correspondence with a well-known British alchemist and economic theorist named Samuel Hartlib, Winthrop Jr. helped promote the founding of a colonial land bank—i.e., a plan to mint currency on the basis of the fluctuating value of the colonies' most ample commodity, land. The younger Winthrop put the plan before the Royal Society in 1661.

That proposal went nowhere, but as John L. Brooke notes, Winthrop Jr.'s alchemical recasting of monetary value caught on more broadly in the colonies. The land-bank plan was revived in Winthrop's native Connecticut and neighboring colonies. By the 1740s, the first land bank was founded in the Massachusetts colony. As support for a land bank continued to gather steam among the disenfranchised farmers and speculators of New England, a Connecticut preacher named John Wise summed up the commonsensical appeal of the plan for a New England populace long convinced of its own mystic ability to conjure money from the earth. We carry "the *Lapis Aurificus* or *Philosophers Stone* in our heads," he wrote in 1721, "and can turn matter into Silver and Gold by the Power of thought as soon as any other People, or else I must own I have not yet Learnt the Character of my Country."[27]

This was a remarkable transport of material and metaphysical speculation to come from the pen of an orthodox Congregationalist minister like Wise, as much a direct heir to the elder Winthrop's sacred covenant as Winthrop Jr. was. Still, the leaders of the land-rich American colonies could see little point in anchoring an exchange currency to such an abundant resource—the effect would likely be akin to the sunny forecasts of the alchemists who predicted that by flooding the gold market with their spiritually refined product, they would drive all money out of circulation altogether and usher in a millennial age of universal abundance. Instead, the Bay Colony latched onto the creditor-friendly currency theories that John Locke had advanced in his celebrated *Second Treatise on Civil Government*. Like many a latter-day hard-money theorist and goldbug, Locke insisted that there was simply "an immutable, intrinsic value of silver and gold, determined for all time in the state of society preceding the formation of governments"—a view that, as Brooke observes, "would stand for centuries to protect the interests of the propertied."

The quarrel over the contingent worth of paper currency versus the ostensible permanent value of precious metals would fuel a great deal of future controversy over the nation's economic fortunes—down, indeed, through the present-day cult of gold worship on the Tea Party right. But in this formative guise, it's vital to recall how deeply the spiritual dimension of the question took hold. It's also important to note that the basic coordinates of this founding colonial conflict over currency and banking would reverse over time. As American believers came increasingly to recognize their eternal interests aligning with market prerogatives, they would fetishize the Lockean ideal of gold-standard exchange as an alchemical wonder in its own right. The modern explosion of paper currency, and the inflationary fears that it stoked in the investor class, would orient the primal gnostic energies roused by Winthrop and the land-bank schemers in a new direction entirely. Now precious metals would themselves be imbued with mystic properties of transfiguration; they would hedge against inflation in dark times, to be sure, but more than that, they would redeem the many worldly struggles of the true-believing Money Cult. Here again, the Mormon experience would prove prophetic, as the esoteric strains of the counter-Puritan money faith would converge in the founding of America's first native-born church and its improbable evolution into a worldwide conservative spiritual corporation.

But this was just one among many respects in which the restless corps of New World Protestants would contrive to sanctify the workings of a new national market economy. And to get a close-up sense of how that process began to gain traction in colonial America, it's worth taking a fresh look at the great spiritual icon of the capitalist takeoff in America, Benjamin Franklin.

The tirelessly pragmatic Franklin would seem at first glance an improbable consort of the hermetic visionaries assigning fluid and contingent value to mutable metals. Of course, as a printer himself, Franklin had a vested interest in the minting of paper currency, and his case was made in entirely secular terms of promoting domestic manufacture and consumer markets. But his support of the land-bank system furnishes a vital vantage on the actual character of religious and economic thinking in a colonial America groping its way toward a broader sanctification of market values.

Like most of the forces that would go on to shape the sanctified market economy, Franklin's ideas on both religion and economics are far more complicated than his starring role in Max Weber's *The Protestant Ethic and the Spirit of Capitalism* has led us to believe. Franklin was far from a principled Deist who happened to retain the character structure of the Puritan divines; he was, rather an acolyte of a peculiarly American strain of worldly piety. Defying both the strictures of Calvinism and the classical conception of republican virtue, he celebrated the idea of luxury as a crucial "Spur" to individual economic effort, much in the vein that his Scottish contemporary Adam Smith did in his later speculations on the mystical (if not quite alchemical) transmutation of material self-interest as a beneficent social force, guided by a quasi-divine "invisible hand." Should we consider, Franklin asked, whether luxury "may not produce more than it consumes, if without such a Spur people would be, as they are naturally enough inclined to be, lazy and indolent?"[28]

Yet Franklin also advocated for a surprisingly communitarian view of the nature of property, in line with the first John Winthrop's views on the organic priority of the social disposition of wealth. Property is simply a "Creature of Society and is subject to the Calls of that Society whenever its Necessities shall require it, even to its last Farthing," Franklin insisted in a paper completed a few months before his death in 1790. And when he presided over Pennsylvania's Constitutional Convention, he endorsed a failed resolution declaring "That an enormous Proportion of Property vested in a few Individuals is dangerous to the Rights, and destructive to the Common Happiness, of Mankind; and therefore every free State hath a Right by its Laws to discourage the Possession of such Property."[29]

Franklin's religious views were also far more complicated and ambivalent than what's typically ascribed to him via his residual Calvinist character. In latter-day political and religious controversy, Franklin, like nearly all the other colonial founders, has largely been conscripted into role-model duty for one tendency or another: Tea Party acolytes scour the details of his life story for evidence of elevated piety (an especially tough sell in Franklin's case), while secularists and atheists glory in his numerous pronouncements on the rational shortcomings of revealed religion.

Franklin's actual spiritual life was far different than either of these culture-war fantasias suggests. In the economic and religious spheres alike, Franklin was far less of a poster boy for any historical tendency than he was a man of several contradictory yet overlapping mindsets—which is to say that he very much embodied the spirit of his peculiar, transitional age.

A brief overview of Franklin's actual spiritual odyssey serves to remind us of this crucial point. The son of a Presbyterian clergyman, Franklin started out training, like so many other colonial men of learning, to be a minister. He then had a youthful dalliance with strictly doctrinaire Deism, which he later repudiated as foolish. He harbored doubts about the efficacy of prayer during the French-Indian War, but during the Constitutional Convention, he sponsored a proposal to have a chaplain lead the proceedings in prayer—a plan duly outvoted by putatively more pious founders such as James Madison, a graduate of the then-Calvinist-leaning College of New Jersey.

When Congress appointed Franklin, together with John Adams and Thomas Jefferson, to design the "Great Seal" for the new American Republic, he did not, as one might expect, alight on the rationalist-Illuminist image of the eye atop the pyramid that now glowers in Enlightenment splendor on the back of the dollar bill; no, this arch-individualist seer of the colonial capitalist order proposed a depiction of the great miracle of collective liberation in the Book of Exodus: "Moses lifting his hand and the Red Sea dividing, with Pharaoh in his chariot being overwhelmed by the waters, and with a motto . . . 'Rebellion to tyrants is obedience to God.'"[30] Toward the end of his life, Franklin harbored private doubts about Jesus' divinity, but he continued to believe in the immortality of the soul and a scheme of otherworldly reward and punishment. "What Franklin liked least was dogma of any kind," notes colonial historian Patricia U. Bonomi, "including the dogma of deism. His youthful view that 'vital religion has always suffer'd, when Orthodoxy was more regarded than Virtue' changed little over a long life."[31] Franklin was also initiated into Freemasonry in

1731, and by at least some accounts, possessed a passing familiarity with alchemy, via both the materials collected in *Poor Richard's Almanac* and his correspondence with such gentlemen seekers after hermetic wisdom such as the Yale University divine Ezra Stiles.

The point here is not that Franklin was a confused thinker, a hypocrite, or an undercover alchemist—nor that his market-friendly *Poor Richard* nostrums were an unimportant feature of his spiritual makeup. It is, rather, to underline the critical point that the features of our economic and religious past that we typically view in isolation were, in fact, in unresolved dialogue with each other. Steeped in the imagery and rhetoric of the Puritan errand, Franklin's spiritual outlook nonetheless strained to take in the full sweep of the new world taking shape before him—from the dizzying profusion of new Protestant sects to the logic of individual achievement in a polity still founded (in Franklin's view, at least) on a socially revocable conception of property. It's small wonder, then, that Franklin, like many far less celebrated founders, should himself give a contradictory account of the spiritual evidence before him—and that he should fail to settle on a definitive account of worldly success, spiritual works, or indeed, the spirit of capitalism.

Meanwhile, if it's viewed from another vantage, Franklin's somewhat motley religious life serves as a fuller template of the capitalist piety of our own age. While the content of Franklin's faith was heterodox, his method was as mainstream as the practices of any of the dissenting sects taking shape around him in the Middle Colonies. Franklin endorsed a restlessly experimental brand of faith, whose precepts were largely borne out by their practical civic uses; once public prayer, for example, had demonstrated its value over Franklin's own inward skepticism, he was happy to advocate for it at the 1787 Convention. Similarly, when he had joined a rationalist social club during his tour of duty in London as colonial ambassador to England, Franklin introduced a characteristically American innovation into the group's protocols: a "public liturgy," which held in part that the "local Gods" who inspired devotion among nations, sects and hairsplitting theologians were inferior to—and indeed, fugitive emanations of—the universe's "governing Principle" that functioned, as Newtonian cosmology then suggested, as "the Universal God."[32]

That's right: Just as the rationalist Franklin thought to draft the national seal in the image of an Old Testament miracle, so did Franklin the diplomat of reason seek to codify his impersonal, science minded faith in the trappings of churchly observance. He was, moreover, quite explicit on the benefits of this will-to-public-communion, according to the club's founder and host, the dissenting Welsh minister David Williams: "Franklin, with some emotion, declared he never passed a Church, during Public Service, without regretting that he could not join in it honestly and cordially."[33]

The formation of the Protestant American Money Cult, in other words, was anything but a schematic fulfillment of a simple Protestant ethic, or a diffuse "spirit of capitalism." The communitarian ideas of John Winthrop were to suffer a far more punishing crucible, one that pitted the dynamic newfound prosperity of colonial life against the fast-ossifying hierarchies of the New England Way. It's important to fix this point clearly as the crucial, post-colonial phase of the Money Cult comes into view: As Franklin's example clearly shows—and as the experience of scores of subsequent Money Cult prophets went on to drive home—the Money Cult was to be an improvised work of syncretism more than the triumph of any one orthodoxy, bringing the dogmas of Puritan achievement into strange new accord with the heresies of counter-Puritan folk religion. The American religious scene didn't traffic uniformly in the gospel of the self-made man as first hymned by Franklin; instead, it created a new nation teeming with self-made gospels. This process began in earnest during the First Great Awakening, which revived many of the lines of class conflict that had shaped the original radical Puritan movements in Britain, even as it sought to call the reprobate colonies back to the one true faith.

2

NATION BUILDING

Benjamin Franklin was a divided soul, but also a tireless entrepreneur. As he pondered the fallout from the religious upheaval known as the First Great Awakening—a dramatic outpouring of piety that derided the colonies' traditional clerical leaders as aloof and privileged guardians of a dead, rationalist faith—Franklin had an inspiration. In 1756, he wrote to his close friend George Whitefield—the great British revivalist who'd touched off the Awakening during his tour of the colonies in 1739 and 1740—with a remarkable proposal: The two men should join forces to settle a brand-new colony of their own, dedicated to the spread of Christian prosperity.

The prospective collaboration between the rationalist patriot and the diehard evangelist spoke volumes about the changes that Whitefield's revival had wrought in the nation's social fabric—a transformation that Franklin, a reliable judge of the popular political mood, grasped intuitively. The unsettled Ohio territory would be an ideal spot to showcase the worldly dividends of Christian virtue, Franklin wrote. What's more, investors in the colony could realize handsome profits along the way—a mutually satisfying arrangement for both evangelicals and speculators.

The material and spiritual returns for the Anglo settlers of this New World colony would be downright staggering: "What a glorious Thing it would be, to settle in that fine country a large Strong Body of Religious and Industrious People! . . . God would bless us with Success, if we undertook it with a sincere Regard to his honour."[34] Besides, the work of converting the Native American population—a key goal for missionary-minded ministers like Whitefield—would be more successful "if we could, by such a colony, shew them a better sample of Christians than they commonly see in our Indian traders."[35]

In advancing this vision of purified colonial commerce along the Ohio interior, Franklin projected a bold new sense of the American colonies' economic power. Here was a "Strong Body of Religious and Industrious People" poised to make good on what looked on all sides to be a glorious commercial millennium-in-the-making. There was a world of ambitious new assumptions about the intertwining paths of spiritual and commercial progress contained within Franklin's proposal—and more than that, there was the simple audacity of the thing. The colonial age's greatest prophet of worldly enterprise was promoting a model community of Christianized commerce, to be co-founded by the best-known evangelist of the age. Here, if anywhere, was powerful testimony to the great primal appeal of the faith that would eventually ripen into the American Money Cult.

There's no record of what Whitefield—a restless spiritual entrepreneur in his own right—thought of Franklin's scheme to plant a missionary business colony in the Ohio territories. It's tempting to suggest, though, that he regarded the idea as largely redundant. It had been Whitefield's own electrifying preaching that had sparked the Awakening, after all—and by all appearances, the greatest legacy of the revival was a newly roused corps of believers, determined to transform the scattered British colonies of the New World into a Christian commercial power of unparalleled abundance. All an impassioned exhorter like Whitefield would have to do was urge them on.

The Clerical Culture War

In strictly intellectual terms, Franklin was no revivalist. He instinctively aligned with the statelier, more reasonable doctrines of the New England establishment. But Franklin was hardly an abstruse theologian—and the First Great Awakening was much more than a seminar-room discussion of the relative merits of reason and emotion in Protestant religion. At bottom, this first great revival movement on American shores was nothing less than an argument over how faith should be affirmed in public, and the extent to which it would now infuse the daily lives of ordinary Americans.

And with the precepts of faith still directing the course of the colonies' political economy, the questions of religious authority at the Awakening's heart were also, inevitably, economic and political propositions, cloaked in the sturdy Protestant rhetoric of personal salvation and millennial striving. In lieu of a divinely appointed calling, and a well-fortified place of authority within the old Puritan communion of saints, the First Awakening offered its evangelical converts something far more immediate, dramatic, and (not least by a long shot) abundant: the sudden deliverance of depraved sinners into the boundless grace of God's love, and the opportunity to topple the unresponsive elites who administered the first New World covenant. In their place, the adherents of the Whitefield revival set out to reshape the intimate experience of Protestant salvation in the image of a new age of market relations.

The First Awakening was, in other words, the first in a long line of moral and political conflicts in America that would pit a fervid evangelical born-again faith against an allegedly hidebound cultural establishment, led by a dry and analytical group of diehard elitists. This revivial's rival camps were known familiarly as "New Light" evangelicals and "Old Light" rationalists, but at the level of pulpit delivery and audience response, they were perhaps better characterized by their less-well-known shorthand designations for their preaching styles. Calvinist evangelicals were known as "hot" preachers, while their rationalist Congregational counterparts were saddled with the dismissive epithet of "cold." These terms applied with equal force to the socioeconomic outlook of their adherents; revival supporters were hot, in the sense of being eager to profess an experiential faith that matched up to the materially gratifying tenets of New World social mobility, and the rationalist old guard was cold, in the sense of preferring that the deferential modes of conduct and commerce that had governed the original colonies remain more or less frozen in place.

This, indeed, was the significant difference that sets the First Awakening apart from the familiar battles royal of modern culture warfare: The great Calvinist uprising in the pulpits of the New World was also a stealth vehicle for a fundamental dispute over what counted as legitimate social power in the new commercial society of the colonies. The revival's main controversies might have cited the venerable warhorses of Protestant theology, from Martin Luther to Jacob Zwingli to John Calvin, but ultimately they pivoted around the newly fluid markers of status and privilege in the emerging market economy of pre–Revolutionary America. As insurgent New Lights railed against the cold and arid certainties of Congregational rationalists, they also assailed many institutions of inherited colonial privilege—the seminaries that churned out a ministerial elite of terminally deficient piety, to be sure, but more broadly, the colleges, landed gentries, and legislatures that presided over the colonies' fragmenting commercial and political life. With these evangelical indictments of the standing order calling down the holy wrath of God—and furnishing the only available rhetoric of popular political dissent—the confident middle-class leaders of the future American Revolution were finding their first authoritative voice of rebellion.

The American Jeremiad

In the decade prior to Whitefield's arrival in the colonies in 1739, this uprising was already brewing, chiefly among evangelical ministers and congregations who'd begun openly to protest the reign of the old Congregationalist order. (By the early eighteenth century, most former Puritan congregations had rechristened themselves as Congregationalist. As it took on the trappings of established religion in New England, Congregationalism mellowed into a more rationalist and generically civic form of Christian worship. The more emotional and experiential preachers of the early eighteenth century, meanwhile, identified as Calvinists. Like most of the generations of evangelical dissenters who would come in their wake, they were backward-looking innovators, depicting themselves as reviving a traditional faith centered on the redemption of sinners even as they pioneered revolutionary new ways of delivering their message to ever larger and more restless audiences.)

As the American colonies blossomed into prosperous port communities and trade centers, the regular rounds of churchly Congregational worship started to seem dull. Basic tenets of the faith, such as the conventions of communally monitored conversion and the rigorous religious control of civic life—seemed to be decomposing into hollow, and unjust, social forms. The sustained and robust rebellion against such formal piety mounted by pre-Awakening Calvinists further loosened the already weakening strictures of communal conversion within New England Congregationalism.

This rebellion found its most persuasive voice in the unique American preaching tradition known as the jeremiad. Named for the angry excoriations of injustice by the Old Testament prophet Jeremiah, the jeremiad was the most prominent public forum for assessing the progress of the Puritan covenant—something like a colonial version of the latter-day State of the Union address, but decidedly less upbeat. Typically scheduled for election days and days set aside in the calendars of colonial legislatures for public fasting and atonement, the jeremiads of the earlier colonial settlement served as dual pleas for restoration. After castigating the populace for all manner of worldly sin and covetousness, jeremiad preachers recalled their guilt-ridden audiences to the basic terms of the covenant, as laid out in Winthrop's *Modell of Christian Charity*. The jeremiad message also mined Scripture for reassuring evidence of God's long-suffering patience with His chosen people, and His miraculous capacity for grace. The basic structure of the sermon served to remind Puritan settlers of their special standing before God via the somewhat perverse method of cataloging the Lord's seemingly unappeasable anger toward their communal failure to uphold the terms of their covenant.

In the decade or so prior to the Awakening, the jeremiad took on a more pointed social message. As the American colonies began to prosper in earnest, their commercial and spiritual leaders were starting to look distinctly sinful. Preachers of jeremiads isolated the spirit of acquisition as the chief cause of the colonies' fatal backsliding. In one representative sermon titled "An Essay for the Reviving of Religion," Samuel Wigglesworth went before the Massachusetts legislature in 1733 to explain that the colony was turning away from the Lord because the "Exorbitant Reach after Riches" was now "the Reigning Temper in All Persons of All Ranks in the Land."[36]

The Calvinist theologians of the pre-revival decade didn't go so far as to identify the age's grasping spirit with deviltry, but they came close. Gilbert Tennent, a graduate of the influential Log College of revivalist Calvinism in Bucks County, Pennsylvania, founded by his father William, bluntly noted that men "grow in wickedness in Proportion to the Increase of their Wealth." Jonathan Edwards—Whitefield's key theological collaborator in the Awakening—marveled at how the leveling, universal condition of human sinfulness made a mockery of the carefully tended social distinctions of the age. "If one worm be a little exalted above another, by having more dust, or a bigger dunghill, how much does he make of himself!" Edwards exclaimed. "What a distance does he keep from those that are below him!"[37]

Calvinist supporters of revived religion in the 1730s were quick to tease out the deeper spiritual sources of such covetousness. Tennent observed, for example, that the mania for luxury was but a symptom of the more fundamental condition of self-idolatry, the longing "to be a little demigod in the World, a sort of independent Being, by having many dependent on thee, counting thy Smiles, and trembling at thy Frowns."[38]

Whitefield adroitly reversed the logic of the jeremiad. The real source of the colonies' ills wasn't a shallow, materialist populace, he stressed; it was, instead, a lifeless and indolent class of preachers. In the process, he made a fundamental dispute about social privilege come across as a fight over theological doctrine, and he focused the populist ire of the Calvinist insurgency on the conduct of a lazy and disdainful ministerial elite in the pulpit.

More fundamentally, though, Whitefield channeled the inchoate mood of class confrontation taking shape before the pulpits of New England into a powerful new social force: the transatlantic market economy. Where the preachers in the jeremiad tradition excoriated the communal pride and vanity associated with the accumulation of personal wealth, Whitefield pared down the covenant vision of a communal faith into a one-on-one transaction binding the individual believer to God. This transaction was what Whitefield famously dubbed the New Birth in Christ. The New Birth, as Whitefield preached it, was predicated on the conviction that believers were facing certain damnation based on a life of incorrigible sin. But from the depths of this despair, the believer could ascend to a no-less-transporting vision of his completely unearned, and divinely assured, salvation in the world to come—redeeming him not just from his own sinful nature, but also from the networks of piety and authority that governed public faith in the earlier phase of colonial life. In theological terms, there was nothing terribly new about the New Birth—Calvinist conversion had long been the mainstay of Puritan social and religious order. But Whitefield's genius was to present the old message of Calvinist salvation in the new wineskins of the transatlantic world's commercial society. He described the theology of the New Birth in the imagery of market exchange, and promoted it via the new communication that bound the American colonies to the expanding mercantile interests of the British crown. Thanks to his efforts, Americans understood their personal redemption to be of a piece with their standing in the colonies' new commercial order. Salvation, and America's bountiful economic life, would never look quite the same again.

The power of direct access to divinity was embodied in Whitefield's ministry itself. The Great Itinerant, as his admirers came to call him, propagated a new kind of public worship. Via the Atlantic world's new markets in book and newspaper publishing, the mode of delivery for Whitefield's gospel of the New Birth became far more uniform and impersonal—even as its content, at the level of individual experience, became much more intensely personal. With the communal structures of conversion and observance derided and discredited in Whitefield's sensational and expertly promoted sermons, the rites of the New Birth were likewise marketed overtly as commodities, in a new religious public sphere where Whitefield depicted the central drama of salvation in a self-conscious new rhetoric of expanded market access. "I counsel you to come and buy of Jesus Christ gold, white raiment, and eye-salve," he preached to revival crowds, portraying the savior of humankind as a merchant of spiritual truths transfigured into human comforts. In a similar register, Whitefield described God as the ultimate angel investor: "God trusted man once . . . He set Adam up, gave him a blessed stock, placed him in a paradise of love, and he soon became a bankrupt." Still, he rejoiced that, in Christ, God had elected to wipe humanity's ledger clean of the consequences of original sin: "Now, blessed be God, we are under a better dispensation . . . our stock is put into Christ's hand, [and] he knows how to keep it." And the lesson of this for enterprising colonial believers couldn't be plainer: They should, Whitefield preached, be "laudably ambitious, and get as rich as [they could] towards God." The "bank of Heaven" Whitefield proclaimed was "a sure bank"; in his own spiritual ventures, he had "drawn thousands of bills . . . and never had one sent back protested."[39]

It is difficult to imagine an account of the atonement of Jesus further in language or spirit from John Winthrop's vision of the Church as a living extension of the savior's own infinitely "liberal" spirit of charity—but Whitefield, just like Winthrop, was a preacher who embodied the spirit of his age. In such performances, and countless others like them, Whitefield was plumbing a new, radically individualist idea of salvation, in which its divine authors were patient, far-seeing investors, and anxious sinners were errant credit risks who might, in a moment of miraculous accord with the true financial order of things, be restored to the "blessed stock" that had been humanity's windfall at the moment of Creation. As a new mercantile economic order stirred to life in England and in the American colonies, Whitefield furnished a briskly efficient, yet powerfully dramatic, model of Protestant piety all but tailor-made for a rising middle class, convinced that it might well be colonizing the Christian millennium as its next great market conquest.

A Market for Salvation

Whitefield was in no sense a great theological thinker or innovator. His sermons typically oscillated, in the great Calvinist tradition, between the terrors of eternal damnation and the wondrous promise of salvation and grace. Among the 18,000 or so sermons he delivered during his career, he rarely deviated from the same basic gospel appeals he'd drafted during the first five years of his ministry.

He was, however, a revolutionary marketer of a gospel message that, in turn, pivoted on a vision of salvation firmly embedded in the marketplace. In place of the jeremiad's laments over a broken covenant, and its pleas for greater communal obedience to God's will, Whitefield substituted a raw, vitalist account of the individual soul in torment, and directed that pilgrim soul out into the public thoroughfares and consumer bazaars of a new commercial society to seek out the terms of a new individualist salvation.

Whitefield's opponents likewise understood that the revival crowds that made up the Awakening were the deliberate contrivance of a new, and dangerous, approach to the cultivation of piety. As was usually the case in Whitefield's preaching, Exhibit A for how this operated on new converts was Whitefield's own vast renown. As he recorded in his bestselling *Jour-*

nals (which, like most of his written work, was self-consciously composed for eventual purchase by his transatlantic mass readership), one of the first things he did after his own moment of conversion was to devote himself with renewed fervor to the study of the Bible—and, as he noted none too modestly, the results spoke for themselves: "I meditated therein day in and day out; and ever since that, God has made my way signally prosperous, and given me abundant success."[40] Throughout his career, Whitefield would continue to see God's hand in the story of his own success; once, as he faced "extraordinary and unavoidable expenses" at the outset of his ministry, his own brother unexpectedly came forward to liquidate the debt. Here, once more, was confirmation of the simple gospel injunction to "seek first the Kingdom of God and his Righteousness, and all things shall be added to you."[41]

While the Bible had worked wonders on both Whitefield's own soul and his standing in the world, he owed much of his American celebrity to a different kind of reading matter—the newspaper, which circulated dramatic reports of his phenomenal London revival crusades well ahead of his colonial preaching campaign in 1739–40, and tirelessly advertised his clashes with the colonial religious establishment as he evangelized through all of the New World colonies.

Britain's sprawling commercial empire had come to rely heavily on the dispersal of information across the Atlantic, to develop new markets for goods distributed back and forth between London and the Crown's colonies. Consumption of British goods in the American colonies was skyrocketing at the time when Whitefield began his New World ministry, from goods valued at one pound per New World consumer in 1740 to more than double that sum in 1760.

Newsprint lubricated this far-flung commercial empire, reporting trends in currency exchanges and commodities markets alongside news of shifting fashions and consumer taste preferences. The London market for newspapers was insatiable, fueling booms in both commercial and literary writing; a similar boomlet of cheap and widely available print took hold in the American colonies, which were publishing eleven major newspapers by the time Whitefield arrived in 1739—up from zero in 1700.[42] The newspaper explosion created attractive new consumer markets for merchants of all descriptions, on both sides of the Atlantic—and George Whitefield, as it happened, was the premier entrepreneur of the coveted transatlantic commodity of the individual believer's personal rebirth in Christ.

Whitefield's genius for marketing was evident from the moment of his arrival at the port of Philadelphia. He had traveled with his successful elder brother James—the same merchant-benefactor who had rescued Whitefield's ministry from its first (and far from last) moment of acute financial distress. On their passage across the Atlantic, James had arranged for George to transport an enormous cache of British manufactured goods, which London converts had donated in charitable support of the great orphanage that the evangelist was founding in the Georgia colony. So George Whitefield's itinerant preaching career in America began, suitably enough, with a detailed ad in the *Pennsylvania Gazette* listing the tempting items he would be offering up for portside auction. These included "Brass candlesticks, Snuffers and snuff dishes . . . English Cordage, Ratling, Worming, Marline and Spun-yarn rugs and Blankets . . . Scotch cloth, cotton romalls, Siersuckers . . . colour'd Ginghams, . . . broad cloth, Shalloons, long Ells, Buttons, Buckrams, and sewing-Silk."[43]

The idea was to induce people to come out to bid on the beguiling hoard of consumer goods, and then for them to stay for a foretaste of what they could expect from an impassioned Whitefield revival sermon—and neither Whitefield nor his audiences were much inclined to draw any clear distinction between the two pastimes. The two Whitefield brothers indeed pioneered a striking form of spiritual and commercial synergy in their New World exploits. James Whitefield, a sailor turned wine merchant, was able to cultivate commercial ties in the colonies on the strength of his celebrity brother's great local renown. Eventually, these contacts were lucrative enough for him to settle permanently in the commercial hub of Savannah. With James's famous evangelist brother working close by at Bethesda, the site of his costly and ambitious orphanage, the Whitefields typified the kind of commercial-evangelical alliance of power that would become commonplace in American Protestantism.

There might seem to be an obvious contradiction at play in the vocation of a preacher who enthusiastically marketed the very baubles of luxury

that he righteously condemned as telltale signs of decadence and idola-
try in the heat of his revival sermons. But as a social prophet, Whitefield had no quarrel with commerce per se. He chiefly took aim at the
personal indulgences most likely to sway believers from their true divine
allegiances—such as theater-going and attendance at fashionable balls
and social gatherings. But he strenuously promoted consumer choices
that enhanced piety and right conduct, such as purchase of his sprawling
published corpus of journals, sermons, and pamphlets, or donations to his
Georgia orphanage and other pet evangelical charities.

Importantly, Whitefield neither evangelized nor raised funds under
retainer from his mother denomination; as both exhorter and fund-raiser,
he was a new sort of religious leader—a faith-building entrepreneur,
whose transatlantic mission was mainly bankrolled by private sources of
funding.[44] Thus he was far more apt to regard consumer excess as something more than simply a spiritual failing—it also represented a sunken
opportunity cost, money that might otherwise help fund his orphanage
or various missionary enterprises. As he solicited donations on his Awakening tour, he pleaded with believers to "let that money, which you might
expend to pamper your own bodies, be given to feed the poor"—inadvertently underlining the notion that charity was a personal choice, and not
a communal obligation, as Winthrop had exhorted. In the same register,
Whitefield bemoaned traditional aristocratic pastimes—not so much as
telltale signs of material injustice, but rather as distractions. He bemoaned
"the misspending [of] precious time [in] play-houses, horse-racing, balls
and assemblies."[45]

One of the defining Old and New Light battles of Whitefield's revival
tour occurred at a 1739 revival gathering in Charleston, South Carolina.
There, Whitefield attacked the local Anglican leader, Commissary Alex-
ander Garden, for his corrupt and un-Christian tolerance for the "sinful diversions" of the town's planter aristocracy. Garden replied with the
dismissive hauteur of a career court preacher that the balls and parties
of Charleston's court society were "innocent" amusements, reserved for
noble Charlestonians of the "first *Figure* and *Character* "—and that, much
more to the point, Whitefield's "*Mobb-Preaching*" was the real "Danger to

Religion and the *Peace* and *Happiness* of Society." The center of that threat, as Garden saw it, was the crudely articulated doctrine of what Whitefield called the New Birth in Christ—"the Belief and Expectation of a certain happy *Moment*, when, by the *sole* and *specific* Work of the *Holy Spirit*, you shall at once (as 'twere by Magic Charm) be metamorphosed."[46]

As is often the case, the alarmist cry of an entrenched establishment neatly captured the deeper social import of a new religious idea. Whitefield's insistence on the intensely personal, all-but-instantaneous experience of the New Birth was indeed disruptive and dangerous, for it represented the emergence of a new ethos of religious expression and redemption—a sphere in which, as Garden spelled out in admirably precise detail, a new mass of believers could claim to be communing directly with the Holy Spirit without the intercession of Garden's own respectable ministerial caste. The leisured amusements that Whitefield was castigating were, at bottom, proxies for this exercise of hierarchical power in the life of the spirit; Garden could look placidly on the balls and other fripperies of the social elite in his pastoral care because they represented a natural extension of his own place in the pecking order of colonial social deference.

In just the same manner, in likening Whitefield's New Birth theology to a "Magic Charm," Garden pointedly sought to remind his hearers that this dangerous itinerant preacher also embodied the pagan sensibilities that were still associated with the underground worship of alchemical metals and monies in the British colonies. The First Awakening, in other words, was simultaneously a remarkable and galvanizing demonstration of popular spiritual power and a pitched battle over religious authority—the always-central question in Protestant faith of just how and why new believers were to be conducted into the defining moment of conversion.

Conversion had once been a badge of inherited privilege. In the early colonial churches, full members of a congregation had to be owners of property, and the families occupying the most prestigious pews, close in to the altar, tended also to be the wealthiest. To come into this exclusive fold, one had to undergo a rigid battery of interrogations into one's spiritual standing and civic character, carried out by the church community at large. "In early New England," Patricia U. Bonomi writes, the elaborate scrutiny of a [church] applicant's life and state of grace had been a kind of community rite. It involved an initial examination of the candidate by church elders and minister, followed by a narration of the individual's conversion experience before the entire congregation. Next came an investigation of a candidate's life and moral conduct, during which church members might question the townspeople at large about his character and reputation. Finally, the candidate was subjected to a close scrutiny of his spiritual development by the body of church members. Only if approved after these various tests was the candidate received into the covenant, at which time he solemnly promised to cleave forever to his fellow members in "brotherly love and holy watchfulnesse."[47]

But just as important, a believer's duly authorized full conversion was the central rite of passage permitting the next generation to accede into full church membership, and to ensure that their successor generations would, in turn, come into their own full guardianship of both their family wealth and the historic covenant that sanctified it. However, this formative experience was to become difficult for successive Puritan generations coming of spiritual age in the more prosperous and worldly social order indicted by jeremiad preachers—so much so that by 1662, Solomon Stoddard, minister of the Congregational Church in Northampton, Massachusetts, had instituted what became known as the Halfway Covenant. The agreement sought to preserve continuity with the founding cohort of Puritan church members by permitting partial church membership to their children and grandchildren—a kind of promissory note of the spirit that would mature into full membership once the younger congregants reported their own full-blown conversions.

Like most accommodations of orthodoxy to the pressures of social change, the Halfway Covenant was doomed to failure. If anything, Stoddard's modified covenant perpetuated the very logic of religious disaffiliation it sought to arrest: Introducing a formal, institutional category of the yet-to-be converted faithful left the work of salvation in something of a permanent holding pattern, while also creating a not-so-subtle incentive

for younger churchgoers to mimic a socially acceptable conversion experience, if only for the sake of reclaiming the pews reserved for the duly saved
and privileged full members of the church.

Whitefield's itinerant preaching of the theology of the New Birth
burst through the spiritual vacuum created by the colonies' declining
church membership and dubious shows of piety. And by hailing the kind
of mass piety enabled by market institutions such as the newspaper and
the outdoor revival meeting, Whitefield's ministry made it urgently and
dramatically clear that wayward sinners could come into their divine station all at once, via the splendors of the New Birth. In lieu of acting out a
spiritual pantomime for the sake of one's neighbors, selectmen, and church
board, the New World's seekers after redemption could now repair to the
colonies' public squares to experience the real thing—or at least the real
article, as marketed faithfully by George Whitefield.

The nervous Congregational divines of the establishment sized up this
direct threat to their own public authority as they pondered the new crowds
thronging to Whitefield's sensational revival meetings. The Awakening's
following drew heavily from the colonies' rising middle classes: small farmers in the South, and urban merchants and workers like Franklin in the
North. These were not the property owners and civic leaders who claimed
pride of place in the pews of Congregational New England. And everywhere
Whitefield preached, newly converted souls came away with the confident
conviction that they were chosen by God to hasten the millennium along
in the glorious image of the New World's own divinely authored prosperity.

Beside this confident vision of the future, the jeremiad's anguished
litany of past covenantal sins simply paled into insignificance—sometimes in the work of the selfsame preacher. The historian Alan Heimert
notes that in 1730, the New Light Boston preacher Thomas Foxcroft had
"commemorated the first century of New England with a lamentation for
departed spiritual glories," but on New Year's Day in 1747, he delivered
a "recapitulation of Christian history in which the Reformation and the
Puritan experiments loomed as forerunners of the Spirit's triumph in the
Great Revival of the 1740's . . . in the course of the Awakening the themes
of the jeremiad all but disappeared from Calvinist sermons."[48]

To the Market Born

Whitefield's insurgent gospel of commercially produced piety, and his cri-
tiques of misspent market resources, came naturally to him. As his close
collaboration with James suggests, the world of commerce was in many
ways Whitefield's native habitat. His father broke away from the Whitefield clan's long line of service to the Anglican church to try his fortune
as a merchant, and when that career choice didn't pan out, he became a
prominent innkeeper in Gloucester—a host, in other words, to many of
the merchants, salesmen, and wholesalers who began to blanket England
during the country's great eighteenth-century commercial revolution. All
five of Whitefield's siblings likewise either pursued mercantile careers or
married into merchant families (and all but one, the second-eldest brother
Thomas, did so with agreeably prosperous results).[49] So by the time Whitefield had risen to fame as the transatlantic world's leading revival preacher,
he was very much the opposite number to what his father had been in
the family hierarchy: the outlier spiritual leader in a family of dedicated
entrepreneurs. And even so, as Whitefield himself regularly reminded his
followers, he was a tremendous success in his chosen field.

In his sermons and writings, Whitefield likewise seamlessly adapted
the language of the era's burgeoning consumer market to the evangelical
cause. Describing the ambitions he'd laid out for his ministry at its outset,
he recalled that "I intended to make an hundred and fifty sermons, and
thought that I would set up a good stock in trade." In the advance publicity
for the 1739–40 revival tour, he dubbed it "a trading voyage [wherein he
would] sail into harbor with a well and full choice of heavenly wares."[50]

His direct appeals to the souls in his care were still more strikingly
cast in the rhetoric of market relations. During a Philadelphia sermon, he
announced that he would "turn merchant" for the Lord's cause; he had
"valuable commodities to offer for sale"—and the best part of the bargain,
he explained, was that in order for his hearers "to *buy* the truth," they could
transact business with the Lord "without money and without price."[51] Preaching before a crowd of believers along the aristocratic planters' preserves of
the Chesapeake, Whitefield again stressed the market utility of the gospel
message, and again contrasted it pointedly with the aristocracy's trademark

excesses. The New Birth, he argued, was the "one Thing needful" for all humanity—a "product" engineered from on high to bring "Satisfaction and Profit." In his studies of the work of fellow evangelical preachers, Whitefield singled out for special praise the work of one Dr. Marryat, on the basis of his facility with "market language"—i.e., easily grasped metaphors and similes drawn from the worlds of agriculture, manufacturing and trade.[52]

In the Beginning Was the Word

Whitefield was justly renowned for his dramatic preaching style—his legendary booming voice could be heard from a distance of several miles as he held audiences of thousands of believers in spellbound silence. Popular evangelical lore has long suggested that Whitefield largely converted the colonies to the New Birth by the sheer charismatic sound of his own voice. But as spectacular as his sermons were, Whitefield's revival owed more of its success to his tireless promotional efforts, and to his innovative grasp of how to harness the age's new transatlantic communications network to spread the word about his appearances among a widely dispersed American audience. Whitefield and his traveling publicist William Seward—a British convert who'd earned no small amount of notoriety in his pre-salvation career as a stock-jobber during the great collapse of the South Sea bubble in 1720—unloosed an amazing barrage of print notices to rouse public interest in Whitfield's sermons.

Since journalism on both sides of the Atlantic was still in its infancy and had few established professional standards in place, Seward and Whitefield were able to draft unsigned dispatches about the miraculous results of Whitefield's preaching during the Awakening, and to get them printed as straight newspaper reports. Many of these stories were misleadingly rendered in third-person prose, as though composed by a dispassionate journalistic observer rather than the revival's principal preacher and/or publicist. All told, Seward and Whitefield composed more than one hundred letters, press reports, and journal entries per day during the American tour. The end result was a saturated literary market: In 1740, an amazing 30 percent of all published work in the colonies was either about Whitefield himself, or was inspired by his preaching.[53] By the end of this promotional blitz, the American reading public could be counted on to know the subject firsthand—during the 1739–40 tour, Whitefield had preached more than 175 sermons, making it likely that every adult in the colonies had heard him at some point. (Later estimates were downscaled to roughly 80 percent of the colonial adult population.)

On principle, Whitefield kept no similar counts of the number of converts he won over to the New Birth at his revivals; the traffic in souls still remained a strictly confidential matter between God and the saved, he believed. Whitefield did, however, keep a running inventory of all the other measures of his success, from crowd turnouts (numbers that he and Seward would puff ever higher in their colonial news dispatches), to fund-raising returns for the Bethesda orphanage, to the number of sermons he'd delivered in a day or week. He was so devoted to the ritual accounting of all the measures of his success that he urged new believers to transpose the same basic bookkeeping method—known in the tradesman's argot of the day as a daybook—into a spiritual register, in order to conduct inward inventories of the state of their souls. "I think a good tradesman, whether he deals largely or not, will take care to keep his day-book well," he advised; but "if a man will not keep his day-book well, it is ten to one but he loses a good deal when he comes to count up his things at Christmas." Following the same calculus in matters of the spirit, Whitefield announced that "now I take it for granted, a good spiritual tradesman will keep his spiritual day-book well," so as to mark his or her incremental progress toward redemption: "I have died a little more to the world than yesterday," an optimistic Christian tradesman of the soul might report; "this day I hope that I have been a little more alive to God than I was yesterday."[54]

It was to be expected that a tradesman conducting such closely calculated self-inspections would benefit greatly from having a volume, or several volumes, of Whitefield's published works in a home library—together with pamphlets, news dispatches, and evangelical periodicals. At the height of Whitefield's transatlantic celebrity, from 1737 to 1745, publishers released as astonishing 300 editions of his work. While the figures on individual print runs are fragmentary, a conservative estimate of the total over this period works out to a minimum of 300,000 individual volumes. Of this total, roughly 80,000 would have been printed and circulated within the American colonies—one Whitefield volume for every 11 men, women, and children living in the colonies in 1740.[55] Printing costs were far and away the greatest expense in his ministry, and his publishing empire—over which he assumed control after his British publisher, James Hutton, turned away from Calvinism and therefore had to distance himself from Whitefield and his message—permitted him to tightly control the print runs and distribution of his books, and to use his latest published work to promote reader interest in forthcoming Whitefield titles. Meanwhile, Whitefield had also acquired control of a British evangelical magazine, the *Weekly History*, that circulated widely among Protestant readers on both sides of the Atlantic, and served as an invaluable tool of cross-promotion within the free-standing battery of evangelical cultural enterprises that now spanned the Atlantic. This tremendous flood of books, tracts, and journals pouring from the presses also gives the lie to the long-standing stereotype of the evangelical preacher as a fire-breathing prophet of "anti-intellectualism." The demand for the printed word, and for closely argued theological polemics, has always run high in the evangelical world, in Whitefield's day as well as our own. As with the castigation of worldly gain, the decisive question in assessing the value of learning was the larger designs—spiritual or worldly, devotional or rationalist—that lurked behind it.

Inventing a Religious Public

A Whitefield revival was also, importantly, a public event, and a rare demonstration of the power of crowds in colonial society—another portent of the new market society taking shape in the colonies' robust trade centers. As he barnstormed through the colonies, Whitefield marveled at how a crowd "so scattered abroad, can be gathered at so short a warning"— even though, of course, these crowds were largely conjured by Seward and Whitefield's relentless publicity machine.[56] One well-known eyewitness account of an outdoor Whitefield revival, from the 1740 journal of a Connecticut farmer named Nathan Cole, is especially striking for how it characterizes the seemingly spontaneous gathering of a colonial public in a makeshift market square. Once he got word that Whitefield would be preaching nearby, Cole had frantically thrust his farm work aside and gathered up his wife to rush on horseback to the revival site just outside Middletown. As he describes the scene, the massing of souls that materialized in his path seems almost a kind of miracle unto itself:

> I saw before me a cloud of fog arising. I first thought that it came
> from the great river [near central Middletown], but as I came nearer
> the road, I heard the sound of horse's feet coming down the road, and
> this cloud was a cloud of dust made by horse's feet . . . When I came
> within about 20 rods of the road, I could see men and horses slipping
> along in the cloud like shadows, and as I drew nearer it seemed like
> a steady stream of horses and their riders, scarcely a horse more than
> his length behind another, all of a lather and foam with sweat, their
> breath rolling out of their nostrils every jump. Every horse seemed to
> go with all his might for the saving of souls.[57]

Small wonder that when Whitefield appeared before the crowd, he struck Cole as "a figure almost angelical," who "looked as though he were cloaked with the authority of the Great God." Small wonder as well that the text of Whitefield's well practiced sermon struck Cole with the force of "a heart wound . . . I felt that my righteousness would not save me."[58] Cole, like countless other New World believers thronging to Whitefield's message, was experiencing the divine presence in a radically new setting: in a public sphere, amid an unfamiliar fellowship of spiritual seekers, bound neither by traditional denominational affiliation nor church discipline. No one could have foreseen it then, but this was to be, in large part, the future of evangelical worship in America: a very public spectacle of mass conversion meant to line up with an individual believer's intense inner conviction of sin, and final assurance of divine deliverance.

In his best known orations, Whitefield would act out the part of Abraham during the Genesis account of the biblical patriarch's abortive sacrifice of his son Isaac, or the role of a poor and obscure follower of Jesus, in order to bring home the miracle of divine intervention in human affairs. This was an especially powerful message for a colonial population that was finding the mandatory rites of Puritan conversion increasingly burdensome, and the experiences meant to justify them maddeningly elusive. For these seekers, Whitefield brought the irresistible message that the New Birth was available here and now, in the marketplace of American faith.

Against this backdrop, Whitefield's dramatized gospel doubled as a message of personal liberation. Instead of being lectured at about their persistent failure to live up to the hallowed communal obligations preserved in the covenant, Whitefield's audience was freed up to enter directly and imaginatively into the world of his sermon's central characters, as any other audience for any other dramatic performance might. In this way, religion stopped being a piously intoned set of verbal formulations, and started to seem more of a lived presence, calling down a revived ethos of immediate salvation on a new spiritual frontier. Whitefield's hearers and readers could go from seeing themselves as obedient members of a body of faith to experiencing salvation in the mode of revived patriarchs and New Testament disciples—even, at times, as living extensions of the Godhead itself.

This powerful allure of experiencing a new sort of personal connection to God in a new kind of public religious sphere was what drew such enormous crowds to Whitefield's pulpit appearances. It was also what unsettled a Congregationalist establishment that well understood the threat that ungoverned religious publics would pose to their traditional civic and spiritual authority. Whitefield had already established himself, in the sensational British phase of his career, as a populist social menace, profoundly disruptive to traditional conceptions of public piety and civic order. Anglican officials in his British homeland sought to ban his outdoor revival crusades, because their sheer spectacular scale—and the diverse socioeconomic character of Whitefield's public—seemed an invitation to social chaos. In England and the colonies alike, Whitefield's revival gatherings would commonly erupt into unnerving displays of religious emotion, and occasionally into mob violence. The very traits that made Whitefield seem dangerous to British officialdom helped reassure America's evangelical New Light divines that, regardless of his Old World denominational pedigree, he was one of their own in spirit.

Whitefield's remarkable career also rendered him the first celebrity and culture hero of the British colonies. On his tour of 1739–40, his average crowd was some 8,000 people, far too great a number for any church to hold. So of necessity, he produced the first great devotional innovation of the Awakening years, by forcing his crowds to come and worship in makeshift revival meetings, in the open fields and public squares of the American colonies.

This was a significant beachhead for evangelical faith to claim as its own, if for no other reason than that the American colonies had so few other outlets for expressing dissent in public. In most colonial towns, civic life was basically the monopoly of town meetings and church boards—venues over which the clerical establishments of New World communities exerted tight control. And they used this power ruthlessly to make the appearance of complete communal harmony something of a neurotic fetish. Even when civic disputes erupted over questions of property ownership or church leadership, they would be swiftly stricken from the public record "in order to . . . cultivate a good understanding and harmony among ourselves," as the colonial Massachusetts code put it. In the town of Springfield, Massachusetts, selectmen warned residents that they could be forced to remain there against their will should it "appear best for the whole." In Ipswich, meanwhile, the town leaders actually sold one local man's farm out from under him when he didn't attend church frequently enough; the move was justified on the grounds "that he may be compelled to live near the sanctuary" and therefore turn up for public worship more regularly.[59]

Religious schism was clearly (and quite literally) an intolerable thought in such communities; it was the main threat that drove colonial leaders to these panicked and autocratic extremes. Many churches banned Whitefield from preaching within their parishes not so much because of his professed doctrines—which were very much in the mainstream of Calvinist teaching—but rather for what the spectacle of his preaching tour symbolized: a roving mass of believers untethered by the usual bonds of communal discipline.

That Old-Time Religion

For all the revolutionary implications that Whitefield's preaching career presented to the established orders of spiritual and civic harmony, Whitefield nonetheless kept close faith with one important Puritan tradition: the idealized image of the apostolic Primitive Church as a model of New World piety. This is an important point of continuity—one that will run through the whole story of the Money Cult's distinctive theological out-look. In the same sense that modern capitalism has relied on the rigors of what Joseph Schumpeter has called "creative destruction"—the relentless dismantling of old structures of enterprise in the perennial quest for new and improved systems of production—so has the inner life of America's Protestants reliably grounded itself in a scripture-based version of the same process. Revival preachers and congregations have instinctively embraced the Primitive Church as the great scriptural origin site of this restoration-ist gospel, furnishing them the proofs of their salvation. These may be the literal, and miraculous, rites of speaking in tongues or handling snakes, or the far more common, and reputable, notion of a small-d democratic com-munion of apostles claiming the same first-hand connection to God and Christ that Whitefield preached. By its very nature as the mystic recon-stitution of the original body of witnesses present at the Christian world's creation, the Primitive Church would be equally resistant to the corro-sive influences of grasping ambition, institutional corruption, and (in the final analysis) history itself. Such a time-resistant and sin-allergic tradition would clearly serve to reconstitute a compromised into a "priesthood of all believers," in the famous primitivist formulation of Martin Luther.

The venerable American image of the Primitive Church presented another central virtue to Whitefield and his revival generation: It could be summoned to serve a very pliable set of social imperatives and preaching demands, and readily adapted to the shifting conditions of consumption in the commercial rounds of colonial life. Every time eighteenth-century believers picked up a Whitefield pamphlet or read through a volume of the Great Itinerant's sermons, they could picture themselves as heroic defend-ers of an embattled true faith, beset on all sides by persecutors and spiri-tual pretenders. And every time Whitefield would preach in the guise and voice of an ancient biblical hero, his rapt audience could feel themselves transported back to the defining trials of the first apostles, preserving their pure communion with the Savior against a corrupt and murderous Roman Empire. For it was also the nature of Primitive Church piety to be in perpetual peril as its devotees sought to preserve it in a sin-addled world; throughout the epic historical struggle to preserve this one, true, redeemed Christianity, vigilant believers continually had to snatch it away and reclaim it from the dead hand of priestly hierarchy.

It was not for nothing, after all, that Whitefield routinely referred to his ministry as the landmark crusade of a "Second Reformation" Just as in the historic Protestant Reformation of two centuries past, Whitefield's revival was devoted to eradicating the corrupt and irreligious practices of a self-interested clerical caste. (Just how this corruption had grown so dire, over such a comparatively abbreviated span of time under the authority of radical Protestant dissenters, was rarely explained, beyond the ritual invocation of the ever-worsening depravity of human nature.) As with the heady early promise of Luther's revival, Whitefield's crusade might well have seemed sure to culminate in the deliverance of all humankind, as the millennium advanced ever closer; all that such a devoutly longed-for out-come would require were newer and purer modes of belief, reflecting back the glories of the one true primitive Christian faith.

The Primitive Church ideal proved as accommodating to free-market innovation in economic matters as it was hostile to institutional structures of worship in the religious sphere—and this strategic advantage, as Whitefield's ministry shows, was far from a coincidence. As if by a sort of inverse law of development, American believers have retreated, over and over again, to ever simpler images of worship in their spiritual imaginations as the larger-scale institutions of commerce and finance have bulked ever more menacingly around their secular working lives.

Virtually any discussion of institutional life would find Whitefield reaching back to the first principles of his biblical primitivism. In an exchange of letters with Franklin, concerning the latter's plans to found a new American academy of arts and sciences, Whitefield voiced a charac-teristic indifference to the novelties of higher learning and cultural inquiry, chiding Franklin for treating religious instruction in his proposal in a way that "is mentioned too late, and too soon passed over":

> As we are all creatures of a day, as our whole life is but one small point between two eternities, it is reasonable to suppose that the grand end of every Christian institution for forming tender minds

should be to convince them of their natural depravity, of the means of recovering out of it, and of the necessity of preparing for the enjoyment of the Supreme Being in a future state. These are the grand points in which Christianity centers. Arts and sciences may be built on this, and serve to embellish the superstructure, but without this, there cannot be any good foundation.[60]

The anti-institutional currents of thought in the New World flowed in two directions, however: As Whitefield presided over the dramatic public conversion of a new generation of Protestant believers, the brewing suspicions of royal prerogative in the British colonies reciprocally shaped his own spiritual and political outlook. He famously converted to Calvinist orthodoxy under the tutelage of Gilbert Tennent, the fire-breathing assailant of social privilege who was helping to raise up a new generation of revivalists at his father's New Jersey Log College. And by the end of his career, Whitefield, who'd been as loyal a royal subject as any major figure in the transatlantic world, openly sympathized with the 1763 Stamp Act rebellion—the key event anticipating the colonies' formal break with the British crown in the following decade. By the time of his death in 1770, Whitefield had become a powerful and beloved symbol of the restive, soon-to-be independent American nation—eclipsed only by the great revolutionary war hero (and fellow Anglican, as it happens) George Washington. Indeed, in one of the more bizarre episodes of the Revolution, a band of American officers prevailed upon the sexton of the church where Whitefield was buried in Newbury, Massachusetts, to unearth the great man's coffin; they then spirited away Whitefield's collar and wristbands to carry into battle as sanctifying relics.[61] It's no great exaggeration to say that George Whitefield, the grand prophet of Primitive Church revival in the American colonies, had himself become an object of cultic worship in a potent new primitivist faith.

The Signs and Wonders of the Marketplace

For all the political significance posthumously ascribed to Whitefield's person, his New World ministry also represented a crucial stage in the gradual sanctification of the market order—a central focus of the Money Cult's later maturation. Henceforward, the institutions of colonial market society would help enable the concerted mass conversion of individual souls, not obstruct it.

The raw market synergy that conjoined revivalism to a new privately funded sphere of worship was at times quite literal, as with Whitefield's frequent fund-raising appeals for the Georgia orphanage, or for the new academy Franklin was sketching out in consultation with Whitefield. This latter facility was to be constructed on the site of a meeting hall that Franklin had recruited private investors to fund to house the overflow crowds that turned out during the revivalist's triumphant 1740 sweep through the Northern colonies. The building would later anchor Franklin's grand design for the Philadelphia Academy—which would, in turn, later become the University of Pennsylvania.

Prophets of the ascendancy of the market and its values—the primacy of the individual and profit-making activity, the principles of self-reliance within private models of charity, and the reign of individual market liberty over claims of collective obligation—instinctively understood that their faith was not to be redeemed in the familiar rites of institutional worship. Their new gospels were devoted to directly calling down a New Heaven and New Earth, on the basis of their personal apprehension of God's higher purposes. The great New World Protestant dispensation was to be not so much a sturdy, chastening faith of self-made men as an amazing new profusion of self-made gospels, all prophesying a tremendous upsurge of Primitive Church piety, delivered through the New World's brave new channels of commerce.

Beneath all the tumult of church schism and theological controversy that makes up the official history of the First Great Awakening, a new and radically anti-institutional form of spiritual individualism was taking root. No longer, it seemed, could any Old Light divine assert with any great scriptural assurance that the church constituted a single, great mystical body betrothed to Christ; the abundant evidence of their own senses demonstrated to believers at all levels of American life that the truest and purest incarnation of the ancient Christian faith resided in their own restlessly striving hearts. Under the dispensations of revival, the Connecticut New Light preacher Ebenezer Frothingham proclaimed, God had established "the absolute necessity for every person to act singly . . . as if there was not another human Creature on Earth."[62]

Few New Light divines put the proposition of spiritual self-invention quite as baldly as that, but the fact remains that the Awakening's chief theological legacy was to firmly recast Protestant experience in America as a dramatically individualist article of faith, a Primitive Church gospel that could reliably smite down any competing vision of Christian fellowship by declaring it a corrupt survival of an illegitimate priestly regime.

In a sense, the whole of Whitefield's career was devoted to the rehabilitation of the Primitive Church ideal in just these terms—to make the dry bones of the true faith's dead ancestors jump up and declaim the wonder-working might of the Lord Our Righteousness (to borrow the title of the Great Itinerant's best-known sermon). In this vein, Whitefield did not so much wield the authority of revived religion as act it out. His revival performances transformed arcane biblical history and theological doctrines into emotionally exhilarating set pieces.

Whitefield dramatized the close identification of the New Birth with the true ancient faith by performing key scenes of biblical history from the makeshift pulpits of the Awakening. As a young man, Whitefield—a gifted mimic and dramatic performer—had been infatuated with the theater, and famously experienced his first premonition of his preaching vocation when he was reading a play aloud to his sister. While Whitefield joined with his clerical brethren in denouncing the dangerous license of the theater, he never stopped acting—he just transposed his prodigious dramatic talents into the powerful, perpetually renewable, register of divine witness.

Whitefield also embodied these imaginative transports in his own writings and expostulations. In the midst of one heated public dispute with an Old Light antagonist, Whitefield immodestly announced that he prayed for the man's own conversion to the New Birth, so that he might realize "it is Jesus whom he persecutes."[63] The more frequent primitive touchstone of Whitefield's career, though, was the Apostle Paul—the original itinerant revivalist of the Christian faith. When something as mundane as a shortage of provisions on board one of his America-bound ships occurred, Whitefield set down the particulars of the episode in his journal, "so that I can say, with the Apostle [Paul], I am 'in hunger and thirst, cold and fastings often.'"[64] Much as Paul had presided over the conversion of many former skeptics in the first century, Whitefield would look out upon the souls he would steer so expertly toward the successive stages of the New Birth—conviction in sin, repentance, and the indwelling of divine grace and deliverance—and rejoice at the clear Primitive Church precedent before him: "The Lord comes down as in the days of old, and the shout of a king is amongst us."[65]

Public Offerings

It's easy to mistake all the drama of Whitefield's primitivist dust-ups with the Old Light clergy of New England for the tumult of a broad-based rebellion of class and manners in the American colonies. But in reality, Whitefield's legacy, like the devotional contours of his own personal faith, was profoundly conservative.

His ministry pointed the way forward for the Protestant mainstream to contain and sublimate any threatened confrontations over moneyed privilege in America that might stray into the region: The market didn't shrink your life chances or abet an unjust concentration of wealth among its masters, Whitefield preached; it *was your salvation*, and its language and transactional logic directly illuminated God's higher purposes and plans for your personal salvation.

Just as the culture wars of our own age have furnished a reliable safety valve for antagonisms of social class to find muffled expression in a rhetoric of pseudo-populist social confrontation, so did the founding Pulpit Wars of the First Awakening dispel the jeremiad's heated denunciations of wealth and wickedness into the pleasant, billowing reveries of the millennial prosperity awaiting the great redeemed American nation. Guardians of Primitive Church piety would be the guiding authorities of this proxy conflict. It was a much more spiritually decorous, and socially acceptable, to complain about the deficient piety of one's social betters than about their overweening privilege, especially in a polity as tightly governed by the canons of social deference as the British colonies were in the eighteenth century.

In this regard, the de-institutional thrust of Whitefield's primitivist gospel helped smooth over the more stubborn social tensions that originally helped stir the Awakening to life. In his sermons, the Great Itinerant cheerfully consigned not merely the Old Light ministry but most existing institutions to history's dustbin. To be sure, charity would still be carried out—as in the enormous and costly orphanage that Whitefield founded in the Georgia colony. But already, in Whitefield's radically individualist accounts of salvation in righteousness, we see the future complexion of Protestant social uplift taking shape, in which believers rely on their own private purses and organizational skills to cure the world's ills.

We also see the fantastic returns of a purely voluntarist model of Christian charity. In a single afternoon of fund-raising, Whitefield was able to collect more than the entire New England clergy earned over the course of a year.[66] Whitefield's unique entrepreneurial ministry was bearing abundant dividends in the market where his gospel originated—so much so that one of the most common charges that Whitefield's Old Light detractors lodged against him concerned the improper accounting and use of the largess he gathered on behalf of the Bethesda orphanage. (None of these charges was borne out, and Whitefield's estate after his death showed that, for all his fame, his personal fortune was modest.[67]) Still, the larger point was unmistakable, and would serve as a potent lesson for a new class of entrepreneurial preachers arising out of the dissolution of America's last state-established churches in the following century: Any ministry designed to attract a mass following could stand assured that "God will provide," as Whitefield himself announced to his sister in the moment that he felt called to preach the gospel.

But the cash yields of Whitefield's ministry were just its most visible fruit. The most enduring legacy of his long career was to bring the fundamental background tenets of the Money Cult faith into the center of American religious life. For the first colonial augurs of the Money Cult—the prophets experimenting with occult hermetic beliefs, alchemy, or the image of Adam as an inspired nature divinity—the deeper connections between spiritual and market values had largely been speculative, fugitive, and dangerous. They hinted only obscurely at the kinds of personal liberation of the spirit to be won in opposition to the Puritan establishment, and as a result, the inchoate elements of the money faith were typically forced to the surface only in moments of heresy-haunted scandal, such as the Salem witch hunt, or via efforts to produce wealth on the principles of alchemy, such as the original proposal for the Massachusetts land bank.

But by translating the foundational experience of conversion into a readily accessed commodity, Whitefield also transformed this scattered and forbidden body of folk beliefs into the stuff of orthodox experiential piety, via a sort of alchemy all his own. Colonists were witnessing their world turned magically into a site of living worship: an open-air temple of mass revival, bringing to thousands upon thousands of believers a revolutionary account of eternal life in the New Birth. And because Whitefield also masterfully evoked—and more than that, brought to life—all the familiar images associated with the Primitive Church's hallowed faith, the New World souls marshaled into his New Birth could profess a spiritual allegiance to market values entirely in line with hallowed Calvinist tradition.

In this way, indeed, the Awakening's overheated Pulpit Wars gradually yielded to something new under the American Protestant sun: an image of American believers as the chosen people of plenty. In the terms of Winthrop's covenant, the divinely chosen status of the Puritan exiles to the New World chiefly worked out into an ethical injunction—a directive to love all sojourning pilgrim souls equally, and to practice a liberal charity to sustain them in their needs. Whitefield's more immediate and primitivist gospel, by contrast, supplied a vision of an abiding abundance of spirit and wealth alike, in which ordinary believers could access the Godhead, as Whitefield had, by mimicking the rites and personalities of the very first Christians.

Whitefield's theatrical style and his chosen medium—the innovative open-air revival—would likewise augur a permanent shift in the public face of Protestant worship. From Whitefield's day forward, American Protestantism would be a revival faith—always offering a variation of Whitefield's foundational creed of the New Birth, while also propelling believers outward into the country's closely contiguous commercial and public spheres. Protestant faith in America would, just as importantly, be a *dramatic* faith, as the core rites of conversion would be acted out, over and again, among new generations of believers in radically shifting economic and social conditions.

We can take stock of just how the political dimensions of this new

revival faith played out in what's commonly regarded as the most important historical legacy of the Great Awakening: the stirring of revolutionary
sentiment among American civic and religious leaders. Historians have
long treated the First Awakening as something of a cultural dry run for the
American Revolution—a widespread revolt against an established order
of faith that eventually allowed New World colonists to experiment with
other significant forms of protest against allied forms of political authority.
But the reality of the Awakening is much more complicated than that. For
one thing, not only were many political leaders of the revolutionary generation inclined to the same rationalist faith that Franklin held, but many
of the best-known Old Light opponents of the revival in the pulpits of
New England, such as the renowned Boston Congregationalist preachers
Charles Chauncy and Jonathan Mayhew, also went on to preach a gospel
of disobedience to civil authority in the series of disputes over the taxing
powers of the Crown that led up to the American Revolution.

What's more, the dissenting ardor that fueled both the Awakening
and the Revolution was rooted much more deeply in the emerging theology of property and free enterprise than in any spontaneous eruption
of social egalitarianism. The American Revolution bore very little resemblance to the later uprising of the former feudal orders in France. Far from
upending any colonial socioeconomic hierarchies, it solidified the rule of
the colonies' landed and mercantile elites—its tax protests and calls for
greater colonial representation in Parliament were famously the plaints of
aggrieved mercantile leaders, landed gentry, and slaveholders.

The Revolution's religious character was real, however, and its unique
spiritual temper bequeathed to later American believers a potent sense of
millennial-minded religious nationalism. This legacy is a key explanation
for a crucial paradox of the time: For all of the doctrinal disputes and social
upheavals that attended the Whitefield crusade and subsequent divisions
of churches and parishes in the colonies along strict Old and New Light
lines, the colonies' many class-inflected confrontations over revival preaching succumbed quite rapidly to a broader sense of shared national identity
among embattled American patriots of all Protestant persuasions. The idea
of the American nation, even before the Revolution's onset, had come to

claim pride of place in a confident new millennial faith that stretched far beyond the provincial boundaries of the old New England covenant.

The Work of Redemption

One of the principal New World prophets of this faith was Jonathan Edwards, the lead theologian of the Awakening and still the most significant religious thinker in our history. Edwards was far and away the most influential colonial preacher to defend the new revival measures of the First Awakening, and he lent enormous credibility to Whitefield's cause by sponsoring a Whitefield-led revival in his home pulpit in Northampton, Massachusetts.

Edwards—best known for his own chilling revival sermons such as "Sinners in the Hands of an Angry God"—ably translated the itinerant spirit of the Whitefield revival into a grand theological system. And at the center of Edwards's own theology was the notion that God was using the colonies' revived religion to disclose the higher purpose of human history. In short, Edwards seized on the miraculous event of the First Awakening as evidence that God was finally bringing the millennium—the final divine redemption of history—to pass.

The final act of history, as it's famously (if also quite confusingly) spelled out in the dense and symbolic passages of the Book of Revelation, is a central touchstone for the social faith of Protestant believers. The Protestant obsession with the precise timing and the social significance of the Last Judgment provided a powerful focal point for believers to right the great wrongs of human history—or refrain from such activity altogether, as their respective interpretations of prophecy dictated.

Broadly, these millennial believers fell into two camps. The *premillennialists* argued that the great moment of cosmic reckoning foretold in Revelation would be swift and epically indifferent to puny human efforts to urge on its arrival. In their view, based on their reading of the recondite language of Revelation, the thousand-year reign of Christ (i.e., the millennium) would come after the Final Judgment—so it made no sense for people to smooth the path for Jesus' return with incremental feints at social reform. At best, such efforts were absurdly self-defeating, since all would be swept away in God's crowning show of wrath; at worst, social reform was a species of hubris, since it placed the upstart reformist conceits of humanity in the presumptuous role of prelude to the main event.

Postmillennial believers, on the other hand, contended that the reign of Christ would precede the final moment of judgment. It therefore behooved concerned Christians to gradually improve human society so that the millennium would be smoothly integrated into the existing order of things. The general sense was that the Savior would take a very dim view of disarrayed social conditions and rampant injustice on his return to Earth; they would represent grossly squandered opportunities for Christian charity, and they'd probably weigh adversely in the balance for the communities of believers hoping to dwell infinitely in God's grace upon the millennium's eventual arrival.

The dissenting sects that founded the Puritan colonies of America were steeped in premillennial belief—an end-times faith that seemed to find abundant confirmation in the bloody and destructive outcome of the recently concluded English Civil War. In European feudal orders, premillennialism generally recommended itself to believers precisely on these grounds—it rescued a larger, intelligible biblical narrative from the common run of war, pestilence, and plague that made up all too much of everyday life in feudal societies. The prospect of a sudden, stage-clearing final act in history was also the closest thing to a revolutionary faith on offer: A far better thing, by premillennial lights, to let God eradicate all human injustice, corruption, and exploitation and finally supplant the fallen course of history with his own harmonious, bountiful and endlessly merciful rule. Premillennial prophets of the apocalypse were thus otherworldly in their view of God's ultimate sovereignty over human history—but also intensely preoccupied with the urgent task of shunting illegitimate human powers out of the way to ensure that God could at last reign on Earth.

But Edwards and the enormous body of American preachers whom he advised and influenced had all come over to the postmillennial side of the great end-times controversy. Much as the Great Awakening shoved aside the grievances of the jeremiad with its powerful new evangelical ambitions, so did Edwards and his fellow postmillennialist divines discard the old premillennialist vision of a righteous final cataclysm in favor of a far sunnier diagnosis of divinely sanctioned prosperity to come. The wondrous achievements of the Awakening itself emboldened its New Light supporters to suspect that Whitefield, Edwards, and company were helping to bend the arc of history toward a benign, overflowing divine justice. Indeed, Edwards's own polemic defense of the Awakening, *Some Thoughts Concerning the Present Revival of Religion in New England* (1743), came close to hailing the Whitefield-led crusade as a foretaste of the millennium—calling it "the dawn of that glorious day," and "the beginning or forerunner of something vastly great."[68]

God and Country

But as the Awakening proper clearly began trending away from harmony and social peace—as New Light and Old Light congregations descended into backbiting rancor over the meaning of the revival itself—Edwards pushed his postmillennial visions further out on the Christian time horizon, stressing that there was still much devotional work for the faithful to do. In a remarkable effort to erect a systematic scheme of universal redemption out of the ardent piety of Whitefield's revival, Edwards published a detailed proposal to establish a worldwide "concert of prayer," in a title-says-it-all tract called *An Humble Attempt to Promote Explicit Agreement and Visible Union of God's People in Extraordinary Prayer for the Revival of Religion and Christ's Kingdom on Earth*. The original idea of a concert of prayer was floated by a minister caught up in Whitefield's revival in Scotland, and in its populist logic, it brought home another respect in which the transatlantic Whitefield revival continued to devolve spiritual authority toward the common believer. All one needed to do to influence the millennial course of history in the proper fashion was to pray, after all, and to induce as many other believers as possible to pray in the same way; seminary degrees and settled clerical hierarchies were largely beside the point.

In Edwards's own account, the concert was to be nothing less than a regular, organized petitioning of the Lord for the gradual realization of the Kingdom of God on Earth—a regular event on the church calendar aimed at calling down the transcendent glory of God to grace all human endeavor, in the church as well as in the broader political economy.

In this view of things, the miraculous mass conversions wrought by the revival still betokened a grand future—but it would take still more concentrated shows of piety to bring the Lord's timetable closer in line with the human one. "With what confidence we may go before God, and pray for that [mercy], of which we have so many precious and exceeding promises to plead!" Edwards exulted before the prospect.[69] Edwards explained that so long as congregants petitioned the Lord with pure, revival-awakened hearts, their prayers would win rapid fulfillment: "God manifests himself . . . as being at the command of earnest prayers"—and that eagerness stemmed from His recognition that such appeals came from "his chosen and beloved people . . . He cannot deny any thing that is asked for their comfort and prosperity."[70]

To demonstrate to his contemporary readers the steady hand of God in colonial affairs, Edwards cited the remarkable recent turn of events in King George's War—a conflict between the French and British crowns over the control of eastern Canada's sea ports, and the region's profitable fishing industry, that spanned the years of the Awakening. Since France was then the most powerful Catholic state in Europe, the preachers of colonial New England—Old and New Light alike—painted their countrymen's divinely ordained role in the conflict in bold millennial strokes. In 1747—the year that Edwards published *An Humble Attempt*—colonial forces defeated a numerically superior but badly under-provisioned French contingent at the Canadian outpost of Fort Louisburg, near Cape Breton. And Edwards read an amazing prophetic moral into the story of Louisburg's defeat:

> Such remarkable appearances of a spirit of prayer, on any particu-
> lar publick occasion, have not been in the land, at any time within
> my observation and memory, as on occasion of the affair of *Cape-
> Breton* . . . He that has done such great things, and has so wonder-
> fully and speedily answered prayers for temporal mercies, will much
> more give the Holy Spirit if we ask him. He marvelously preserves
> us, and waits to be gracious to us, as though he chose to make us
> monuments of his grace, and not his vengeance, and waits only to
> have our mouths open wide, that he may fill them.[71]

The same lesson applied with at least equal force, Edwards argued, to matters of civil order and prosperity, where future American revivalists would indeed have their mouths open wide: "It especially becomes this society, visibly to unite, and expressly to agree together in prayer to God for the common prosperity; and above all, that common prosperity and advancement that is so unspeakably great and glorious, which God has so abundantly promised to fulfill in the latter days."[72] Such a union in prayer, Edwards explained, "would not only be beautiful, but *profitable* too"; in "praying one with and for another, and jointly for the common welfare," he argued, ministers and lay believers alike would awaken to an enlivened spirit of productive worldly and religious activity. "It would naturally tend to awaken in them a concern about things of this nature, and more of a desire after this mercy," Edwards wrote—a sort of virtuous circle, in which heightened desire for improvements of spiritual standing and personal station call forth renewed effort to bring the conditions for the millennium gradually to pass. An ardent, ongoing prayer for the revival of religion on the part of ministers and lay believers "would engage them to more attention to such an affair, make them more inquisitive about it, more ready to use endeavours to promote that which, they, with so many others, spend so much time praying for, and more ready to rejoice, and praise God when they see or hear anything of that nature or tendency."[73]

Here, in the lofty vision of a global Christian communion of prayer, was the seed of faith by which the idea of America's divinely blessed prosperity was coming into full millennial flower. Even as Edwards would grow disenchanted with the millennial promise of the Awakening—and eventually lose his own Northampton pulpit—the basic contours of this vision remained fixed at the heart of the evangelical consensus that steered colonial believers out of the Awakening and into the great unifying crucible of the American Revolution. From here on out, American believers would point to the military rewards of their embattled colonial lives, as well as the overall condition of the American economy, as decisive proof that they continued to enjoy a direct and overweening divine favor.

And if comparatively minor battles like the Louisburg siege set prophecy-minded theologians like Edwards musing on God's plan to pursue his New England covenant into the unparalleled prosperity and harmony of the millennium, the next generation's formal independence from England unmistakably stamped the American nation-in-the-making as God's chosen country.

Thomas Paine sounded the most famous such refrain when he proclaimed in *Common Sense* that "we have it in our power to begin the world over again." In reality, though, the millennial faith that gripped the imaginations of Edwards, Whitefield, and other divines of the Awakening age had long prepared the ground for the kind of revolutionary fervor that Paine—a Quaker often mistaken (like his colonial sponsor Benjamin Franklin) for a doctrinaire unbeliever—summoned to such dramatic effect during the War of Independence.

The revival spirit, as Edwards correctly surmised, would define the future course of Protestant worship—and hence give the Money Cult its own distinctive millennial shape. Already in Edwards's own day, the Awakening's Old Lights were rallying to the same awe-inspiring vision of America's spiritual destiny—demonstrating, in essence, that for the many dramatic changes in store for the American Money Cult as it would come of age in the modern era, its new millennial-nationalist incarnation would remain fixed in place as its permanent scaffolding.

Jonathan Mayhew's politicized preaching from his Old Light pulpit at Boston's West End Church is a revealing case in point. Mayhew "had himself renounced the particular theology of the Awakening," Mark Noll observes, but in his sermons protesting the Stamp Act and celebrating colonial military victories, he "displayed a rhetorical style that was as 'evangelistic' in the service of liberty as Whitefield's was in the service of the gospel."[74] Even rationalist Old Light defenders of the covenantal tradition like Mayhew could appreciate, and mimic, the power of Whitefield's new vernacular revival preaching, mindful of the new ways that religious ecstasy easily bled into the American Revolution's public rites of rebellion.

Preaching a sermon of Thanksgiving on the occasion of another landmark British colonial victory over France in Canada—the 1759 Battle of Quebec—Mayhew left off the now-standard invocation of a glorious Protestant crusade vindicated at the behest of a loving God to deliver a remarkably sweeping millennial vision of the American future. He first hailed the Quebec victory as a foretaste of what would surely be America's unparalleled military strength: "Yea, we may reasonably suspect that this country, which has been in a short time, and under many disadvantages, become so populous and flourishing, will, by the continued blessing of heaven, in another century or two become a mighty empire . . . in numbers little inferior perhaps to the greatest in Europe, and in felicity to none."[75]

Of that felicity, Mayhew waxed positively prophetic in his own right—a striking emotional transport on the part of a preacher who prided himself on his rationalist faith. Mayhew provided so complete and so fulsome an account of a vast redeemed nation blessed by a divinely authored influx of commerce that it bears quoting at length:

> I cannot forbear fancying that I see a great and flourishing kingdom in these parts of America, peopled by our posterity. Methinks that I see mighty cities rising on every hill, and by the side of every commodious port; mighty fleets alternately sailing out and returning, laden with the produce of this, and every other country under heaven; happy fields and villages wherever I turn my eyes, thro' a vast, extended territory; there the pastures cloathed with flocks, and there the valleys covered with corn, while the little hills rejoice on every side! . . . Methinks I see religion practiced and professed throughout this spacious kingdom, in far greater purity and perfection, than since the time of the apostles; the Lord being still as a wall of fire round about, and the glory in the midst of her! O happy country! happy kingdom![76]

Thus was the Kingdom of God conjured as a kingdom of New World prosperity—as would be the case, over and over again, in the actual American centuries that followed on Mayhew's vision. In this promiscuous mingling of the language of secular trade and commerce with the traditional imagery of peaceful millennial blessing, the disparate currents of the Money Cult faith were converging in dramatic fashion. Winthrop's famed city on a hill was transformed here into a whole battery of "mighty cities"; commodious ports that sent fleets of ships coming and going, all "laden with . . . produce." And of course, amid all this hectic trade and towering commercial and military might in this "spacious kingdom," the one true primitive faith was practiced at a level of purity not seen "since the time of the apostles."

That this prophecy of the American colonies' quite worldly deliverance at the hands of a singularly benevolent God, which so richly echoed

Edwards's own rendering of God's unique plan of New World salvation, should come from the pulpit of one of Edwards's principal Old Light antagonists was powerful testimony to the emerging new evangelical consensus. Beneath this consensus, the bitter class-based religious divisions that preceded the Whitefield Revolution had largely melted away—at least so far as the guardians of colonial piety were concerned.

In similar fashion, the most compelling pulpit visions of the ascendant American nation pivoted upon deeper forces of postmillennial accord that bridged the Awakening's great theological divide. Like Edwards's own end-times speculations, Mayhew's reveries of the handsomely settled, gloriously saved America to come stemmed from the news of a stirring military conquest. And like Edwards's ambitious scheme of gradual world salvation, Mayhew's vision alighted finally on the image of America as the redeemed sanctuary for the true primitive faith, in a rousing display of divinely sanctioned peace and prosperity, with the living God "a wall of fire round about."

Next to these strong millennial affinities, the high-profile pulpit battles over the Whitefield Awakening—concerning the place of emotion in the experience of conversion, or the relative merits of a learned clergy—dwindled into so much theological gnat-straining. In this respect, the cross-revival spiritual consensus that Mayhew and Edwards forged around the idea of the redeemed nation was its own great prophetic portent: Theology—the discipline that early modern Protestants still regarded as the queen of the sciences, and the historical record of the intellectual quest to justify the ways of God to man—was ceding the ground of New World piety to the untamed frontier of raw and unmediated spiritual experience. This millennial promise would open onto strange new spiritual worlds—in ways that Benjamin Franklin would never have dared to imagine.

3

FREE WILL AND FREE MARKETS

There is, probably, no people on earth with whom business constitutes pleasure, and industry amusement, in an equal degree with the inhabitants of the United States of America. Active occupation is not only the principal source of their happiness, and the foundation of their national greatness, but they are absolutely wretched without it, and instead of the "dolce far niente," know but the horrors of idleness. Business is the very soul of an American; he pursues it, not as a means of procuring for himself and his family the necessary comforts of life, but as the fountain of all human felicity . . . it is as if all America were but one gigantic workshop, over the entrance of which there is the blazing inscription, "No admission here, except on business."
—Francis Grund, *The Americans*, 1837

If the signature scene of the First Great Awakening was George Whitefield holding forth on the terrors of damnation and the sweetness of divine grace in the Boston Common or along the main thoroughfares of Philadelphia, the defining moment of the country's great successor Awakening occurred at the outset of the new century in an open field in rural Kentucky. The Cane Ridge revival, as it came to be known, was an outdoor crusade that drew as many as 20,000 souls for what was originally conceived as a six-day stretch of prayer.

On the last days of the gathering—which would extend several days beyond its appointed schedule—came an amazing wave of conversion.

Believers fell into near-comatose faints—observers commonly likened them to corpses. In the nomenclature of revival, they had been "slain in the spirit." An eyewitness account by one of the leading preachers of the revival, Richard McNemar, captured the startling work of redemption: "At first they were taken with an inward throbbing of the heart; then with weeping and trembling; from that to crying out, in apparent agony of the soul; falling down and swooning away until every appearance of animal life was suspended, and the person appeared to be in a trance."[77]

When the spirit-slain stirred back to life, it was often with exultant shows of enthusiasm. They would break out into violent jerks of the head and body, fits of unrestrained laughter, prolonged dances, even the barking and howling of dogs. As the evangelistic fervor spread over the weeklong proceedings, revival organizers estimated that as many as 3,000 of the 20,000 were won over for God.

To McNemar, the widespread bodily transports and visionary enthusiasms were signs and wonders that meant the Kingdom of God was at hand. In his telling, the revival was a spontaneous communion of souls on the brink of rapture—a state that was at once all-consuming, intimate, and otherworldly:

> Sleeping and waking, the whole topic . . . was the increasing work of God, and the blessed kingdom just about to appear, and each one contemplating it through some special dream or vision, in which they each felt confident that they had a particular revelation of the Lord's Christ. This was the kind of *manna* which they were daily gathering, and out of the infinite abundance that fell on the camp, it may not be improper to deposit a little bit of it in the pot. In some of these rapturous scenes, they professed to be carried clear out of the body, and to be favored with a particular interview with the spirits of their departed friends, and to see and learn their allotments in the invisible world.[78]

The dramatic visitation of abundant grace that seemed to steal unbidden over the crowds at Cane Ridge was a foretaste of the free-will Gnostic transformation of the American religious scene known today as the Second

Great Awakening. Many bewildering cross-currents of Protestant belief were released during the course of this great revival—from the decisive rejection of the Calvinist doctrines of total depravity and predestination to the utopian quest for the perfection of the American social order. But the central defining traits of this decades-long revival were neatly distilled in McNemar's account: the discovery of a new and direct experience of divinity originating within the soul of each individual believer, and the sense that the great work of redemption would spill over by sheer force of its antinomian power into the allied experience of finding one's fortune in the New World amid the worldly allurements of commerce. Here, on the American republic's frontier, the wild visions of prophets and spirit-infused singers and dancers were converging upon the window display of a merchant-God "about to open his everlasting kingdom" to whichever believers had the great good fortune to be transformed into his wares.

It's a surpassingly strange image—until, that is, you take fuller stock of how the Kingdom of God and the kingdoms of American commerce were coming to resemble each other in the eyes of the wayfaring believers of the nineteenth century. Individuals were coming into a powerful certainty that they had uncovered a new model of salvation, keyed to their eager pursuit of prosperity and well-being in the New World.

One simple but telling shift in sensibility demonstrates how far American believers had advanced toward a strictly experiential, individualist account of salvation by the time all those barking, chanting, spirit-slain souls converged at Cane Ridge. During the Whitefield Awakening of the prior century, defenders of the revival such as Jonathan Edwards had expended great effort to verify and publicize the marks of a true conversion, versus the passing symptoms of a false sense of spiritual overstimulation. But confronted with the Gnostic power of Cane Ridge and its many successor revivals, no one showed any great interest in separating out legitimate works of the spirit from the sham variety. That's because the guiding authority of the Second Awakening resided almost entirely within the solitary believer's emotional experience of conversion: Preachers and denominations would henceforth be accepted or rejected largely on the basis of their ability to inwardly move unconverted believers toward the

New Light of redemption—and not on the basis of their standing as theological thinkers or civil authorities. It's crucial to recall in this connection that Edwards carried out his researches into the First Awakening's spiritual transports as a state-supported member of an established clergy—a breed of preacher that was moribund in the early nineteenth century.

In frontier outposts like western Kentucky, however, no religious establishment of note ever took firm root. So it was only logical that this less churched, more footloose part of the country should host a gathering like the one at Cane Ridge. In the same vein, it also made sense that the great "American Pentecost" at Cane Ridge, as its lead historian Paul Conklin has dubbed it, should serve as the defining opening act of the Second Awakening—it was where new converts could commune with the liberated spirit of a market-bred New World God with no threat of meddling from the spiritual and civic leaders of their church or village. In a few decades, the Gnostic spirits unleashed at Cane Ridge would storm the liberated free markets of faith in the urban Northeast, the upper Midwest, and the remainder of the South, as both the spiritual and mundane economies of the United States entered a prolonged free-market boom phase.

First, however, it bears considering just why and how the Second Awakening was launched as a *Gnostic* revival. The Gnostic strain of American faith had heretofore largely been confined to popular folk traditions such as alchemy and hermetic healing lore. Adherents of this underground faith had preached a counter-Calvinist folk religion premised on the soul's confident *ascent* into divine wisdom, as opposed to its all-but-certain damnation under Puritanism's iron dictates of original sin and predestination.

It's chiefly in this respect that the sudden burst of enthusiasm and conversion at Cane Ridge bore all the earmarks of the ancient heterodox faith of Gnosticism: In falling prey to these strange new convulsions of the spirit, the revival's clamorous following forcefully disowned, almost in spontaneous unison, the older social rites of Puritan piety. The Pentecost at Cane Ridge wasn't necessarily the most self-conscious or articulate rejection of Calvinist doctrine—those would come later, as the more organized and belligerent forces of free-will Protestantism would storm to the forefront of major revival crusades on behalf of the Baptists, Methodists, and other leading denominations of the Second Awakening. But it was hard to surpass the displays at Cane Ridge when it came to eliciting the dramatic power that believers felt themselves coming into, once they were finally able to break the bounds of Calvinist orthodoxy. Here, truly, was an unanswerable vindication of the great promise of the new nation's liberty, unleashed on the untamed frontiers of Protestant faith.

But these individualized transports of the spirit, like the other trappings of American individualism in the secular world, were no simple thing: for seemingly miraculous shows of diving power, they involved a great deal of human effort, and spurred still greater displays of theological dissent. As the opening act of the great sectarian revolution in American faith, Cane Ridge pointed the way forward to a seemingly infinite regress of religious controversy: Where there was free will in matters of the spirit, there would also be all-but-endless disputation. In this sense, calling Cane Ridge a Pentecost is to use something of a misnomer. The New Testament's account of the Pentecost and its own signature miracles—the sudden ability of believers to communicate in unknown languages, or handle deadly serpents without risk of injury—stressed that the powerful new mysteries of faith served to unite the Early Christian Church behind its gospel message. In strong contrast, the Second Awakening's free-will signs and wonders bred a much more fragmented mood of intense rivalry in a new free market of denominational faith. To preach religious liberty, it turned out, meant a lot more than to preach one simple galvanizing truth—even if that truth was the antinomian force that more and more American believers felt to be at the very seat of their self-empowered souls.

There was, just for instance, the delicate matter of how free religious agents could still be held accountable for the less palatable consequences of their choices and actions. A key contradiction lurked at the heart of the free-will dispensation: God's unshackled plan of redemption was both open-ended and all-encompassing—which made it all the more incumbent on the religious seeker to choose it, since the neglect of God under the strict interpretation of free will entailed eternal punishment for which only he or she could be blamed.

Here again, the testimony of Cane Ridge preacher Richard McNemar captures the spirit of this transformation in remarkably vivid terms. One core lesson of the revival, McNemar wrote, was

> that all creeds, confessions, forms of worship and rules of govern-
> ment invented by man, ought to be laid aside; especially the distin-
> guishing doctrines of Calvin. That all that received the true light of
> the spirit in the inner man, and faithfully followed it, would natu-
> rally see eye to eye, and understand things of the spirit, without any
> written tenet or learned expositor. That all who received this true
> light, would plainly see the purity of God, the depravity of man,
> the necessity of a new birth and of a sinless life and conversation to
> evidence it. That God was no respecter of persons, desires the salva-
> tion of all souls, has opened a door of salvation through Christ, for
> all, will have all invited to enter, and such as refuse to come in, must
> blame themselves for their own perdition.[79]

This direct repudiation of the old dogmas of Calvinist election—
which tended to imprison believers in extended, melancholy contempla-
tion of their common lot of likely damnation—was a pivotal moment in
the development of America's religious imagination. McNemar's ringing declaration of spiritual independence upheld the American believer's
right to discover salvation via the raw materials of experience—"the true
light" of the inner man's spirit, easily apprehended through the eye-to-eye
communions among the redeemed, unmediated by "any written tenet or
learned expositor." McNemar was also admirably direct in laying out the
baleful consequences of doubt, backsliding, or indifference in the face of
this radical new experiential gospel: Those who deny its power perversely
"refuse" God's universal plan of salvation, and so have richly earned the
perdition that awaits them. As with the pursuit of more worldly varieties
of success on the American frontier, the stakes of failure for the insurgent,
self-enabled preachers of the free-will gospel were forbiddingly high.

Still, no one was especially deterred by the protests of the residual
Calvinist establishment that the Babel-like confusion of free-will doctrine
was the real road to damnation for American believers, since it spurned the

communal bonds of charity that the Puritans had so carefully wrought for the Protestant sojourners in the New World for the past century and a half. Instead, the reassuring republican rhetoric of equality, boundless opportunity, and spiritual liberty that would thunder from revival pulpits throughout the nineteenth century would serve as a de facto rallying cry for the freewheeling course of the Second Great Awakening. Unloosed from the dead hand of predestination, the American religious imagination allowed itself to entertain all manner of strange new reveries of its own self-enabled liberation.

For all this brewing sectarian discord, however, the vast welter of centripetal movements away from the old Calvinist order had one important thing in common: They all tended to echo the older Gnostic ideals of hermetic progression through successive stages of spiritual enlightenment. The soul's steady upward arc would find telling confirmation in the believer's own deportment: "the necessity of the new birth and of a sinless life and conversation to evidence it," as McNemar described it, in an important elaboration of the perfectionist cult of character discipline that would soon overtake the old Puritan model of conversion as a communal rite of passage.

Such signs were, however, but the outward apparitions of the new wisdom vouchsafed to this generation of evangelical New Lights. And while this higher knowledge was, in theory, universally available to free-will believers of all descriptions, McNemar made it plain that the divine and experiential gifts of Cane Ridge far transcended the mere outward observance of Protestant faith:

> The established opinion in the churches had been, that the *Scriptures*, explained according to sound reason and philosophy, was light sufficient; and simply to believe, what we were thus taught, was the highest evidence we could have of the truth of spiritual things. But [the New Lights at Cane Ridge] adopted a very different faith, and taught, as an important truth, that the will of God was made manifest to each individual who honestly sought after it, by an inward light, which shone into the heart . . . Those who were the subjects of this inward light, did not call it *new light*, but a renewed manifestation of *that*, which at

sundry times and in divers manners, had been opened to those who were willing and desirous to know the truth for themselves.[80]

Both new and democratic, esoteric and ancient, universal and elect: McNemar's own testimony was remarkably faithful to the contradictory spiritual impulses that converged upon the Pentecost at Cane Ridge. These are also the same spiritual tensions that run through the Gnostic tradition. Gnostics historically rejected what they regarded as arid and mindless fealty to the outward rites of orthodox worship in favor of the more ecstatic inward communions available to true seekers after attaining deeper spiritual wisdom. And the ancient Gnostics, while welcoming to otherwise ostracized believers—notably women and slaves, two among many outcast populations in the Roman Empire—also derived from their heightened sense of spiritual knowledge a distinct contempt for believers of a merely orthodox persuasion. The later, ultra-sectarian course of McNemar's preaching career rather precisely traced this same insatiable individualist quest for a perfect communion of like-minded souls able to sustain the heavenward ascent of the New Light. That McNemar himself never alighted on any satisfactory such form beyond the doomed Shaker experiment shows how little the atomistic course of Gnostic worship had changed across the centuries.

But the Second Awakening was much more than just another study in the folly of overvigilant Protestant sectarianism. There was, just for starters, the striking new image of the deity who sent so many of the Cane Ridge faithful clamoring after their own transfigured Gnostic truths. As Harold Bloom, a contemporary Gnostic enthusiast, observes, the transports at Cane Ridge pivoted upon "a fundamental but scarcely avowed principle of the American Religion: creedlessness, or the *doctrine of experience*, as oxymoronic a phrase as even I can imagine." What set apart the communion at Cane Ridge, by Bloom's lights, was "a kind of orgiastic individualism, in which all the holy rolling was the outward mark of an inward grace that traumatically put away frontier loneliness and instead put on the doctrine of experience that exalted such loneliness into a being-alone-with-Jesus."[81]

Or, to put things a bit less floridly: The communicants at Cane Ridge had experienced a new free-will gospel of *inner sanctification*, very much in line with the age-old Gnostic quest for liberation from the old social forms of churchly faith. Under this potent brand of spiritual individualism, believers knew themselves to be entirely saved—or entirely damned, as McNemar stressed—within the hermetic confines of the self. This epiphany would soon go on to serve as the bedrock spirit of a new market-driven American capitalism. Strange as it may seem, the otherworldly fits and dead faints that afflicted the eager congregants at Cane Ridge betokened a much broader retreat from institutional faith and communal charity that would stretch over the next two centuries of American religious history. And the Gnostic revelations at Cane Ridge would gradually spill over, in the manner of most great shows of otherworldly faith in the New World, into the spiritualized conception of the nation's economic life. The great spiritual anxieties of the Puritan order were mooted in a burst of unanswerable, revelatory experience—and the new Protestant scheme of Gnostic redemption would soon be off in search of new worlds to conquer.

Christ in the Counsel Room

If Cane Ridge's Gnostic revival found its signature following among the landed gentry and military caste of the upper South, the Northern phase of the Second Great Awakening found its prophetic voice in the storied career of a charismatic young commercial attorney-turned-preacher. Charles Grandison Finney, the lead revivalist of the Second Awakening, was another Presbyterian divine seeking spiritual assurance on the Market Revolution's frontier. With striking emotional power, the nation's greatest individual revival leader would distill the new individualist turn in American religion into a great reformer's crusade.

Like his eighteenth-century forebear George Whitefield, Finney started out as an ambitious young man pursuing a secular calling, as a fledgling lawyer in the upstate New York village of Adams in 1820. Before long, he fell under the influence of a revival in the region. But despite the fervor, Finney observed that petitions offered up during the meetings at his local Presbyterian congregation were ineffectual. "It struck me that the reason their prayers were not answered was that they did not comply with the revealed conditions upon which God had promised to answer prayer, that they did not pray in faith in the sense of *expecting* God to give them the things they asked for," he wrote.[82]

Tellingly, what Finney found missing in the prayers of his Presbyterian companions was a trust in the abundant capacity of God to bring their wishes to fulfillment. Instead of confidently tapping into this plenitude, the church elders in Adams delivered their prayers in an attitude of beseeching scarcity, which in Finney's view clearly repelled any prospect of true divine assistance:

> When I read my Bible, I learned what Christ had said in regard to prayer and answers to prayer. He had said, "Ask and ye shall receive, seek and ye shall find, knock and it shall be opened unto you. For everyone that asketh receiveth, and he that seeketh findeth, and to him that knocketh it shall be opened. I read also what Christ affirms, that God is more willing to give His Holy Spirit to them than earthly parents are to give good gifts to their children.

So it was a simple thing for the young seeker to grasp that his fellow worshipers had undermined themselves by overlooking God's ample generosity: "I heard them pray continually for an outpouring of the Holy Spirit, and as often confess their leanness, and that they did not receive what they asked for."[83] When his fellow congregants offered to pray on Finney's behalf to secure his full conversion, he brusquely declined, on the grounds that they were going about it all wrong.

Finney's scripture-based intuition that prayer would bear abundant fruit if delivered in something more than a spirit of "leanness" would come to fuel not merely much of the free-will enthusiasms of the Second Awakening, but also the later pietist revolution in business-minded worship, which focused intently on the worldly dividends of prayer. The young seeker would also go on to erect an ambitious new theology of infinite personal self-improvement on the foundational belief that a beneficent, post-Calvinist God would permit faithful worshipers to achieve a state of individual perfection while still on Earth.

Still, that was all to come later. Back in Adams, confident piety wasn't immediately forthcoming to Finney, either. The young lawyer was plunged into an acute state of inner spiritual distress over a number of weeks, a state only made worse by the discovery that he couldn't count on the traditional institutional resources of his church to bring about his longed-for conversion. He desperately wanted to pray, alone in his home closet, removed from any soul-searching discourse with "the elders of my church, or with any Christian people." But he found that he was unable to do so—or for that matter, to talk much at all: "It seemed as if my heart grew harder . . . I was shy and avoided, as much as I could, speaking to anybody on any subject."

He spent one mostly sleepless night tortured by premonitions of sudden death and imminent damnation that left him feeling "almost like screaming." As he walked to work the next morning, an inner voice caught him up short, suggesting that he, too, had let his trust in God's deliverance atrophy in favor of his own earnest efforts to achieve salvation on his terms. "Did you not promise to give your heart up to God?" it seemed to ask; and then, "Are you endeavoring to work out a righteousness of your own?"

It was this last point, in particular, that triggered Finney's moment of conversion. "I think I then saw, as clearly as I ever have in my life, the reality and fullness of the Atonement of Christ," he recalled:

> I saw that his work was a *finished* work, and instead of having, or needing, any righteousness of my own to recommend me to God, I had to *submit myself* to the *righteousness of God through Christ*. Indeed, the offer of Gospel salvation seemed to me to be an offer of *something to be accepted* . . . Salvation, it seemed to me, instead of a thing to be wrought out from my own works, was a thing to be found entirely in the Lord Jesus Christ who presented himself before me to be *accepted*.[84]

Determined to seal this new union with Christ, Finney adjourned to a wooded area near his office to offer himself in the kind of confident petitionary prayer he knew that Scripture required. But here, once more, he seized up at the decisive moment. "When I attempted to pray, I found that my *heart* would not pray . . .When I came to try, I was dumb: that is, I had nothing to say to God; or at least I could say but a few words, and those without heart." Plunged now into yet deeper personal despair, Finney sensed the approach of someone in the woods. Thence came the final reproach to his pitiful human pride: "Such a degraded sinner as I am, on my knees confessing my sins to the great and holy God, and ashamed to have any human being, and a sinner like myself, know it," the inner voice declaimed. "The sin appeared awful, infinite," Finney recalls—but this is where he became infused with a true spirit of prayerful expectation, and was reminded of the great divine guarantee of abundant returns to the properly prayerful:

> Just at that point this passage of scripture seemed to drop into my mind with a flood of light: "Then shall ye go and pray unto me, and I will answer you. Then shall ye seek me and shall find me, when you search for me with all your heart." I instantly seized hold of this with my *heart*. I had *intellectually* believed the Bible before, but never had the truth been in my mind that faith was a *voluntary trust* instead of an *intellectual state*. I was as conscious as I was of my existence of trusting, at that moment, in God's veracity . . . I knew that it was God's Word, and God's voice, as it were, that spoke to me. I cried to him, "Lord, I take Thee at Thy Word; now, Thou *knowest* that I *do* search for Thee with all my heart."[85]

There's much to mark here for the Second Awakening's new model of revival. There is, first of all, the acute isolation of the scene. All Protestant faith is founded on the stark encounter of the individual sinner and the divine presence, but in his quest for the true experience of spiritual rebirth, Finney had deliberately positioned himself beyond the ordinary communal resources that might elicit conversion, in either church-led polities or open-air revivals. When he's unsettled by the seeming approach of an onlooker—i.e., someone who would render his prospective confession of faith a public conversion, in the tradition of the Puritan covenant and the Whitefield revival—Finney is struck anew with the pitiable vanity that holds back his moment of surrender to Christ. Seeing himself as a potentially weak and beseeching seeker of the Lord's favor, like the Presbyterian elders he had scorned and rejected, brings him fully into the free-will gospel's great moment of truth: He embraces the abundant promise of fulfilled prayer, so long as it comes from a confident, completely committed heart. Without this crucial element of *voluntary trust*, as Finney stresses, his piety had remained an arid and unresolved *intellectual state*, an unwelcome relic of the old Calvinist faith of his Presbyterian elders.

Finney's newfound confidence in a voluntarist faith is no doubt part of what's behind the supremely curious choice he makes after he consecrates his heart to Christ. He goes to work. Or, rather, he initially thinks he will get lunch, since he discovers that the entire morning has elapsed as he sought to seal his conversion. But he has no appetite. When he arrives at the office, he learns that his senior law colleague, Esq. Benjamin Wright, has left for lunch, so Finney plays his bass viol, and begins to sing some hymns, but he finds he's too overcome with emotion to continue. When Wright returns, he and the newly enlightened Finney spend the remainder of the afternoon "removing our books and furniture to another office." At the end of this uneventful workday, Wright returns home, but Finney stays on and is again moved to resume prayer—"the rising of my soul was so great that I rushed into the counsel room, back of the front office, to pray." There, he's promptly blessed with a visitation by Christ: "It seemed to me that I met Him face to face and saw Him just as I would see any other man . . . I wept aloud like a child, and made such confessions as I could with my choked utterance. It seemed to me as if I had bathed His feet with my tears, yet I had no distinct impression that I *touched* him."[86]

Finney again lost all track of time, and his "mind was too much absorbed in the interview to recollect scarcely anything I had said." But when he had stirred from this transport and returned to the main office to tend a dying fire, another, equally dramatic, rite of experiential faith was in store.

> As I returned and was about to take a seat by the fire, I received a *mighty baptism of the Holy Ghost*. Without expecting it, without ever having the thought in my mind that there was any such thing for me, without any recollection that I had ever heard the thing mentioned by any person in the world, at a moment entirely unexpected by me, the Holy Spirit descended on me in a manner that seemed to *go through me*, body and soul, I could feel the impression, like *a wave*

of electricity, going through and through me. Indeed, it seemed to come in *waves* and *waves of liquid love*—for I could not express it in any other way. And yet it did not seem like water, but rather as *the breath of God*. I can recollect distinctly that it seemed to *fan* me like immense wings; and it seemed to me, as these waves passed over me, that they *literally moved my hair like a passing breeze*.[87]

Dazed, Finney stayed in his office chair the remainder of the evening. The following morning, a client turned up for an appointment—a member of the Presbyterian church choir that Finney had led. Finding the young lawyer still much disarranged—all he could really manage to tell his client was that "I am so happy that I cannot live"—the choir member sent for a church elder who owned a nearby shop. Later, a young friend of Finney's happened by. Together, they had frequently discussed the finer points of religious doctrine. Instantly, Finney's friend apprehended the young barrister's transformed and beatific state, and begged for him to pray on his behalf. Finney promptly complied.

The events of his conversion, as Finney relates them, are so arresting that it's easy to miss the no-less revealing social background of this Damascus scene. One of the common complaints from opponents of the First Awakening was that Whitefield's revivals drew too many workers away from productive labor; here, strikingly, the most celebrated account of a religious leader's conversion in the Second Awakening takes place entirely on the site of his job. Successive visitations from the Savior and the Holy Ghost, as well as augurs of the great experiential conversions that will distinguish his religious career have come to him all within the confines of his village law office. There he had undergone the same sort of dramatic transformation of the spirit that befell thousands at the Cane Ridge revival; through the entirely voluntary decision to consecrate his innermost heart to Christ. Finney's expectation of abundant personal fulfillment from the attentive free-will God of the post-Calvinist world extended naturally to his own perch in the Market Revolution.

The sagas of Cane Ridge and Finney's come-to-Jesus moment speak volumes about how the defining experience of American Protestant faith—the rite of conversion—was acquiring the protective coloration of market society. In Puritan New England, recall, individual conversion was a matter of urgent collective interest, which drew in nearly every kind of civic and religious authority to monitor and authenticate its progress. By the time of the Cane Ridge gathering, the relevant authority had retreated almost entirely within the individual's personal sense of sanctified grace; converts came to the new birth under their own powers, and increasingly experienced it as something bound up with their own sense of economic agency. Once Finney launched his formal career as a revivalist, and touched off the central phase of the Second Awakening, the virtues and benefits of American Protestant belief would be defined as never before by the logic of the marketplace.

And the new market complexion of the revived American faith was made instantly clear, as Finney seamlessly upgraded his spiritual CV from joyful convert to soul-winning evangelist. In both guises, after all, Finney was clearly caught up in the promise of the emerging national market order. Benjamin Wright, whose law office furnished the backdrop to Finney's conversion, was well known as the lead engineer on the middle section of the Erie Canal, and a prominent booster of market expansion in upstate New York. Wright would soon find that his engineering career held far greater promise than his rural judgeship, and would go on to oversee a great number of canal, highway and railroad projects, becoming New York City's street commissioner in 1834.

There is, of course, nothing sinister or conspiratorial in the connection between Wright and Finney—and even if there were, Finney's legal career was soon concluded anyway. Two days following his conversion, he told a disappointed client that "I have a retainer from the Lord Jesus Christ to plead his case, and I cannot plead yours."[88] Nevertheless, it's significant to note that the most successful revival preacher of the nineteenth century was, at the outset of his career, serving at the confluence of legal and market relations that were then radically reshaping the national economy. (In much the same vein, we might further note, the great paragon of the American civic religion, Abraham Lincoln, would launch his own career as a railroad and corporation attorney along the nation's western frontier a few years later.) Like George Whitefield, Finney was primed to move in concert with the demands of his new commercial age well before he found his true calling in the pulpit.

Finney's Wright connection was significant in another way. The revivalist's former employer would also furnish the first in a long litany of edifying character illustrations that would punctuate Finney's preaching career—all dramatizing the new spiritual struggle for self-control amid the temptations of the market world. As Finney relates, Wright was at first quite averse to follow his young apprentice's bold redemptive leap. Within weeks of Finney's conversion, the wooded spot behind Wright's law office became something of a shrine to the revival-in-the-making, with several members of Finney's church repairing there to replicate the young attorney's already storied moment of surrender to Christ's sovereignty. Wright affected a kind of spiritual hauteur appropriate—or so he thought—to his standing in the social hierarchy of Adams: "When Esq. Wright heard them tell their experiences one after the other in our meetings, he thought that *he* had a *parlor* to pray in; and that he was not going to go up into the woods, and have the same story to tell that he had so often been told."[89]

The spiritual affliction of the village snob is plain enough, by Finney's reading: "It was *pride* that make him take that stand, and that kept him out of the kingdom of God." But even as Wright waved away the implications of his parlor piety, he sank deep into despair, becoming at one point "so enraged that God did not hear his prayer [that] he was tempted to kill himself." At last, he broke down and prayed in Finney's wooded preserve. Rid of his worldly skepticism, his conversion, like so many other to come in Finney's career, was instantaneous and joyful; another recent convert reported seeing the old surveyor-judge clapping his hands, pacing frenetically and yelling "*I will rejoice in the God of my salvation!*" Wright burst shortly thereafter into his office—where Finney was still on hand, but only for the sake of conducting spiritual interviews among would-be and recent converts—to shout "God, I've got it! God I've got it!"[90]

Wright's turn toward the Lord was momentous not merely for him, but for the progress of the revival Finney would go on to lead. The older man's conversion was among the first proofs to Finney that his intense experience of salvation and sanctification could be replicated. Just as important, Wright would become one of the corps of believers who would make up the crucial vanguard of the Second Awakening, especially in the rapidly industrializing North: entrepreneurial elites who occupied the key positions of influence in a mostly rural and artisanal economy that was being rapidly transformed in the service of the new national market In his later career, Finney would come to appreciate how the pride of this fast-rising social class could work great new spiritual and social wonders, once it had been delivered into the Lord's hands. By helping to engineer his former boss's conversion, Finney was discovering American Protestantism's next great calling.

What's more, Finney himself was extraordinarily solicitous to pitch his revival message to the most influential and wealthy members of any community that he barnstormed for Christ. His alliance with the affluent Tappan brothers in New York elevated the pivotal issues of evangelical reform, such as temperance and abolitionism, into bona fide national causes. But the quest for well-heeled evangelical allies was more than an instrumental push for social influence and financial resources. In Finney's reputation-making revival campaign in Rochester, New York—then a booming port city on the Erie Canal—he made his first converts among Rochester's moneyed elite. First one "prominent lady" in Rochester confessed her personal redemption at a Finney sermon, and then another. Soon, it was plain to Finney that his preaching had sparked so much "excitement and interest among that class of people" that

> it was soon seen that the Lord was aiming at the conversion of the
> highest classes of society. My meetings soon became thronged with
> that class. The lawyers, physicians, merchants, and indeed all the
> more intelligent class of society became more and more interested,
> and more and more influenced to giver their hearts to God.[91]

So critical was this constituency to Finney's revival preaching that the most famous of his so-called new measures modernizing the Awakening's gospel message for a new mass following—the "anxious bench" assembling members of the revival crowd plunged into acute personal distress over the unredeemed condition of their souls—was contrived to assuage the delicate sensibilities of the "highest classes." "From my own experiences and observation," Finney recalled, "I had found that with the highest classes especially, the greatest obstacle to be overcome was their fear of being known as anxious inquirers." After winning his first "prominent lady" to

Christ in Rochester, Finney "made a class, I think for the first time, upon that class of persons whose convictions were so ripe that they were willing then and there to renounce their sins and give themselves to God, to come forward to certain seats which I requested to be vacated, and offer themselves to God while we made them subjects of prayer."[92]

It was a finely calibrated flourish of social drama, showcasing in equal parts elite righteousness and class deference—the sort of gesture that Esq. Wright and the countless other princelings of the Market Revolution doubtless savored, as the urgent preaching of Finney and the age's other lead revivalists coaxed them out of their comfortable studies and into the public confession of their newfound evangelical zeal. And sure enough, the legacy of the Rochester revival, much like the Second Great Awakening's general reformist crusade, translated into a concerted assault from the newly saved "highest classes" on the mores, entertainments, and followays of the working masses—from pub crawling to theater going to the innocuous pursuit of work and commercial gain on the Sabbath.[93] Just as tellingly, Finney records that his more materially blessed followers found their perfect states of inner repose as they summoned their own stern to renounced the ornaments and fripperies of their higher station: A well-to-do pastor's soul is cleansed when he lays aside a showy gold ring and his fancy ruffled shirt at the behest of a revived congregant; a woman finds her when she realizes "the ornaments in my hair . . . stood in the way of my conversion." [ibid., p. 141] Austerity for the nation's weak and easily tempted workers, and purified decorousness for a newly roused evangelical leadership class: These were to be the watchwords of the Second Awakening's long, and ongoing, social dispensation.

Meanwhile, as Finney's evangelical vision of divine abundance and human free will continued to gain momentum, it would alight on a distinctly Gnostic theology of pure sanctification eminently suited to the American political economy's next stage of consolidation.

The Imperial Self and the Empire of Reform

There would be many insurgent religious movements devoted to reformist social ideals in the ongoing American quest for Gnostic deliverance;

indeed, the best-known legacies of the Second Awakening all have to do with the postmillennial effort to improve and perfect the integrity of an American social order convulsed by rapidly expanding divisions of class, race, caste, and gender. At the same time, however, these worthy efforts were inextricably bound up with the dictates of a saving faith fashioned by, for, and about the imperial American self.

The successive Protestant assaults on the institutions of the church, the state, and the idea of social welfare would all henceforth be rendered in the telltale spirit of orgiastic individualism. And Gnostic seekers from a wide array of new denominations and religious movements would eventually retool all the features of their Puritan inheritance to move in rhythm to the restless cadences of market capitalism. They would drill down, far beyond all the hated accretions of Old World history, to the solitary, saving knowledge that their unique spiritual destiny was forever beyond the mere bonds of institutional or communal life. In time, this message would come to be a common-sense fixture of American social mythology, mined by ideologues, business and political leaders, garden-variety opportunists, and self-help prophets. It would seem to be rediscovered and foisted, over and over again, on impressionable new generations of American seekers from without, as the indispensable means by which they could disclose and redeem the higher truths buried within their inmost, success-haunted spiritual hearts.

But to paraphrase the moral of the Wizard of Oz, the vision of Gnostic redemption was right there all along, in each new generation's spiritual makeup. It's important to fix the religious origins of this recurring prophecy of individual transcendence clearly in view, since part of what's made the rhetorical tradition of a pristine American economic individualism so durable, so unassailable to sustained critical inquiry, and so resistant to major countervailing trends in our political economy, has been the fundamental conviction that it's integral to the nation's very soul. We commonly speak of it as a folk belief, a fairy tale, or a social myth, but the tight alliance of personal prosperity and spiritual awakening in the American grain is at bottom a gospel of Gnostic deliverance.

The bare outlines of this vision were already present at the creation, so to speak, on the makeshift campgrounds of Cane Ridge. One of the things that made this particular outpouring of the spirit such a compelling show of unrestrained divine power was that the revival in question had been organized around a fairly stringent set of denominational rites and ceremonies. The seemingly spontaneous marshalling of heaven-possessed souls into their own individual rites of yelling, chanting, singing, and comatose silence occurred at a ceremony organized as an extended communion feast, intended to renew believers' fervor within fairly rigid channels of traditional observance.

As the church faithful and the swelling community of onlookers from outside the denomination assembled for the sermons and sessions of public prayer commemorating the sacrament, members of the Presbyterian clergy continued to pay close attention to the spiritual progress of their flocks. They were, in fact, better able to carry out this mission because they had selected likely candidates for conversion in advance, interviewing them at church social gatherings to ascertain the state of their religious development, and handing out communion tokens—key markers of status at Presbyterian revivals—to promising would-be converts. Theologically close to Calvinist tradition, Presbyterian leaders also hewed to traditional Puritan forms of managing the course of younger congregants' spiritual development. A communally monitored experience of conversion within the faith was a social rite of passage as much as a religious one, and treated with the sort of close social attention that today might attach to standardized college admission tests among privileged American youth. Especially in frontier social orders, a socially verified come-to-Jesus moment was often a passport to influence—one of the few surefire signs that the rising generation of elite leaders could be entrusted with social power. That, indeed, was why Whitefield's revival preaching met with pronounced hostility from social elites in the South on his eighteenth-century revival tours there: The Great Itinerant was meddling not just with long-cherished theological convictions about who could be saved in what circumstances, but also with the fabric of the colonial Southern social order.

By the turn of the nineteenth century, however, the south's regional elites were primed for an evangelical gospel far surpassing George Whitefield's most dramatic transports. What had changed was the bedrock conviction that the old Calvinist gospel of acute dependence on God's will and his inviolate plan of salvation would secure the South's most pressing need: the preservation of a thoroughgoing system of economic and social deference. Indeed, the Presbyterian conception of theological and social order was one of the earliest casualties of the Second Awakening, with erstwhile Calvinist preachers like McNemar and Barton W. Stone announcing their break with the denomination almost immediately after the transports they'd witnessed and enabled, much to their own amazement, at the revival campgrounds. But significantly, members of the region's Presbyterian social elite also passed through the transforming crucible of the Cane Ridge Pentecost—and typically went on to follow in the sectarian footsteps blazed by the revival's sponsors.

In what would become a very consistent pattern across the Second Awakening, the apparently egalitarian disbursal of the experiential gifts of the spirit to broader followings and former outcast communities failed to produce anything like a millennial reordering of the worldly economy. Quite the contrary, in fact: The New Light gospel of experience galvanized social elites into a new sense of both personal rectitude and reforming ardor. The first remained first, and if they weren't able to ensure that the last would always remain last, they would at least find ingenious new ways to impress their own values and preferences upon the tenant farmers, slaves, and wage workers amassing around the nation's new economic frontier.

In this regard, the Presbyterian experience at Cane Ridge was indeed prototypical. On one level, Presbyterianism represented an organized system of social deference that broke up virtually on contact with the experiential Gnostic wonders on display at Cane Ridge. Not long after Anglicans had been decisively routed in American pews during the Revolution, Presbyterianism in the South claimed wide allegiance among the region's landed elites and its upwardly mobile merchant class—particularly as Scotch-Irish landowners, like President Andrew Jackson, came into positions of social power. In North Carolina's Piedmont, where Stone, the lead organizer at Cane Ridge, was educated and launched his early ministry, Presbyterians were known as "a landed, literate, politically involved class of people," writes Conklin.[94] The same demographic profile extended to Presbyterian synods around Richmond, Virginia—the capital of the Old Dominion, and the social hub of its plantation-holding "squirearchy."

Presbyterians likewise represented the social elite in the rawer frontier outposts of Kentucky, where the Cane Ridge revival drew its adherents. One of the gathering's best-known early converts was Col. Robert Patterson, a founder of the state's commercial capital of Lexington, and a storied Indian fighter and militia leader. Another Presbyterian preacher at the site, John W. Lyle, kept close note of the conversions he witnessed; his diary recorded that "the people most stricken were often sturdy landowners or prominent women, leaders in the local congregations, people in the upper ranks of early Kentucky society," Conklin writes.[95]

It's certainly easy—and in most historical surveys of the Second Awakening, quite common—to interpret all the obvious heaven-storming energy at Cane Ridge and its many successor revivals as a great upsurge of democratic religious sentiment. And undeniably, the notion of immediate, experiential salvation achieved largely through the believer's free will was a potent source of inward spiritual validation for the lesser-born frontier souls who would come to be identified, amid the political transformations of the Jackson age, with America's suddenly all-powerful "common man." But the social import of Cane Ridge and the Second Awakening was a much more complicated matter—something closer to a series of unruly, but still well appointed, fraternal lodge meetings than a spontaneous spiritual insurgency from below. Into the ranks of the newly enlightened, Cane Ridge alone drew many prominent Kentucky political leaders and landowners, from the governor on down. Indeed, the main sectarian movement that took root in Kentucky in the wake of Cane Ridge—the 1810 founding of the phenomenally successful Cumberland Presbytery by a group of post-Calvinist revival preachers—was led by Finis Ewing, one of the state's largest slaveholders and land-owners. Ewing was a close friend and later patronage appointment of Andrew Jackson; at the time of Ewing's ordination, he was "arguably the most wealthy, socially the most prominent, and politically the most influential of all Presbyterian clergyman in the West," in the judgment of Conklin.[96]

The idea that such a visceral and extended show of experiential faith should yield such a steady stream of socially eminent converts seems more than a little improbable at first glance. Weren't the prime instincts of wealthy believers to seek out the Lord's favor in polite, edifying public discourses—preferably delivered before a congregation's most influential families seated in high-priced rented pews? How was it that Kentucky's rising power elite should be fainting dead away and succumbing to involuntary physical jerks and wailings, and professing a childlike rebirth in Christ's deeply personal love? Even out on the farther reaches of the American republic's western frontier, these were unseemly displays of religious enthusiasm for the leaders of respectable society to indulge in—and especially so, one might argue, for the leaders of the American South's neo-feudal slave economy.

But as is the case with most revival movements in American history, the key to Cane Ridge's elite appeal lay in its deft repackaging of sturdy biblical truths in terms readily adaptable to the nation's rising commercial ethos. Indeed, throughout the course of the ensuing Second Great Awakening, believers from all class backgrounds and walks of life would enact a series of revealing variations of the experiential, Pentecostal drama of redemption played out to such grand effect at Cane Ridge. The class affiliations and political sympathies of the nation's new cohort of revival leaders would diverge wildly over the course of the Second Awakening—from Methodist circuit riders, to reform-minded exhorters promoting campaigns of mass social improvement, to Brahmin divines extolling strange new Gnostic principles of character reform and self-improvement.

But these figures would all share an abiding sense of the market order's metaphysical rightness, and would tailor their own ingenious modifications of the Cane Ridge Pentecost to the needs of a restless spiritual public positioned at the vanguard of the nineteenth century's great Market Revolution—a tremendous upsurge in the nation's trade infrastructure, combined with the sudden breakup of home-based economic manufacture for local markets in favor of newly standardized, national-scale industrial modes of production and work discipline. As every other sphere of American life—from constitutional law to property relations to wage labor and family relations—was realigned with the contractual logic of the great growth spurt of the national economy, the life of the spirit, too, would move increasingly in concert with the convulsions of market demand.

Over the long run of the Second Awakening—which has arguably never come to any official end—the masters of the Market Revolution in American economic life would find their social station and preferences anointed, over and over again, in the image of a new American millennium. Only where the revival adherents of George Whitefield's First Great Awakening recommitted themselves to the core Calvinist principle of obedience to a remote and unfathomable God who lent a higher purpose to their worldly callings, the followers of the Second Awakening fashioned a new God for themselves, one far more attuned to the consolidation of a truly national economy.

This did not mean that the leaders of the Second Awakening were anything close to Deists or skeptics—they affirmed the importance of human agency in creating religious enthusiasm, while attributing the mystic workings of that enthusiasm upon each newly converted soul entirely to the wondrous power of God. The divine will was still an awesome force that dictated the most basic terms of character, morality, and personal advancement for ordinary Americans—but the old Calvinist God was increasingly ill-suited to the new competitive conditions of enterprise that guided the new channels of national commerce. The dread specter of Arminianism—the free will doctrine associated with the sixteenth-century Dutch theologian Jacobus Arminius—was now, with minimal institutional controversy, accepted as an obvious foundation of the revived religion of the nineteenth century.

This revolution in the new nation's theological worldview was itself the product of dramatic new market pressures. By 1833, the last state-supported church establishment, in the old Puritan stronghold of Massachusetts, was finally abolished, as dissenting Baptists in the state finally were able to compete on equal material and cultural terms with the pedigreed former clerical lords of the Bay Colony. And by that point, religious entrepreneurs up and down the former colonies had already rendered the broader logic of state-sponsored religion—the indispensable adjunct to the civic education in republican virtue that the nation's founders prescribed in order to endow the constitutional republic with an engaged and productive citizenry—very much a dead letter. What realistic chance did prim election-day sermons and legislative prayer sessions, or the other collective rites of old New England Puritanism, have of competing with the seemingly unbidden descent of the Holy Spirit before a vast new religious public of individualist believers, working out their own salvations, in terms that they had largely invented and administered for themselves? Once the threshold of disestablishment had been crossed, religion became the first— and is arguably still the greatest—deregulated industry in American life.

The Market's Saving Graces

Ironically, the new free-will prophets of the Second Awakening were pronouncing the glorious dividends of spiritual self-determination at the same moment that many American farmers and mechanics had become more unsettled than ever in the battle for control over their economic fortunes. In an economic upheaval at least as profound as the political changes wrought by the War for Independence, Americans were thrust into what nineteenth-century historians called the Market Revolution. The emergence of a new national market marked a fundamental reorientation of the American legal, political, and economic system that rewarded the same market actors who'd made up the leadership vanguard of the nineteenth century's free-will revivals: a new class of savvy entrepreneurs, positioned at the nation's booming nexus of the nation's new networks of transport, real-estate speculation, interstate commerce, and finance.

The initial origins of the Market Revolution lay, however, in the nineteenth century's diminishing surplus of what had formerly been the most abundant commodity of the American colonies: land. The farm- and village-based economy of the early American republic operated on much the same subsistence principles that governed European peasant life for centuries. And if anything, the folk beliefs and work habits of the yeoman class enjoyed much greater influence in America, thanks to the New World's incredible land riches. "So long as land was assured for rising generations," the historian Charles Sellers writes, "accumulation was pointless and productive effort could be relaxed as soon as conventional standards of consumption were achieved. Work exercised varied skills and alternated with considerable leisure as dictated by season and weather. Often it was interwoven with family and neighborhood sociability."[97]

But the new national market rudely shouldered aside most of the traditions that tethered American settlers to the familiar rhythms of folk worship. As older rural families lost their grip on farms divided by the new American system of fee-simple ownership, the old subsistence order grew unstable. Subdivided land, unable to sustain the rising populations of established rural clans, pushed straitened would-be heirs to uncultivated lands farther west—and south, as the heavily Presbyterian Scotch-Irish migration into Kentucky, North Carolina, and Virginia shows.

Meanwhile, the booms in commercial trade and manufacturing in major port centers such as Boston, Philadelphia, New York, and Baltimore accelerated the demographic pressures squeezing the countryside. As early as 1790, the year of the first American census, the population densities of settlements in the orbit of these rising metropolises were spiking dramatically. "Land prices swelled as farms contracted," Sellers writes. "Although residents were leaving in droves, enough remained to swell an increasingly insecure class of landless tenant farmers, laborers, and craftsmen."[98] In southern New England, the region hit hardest by these trends, "population density exceeded forty persons per square mile in most of the old farming towns, reaching one hundred in some, and land values doubled or trebled," Sellers notes. "A rich 'loaner class' appeared, wealth became more polarized, sons fell below the status of their fathers, and the poor were poorer and more numerous."[99]

In this atmosphere of mounting crisis, the masters of the nineteenth-century Market Revolution seized no end of fresh economic opportunities. Deftly exploiting the resources of state and national governments, entrepreneurs in commercial ports and along the country's western and southern interior knitted together a powerful new system of interstate commerce. The activist Supreme Court majority led by the great Federalist chief justice John Marshall created unprecedented new prerogatives that enabled the Bank of the United States and a host of state-chartered corporations to direct the course of new commercial development in terms immensely favorable to themselves.

Overthrowing a battery of legislative constraints on the power of money, from several state measures of bankruptcy relief to an effort to tax the Baltimore branch of the national bank, the Supreme Court inscribed the new rule of the national market in unmistakable terms. During a single six-week period in 1819, Sellers writes, the court

> forbade the states to interfere with the chartered privileges of corporations, to relieve existing debts, or to impede in any fashion the constitutional functions or instrumentalities of the federal government. Moreover it asserted its own right to define the range of permitted federal functions so broadly as to include not only the national Bank but also by implication internal improvements, protective tariffs, and the rest of the [Federalist/Whig] developmental program. Indeed, the justices all soon took the extraordinary step of informing the President directly that they were "all of the opinion that the decision on the Bank question completely commits" to upholding internal improvements as implied by the enumerated congressional power to establish post offices and post roads.[100]

Capital-heavy transportation projects such as the Erie Canal created a host of boom towns along their main arteries and tributaries, and further spurred rural production to serve the needs of the nation's rising commercial centers. The nation's fledgling postal service made it easier to conduct business across state lines, and to standardize potentially risky channels of regional trade along the countryside. New technological breakthroughs such as Robert Fulton's steam engine and Eli Whitney's cotton gin created quantum leaps in the speed and efficiency of transportation and production, and opened up still bigger markets for cash-crop agriculture. Soon even the most rural and remote outposts of the feudal south had bulked up into an enormously profitable—and completely slave-dependent—Cotton Kingdom, catering to the demand for cheap cotton in both foreign markets and the sprawling new textile mills of New England.

The explosion of credit-backed enterprises and major infrastructure projects also meant that older stigmas on indebtedness were refashioned to meet the financial needs of the Market Revolution. Large-scale debt was now transformed from a moral hazard into a badge of market daring,

with state legislatures extending generous terms of bankruptcy relief to
the captains of enterprise. Meanwhile, the wage-earning working poor
who often ended up as the collateral victims of the massive overextension
of debt and credit were stigmatized as lazy or perverse flouters of market
discipline. Since cash was steadily supplanting the older subsistence-era
ethos of communal self-help, to be left living without it was a sign of acute
moral weakness, particularly for the unfortunate souls who fell under the
spell of gambling, counterfeiting, and other nineteenth-century confidence
schemes. However, in the hands of the new century's credit-backed market
entrepreneurs, the vice of weak-willed individuals became a heroic social
virtue. A good deal of investor class's fabled pluck and resourcefulness now
hinged on its ability to organize its own indebtedness on an enormous scale
and sell it as a stock or bond issue to other investors or state legislatures.[101]

With such visible and profitable networks of commerce now studding the
American landscape—and bringing virtually all the major enterprises along
the chain of New World production into closer regular contact—the attraction of the formerly heretical doctrines of human spiritual agency and free
will became well nigh irresistible. The clear material blessings of concentrated
human effort were to be seen everywhere in the booming centers of American production and trade—from the South and West's commercialized wheat
and cotton fiefdoms, to the textile factories and company towns of Massachusetts, to the ports and financial centers of New York and Philadelphia.

The Awakening's close and abiding affinity for market values helps
explain, among other things, why the feudal labor regime of the South
should have adapted so readily to a revival whose core message seemed,
on the surface of things, a direct democratic threat to the canons of social
deference demanded by the region's slaveholding squirearchies. If evangelical believers could now do so much to lay their hands directly on their
ultimate spiritual destinies, nothing in theory should have prevented
slave populations, or poor Southern whites, from applying the exact same
moral to their economic lives, and carving up cotton estates into the small
free-holding farming parcels of yeoman democratic lore.

Yet as we've seen, the gospel of self-improvement spawned by the
Awakening's free-will vanguard was welcomed at least as heartily along

the Southern planter elite as it was among their sworn foes in the anti-
slavery evangelical vanguard of the North. Southern planters had plenty
of economic complaints about the ways in which they saw the lords of
the Market Revolution diminishing their livelihoods—but curiously,
these were typically laissez-faire protests against the unfair burdens lev-
ied against the region's farming economy by measures such as the tariff
assessed against foreign export markets to support U.S. manufacturers.
Such was the visceral power of the Money Cult's intimate Gnostic gospel
that the Christian beneficiaries of one of the world's most unfree modern
labor regimes unblinkingly endorsed a rhetoric of complete free-market
opportunity to defend their own autocratic interests.

Nor was this the era's only mind-bending bit of ideological acrobatics.
For a revival predicated at first on the rapid spread of ecstatic transports of
divine grace, the Second Awakening segued with remarkable ease into a
programmatic gospel of sober self-discipline and calculation. As though by
some unstated law of spiritual compensation, the country's new affirmation
of the spiritual will served to bind believers to a tight regimen of rational
self-control. A more responsive God would collaborate much more cheerfully in the improvement of the American self—just as the revived American Gnostic believer would now commune with a God brought much more
vividly down to earth. The end result, as historian Jackson Lears notes,
was an entrepreneurial outlook he calls "evangelical rationality"—a boldly
dialectical new force that sought to reconcile the more traditional and austere ideal of God's Providence with the far less stable, but almost equally
awesome, operations of market sovereignty.

This synthesis was expressed most famously in the revival's direct and
unadorned means of communication. While the soul-shaking transports
of the freely professed New Birth swept over revival crowds in seemingly
spontaneous waves of enthusiasm, these displays were carefully managed,
premeditated, and dispassionately chronicled by the Awakening's leaders. The greatest practitioner and theoretician of the Second Awakening's
soul-winning tactics was the master revivalist Charles Finney—another
Presbyterian who threw over most of his denomination's established communions and doctrines in favor of what he called the "new measures" of

experiential revival. While the revivalists of Whitefield's age took great pains to separate out the mysterious workings of divine grace from the infinitely feebler manipulations of passing human passion, Finney cheerfully acknowledged that revivalists, like their prospective converts, could readily employ their own rationally calculating wills to help bring about the great work of salvation—and if those efforts happened to err on the side of other-than-supernatural human agency, Finney argued, why, that was far from a sin in its own right. In a typical and revealing defense of his new measures, Finney argued, like scores of market rationalists ever since, that the end justified the means. To the defenders of the older Calvinist view that the unassailable sovereignty of God had "precluded a rational employment of means for promoting a revival of religion," Finney countered, just as any common-sense philosopher might, that "there is no evidence from the Bible that God exercises any such sovereignty as that. There are no facts to prove it. But everything goes to show that God has connected means with the end through all departments of his government—in nature and in grace." What's more, Finney concluded, to the extent that unforeseen human mischief might distort the gospel message of a revival, that, too, is but a minor setback, in view of the larger calculations of means and ends. "The evils which are sometimes complained of, when they are real," Finney candidly averred, "are incidental and of small importance when compared with the amount of good produced by revivals."[102]

But while these means may have been rationally conceived and assessed, their appearance on the religious scene of the young republic was still plenty raw. As had been the case during Whitefield's Awakening a century earlier, the masters of the Second Awakening determined to retool the rhetorical imagery and communications tools of their version of the New Birth in order to evangelize a national public in a gospel message that readily equated the Lord's kindly labors with their own efforts to tame the market frontier. As the beleaguered defenders of the old Puritan order saw to their shock and dismay, the most effective modes of evangelical preaching were also the most vernacular. Not only did revivals and camp meetings routinely feature the sorts of convulsions and transports among revival crowds that converted the somber communion at Cane Ridge into a latter-day Pentecost; revival preachers were also deliberately stoking the mood of self-sanctified worship with scandalously familiar exhortations. On the revival circuits of the frontier, the apostles of the new century's free-will faith would wheedle, joke, sing, and tearfully pray for the great work of salvation to sweep up still more unconverted souls into their ranks. The new clamor for emotionally demonstrative preaching was neatly captured in a rejoinder from the crowd when the great Methodist circuit rider Peter Cartwright, who'd made the mistake of opening one of his revival sermons with a joke: "Make us cry, make us cry—don't make us laugh."[103]

But like most easy entertainments, the performances of the Second Awakening's charismatic preachers concealed a great deal of unseen effort. For starters, there was the sheer scale of their new national gospel appeal. The great Methodist bishop Francis Asbury—who kept copious records of all his denomination's soul-winning gains—estimated that by 1811, his tireless squadrons of circuit riders had staged camp-meeting revivals reaching between 3 and 4 million believers—one third of the country's total population.[104]

Printed appeals were, if anything, more inescapable. As revived denominations founded missionary and tract societies on a national scale, new breakthroughs in mass-printing technologies permitted them to overrun the frontier with sacred texts. Of some 605 religious journals printed in America in 1839, a scant 14 had existed before 1790. By 1830, the American Bible Society and the American Tract Society, both based in New York and funded by recently converted businessmen, were printing and distributing 1 million bibles and 6 million tracts a year.[105] As Charles Sellers notes, the Tract Society's print runs marked a significant commercial breakthrough as well, in the development of a mass readership for literature produced for the first time on a national scale: The "spiritual missives" pouring off the Tract House presses were "the first standardized, mass-produced commodities to be distributed and promoted for the entire national market."[106] During its heyday, the Tract Society alone managed "to rival the federal government in terms of manpower and resources," John W. Compton writes. "Indeed, the largest reform societies raised a combined total of about $2.81 million during the 1820s—a figure that very nearly equals the $3.59 million spent by the federal government on internal improvements between 1782 and 1830."[107]

As impressive as the scale of the Awakening's system of message delivery was, its most enduring gains occurred thanks to the age's unprecedented boom in charismatic preaching. The lead preachers of the Awakening all perfected powerful methods of channeling and dramatizing the liberating New Birth of a post-Calvinist faith as a face-to-face experience. The signature exhorters of the Second Awakening were "communications entrepreneurs," as Nathan O. Hatch observes—dedicated to bringing an experiential grasp of the free-will gospel to the widest possible audience.[108] The vanguard denominations in this regard were the Methodists—who famously doubled their church membership up to 1 million between 1820 and 1830—and the Mormons, who proselytized with the unique fervor that arose from the conviction of their own persecution at the hands of a sclerotic, corrupt Protestant establishment. But these hard-driving faiths relying on nonstop revival efforts from hastily trained, uncredentialed missionary preachers only represented the extreme form of a new, across-the-board sense among the age's revived denominations that the work of redemption had to be spread far and wide—and rapidly.[109]

This urgent sense of pending deliverance was also the motive force behind the age's signature evangelical reform crusades. Here, too, the sheer clamor of the Awakening's frenetic activity has often drowned out its ultimately conservative economic designs. Despite the hectically leveling character of missionizing activity, church expansion, and spiritual authority in the new century, the Second Awakening cleaved to an elite model of respectable virtue that clearly favored the spiritual outlook and character traits already earmarked for worldly success. Under this dispensation of faith, the age's emerging gospel of Gnostic experience was channeled, under the authority of a new evangelical establishment, into a much broader and influential gospel of character-driven success. The trademark crusades of the Second Awakening all targeted the habits and vices of populations who stood athwart the ideal of spiritual progress that commanded great loyalty from the lords of Northern market capitalism: intemperate drinkers, gamblers, and—far more consequentially—Southern slave-masters.

Low Spirits

These figures all haunted the evangelical imagination not merely as lost souls courting their own certain damnation, but also, significantly, as specters of what the Market Revolution took to be the greatest of all personal sins: lapsed self-control. By indulging in the judgment-clouding, morale-sapping excesses of liquor or tempting the designs of Providence with schemes to link prosperity with the dangerous pagan notion of luck, drinkers and gamblers struck directly at the unspoken social contract at the awakening's heart: *Improve yourself, and the good things of the Earth shall be pledged to you.* As Lears observes: "Gamblers, like drunkards, challenged the emerging mythology of self-made manhood . . . Under the aegis of evangelical rationality, the gambler was recast from an epitome of masculine selfhood to a pathetic anti-self—a slave to his destructive habit and frequently a suicide . . . The gambler's manic-depressive oscillation between joy and sorrow comported ill with the secularized Protestant ethic of unending improvement, civic or personal."[110]

In a steady stream of sermons, tracts, and didactic plays and novels, the gambler and his close cousin the drunkard came to stand in for all the indulgences firmly repudiated by the sober guardians of market virtue, dead-set on implementing a tireless Gnostic regimen of self-improvement and self-control. Perhaps most damningly, these sinners were heedless of the scarcest and most precious commodity available to an enterprising Gnostic believer: the gift of time. An anti-gambling sermon that the Reverend Eli Hyde delivered in 1819 excoriated the "perpetual and increasing incitement" that came with the compulsive pursuit of victory in games of chance. While more sober amusements succumb at the end of their appointed rounds to "the business of life," gambling was a different proposition entirely, as Hyde explained: "It tempts, fascinates, absorbs. The glass runs out unheeded: hour is added to hour, and the party rises fatigued and exhausted." Such amusements, Hyde darkly warned, were "a sinful mispense [sic] of time." This offense was especially unforgivable for divines such as Hyde, since the time squandered in chasing intoxication and/or the turn of a friendly card was forever lost to the far more worthy pursuit of profitable enterprise or (what increasingly amounted to the same thing) the provident believer's regimen of moral self-improvement.[111]

Hence the strenuous efforts of evangelical leaders of the Second Awakening to ban outright, as opposed to merely regulating, the liquor traffic and state lotteries: As the evangelical conscience of the age saw things, individual reform *was* social reform, and the apparatus of the state is morally obliged to eliminate the most detrimental institutions and practices that undermine the sanctified progress of the individual believer. The anti-lottery crusade in particular dramatized the intensity of the age's new evangelical determination to refashion the striving character of the American believer from the ground up: Evangelical leaders committed themselves to the quixotic bid to eradicate all existing state lottery contracts via court challenges and federal legislation—even though they had already succeeded in revoking such charters in all but three of the republic's states, and even though such charters were clearly protected by the contracts clause of the U.S. Constitution. Indeed, a central if little-known legacy of the age's heroic reform efforts was the steady onslaught of evangelical court challenges to previously settled law on limits to regulation of lotteries and liquor sales; these concerted legal challenges eventually so unsettled the foundations of Federalist judicial review that they gave rise to the Progressive era's later embrace of the idea of the "living Constitution"—i.e., a judicial philosophy less bound by precedent and interpretations of the Framers' original intent than by the sense that lawmakers and courts needed to rally to the shifting public understanding of what moral or ethical reforms can and should be enacted by law.[112]

On the strict constitutional level, these creative assaults on the public toleration of vice also appeared to strike at the conceptual heart of the American legal system's basic protections of property and contract. But that perception, too, hinges upon a hard-and-fast division between expropriating means and spiritual ends that the evangelical revolution of the nineteenth century didn't recognize. For the Second Awakening's leaders, the mission before them was never to challenge the lawful sovereignty of property per se; it was, rather, to infuse the canons of enterprise with the awakened spirit of revival. If the trade in liquor or the contracts endowing a state lottery interfered with that aim, they became dangerous and illegitimate—not so much because they profiteered off vice and moral decline, but because they dismantled the sort of aspirational and tirelessly improving character that accumulated profit in the first place.

The deeper logic of this stance becomes especially clear when it's applied to the great evangelical campaign against slavery. While the continued practice of slavery was a far greater trespass against Christian morality than the private vices of drinking and gambling, the Second Awakening sparked little in the way of outright bids to eradicate the South's great social sin. Evangelical opponents of slavery didn't mount ingenious efforts to attack the peculiar institution's constitutional protections in the same ways that they pursued legal end runs around lottery contracts and state statutes that regulated grog shops. In part, of course, this was because any head-on legal assault against slavery was a daunting prospect; the radical abolitionist William Lloyd Garrison famously dramatized this dilemma by burning copies of the Constitution and denouncing the document as an instrument of the devil for explicitly recognizing and rewarding the practice of slavery. And the confrontational and violent rhetoric that Garrison and other abolitionists provoked among Southern slave-owners and their congressional defenders supplied further proof to skittish Northern reformers that a sustained battle over the slave economy could place the union in jeopardy. Human slaves, after all, represented the single most valuable form of property in the antebellum United States.

Still, for fire-breathing evangelists who had imbibed the spirit of postmillennial reform, the specter of such resistance might well have been, if anything, an additional spur to righteous action. After all, truly dedicated prophets of reform expect not to be loved in their own country. Indeed, reformers already targeting the deep-seated human impulses to drown one's sorrows and put hard-earned money to sporting use would logically have been expected to rally behind the abolition of a barbarous and profoundly antidemocratic labor regime that destroyed the central plank of faith in the emerging Money Cult: the myth of the individual worker's hypothetical ascent into market titanhood. If free will in matters of earthly enterprise meant anything at all, it seemed, it meant setting one's entire heart and spirit intractably against the perpetuation of slave labor.

Instead, the main run of evangelical reformers sought during the

nineteenth century to confine the geographic spread (and hence the political influence) of the peculiar institution, while promoting schemes such
as the mass emigration of former American slaves to the African colony
of Liberia. The quarantine of slavery within the borders of the old South
would, they reasoned, promote the peculiar institution's likely organic
dissolution under its own lethargic noncompetitive steam. Likewise, the
schemes of mass slave deportation sidestepped any sustained responsibility for the condition of former slaves as fellow human beings and children of God. While the continuance of slavery was a perverse affront to
the Northern Protestant work ethic, it didn't need to provoke abolitionist
outrage—an argument that gained currency for respectably middle-class
evangelical leaders as religious abolitionism became identified with radical
figures such as Garrison and John Brown.

Notably, this class myopia extended to the tactics employed in the
evangelical sphere of public reform. The close attention that evangelists
such as Finney paid to means-and-ends rationality simply did not apply
with the same force in the case of the antislavery crusade. In the decades-
long push for prohibition of liquor sales, evangelical reformers advocated
both "local control" initiative votes to approve or abolish liquor sales,
together with laws endorsed by state legislatures to ban the liquor traffic—i.e., the very measures of local control they sought to subdue in the
hands of the expanding slave power in the South.

This same political worldview has largely remained intact among
evangelical reformers, and accounts for one of the great seeming contradictions in the strategic thinking of today's evangelical right: a stridently
individualist social ethic that nevertheless promotes the ready embrace
of draconian state-backed measures to promote putative moral reform at
the most basic levels of individual conduct, such as bans on gay marriage,
reproductive choice, and the teaching of evolution in charter and public schools. Nevertheless, the same activists perceive no logical difficulty
in mounting pleas for the preservation of conscientious "religious liberty"
when the state will advance policies less congenial to their own morality
in the name of pluralist choice. They see no contradiction here because, for
them, none exists: The overriding challenge for evangelical reformers in

the twenty-first century, as in the nineteenth, is to harness any available means to the urgent project of the American self's Gnostic reclamation.

Most of these awkward circles were squared in the Second Awakening's dominant image of slavery as an affront to the Northern Protestant work ethic. Evangelical Northern foes of slavery, who were typically unfamiliar with the daily working lives of black slaves, often preferred to zero in on the debauched figure of the slave-master as the most potent symbol of the moral bankruptcy of the South's peculiar institution. And here, too, the dominant imagery stressed unbridled self-indulgence over sinful exploitation. The slaveholder's most damning legacy was the unproductive economic example he set for his social inferiors. "Wealth is the natural fruit of industry, poverty of slave labor," the Yankee theologian Horace Bushnell famously preached. As Richard W. Carawardine notes, these sentiments became commonplace among Northern evangelicals as the case against slavery's territorial expansion matured into a national political cause:

> Slavery was synonymous not only with moral degradation, but "indolence," "lethargy," and "dishonor to honest toil." As such it directly contradicted the laws of God. It demoralized white laborers even more than black, keeping them illiterate and debased. A northern Methodist visitor to Georgia wrote home to tell of "indolent, improvident, and overbearing" whites who had kept as an agricultural desert land around Savannah which under Yankee cultivation would have flourished. Put St. Louis in a free state, James Finley insisted, and it would double in prosperity.[113]

It bears noting here that Finley, an Ohio Methodist minister, was only a transplanted Northerner; he was born in North Carolina and launched his preaching career in Kentucky. Indeed, like many middle-state evangelical preachers of his generation, he underwent his great moment of conversion at Cane Ridge. But his denunciation of his home region's lax productivity was atypical for evangelical sons of the South mainly by virtue of its explicit mention of slavery. Many evangelical boosters of the Southern highlands, keen to latch on to the boom conditions of the Market Revolution, sought, in flourishes of revivalist rhetoric, to instill more sturdy habits of industry and investment as part of the region's conversion to a free-will code of moral self-control—while maintaining a circumspect silence on the key questions of slavery and its expansion. As Tennessee Methodist William Brownlow put it in one typically overheated appeal to investors:

> We want less *idleness* and more *industry*; . . . less *extravagance* and more *economy*; . . . more *honest men* and fewer *rogues*; . . . more *capital* and less *credit*; . . . more *shirts* and fewer *ruffles*; . . . more *Christian morality* and fewer *grog shops*; . . . more *laboring men* and fewer *loafers*; . . . more *mechanics* and fewer *dandies*; . . . less *ignorance* and more *education*; . . . less *aristocracy* and more *democracy*.[114]

These sentiments took such powerful hold among evangelical elites that it mattered little just where and to what populations they might be applied. Indeed, the prescription for the rescue of southern whites from the indolent clutches of slaveholding civilization was identical, in the moral pleas of Northern abolitionists, to the path of self-improvement that freed slaves themselves must follow when they, too, would encounter the salubrious Yankee middle-class culture of the main chance. As the Unitarian minister James Freeman Clarke preached in 1842, the true evil of the system of slave labor was to put slaves at odds with the powerful means of self-regeneration that would permit them to rise above their fallen "animal" natures. This state of forsaken moral promise was, indeed, worse than the slave system's physical horrors; the slave, in this fanciful account of spiritual exploitation, was the ultimate specimen of lapsed self-control:

> A worse evil to the slave, than the cruelty he sometimes endures, is the moral degradation that results from his condition. Falsehood, theft, licentiousness, are the natural consequences of his situation . . . He goes to excess in eating, drinking, and animal pleasures; for he has no access to any higher pleasures, and a man cannot be an animal without sinking below an animal,—a brutal man is worse than a brute . . . Slavery is the parent of the vices.[115]

It therefore followed, in the rigid evangelical scheme of individual self-improvement, that freed slaves would have to become an absurd sort of super-American striver, fulfilling a script of scrupulously rational and accumulation-driven conduct that any self-respecting white American of the privileged middle class would find daunting indeed. One editorialist in William Lloyd Garrison's flagship abolitionist newspaper *The Liberator* counseled a profoundly imaginary audience of Northern African-Americans on the subject of their disproportionate incarceration in Massachusetts. This unequal disbursal of life outcomes simply meant that freed black Americans would have to embody each and every immaculate virtue of the redeemed Protestant faith. "It is time for you to awake," this paternalist writer explained, in the airy confidence of one of Job's biblical consolers:

> Be industrious. Let no hour pass unemployed . . . Be virtuous . . .
> Use no bad language. Let no foolish jesting be heard from you, but
> be sober men, who have characters to form for eternity . . . In a word,
> endeavor to be good Christians, and good citizens, that all reproach
> may be taken from you, and that your enemies, seeing your good
> conduct, may be ashamed.[116]

In the same vein, the executive committee of the American Anti-Slavery Society had issued instructions to its agents that the first order of business in the rehabilitation of freed slaves was the strict inculcation of the calculating yet pious outlook of evangelical rationality. The curriculum adopted by the moral instructors of freedmen must stress "the importance of domestic order and the performance of relative duties in families; of correct habits; command of temper and courteous manners." The society's agents were also charged to teach freed slaves "industry and economy; promptness and fidelity in the fulfillment of contracts or obligation" while also encouraging them "in the acquisition of property."[117]

This preaching of maximized personal utility in the service of a deeply hypothetical regime of free labor would have had a sickeningly familiar ring to recently freed slaves; what were the bywords of the grueling unfree field work of the Southern slavocracy if not "Be industrious" and "Let no hour pass unemployed"? There is likewise a universe of presumptuous social privilege contained within the notion that a population who until recently had been treated *as* property required patient tutelage in the observance of contract language and the acquisition of property. But this was the great unseen consensus that lay beneath much of the sectional rancor over the expansion of the southern Slave Power: The rhetoric of Gnostic evangelical self-improvement papered over a multitude of other social sins, as American preachers settled on a strikingly uniform regimen of pious and upright self-control for all citizens, regardless of social background or economic station.

It made sense, then, that after the South had finally been routed, the reflex among pious Northern reformers was to define the central task at hand as something very far afield from achieving a semblance of racial equity within the blighted former Confederacy. The central economic-cum-moral challenge here remained largely what it had been prior to the war: to conduct among devoted residents of the former Confederacy a campaign of individual moral reconstruction. The idea was to revive the old evangelical dream of rousing laggard Southern sensibilities to the charge of redeeming their land and culture alike. Here, the colonial spirit of Northern capitalist enterprise merged indistinguishably with the project of reviving the imperiled souls of the South's slaveholding civilization who had allowed themselves to sink into the mire of feudal indolence. As the *Nation* editorialized three months after the Confederacy's surrender at Appomattox, earnest reformers from the North now had to do nothing less than "to renew [the South's] soil, to raise unheard-of crops, to clear the forest and drain the swamp, to impress the water-power into service, to set up the cotton-mill alongside the cornfield, to build highways, to explore mines, and in short, to turn the slothful, shiftless Southern world upside down."[118]

This all seems, from our vantage on the other side of both the hard-fought Civil War and the civil rights revolution, an oddly self-involved rationale for vanquishing a barbarous and inhuman labor regime. But this is how the antislavery cause flowed naturally from the larger social premises of the Second Awakening: It would achieve the South's redemption one drained swamp, and one enterprising soul, at a time.

The ruinous consequences of this stalwart individualism soon became plain enough, in the century of malign neglect of black political and economic rights from the Reconstruction era onward, which worked to shore up both the political ideology of white supremacy and the systemic economic degradation of the freedmen and their descendants in the South. When it was toted up in the historical calculus of Northern evangelical faith, the sin of slavery was yet another instance of a wayward and unaccountable lapse of personal self-control, in precisely the same debilitating manner that drinking or gambling was. This resolutely personalized approach to this issue, together with the persistent racist outlook of most Northern opponents of the Slave Power, explains how the central goal of the Reconstruction years became, in remarkably short order, not to make the South, or the American economy more generally, more equitable for black and working-class labor; it was, instead, to make a New South over in the image of the old industrial and evangelical North.

American Jitters

But something gnawed away at all this world-conquering evangelical certainty, just beneath its surface: How free *was* free labor, really? Just as evangelical reformers were heeding the clarion call of free labor in the early decades of the nineteenth century, the rise of the new industrial workplace deskilled many manufacturing vocations; it is, indeed, inadvertent testament to the sweeping nature of this change that scarcely anyone today recalls that "manufacture" meant "made by hand," in the original usages of skilled craftsmen and commercial masters. Former guild-supervised trades, from shoemaking to barrel-staving, were now routinely hired out to households; and new textile mills, such as the great works at Lowell, Massachusetts, which opened in 1826, raised the fear that the industrializing United States would be home to a permanent wage-earning class—a scenario that never entered the minds of the defenders of the Northern work ethic. These apostles of heroic Protestant individualism were, indeed, lionizing the figures of the enterprising business owner, plucky office worker, and small farmer as symbols of untrammeled American opportunity at just the moment that their dreams of future improvement were being threatened on a scale never before imagined.

This was more than a matter of purely academic or theological speculation. As more Americans came face to face with an impersonal new regime of wealth creation, which was impervious to older spiritual notions of virtue and communal obligation, the individualism of the Gnostic revival became distinctly less orgiastic—and much more anxious. But free-will salvation admitted precious little room for sustained doubt, in either the careful cultivation of the self or the restless pursuit of worldly opportunity. Under this new form of market pressure, the striving Protestant self became more, not less, convinced of the awesome powers of self-reinvention contained within its reborn heart. For the energetic young men who would struggle to move into the Market Revolution's vanguard, the promise of free-will salvation imposed a paradoxically more demanding sort of character discipline. To please the new lords of the market, they appealed to the kinder and more accessible God of the Second Awakening for detailed guidance on proper behavior and self-improvement. While well-connected and firmly established capitalists of the nineteenth century could—and often did—fail repeatedly en route to their eventual fortunes, the young would-be entrepreneurs of the new market order, just like the former slave recruits to the Market Revolution's rank and file, had to make the most of whatever opportunities might materialize in their paths. Thus was born one of the longest-lasting legacies of the Second Awakening—the intensely individualist American gospel of self-help. Here's how historian John Lauritz Larson sums up the demand for pious new measures of self-advancement among the ambitious young men of the age as they scraped doggedly in search of the main chance in New York:

> Finding a good situation, acquiring a living, comfort, security, wife, family, and respectability, rewarded those who could thread the eye of a very small needle. Permanent success seemed especially elusive; a few false steps, however, resulted in consignment to the wage-earning class, whose comfort remained forever contingent upon the success of somebody else. By the 1830s, those youths who resisted the temptations of New York's "sporting society," strove to keep themselves on the straight and narrow path. They pored over self-help books and

listened to evangelical sermons intended for their guidance. Industry and frugality, as in former times, loomed large in all of this advice, but so did injunctions to forgo all kinds of gratification—especially courtship, sex, and marriage—until one's *economic* success had earned him the rights to enjoy the fruits of adult life . . . Middle-class virtues of self-control, hard work, and chastity, shored up with piety and temperance, became by the 1850s the standard of admission into the ranks of polite society; they marked for some a bright line between acceptable behavior and the self-destructive ways of the working poor.[119]

Over time, this bright line would come to cordon off the sanctums of inward Gnostic experience for new generations of evangelical believers. We tend today to interpret the emergence of a self-conscious middle-class piety as a shallow, outward thing—hinging on the sort of perfunctory check-list regimen of personal reform that now fuels the multibillion-dollar self-help industry. But to approach the Second Awakening's free-will revolution merely as another variation of the stalwart Benjamin Franklin program of upward-striving self-improvement misses the real nature of the Second Awakening's character-based faith, and downplays the deeper appeal of the nineteenth century's self-enabled gospels of success. There remained enough of the febrile spirit of orgiastic individualism in the age's trademark evangelical quest for self-control to make the rote rewards of upward mobility seem as though they were imbued with an immediate and electrifying promise of salvation.

To worship a God who could vouchsafe both your worldly and your eternal redemption was, indeed, a revolutionary prospect. It also involved a complete inversion of the old logic behind the Protestant ethic. No longer were believers propelled forward by the windfall of productive activity that Weber saw arising from the evacuation of the medieval monasteries. No longer would capitalism continue to expand on a largely covert identification of secular enterprise with divinely sanctioned personal callings. The Calvinist tradition had died on the Gnostic frontiers of the American spirit, and with it had the old model of salvation won through the earnest pursuit of a divine vocation. Now the believer's vocation and the believer's self merged into the same core project of Gnostic self-regeneration. Hardworking Protestants could best do God's bidding by improving their characters—not by doggedly burrowing into this or that worldly version of diligent and prayerful work in order to sidestep the grimmer disciplines to be exacted someday by a remote and unknowable Father God. The interlocking Puritan work disciplines of worldly austerity and self-denial belonged to a vanishing age of subsistence. In the Market Revolution's vision of saving abundance, the self wasn't to be hemmed in at all. It was to be perfected.

The Gnostic Reformation

This self-scrutinizing, tirelessly entrepreneurial theology of the striving self has become so tightly identified with American success thinking, and American faith more broadly, that it's now difficult to recognize as the product of a particularly strange moment of Gnostic retreat. In this new self-conscious phase of the spiritualized Market Revolution, the ideal-type of the believer-on-the-make was required to blot out enormous swaths of economic and social causation as they actually existed, and to invest the heroic, market-attuned features of the self with a correspondingly greater power— in much the same fashion that the freed slave and former southern slave-master had to reinvent themselves as pious accumulators of marginal advantage, unto infinity. The intensively personalized regimen of success pivoted on a stridently depoliticized understanding of how the basic conditions of earthly prosperity could be met, and teased out into a millennial future of abundance and achievement that would rescue the solitary believer and the Christian nation alike. The self was becoming the principal site of anxiety for the apostles of American success; it therefore stood to reason that, for a surprisingly wide sweep of spiritual thinkers, the self also served as the chief avenue of redemption in the aftermath of the Market Revolution.

The strange new nineteenth-century ideal of self-perfection marks a vital point of contact across the old evangelical-rationalist divide, uniting the raw preachments of fire-breathing evangelists such as Charles Finney with the far more refined musings of the age's armchair theologians—public intellectuals such as the Brahmin Unitarian preacher William Ellery Channing, and the great transcendental sage of Concord, Ralph Waldo Emerson. Here was a great, infinitely renewable mission for the spirit of evangelical rationalism that had first found its public voice in the era's reform crusades.

As at the end of the First Awakening, the Second Awakening's divide separating the emotional outbursts of the saved and the rational speculations of the scholarly proved to be far more illusory than real. The partisans of rational and evangelical faith had drawn far closer in their social philosophies than they had been when the pitched battles over the Calvinist and Congregationalist visions of salvation had divided eighteenth-century seminaries and congregations. In the new free-will dispensation of the Second Awakening, evangelicals and rationalists alike were pietists, privileging the more authentic, inward disposition of spiritual seekers—the gospel of the heart—above the artifices and contrivances of doctrine and institutional worship. They likewise shared the same broad postmillennial allegiance to the ideal of social reform carried out at the behest of a sanctified or enlightened band of activists.

Most of all, these unlikely nineteenth-century partners in uplift had strikingly similar theological outlooks. By far the least-known legacy of Charles Finney—and, among latter-day evangelicals, the most deliberately downplayed one—is his adherence to the then-heterodox teachings of Wesleyan perfectionism. This tradition, also known as "holiness" theology, went beyond the great moment of conversion plied by traditional revivalists to examine just how Christians should comport themselves in the world after they had handed their wills over to the Lord's sovereignty. In the view of holiness doctrine, humans were capable of gradually achieving a state of sinless conduct—once sanctified by the Holy Spirit, they were on the path to discovering a more permanent, metaphysical repose not merely in the Lord's care, but in his very being.

Of course, perfectionism was by no means moral license—its adherents took great pains to distinguish it from the "sin now, repent later" caricatures of Christian redemption propagated by rationalist and atheist cynics. If anything, the perfectionist ideal required far greater rigors of inward self-control than those summoned under the more straightforward exhortations from revival preachers to honor sobriety, thrift, and sexual modesty. After a long career of such pulpit harangues, Finney found himself growing restless and wondering whether there might be some sort of heightened, annealing spiritual experience awaiting already disciplined Protestant souls in the wake of their the rites of passage into Christian conversion.

Always a close chronicler of his own inward religious state, Finney reported that during the more reflective phase of his career as president of the abolitionist Oberlin College, he discovered, in the act of praying for the health of his ailing wife, that his own sense of spiritual power was expanding in virtual unison with the Lord's: "I felt a kind of holy boldness in telling him to do with me just as seemed good to him . . . I gave up hope from any past experience, and remember telling the Lord that I did not know whether he intended to save me or not. Nor did I feel concerned to know . . . My confidence in God was perfect, my acceptance of his will was perfect, and my mind was as calm as heaven."[120]

Here, in a vastly different social setting and intellectual inquiry, Finney had worked through the same sanctified sense of unchurched, primitivist communion with God that had been unleashed at Cane Ridge into a central principle of self-reform. After a long career of replenishing the ranks of organized religious observance and building new institutions of revived worship and education, Finney now concluded that "there was something higher and more enduring than the Christian church was aware of" and that "there were promises and means provided in the Gospel for the establishment of Christians in an altogether higher form of Christian life."[121] What's more, he discovered that, in contrast to his earlier encounters with the divine, this beatific condition was infinitely renewable, and never truly diminished. "I not only had all the freshness of my first love [of God], but a vast access to it continually . . . I then realized that I knew what is meant by the saying that he 'is able to exceedingly abundantly above all that we ask or think' . . . I had had no conception of the length and breadth, and the height and depth and efficiency of his grace."[122]

This God of transcendent abundance differs significantly from the gracious divine guardian of American prosperity who emerged out of the consensus that followed the First Awakening. The doctrines of perfectionism were more than simply anti-Calvinist; they were affirmatively Gnostic. In extending the vision of personal redemption as an immutable and abundant state of being, the perfectionist notion of spiritual selfhood possessed radical implications for American Protestantism. For starters, nineteenth-century perfectionism staged the central dramas of conversion—the sinful believer's broken-willed abjection and the ensuing moment of pure sanctification— entirely within the confines of the self. This represented a final stage of the inward migration of the work of redemption. Finney was hymning the soul's capacity to withdraw into itself, and to retreat behind the veil of earthly existence to access a boundless fund of divine grace from within.

With this retreat inward came a corresponding rejection of engagement with the created world. Regenerated within American Protestantism, this central article of Gnostic faith produced a lush, hothouse brand of spiritual individualism, allowing believers of the industrial age to contemplate their own communions with the divine virtually into infinity.

The path traversed by Finney in his own upward journey into sanctification would set the American religious mind off on a binge of self-reinvention—a process that closely tracked the steady advance of a mass consumer society that privileged individual experience above nearly every other notion of redemption and spiritual community. The basic notion of self-improvement had always, of course, been a key precept of American social mythology, dating at least back to the days of Franklin. But Finney's cohort of spiritual entrepreneurs had propelled the idea one glorious metaphysical step further.

Finney occupied a pivotal position in this new theology of self-reinvention and abundance. He was still enough of an ardent evangelist to conceive of his own inner sanctification wholly in terms of trust in Jesus as the alpha and omega. At the same time, he had flirted with more esoteric and elitist conceptions of faith. "In preaching, I have found that nowhere can I preach those truths on which my soul delights to live, and to be understood, except by a very small number," he confessed near the end of his memoir.

> I have found only a few, even of my own people, appreciate and receive those views of God and Christ and the fullness of his free salvation on which my own soul still delights to feed. Everywhere I am obliged to come down to where the people are in order to make

them understand me . . . When I preach the Gospel, I can preach the conversion, the atonement, and many of the prominent views of the Gospel that are appreciated and accepted by those who are still young in the religious life, and by those who have been long in the church of God and have made very little advancement in the knowledge of Christ. But it is only now and then that I find it really profitable to the people to pour out to them the fullness that my own soul sees in Christ. Everywhere the majority of professing Christians do not understandingly embrace those truths. They do not object, they do not oppose, and so far as they understand, they are convinced. But as a matter of experience, they are ignorant of the power of the highest and most precious truths of the Gospel of salvation in Christ Jesus.[123]

This was a remarkable confession for a career revivalist to make— something akin to St. Thomas's famous declaration on his deathbed that the vast achievement of the Summa Theologica and all his other apologetic works of Catholic theology now seemed like straw in a blazing fire. But in a larger sense, Finney's confession—published the year after his own death—was, like nearly everything he had done, very much in the grain of the Protestant mainstream of his day. In the South and West, primitivist prophets in the Baptist, Methodist, and Presbyterian traditions set about carrying forth the great work of the Cane Ridge encampment via elaborate Gnostic rejections of all prior church history, enshrining the irreducible, deeply individualist experience of personal imbuement with the Holy Ghost in its place. Utopian perfectionists, like the Shakers, the communitarian Christians quartered in Charles Humphrey Noyes's experimental Oneida settlement, along with the more spiritually minded apostles of New England's Transcendentalist movement, adhered in different ways to the great enabling mythos of Gnostic faith—that salvation was an arduous higher experience, not merely of self-discipline, but self-*transformation*, reserved for those properly instructed to form themselves into a spiritual elect. Like Charles Finney, these believers chased down the sanctioned religious promise of individualist reform. And with Finney, they concluded that some grander spiritual synthesis lurked within their own breasts, and it was there that they clung to the secret conviction that they were one with a transfiguring Christ.

Two of their number, William Ellery Channing and Emerson, serve to show how the tangled Gnostic encounter with the sanctified American market would take more coherent shape in the years ahead. Channing and Emerson were among the founding apostles of the movement known as self-culture—and their idiosyncratic respective meditations on religion and self-transformation served as a vital coming-of-age moment for Gnostic faith in America. In their hands, the intimations of Gnostic immortality plumbed by Finney and the prophets of Cane Ridge were reworked into the stuff of a proper literary-intellectual reformation—an American declaration of principles tailored to the Market Revolution, and nailed to the entrances of the entrepreneurial workshops haunted by the industrially disciplined, culturally expansive American self.

The self-culture movement was founded on the stalwart Brahmin conviction that the full promise of American democracy could only be realized by giving the ordinary American striver a thorough grounding in the culture of his—and increasingly, her—betters. As it turned out, this precious inheritance came bound up with a very peculiar sort of Protestant faith.

As the fervor of the Second Awakening began to wane at the end of its third decade, the great Unitarian theologian William Ellery Channing delivered an address to the artisan-workers of Boston in 1838. Like Jonathan Mayhew in the past century, Channing was a religious rationalist who had readily adapted the substance of his theology to the rhetorical demands of audiences in a new revival age.

The timing of his address was important, since America was then in the throes of its first major national depression, in the wake of the bank crisis; seeking to force Jackson's hand to withdraw his opposition to the bank's reauthorization, bank president Nicholas Biddle withdrew deposits from all the state branches in the national system and thereby created a precipitate credit freeze, which led to the great panic of 1837. Heavily dependent on credit-intensive industries such as textile manufacturing and shipping, Boston's working population was suffering a wave of mass unemployment. So it came to pass that Channing delivered a sermon directed at the working man's prospects for "Self-Culture" as that year's opening oration in the local Franklin lecture series—modeled, as many similarly dubbed mercantile libraries and workingmen's associations in other major cities were at the time, on Benjamin Franklin's legacy of personal improvement in the name of prosperity.

The subject was a new one, in several important respects. As the historian Daniel Walker Howe notes, it marked the first major effort to extend the Victorian ideals of "polite culture"—the refinement of taste, the benefits of education, the mandate of enlightened public service—to a working-class American audience. Channing's exposition of the theme "deserves to be ranked as a minor classic of American culture and the Protestant ethic," Howe writes, "bridging the worlds of Benjamin Franklin and Horatio Alger, popularizing faculty psychology, and synthesizing the Enlightenment with Christianity."[124]

With this ambitious aim in view, Channing launched into a strikingly Gnostic account of the soul's ascent into a kind of post-material enlightenment. To be sure, he counseled his audience of distressed laborers, we all must earn our livings, in earnest Protestant fashion; but it is also a signal error to suppose that self-culture exists merely "as a means or instrument of something else"—i.e., a material scheme of uplift to correspond with the spiritual one that Channing urged on his listeners. "Not a few persons desire to improve themselves only to get property and to rise in the world," he preached,

> but such do not properly choose improvement, but something outward and foreign to themselves; and so low an impulse can only produce a stinted, partial, uncertain growth. A man . . . is to cultivate himself because he is a man. He is to start with the conviction, that there is something greater within him than in the whole material creation, than in all the worlds which press on his eye and ear.

This was not, Channing cautioned, a reckless plan to disregard material advancement altogether. Since want and poverty foster anxiety over material deliverance, it is, of course, honorable to improve one's lot; here, he sounded many of the same reassuring notes that Finney had struck in his preaching before business audiences. "Multiply comforts," Channing stressed, "and still more, get wealth by honorable means, and if it do not cost too much. A true cultivation of the mind is fitted to forward you in your worldly concerns, and you ought to use it toward that end." But it is fatal, he warned, to confuse material well-being with the true divine provenance of your soul. As you advance, Channing preached, "feel that your nature is worth more than everything which is foreign to you. He who has not caught a glimpse of his own rational and spiritual being, of something within himself superior to the world, and allied to the divinity, wants the true spring of that purpose of self-culture, on which I have insisted as the first of all the means of improvement."[125]

In this distinctly Gnostic account of salvation-through-self-realization, the saving knowledge of self is the heart of redemption—the believer's inspired discovery of "something within himself superior to the world, and allied to divinity."

By explicitly casting spiritual self-disclosure as the alpha and omega of all worldly enterprise, Channing furnished both mission and alibi to the sprawling contemporary genre of business-minded self-help literature. "What we have actually gained to," he insists in high Gnostic fashion, is

> the idea of Perfection as the end of our being . . . We have the power not only of tracing our powers, but of guiding and impelling them; not only of watching our passions, but of controlling them; not only of seeing our faculties grow, but of applying to them means and ends to make them grow"—a remarkable inward capacity for self-reinvention that "transcends in importance all our power over outward nature. There is more of divinity in it, than in the force which impels the outward universe.[126]

In striking contrast to past apostles of market uplift such as Franklin, Channing wasn't proposing a ground-up *rehabilitation* of the earnestly striving character; rather, he depicted the individual's progress toward success and self-culture as a kind of mystic *revelation* of self-generating qualities already inherent in the secret recesses of one's soul. This is an all-too familiar strain of latter-day success literature, from *The Secret* to *The Prayer of Jabez*: Rather than fostering a visible, measurable regimen of altered behavior, the main challenge in a culture increasingly driven by the consumer market is to tap the hidden resources of self-enlightenment—to "awaken the giant within," to quote a contemporary bestselling book by success prophet Tony Robbins. For such common refrains in our latter day business culture, we owe direct thanks to the visionary soundings of thinkers such as Channing—just as we now reflexively accept the publishing market's own packaging of business advice books and inspirational works about self-help as essentially the same genre.

Nor did Channing speak as a lone cultivated voice in the Second Awakening's spiritual wilderness. By far the best-known Victorian-age exponent of spiritual self-help—and of cheerful accommodation to the new capitalist national market—was Channing's Boston contemporary, Ralph Waldo Emerson. America's most distinguished philosopher of the spirit was famously a dropout from the Harvard Divinity School, where he, too, had been training to be a Unitarian minister. During the same year that Channing was instructing Boston's artisan-merchant class in the spiritual meanings of self-culture, Emerson returned to the Harvard Divinity School (at the behest of its senior class, not its faculty) to deliver his famous "Divinity School address," which rehearsed the principles of Gnostic divinity before the earnest sons of New England privilege.

In his Divinity School address, Emerson first warmed to his subject by depicting the Christian Savior as nothing less than a Gnostic seer:

> Alone in all history, he estimated the greatness of man. One man was true to what is in you and me. He saw that God incarnates himself in man, and evermore goes forth anew to take possession of his World . . . He spoke of miracles; for he felt that man's life was a miracle, and all that man doth, and he knew that this daily miracle shines as the character ascends.

But as Christianity hardened into dogmatic worship, inevitably the Savior became a dead object of reverence in his own right, thanks to "the noxious exaggeration about the *person* of Jesus . . . Accept the injurious impositions of our early catechetical instruction, and even honesty and self-denial were but splendid sins, if they did not wear the Christian name." Emerson further declared that under this fraudulent dispensation, believers were cheated of their own divine natures: "You shall not be a man even. You shall not own the world; you shall not dare and live after the infinite Law that is within you, and in company with the infinite Beauty which heaven and earth reflect to you in all lovely forms; but you must subordinate your nature to Christ's nature; you must accept our interpretations, and take his portrait as the vulgar draw it."[127]

On one level, of course, Emerson's own idiosyncratic principle of new divinity was of a piece with the dictum he'd famously laid out in his land-mark essay "Nature"—that citizens of the New World were to seek "an original relation with the universe," unbounded by conventional authority or tradition. More fundamentally, though, Emerson preached the same Gnostic gospel as Channing: Believers must reclaim their unconditioned true identity, as children of a higher order of things that lay beyond the stuff of mere history, politics, and ritual. From here it was a short step to a more thoroughgoing social quietism, as Emerson made plain in his 1844 essay, "Self-reliance"—his most complete accounting of the Transcendental-ist faith as a philosophy, and like "Self-Culture," a key future touchstone for the unique American genre of the spiritualized self-help manual. "Society never advances," Emerson declared flatly in that treatise; "All men plume themselves on the improvement of society, and no man improves."[128] The real center of spiritual activity is, again, the individual self, which must effec-tively lay waste to its own social background in order to continue growing:

> This one fact the world hates; that the soul *becomes*; for that forever degrades the past, turns all riches to poverty, all reputation to shame, confounds the saint with the rogue, shoves Jesus and Judas equally aside . . . Self-existence is the attribute of the Supreme Cause, and it constitutes the measure of good by the degree in which it enters into all lower forms.[129]

It therefore follows that the true nonconformist must greet the smallest claims of social obligation with the utmost scorn. Hence Emerson assailed the Second Awakening's reformist crusades, not on grounds of class hypoc-risy, but rather because their patrician spirit belonged more properly within the confines of a higher vision of Gnostic "spiritual affinity":

If an angry bigot assumes this bountiful cause of Abolition, and comes to me with his last news from Barbados, why should I not say to him, "Go love thy infant; love thy wood-chopper, be good-natured and modest; have that grace; and never varnish your hard, uncharitable ambition with this incredible tenderness for black folk a thousand miles off. Thy love affair is spite at home" . . . Then again, do not tell me, as a good man did to-day, of my obligation to put all poor men in good situations. Are they *my* poor? There is a class of persons to whom by all spiritual affinity I am bought and sold; for them I will go to prison if need be; but your miscellaneous popular charities; the education at the college of fools; the building of meeting-houses to the vain end to which many now stand; alms to sots, and the thousand-fold Relief Societies; though I confess with shame I sometimes succumb and give the dollar, it is a wicked dollar, which by and by I shall have the manhood to withhold.[130]

Emerson's manfully guarded dollar and imperious defense of "hard, uncharitable ambition"—"Are they *my* poor?"—speaks volumes about how far the country had come through its unique Protestant spiritual odyssey in a century and a half. It never would have occurred to John Winthrop to think of the less-fortunate members of his covenantal community as belonging anywhere else. As the dispersed spiritual authority unleashed by the great revival devolved onto individual believers, they didn't spontaneously cluster into movements of democratic reform; instead they intuited new ways of elevating the believing self into the vicinity of the godhead. No longer was the New World Protestant ideal a priesthood of all believers; now, it was something closer to every man and his own divinity.

As it turned out, this bold faith dispensation had already called forth a new prophet who would synthesize many of the scattered Gnostic strands of the American market faith into a powerful new revelation. Like most prophets, Joseph Smith would fail to win honor within his own country in his lifetime. But along the free-will frontiers of the American spirit, he would conjure an entirely new American revelation just outside of Palmyra, New York.

4

OF LOST TRIBES AND LATTER DAYS

Like many souls swept up in the Second Great Awakening, young Joseph Smith was haunted by the paradoxes of denominational division. The question was really lurking at the heart of Protestantism from the moment the Reformation began: Having broken away from the universal and absolute assurances of Catholicism, how could any Protestant lay claim to anything so exclusive as divine truth? Isn't God's truth one—and shouldn't it unite all humanity in a single community of belief?

A teenager in the rural upstate New York town of Palmyra, Smith put his distress before God in prayer, and soon was granted a vision. One day early in 1820, he beheld a pillar of light above the sun at high noon; it descended upon him and, as he later recounted, "I was filled with the spirit of God and the Lord opened the heavens upon me." First the light announced to the young man that all of his sins were forgiven; it then went on to lay out the dismal state of religion in Smith's day: "the world lieth in sin at this time and none doeth good no not one they have turned aside from the Gospel and keep not my commandments they draw near to me with their lips while their hearts are far from me and my anger is kindling against the inhabitants of the earth."[131]

It was a lot to take in for a teenager (Smith claimed he was sixteen at the time, though in the two separate accounts he offered of this canonical "first vision" in his later adulthood, the timing and other narrative details vary). But Smith's vision was fully in line with the forces behind the Awakening's broader quest for the Primitive Church and the apostolic succession of the one true faith: the fear of sectarian error, the neglected true Gospel, and the promise (or threat) of a great, and pending, millennial reckoning.

Visions of this sort weren't uncommon in Smith's family, which bore its own distinctive spiritual pedigree, entirely representative of both its era and the family's hardscrabble social station. Both of his parents, Joseph Smith Sr., and Lucy Smith (nee Mack), had experienced religious visions in their dreams—typically concerning the Tree of Knowledge and Tree of Life in their unsullied Edenic state. (In Joseph Sr.'s case, the lush dream of the divine realm contrasted pointedly with his vision of the fallen world as a vast and desolate wasteland, where large-tusked beasts were "bellowing most terrifically." An attending spirit told the elder Smith that this scene signified "the world which now lieth inanimate and dumb, in regard to the true religion or plan of salvation."[132]) Joseph's paternal grandfather, Asael Smith, a renegade Universalist who'd settled in Topsfield, Massachusetts, around the time of the Revolution, worked in the orbit of a nearby copper mine, whose proprietors endorsed the alchemical principles of mining still common at the time, holding that precious metals reproduced themselves organically in the earth, by seeding and gestation. Further back still, Asael's father, Samuel Smith, had propelled the family out of their prior home in Boxford, Massachusetts, after testifying to the occult powers of a maternal aunt who was on trial for witchcraft. Not surprisingly, Samuel's testimony produced a falling out with his in-laws, the Townes family, and he and the extended Smith clan shifted their local allegiances to the Gould family, who were ardent New Light supporters of the First Awakening—and proprietors of an area ironworks, also steeped in alchemical lore. Smith's maternal uncle Jason Mack struck out in his teens to become a lay preacher, and later a faith healer, "pursuing the spiritual gifts of early Christianity outside of established churches," as Richard L. Bushman writes.[133]

All this family history locates Smith in the Gnostic and alchemical side of American popular religion—a lineage that, as John Brooke shows in his path-breaking study of Mormonism's occult origins, *Refiner's Fire*, would directly shape future Mormon revelation and social thought.[134] The modest-born forebears of other Mormon leaders, such as Brigham Young and Parley Pratt, likewise experienced brushes with witchcraft and alchemy—both common enough forms of folk belief, as we've seen, in the early phases of the colonial settlement of New England.

The Gold Testament

But Joseph Smith was that rare religious genius, who took the raw materials of his inherited parochial faith and transmuted them into a universalist vision that would go on to supply the basis of a sprawling religious empire. And in his adolescent seeking, he intuited that restoring the broken unity of the Christian faith required a wholesale spiritual revolution. While very much in the vein of the dispensations announced by the Second Awakening's apostolic primitivists, Smith's visionary breakthrough was more ambitious still: a fully recovered primitive faith, grounded in what Smith believed was a New World scripture, attesting to a transfigured spiritual order, destined not only to govern American society, but the cosmos at large.

In Smith's second vision, during the fall of 1823, he encountered the Angel Moroni, who told him that a new revelation awaited him, buried beneath a hill outside of Palmyra; this was a testament "written upon gold plates, giving an account of the former inhabitants of this continent and the sources from which they sprang. He also said that the fullness of the everlasting Gospel was contained in it as delivered by the Savior to the ancient inhabitants."[135]

This terse angelic summary of *The Book of Mormon*—as the famous translated account of that scripture's message would become known after it was published in 1830—makes it clear that Smith's revelation was all but custom-made to fulfill the spiritual longings unloosed by the Second Awakening. It was to be both a confirmation of America's exceptional place in the divine scheme of history, and a restoration of the true Christian faith as observed by the ancients—badly misunderstood, maligned and distorted by nineteen centuries of denominational sniping, rivalry, warfare, and infighting.

It was also, not to put too fine a point on things, made of gold. Like much else concerning both the origin myth and contents of *The Book of Mormon*, the saga of the precious-metal plates Smith allegedly recovered four years later, in 1827 (per the angel's instructions) strains credulity. But the truth claims of Mormonism—or for that matter, those of any other variant of the Money Cult faith—aren't the point here. The gold-hewn state of the Mormon revelation was significant as both a religious and material symbol. Gold is, after all, the crowning, divinely sanctioned substance in the alchemical tradition to which Smith was an heir. Smith's own reported discovery followed upon rumors then circulating through upstate New York that a similar "Golden Bible" had been unearthed in Canada. Smith himself was working around Palmyra as a money-digger—i.e., a folk diviner professing to locate and retrieve enchanted treasures from beneath the area farmland. In an epilogue to the visitation announcing the true whereabouts of the lost Golden Bible, the Angel Moroni returned from his heavenly chamber to pointedly instruct the resourceful youth that "Satan would try to tempt me (in consequence of the indigent circumstances of my father's family) to get the plates for the purposes of getting rich." Perhaps alone in the annals of recorded prophecy, Smith had rated a return annunciation from the divine realm explicitly to prevent the exploitation of his revelation for undue personal gain.[136]

The angel's cautions were well founded, as it turned out. By the time *The Book of Mormon* was published, Smith's parents were about to lose the mortgage on their farm; he was only able to pay for the book's publication by persuading one of his early followers, an area farmer named Marvin Harris, to take out a new mortgage on *his* farm. It's unlikely that Smith conceived of his new church as any sort of get-rich-quick scheme—though the angel's warning is certainly ample suggestion that personal gain was, at the very least, a subconscious temptation. At the same time, though, the Mormon faith harnessed a powerful new vision of unparalleled divine abundance to a scheme of salvation binding communal and individual enterprise together in a dramatic New World revelation.

In this respect, Smith's revelation worked a twofold revolution in American spiritual life. It was, first, the most significant eruption of a Gnostic theology of self-advancement on American shores. If American religious life had conjured any truly self-made man, Joseph Smith was it—a resourceful son of the striving American frontier who went on to be both a prophet and a presidential candidate. The Mormon tradition's evolving gospel of self-engineered transcendence recapitulated the basic features of the founding New World Gnostic faith in a remarkably confident and comprehensive manner. This meant that unlike other permutations of the Money Cult, which endowed wealth with spiritual significance on a largely ex post facto basis, winning converts looking for new and inventive ways to catechize the market's blessings, Mormonism was in every sense a religion for spiritual and material *pioneers,* with its own founding revelation, scripture, cosmology, and promises of worldly abundance. As the Mormons endured decades of exile en route to their New World promised land, the alchemy imbued within their vision of redemptive plenty was explicitly incorporated into rites of Mormon faith—or, as they would come to be known, the "secrets of the temple."

Just as important, Mormonism was a version of the nineteenth century's free-will gospel of improvement administered by and for believers who'd otherwise been displaced by the market revolution. Faced with the economic upheavals that rendered the small-farming economy of the Northeast yet more precarious, Smith and the founding band of Mormon faithful assayed more than a radical revision of biblical history and revelation; they also pioneered a remarkably disciplined and profitable model of spiritualized enterprise. From the pinched margins of upstate New York's famed "burned-over district" (so called because of its susceptibility to waves of religious enthusiasm during the Second Awakening), Smith and his powerful cadre of lieutenants in the Mormon apostolate erected a new religion that also functioned as a joint-stock investment opportunity; by pooling their own labor, land holdings, and capital, the patriarchs of the Mormon faith reinvented the utopian perfectionist faith of the Second Awakening as the spiritual equivalent of a publicly traded corporation.

If George Whitefield had created a new revival faith for the mercantile age, and Charles Finney had laid out a post-Calvinist perfectionist gospel for the market revolution's hardy free-will entrepreneurs, then Joseph Smith founded an ingenious, self-engineered brand of worship for American strivers who were conspicuously denied the advantages of believers on the vanguards of the first great American revivals. Mormonism would adopt many curious new guises over the course of its dramatic founding decades, but it was, more than any other faith tradition founded during the Second Awakening, a folk religion of American corporate capitalism.

But like every other feature of the Mormon faith, its attitude toward entrepreneurial activity was very much a work in progress—improvised, in large part, in response to the church's urgent mission of planting and gathering its ranks in a quasi-Zionist model of communal enterprise, with labor and land pooled among the tithing masses and the church's wealth and productivity managed from the top down by the religion's tightly knit apostolate. Church fathers debated the finer points of reconciling their radical New World revelation with the model of enterprise then known as "joint stockism," but in the critical formative years of the Mormon inland hejira, they had little choice but to install themselves as the managers of a new kind of frontier capitalism.

This task was prompted in part by the Mormon scripture's detailed portrait of primitivist faith as a colonizing force, and also as a necessary response to the vicious persecution that Mormons faced from the nation's Protestant mainstream. But it marked Mormonism as not merely a mode of worship but an entire, vertically integrated model of divinely consecrated shared enterprise. American business thinkers have long hailed our capitalist heritage as something possessed of a unique spiritual genius—honoring core principles of ingenuity, creativity, and market disruption. But as the Mormon example shows, the corporate stage of our business history partakes of a radically different sort of Protestant spirit, centered more around the elusive but beguiling promise of an infinitely renewable state of redemption for an otherworldly kind of American self, planted decisively athwart the homely historical limits of time, place, and error-ridden formal piety.

This core innovation was very much founded on a trial-and-error basis, with necessity dictating most of its basic terms. Along each stage of the Mormon's Western exile, Smith and his inner circle of patriarchs were dogged by the insistent claims of creditors, and would abandon a significant share of their capital stock and enormous land holdings each time the vicious persecution of authorities aligned with the mainline Protestant majority drove them from their latest effort to realize Smith's vision of a New World Zion. It was only after Smith's martyrdom, when they began their final trek into the Utah territory in 1847–48, that the Mormons' organizational genius yielded firm and lasting worldly returns, together with a centralized church equipped to spread the Mormon gospel across the world. But for that very reason, the history of Mormonism's founding grants us an invaluable vantage on how the powerfully yoked central articles of the Money Cult faith—the primitivist allergy to traditional church hierarchies, and the Gnostic determination to redeem the transcendent essence of the American self—helped to produce what would soon become the fastest-growing religion in the world.

The Protestant Ethic Reborn

Whatever the rarefied and speculative nature of the later Mormon spirit of enterprise, there's no doubt about its quasi-populist roots among the dispossessed small landowners of the nation's inland agrarian territory. Smith's revelation itself teems with incendiary pronouncements that appear to be all but cribbed from the mood of uneasy class confrontation unloosed along the commercial frontiers of America in the Jackson age. In its closing pages, *The Book of Mormon* features a climactic prophetic appeal from the final recorder of the New World chronicles of covenant-breaking, backsliding, war-making and (most commonly) material vanity and pride. These classical themes of ancient Old Testament prophecy are underlined one last time prior to their burial at the behest of the author (who, like the angel who delivered the revelation to Smith, is named Moroni). Addressing the nineteenth-century audience of backsliding Protestants whom he knows, via his own prophetic gifts, are destined to uncover his record, Moroni excoriates the myopic greed and boundless self-seeking of the religious in Smith's own age:

> Behold, I speak unto you as if ye were present, and yet ye are not. But behold, Jesus Christ has shown you unto me, and I know your doing.
>
> And I know that ye do walk in the pride of your hearts; and there are none save a few only who do not lift themselves up in the pride of their hearts, unto the wearing of very fine apparel, unto envying, and strifes, and malice, and persecutions, and all manner of iniquities; and your churches, yea, even every one, have become polluted because the pride of your hearts.
>
> For behold, ye do love money, and your substance, and your fine apparel, and the adorning of your churches, more than ye love the poor and the needy, the sick and the afflicted . . . Why do you adorn yourselves with that which hath no life, and yet suffer the hungry, the needy, and the naked, and the sick and the afflicted to pass by you, and notice them not?

Yea, why do you build up your secret abominations to get gain, and cause that widows should mourn before the Lord, and also orphans to mourn before the Lord, and also the blood of their fathers and their husbands to cry from the ground, for vengeance upon their heads?[137]

In other words: Strong stuff, seemingly aimed at the same comfortable, meddlesome souls who were thronging to Charles Finney's anxious benches in the new citadels of American commerce. But while some interpreters have seized upon the many heated prophetic outbursts against well-heeled spiritual complacency in Smith's testament as evidence that the Mormons were proto-populists, and angry scourges of economic privilege, the actual history of the church's inland American diaspora tells another, far more complicated story.[138]

It's true that Mormonism began life as an outcast faith, and many of its early converts were desperate, downwardly mobile descendants of Yankee farm families faring poorly in the quest for stable cash crops, market share, and reliable credit—all elusive after a series of early nineteenth-century agricultural depressions in the upper Northeast. But while Smith and his followers were acutely conscious of their declining fortunes and tenuous social status, they didn't embrace a program of radical redistribution of wealth. Quite the contrary: The Mormon Church, which began as a quasi-socialist concern, consigning its members' individual wealth to the collective use of believers on the hallowed model of the Primitive Church, soon metamorphosed into a land-hungry, labor-intensive model of worldly enterprise, aiming to secure every advantage it could over its competitors in the Gentile world.

The Mormon experience, probably more than any other chapter in our religious past, systematized the key elements of the Money Cult faith in radical fashion. In their determination to plant the model of Primitive Church on the fresh territory of the American continent, Mormons went further than any other denomination claiming the authority of the Bible's usable past, by adopting an entirely new scripture and cosmology grounded in the saga of the lost tribes of Israel—recreated in Smith's new scripture as the exploits of the New World's first sojourners from the East, who'd arrived several centuries ahead of Jesus' birth. Among other things, this parallel primitivist legacy gave the first Mormons a redoubled version of the same wilderness-conquering faith that had propelled the original Puritans into such tireless and profitable worldly effort. Recognizing no legitimacy in the institutional structures that lorded it over rival Protestant worldly endeavors, Mormons simply invented their own—from Church-based currencies to Church-driven cities, factories, and architectural plans.

In political terms, as well, Mormons undertook a full-scale Puritan revival. Like the Puritans, they recognized no real distinction between religious and civil authority. The Prophet and his hand-picked apostolate ruled over virtually every feature of the Mormon community's economic and political life, organizing real estate and commercial ventures, drafting city charters, mounting global missionary campaigns, marshalling corporate-funded supply lines for overland and transatlantic migrants, and even specifying standard house and lot sizes in the city plans for the Church's settlements in Nauvoo, Illinois, and Salt Lake City.

It was, indeed, the organizational genius of the Mormon diaspora that permitted the religion to survive and thrive, whereas so many other perfectionist movements arising from the tumult of the Second Awakening ran aground. Some movements, like the celibate Shakers, succumbed to the logic of their own perfectionist manias; others, like the purist and primitivist leaders of Landmark Baptism and the "Christian" (later Disciples of Christ) denominations, fell out amid tortured literalist interpretations of millennial prophecy and warring models of authentically apostolic worship; still others, such as the free-will Methodists and the holiness Wesleyans, merged indistinguishably into the teachings of mainline denominations.

The Mormons, however, vigilantly preserved their identities from the pressures of both denominational strife and mainstream assimilation. Thanks to their new sanctified status as the rightful heirs to the legacy of the lost tribes, they knew just how much was riding on maintaining their spiritual kingdom as a separate, self-determined entity. And as the Mormon revelation continued to expand during the prophet's life, so did its potent New World mythos. Joseph Smith not only uncovered a New World scripture in which his followers were to play leading parts; he also announced that the New World had hosted Adam and Eve after their expulsion from the Garden of Eden—and prophesied that this same site, just outside the Mormons' provisional settlement near Independence, Missouri, would also be a principal venue for the gathering of the saints at the dawn of the millennium.

This compound of spiritual primitivism and millennial confidence help explains a singular paradox: Mormonism, for all its seeming apostasy from Protestant tradition, is the most intense form of American Protestant prophecy in the American grain. Even though the Mormon faithful were relentlessly persecuted by the authorities of mainstream America, they were a kind of super-Americans. No other religious group so thoroughly embodied the ethos of American exceptionalism, and in later revelations that were disseminated during the church's stay in Kirtland, Ohio, Smith had pronounced that the drafters of U.S. Constitution were divinely inspired. By the time Smith announced his own candidacy for president in 1844, the church patriarchs who tirelessly campaigned for him in hostile Gentile outposts throughout the union regarded the Oval Office as but a natural extension of his prophetic calling.[139]

Most of all, thanks in large part to Mormonism's humble beginnings in the lower reaches of the burned-over district, the followers of the Latter-Day saints (LDS) church instinctively grasped the significance of wealth as liberation of the spirit—and indeed, as a species of divine magic. Just as the precious metals concealed beneath the earth's surface possessed magical properties of individual transformation in the alchemical traditions of the Smith clan, so was the hard-won prosperity of Mormon sojourners to serve as the primary evidence of their prophetic destiny. While *The Book of Mormon* castigated the greed and vanity of the godless, it also repeatedly stressed that God had pronounced worldly gain the just reward of the faithful. As the Mormon economist Mark Skousen notes, the most frequently occurring phrase in the Mormon scripture—apart from the place-holding King James–style clause "And so it came to pass"—is "if ye keep my commandments, ye shall prosper in the land."[140] This vow contains obvious echoes of the original covenant with Abraham, in which the Lord pledges a desert kingdom to the Old Testament patriarch and his descendants in exchange for their faith—but more than that, the Mormon revelation sought to bind the Promised Land's lost tribes to a far more otherworldly promise of ascension beyond the limitations of both their worldly and cosmic stations. From the moment of its unlikely founding in the Palmyra back country, the Mormon church had adopted an explicitly Gnostic theology of individual redemption predicated on the erection of its own worldly empire. It is no coincidence that the first full-blown religion founded on American soil was a breathtaking work of Gnostic alchemy—a transmutation of debt, invention, and the well-documented spiritual solitude of the Protestant believer into new corporate forms of religious community and prosperity.

Alchemical Romance

It's difficult to overestimate the role that the pursuit of precious metals played in the saga of Mormonism's founding. In the decade prior to *The Book of Mormon*'s publication, in his career as a money-digger, Joseph Smith had persuaded gullible landowners to fund digging expeditions to recover alleged pirate or Native American treasure buried in the ground of the New World. Brooke writes that

> throughout the postrevolutionary Northeast, the unsettled economic and religious conditions of the 1780s and 1790s drew hundreds of people into "money-digging companies" in a futile search for an easy way to wealth . . . Legends of treasures buried by Spaniards and pirates, even the wording of colonial charters, contributed to a fascination with precious metals. Diviners located metallic treasure with stones and rods and then attempted to overpower guardian spirits by casting magic circles and invoking astrological influences.[141]

What's more, Brooke notes, the money-diggers on the New England frontier ascribed volatile spiritual qualities to the metals themselves—an understanding entirely in line with a social order that often made wealth seem a random blessing issued by remote household gods.

> One of the central themes in the treasure-hunting sagas was the volatility of precious metal: chests of money "bloom" to the surface of the earth only to fall away when the diggers utter a sound or violate a ritual

practice. Joseph Smith Sr., father of the Mormon prophet, told his Palmyra neighbor Peter Ingersoll that "the best time for digging money
was in the heat of the summer, when the heat of the sun caused the
chests of money to rise to the top of the ground." Smith also claimed
that the chests were ruined by the summer sun when they reached the
surface, the heat transmuting them into "large stones on the top of the
ground." More usually, such chests would disappear into the earth from
which they had risen, controlled by spirits that resisted the money-
diggers' efforts; Joshua Stafford recalled Joseph Smith [Jr.] showing
him "a piece of wood which he said he took from a box of money"
that had slipped away; far into the nineteenth century, Brigham Young
recounted the story of Mormons Porter Rockwell and Martin Harris
breaking off a corner of a chest as it sank into a money-diggers pit.[142]

The maddeningly unobtainable character of gold treasure clearly left a
profound, and lifelong, impression on Smith. As his biographer Fawn Brodie
observes, "the desire for money in gold and silver became almost an obsession" for the Mormon prophet[143]—especially after he sought to capitalize on
rampant real-estate speculation in the church's first provisional exilic home in
Kirtland, Ohio. The church sought, bizarrely, to incorporate its own bank—
and when a bill from the Ohio legislature blocked the launch of the bank
and its circulating notes, Smith sought to sidestep its strictures by printing
the prefix "anti-" and the suffix "-ing" after the word "bank" on the currency
issued by the institution—so that he could legally claim to be trading, not in
unauthorized bank-issued currency, but rather in "anti-banking" notes.

No amount of semantic subterfuge, however, could rescue the flailing
Mormon bank in Kirtland from the collapse of the local real-estate bubble and the staggering depreciation of bank assets that ensued. So Smith,
who had picked up word in 1836 of a reported cache of buried gold outside
Salem, Massachusetts—the port city that Smith had always regarded as
vaguely enchanted ever since his family had sent him as an eight-year-old
boy to convalesce with an uncle there—organized a secret expedition, led
by himself and senior Church lieutenants, to try to rescue the glittering
prize. (The group employed the cover story of visiting Salem on a mission-

izing trip, since even Smith sensed that it would be unseemly for outsiders
to hear that the founder of the great remnant church of the New World
was scouring the East Coast in search of buried gold treasure.) When the
search proved a bust, Smith issued another prophecy—one of the rare
utterances in which he professed to speak in the Lord's name—clearing
the whole contretemps from the divine memory bank, while guaranteeing
an eventual gold cache in Salem for His faithful followers: "I, the Lord
your God," the revelation read, "am not displeased with your coming on
this journey, notwithstanding your follies. I have much treasure in this city
for you, for the benefit of Zion . . . I will give the city into your hands, that
you shall have power over it, insomuch that they shall not discover your
secret parts; and its wealth pertaining to gold and silver shall be yours."[144]

The quest for hard-money prosperity would color the whole of Smith's
career—but as the conclusion of the Salem gold-digging foray showed, the
rougher edges of the Mormon quest for prosperity would always shade off
into the more reassuring language of revelation. Indeed, in Smith's vocation, the directives of God were themselves readily tailored to the communal quest for economic security: A central, indispensable innovation of the
faith was the doctrine of continuing revelation, which permitted Smith to
channel the larger divine plan that guided the eventful trek of the Mormons into the nation's western interior. And a centerpiece of that plan was
"erecting and maintaining an improved economic system for its members,"
according to Mormon historian Leonard J. Arrington, who notes that of
the 112 revelations Smith had pronounced, 88 were either directly or indi-
rectly concerned with economic matters.[145] (Continuing revelation would
also prove instrumental in altering received Mormon orthodoxy to comport with modern sensibilities, such as the successive revelations ending
the prior divine sanctions of plural marriage and the denial of any office of
bishop or higher to black members of the church.)

It's too easy, however, to dismiss the successive revelations tendered
by Smith as opportunistic efforts to dress up worldly ambition in
the rhetoric of a divine commandment. For Smith's rapidly growing
following, the teaching that God was continuing to reveal his purposes
in the New World was at the heart of Mormonism's appeal—and the fact

that Smith was channeling that purpose in the arrangement of the church's worldly affairs was, far from a suspicious constriction of the divine will, simply additional evidence that the Mormon prophet, and the Mormon community, were blessed with a special prophetic calling.

And after all, the Mormons' updated glosses on biblical revelation don't look much different from the parallel movements of Protestant faith in concert with the demands of new market society of the Jackson years. Smith's continuing revelation differed from the perfectionist and utopian strains of Second Awakening faith more in degree than in kind. In preaching the close affinities—indeed, the physical relation—of humanity and God, Smith had supplied a powerful divine sanction for the holiness speculations of Charles Finney. And in his most controversial teachings—instituting practices such as plural marriage and the posthumous conversion of Mormon ancestors—Smith was following through on the Gnostic intuitions aired by more reputable thinkers such as Channing and Emerson, and pressing them to consistent, if at times outlandish, conclusions. As with so many other features of the Mormon story, the operative question here shouldn't be how such a strange, prosperity-driven faith could find such a permanent footing in the American religious scene. In tracking the evolution of the Money Cult, we'd do better to stand that question on its head, and ask why believers in the Protestant mainstream have taken so long to recognize in the Mormon tradition a version of the primitive Christian faith scored so deeply in the American grain.

In part, Mormonism seems so unfamiliar from the outside because of its motley and obscure theological pedigree. Joseph Smith, after all, didn't have the luxury of framing his Gnostic speculations in a Boston study or an Oberlin library; he acquired, and synthesized, his beliefs on the fly, as the specters of debt, persecution, and scandal hounded him into exile and an early death.

He also encountered his first ideas about God, creation, and biblical faith from a deeply heterodox source—namely, the occult strain of folk religion that permeated popular belief in the upper New England frontier where he came of age. As Brooke demonstrates, the young Smith was steeped, like his father, in a syncretic, superstitious folk religion of radical self-improvement, under which individual believers gradually ascended to higher states of spiritual wisdom. This tradition, which crossed the Atlantic via "the most extreme fringe" of England's radical Reformation in Brooke's telling, was a curious compound of Masonic symbolism, hermeticism, astrology, and Gnostic speculation, fundamentally distinct from the dominant Calvinist outlook of the divines who controlled the political and religious institutions of New England.

This folk tradition possessed little in the way of systematic theology. Its most vital and articulate tributary was hermeticism—which, by way of review, was the Renaissance-era doctrine of human perfectibility that gave rise to alchemy, among other humanist fields of inquiry. As we've seen, the figure of Adam was central to hermetic speculation, only not as the original sinner of the Genesis account, but rather as a seeker after spiritual knowledge who voluntarily renounced his Edenic state to mate with nature. This peculiar image reflects another distinctive feature of hermetic thought: it held that the natural world was something of divine origin, not dead matter, as was the belief of many orthodox Christian scholars. (Hence the tradition across the generations in the Smith family holding that precious metals were organic, self-regenerating forms of subterranean life, apt to decompose rapidly under the light and heat of the sun.)

Adam's renunciation opened the path, according to hermetic believers, for the individual to reconstruct and recover the divine origins of humanity—one of the central projects of the great alchemist researches of the seventeenth century. Adam's exile from the Garden was, in other words, not a calamity for the human condition, but rather a "fortunate Fall," since it would point the path to universal salvation and godhood. In later works of revelation, such as the revised account of Genesis, called the Book of Moses, generated in 1830 and 1831, Smith would stress the central importance of the figure of Adam, depicting him as the semi-divine conduit of spiritual wisdom handed down from hermetic and Masonic lore: "after the order of him who was without beginning of days or end of years, from all eternity to all eternity"—a vision that also commanded the die-hard allegiance of Smith's successor at the head of the church, Brigham Young.[146]

The Adam-centric reading of Genesis is the most dramatic illustration of the Gnostic temper of the new Mormon religion—though in Smith's teachings the metaphysical despair of the ancient Gnostics was fused with the more upbeat Renaissance doctrines of hermeticism. Hermetic thought, Brooke writes,

> was at its core an optimistic, expansive philosophy, celebrating the potential divinity and power of humanity . . . The Mormon cosmology constructed by Joseph Smith was as optimistic as Renaissance hermeticism and shared with it a startling number of common themes. As he was gathering his church in Fayette, New York, in December 1830, Smith announced that he had been given "the keys and mysteries of those things which have been sealed, even things which were from the foundation of the world." . . . Three centuries after the height of the Renaissance, Mormonism echoed the hermetics—and explicitly rejected Calvinism—in its advocacy of universal salvation and freedom of the will, its replacement of the doctrine of original sin with that of the fortunate Fall, and its denial of the efficacy of grace alone. In granting priestly powers "to seal up the Saints unto eternal life," Joseph Smith gave the Mormon hierarchy the same authority that the hermetic alchemist assumed: human means to immortality, even divinity.[147]

The full Gnostic implications of this spiritual outlook found expression in a funeral oration that Smith gave in 1844 in Nauvoo just two months before his death. As he memorialized his old friend King Follet, the prophet detoured into a far-reaching explication of the Mormon doctrine that would later become known as "the soul's eternal progression." Smith explained that humanity was not merely bound to recover its divine origins (as hermeticism taught), but to ascend to divinity in its own right, in the Gnostic tradition. "If you were to see the great God who holds this world in his orbit," Smith preached,

> you would see him in the very image and the very form of a man; for Adam was created in the very fashion and image of God. He received instruction from and walked, talked and conversed with him as one man talks and communes with another . . . The mind of man is as

immortal as God himself . . . I might with boldness proclaim from the
housetops that God never did have the power to create the spirit of man
at all. God himself could not create himself . . . God found himself in
the midst of spirits and glory, and because he was greater, he saw proper
to institute laws whereby the rest could have the privilege of advancing
like himself—that they might have one glory upon another and all the
knowledge, power, and glory necessary to save the world of spirits.[148]

This alternate myth of creation—laying out the full spiritual equiv-
alence of God and the first human, Adam—brought the restive Gnostic
spirit of the Second Awakening to a new and self-conscious head. And
when it was wedded to the singular Mormon ethos of frenetic material
improvement, this radical theology of the higher Gnostic self would
redound far beyond the bounds of LDS ritual, into the heart of the corporate American dreamscape.

The Mormon American Dream

Much like the other great denominational innovators of the Second Awakening, Joseph Smith was laying claim to a recovered primitive Christianity in the heart of the New World Protestant errand—a project that here
resulted in the erection of an entirely new faith out of an entirely new (or, as
the Mormon faithful would have it, newly discovered) American scripture.

In this sense, the whole burning question of Mormonism's assimilation into the American mainstream—which religious and political pundits
alike debated in exhaustive detail during the height of Mitt Romney's 2012
run for the presidency—comes about a century and a half late. Mormonism was already a preeminently American synthesis of the core beliefs of
the Money Cult, from the moment when Joseph Smith began to publish
his translations of the gospel on the golden tablets. Mormonism broke
through the welter of new religions and sects that arose over the Second
Great Awakening largely because it deftly drew upon venerable Gnostic
visions of land-and-metal alchemy in an ultramodern, serially revised theology grounded in the very soil of the New World.

Small wonder that this syncretism took root among the dispossessed

landowners of upstate New York, who had every reason to regard the fugitive boom-and-bust cycles of frontier existence in the burned-over district
as a sequence of events governed by quasi-magical forces. Small wonder,
too, that the faith's economic appeal would later form an important basis
for the Mormon Church's stupendously successful missionizing efforts in
England and Western Europe, which would in turn send thousands of
immigrants from the Old World to settle in the Utah territory.

The importance of the English emigration was more than a question
of spreading the Mormon gospel around the world. British converts to
the faith—who came overwhelmingly from the depressed northern industrial cities of Manchester and Liverpool—represented critical infusions of
capital and skilled labor to the Nauvoo settlement. In a remarkable 1844
letter to the leader of the British mission, Smith's then-lieutenant Young
exhorted him to "make all the money you can in righteousness" and painted
the enterprise in stark millennial terms:

> Make enough to support yourselves and help us a bit . . . We will
> by-and-by have offices from the rivers to the ends of the earth, and we
> will begin at Liverpool . . . and increase and increase and *increase* the
> business . . . Employ a runner, if necessary, and show the world you can
> do a better and more honorable business than anybody else, and more of
> it . . . Let nobody know your business but the underwriters. Our wives
> know not all our business, neither does any wise man's wife . . . for the
> secret of the Lord is with those who fear Him and do His business . . .[149]

Such commands were very much of a piece with Smith's unique vision
of the Mormon faith not merely as a preserve of restorationist worship
but as a powerhouse of economic influence. Each of these impulses was
embodied in the two major construction projects that Smith conceived and
personally oversaw in the great Mormon settlement of Nauvoo. The best
known of these constructions was the great temple, where believers would
be initiated into the Gnostic mysteries of Smith's revised rites of worship
(including the marriage rituals sealing two conjoined souls into eternal
union, and the mass baptism of the Mormons' dead ancestors into the

faith). The Temple occupied such a central place in the emerging Mormon cosmology that the Nauvoo Mormons remained in the city long past the point at which local authorities advised that they stay for the sake of their own personal safety, in order to undergo the secret rites of worship upon the Temple's completion several months after Smith's assassination.

But Smith's other major building project—a Nauvoo visitors' facility, designed to house travelers to the settlement and showcase the worldly abundance of Mormonism to the Gentile world—was, as the historical record suggests, much closer to the prophet's heart. This banner project, called Nauvoo House, was to be constructed on the site of Smith's own provisional home in Nauvoo, and commanded the lion's share of the prophet's interest as he continued to coordinate the city's economic and civic life.

Smith had always been greatly preoccupied with the impression that his new religion was making on influential and wealthy outsiders. He graciously hosted a steady stream of celebrity visitors, from newspaper publisher Horace Greeley to the Brahmin historian Charles Francis Adams (son of former president John Quincy Adams), curious to get a close-up sense of how the bustling Mormon colony was prospering. So when work on the Nauvoo House fell badly behind schedule, and looked to be running out of money—and as better-situated construction on the hillier reaches of Nauvoo (where the Temple was being constructed) ate up more of the community's cash and labor—Smith issued a ringing public defense of the centrality of the Nauvoo House in his vision of the Mormon future.

> There may be some speculation about the Nauvoo House, say some . . . that the people on the flats are aggrandizing themselves by the Nauvoo House . . . Some think [aggrandizement] unlawful . . . [but] everything that God does is to aggrandize the kingdom. And how does he lay the foundation? "Build a temple to my great name, and call the attention of the rich, the great, and the powerful." But where shall we lay our heads? In an old log cabin [referring perhaps to his own house] . . . when men have done what they can or will for the Temple, let them do what they can for Nauvoo House. We can never accomplish one work at the expense of the other . . . The building of the

Nauvoo House is just as sacred in my view as the Temple. I want the
Nauvoo House built. It *must* be built. Our salvation depends on it.[150]

Smith spelled out just how that salvation would work itself out, if
only the hard-pressed backers of the Nauvoo House project would stay the
course. The rewards would arise from a prototypically Mormon mingling of
spiritual and financial favor, Smith explained; once the overseers of Nauvoo
House finished their work, he predicted that "You will then be on Pisgah's
top, and the great men will come from the four quarters of the earth—will
pile up the gold and silver into it until you are weary of receiving them . . .
and they will cover up and hide all your former sins and, according to scripture, will hide a multitude of sins; and you will shine forth, fair as the sun,
clear as the moon, and you will become terrible, as an army with banners."[151]
   This remarkable flight of millennial prophecy in the service of a hotel
development alighted finally on Smith's other economic obsession: the need
to fund this soul-saving enterprise with hard money. Deriding the building
committee's failed joint-stock efforts to fund the project, Smith reminded
its members that "I would not do as the Nauvoo House committee have
done—sell stock for an old store-house, where all the people who tried to
live in it died, [or] put that stock into a man's hands to purchase rags [sell
stocks for paper currency] to come here and build mammoth bones with . . .
I command the Nauvoo House Committee not to sell stock . . . without the
gold or silver."[152] When Smith's impassioned case for the project's completion failed to produce results, he resumed his crusade at the annual Mormon
conference a few months later. "There is no place in the city where men of
wealth, character, and influence from abroad can go and repose themselves,
and it is necessary that we provide such a place," he commanded. "This is
the most important matter for the time being . . . The Church must build it
or abide the result of not obeying the commandment."[153]
   Smith lost this battle in the short term—the Nauvoo House was never
finished, and was abandoned with the rest of the city when the Mormons
uprooted themselves again to settle in the Utah territory after Smith's mur-
der. In the larger scheme of things, though, the Mormon empire that Young
went on to found in the West would never again suffer this perceived ten-

sion between spiritual and commercial enterprises. Smith's vision of a pres-tigious hub of Mormon activity to anchor the faith's dealings with the wider world—made up in equal parts of "gold and silver" returns on investment and the miraculous remission of "a multitude of sins" for a robust and "ter-rible" new Christian "army with banners"—would serve as the watchword of Young's new authoritarian and militia-run kingdom on the Utah frontier.

Young and the Restless

Young, indeed, was the Mormon leader ideally suited to bring Smith's pro-tean vision of a prosperous community of saints to full fruition. Though he was a devoted adherent of Smith and the Mormon revelations, Young himself was no prophet, at least not as measured by the standard set by his martyred predecessor. Like Smith, Young had grown up on the economic margins of the burned-over district, the youngest child in a farming family of ten children. He'd been turned out of his home to apprentice as a carpen-ter in his teens after his mother died of tuberculosis. After Young's conver-sion, Smith soon recognized his prowess as a stern administrator, and placed him in charge of the church's crucial British mission. During that tour of duty, Young displayed some charismatic gifts of the spirit, such as speaking in tongues and the performance of some healing rites for the sick, but he was principally, and fanatically, devoted to securing a steady flow of converts pre-pared to forsake the grinding oppression of the Old World's industrial order and tithe their capital and labor to the great ingathering of Saints at Nauvoo.

Once installed as Smith's successor, Young directed the Mormon faith-ful with the same no-nonsense worldly authority that the faith's founding Prophet had wielded—though as was always the case in the Mormon expe-rience, the consolidation of the temporal was indistinguishably merged with higher spiritual precepts. As Young campaigned for the mantle of Mormon leadership against his chief rival, the former Christian socialist Sidney Rig-don, he appealed to the demoralized on a brusque of managerial compe-tence: "Do you want the church organized," he asked the assembled crowd derisively, "or do you want a Spokesman, Cook, and Bottle-Washer?" But he also professed to serve as a fully licensed safe-keeper of Smith's higher Gnostic legacy: Without compromising the jealously guarded secrecy of

Smith's hand-picked inner circle of chief apostles, known as the Twelve, Young alluded to "an organization you have not seen," and explained that its members alone could procure entry for ordinary Mormon believers into the transfigured godhood prophesied by Smith. "We have all the signs and tokens to give to the Porter [of Heaven]," Young explained in a characteristically homely metaphor, "and he will let us in." Young's appeal was so persuasive that several congregants were convinced that he had become mystically possessed by Smith's spirit—and that his voice and visage indeed had changed completely into Smith's. The bewildered, leaderless, and soon to be homeless Mormon believers at Nauvoo duly consecrated leadership of the church henceforward to the charmed circle of the Twelve, and appointed Young as the church's head prophet; the vote was nearly unanimous.[154]

Throughout his long and eventful presidency of the church, Young displayed the same single-minded will to spiritualized organization. Unlike Smith, he placed little stock in how the LDS church maintained its image in the eyes of the Gentile world; "You don't know how I detest and despise them," he candidly announced to one of the initial band of Mormon pioneers to Utah as they debated the community's posture of toleration toward non-Mormons. For the newly displaced Mormon sojourners in Utah, Young's ready vindication of their status as a self-segregating spiritual elect fused with his intensive focus on the many practical tasks at hand to create a new sense of spiritual selfhood, readily confirmed by the wilderness-conquering wonders that the Mormon faithful would bring to pass in their desert kingdom. For the practical-minded Young, there was no distinction at all between the church's spiritual exploits and its rapidly expanding worldly dominion. He warmed to discussions of economic life with a spiritual (and nakedly self-promoting) fervor; "I dream about it," he said, "and understand it by vision and all the principles." These first precepts translated readily, he insisted into a wide-ranging managerial prowess: "I know what would be good for a farmer, blacksmith, wheelright, or tannery," he pronounced—and "in regard to merchandizing, I know better than all other men unless they think as I do."[155]

The point isn't so much that the Mormon patriarch was an entrepreneurial wizard; rather, it's that the Mormon Church desperately needed a leader who could position himself as an all-knowing economic czar—and inspire faith in his own worldly leadership among the scattered, hard-pressed ranks of the Utah faithful. In this respect, Young was indeed the man for the job. In the same way that the alchemist cult of hard specie had bewitched the young Joseph Smith, the specter of sovereign economic independence for the new Mormon territory haunted Young's dreams of spiritual-cum-economic order. He repeatedly exhorted his followers to boycott non-Mormon business, and in the mid-1860s, he founded a School of the Prophets to enforce economic policies enforcing Mormon separation from the Gentile world, while also reprising his own pet Adam-centric theological teachings on the relations between humankind and divinity. The school brought hundreds of Mormon commercial and religious leaders together in fortnightly meetings at Salt Lake's city hall, and soon fanned out into satellite centers of instruction in at least a dozen other Mormon settlements. If any members of the school were found to be doing business with Gentiles—"trading with our enemies," as Young put it—they were immediately expelled. (Young's anti-Gentile rhetoric had reached something of a fever pitch during the 1857–58 "Mormon War" with the federal government; by some accounts it was at least an indirect factor in fomenting the horrifying Mountain Meadows massacre, in which a group of Mormons attacked an Arkansas-based traveling party, killing more than 140 in their number, many of them women and children.)

Which is not to say that Young himself shied away from commercial concerns spreading west into Utah. After Young failed to yield significant returns from his initial plans to make Utah bloom with cash-crop staples such as cotton and tobacco, he and other church leaders brokered labor contracts with the nation's first transcontinental telegraph and railroad concerns as they prepared to cross the state. Because many Mormons were working off their passage into Utah with tithed labor, Mormon leaders were able to significantly underbid other regional competitors for the lucrative contracts. He portrayed these deals—which netted more than $2 million from the Union Pacific railroad and $4 million from the Central Pacific line—as preventive feints against deeper Gentile incursions into the Mormon kingdom, while also improving the church's fraught relationship with the U.S. Congress.[156]

But when the Union Pacific failed to honor its contract payments in a timely fashion, Young hit upon a characteristically ambitious solution: The Church would start its own railroad within the territory, first connecting Salt Lake City with the Union Pacific hub in Ogden, 40 miles to the north. With the Union Pacific contributing rails and other construction materials for the line, known as the Utah Central Railroad, church members would again supply their labor to grade the rails—this time in exchange for Utah Central bonds floating the initial capital investment. When an apostle skeptical of the plan aired his doubts at a School of the Prophets meeting, Young replied in much the same millennial fervor that Joseph Smith had brought to the defense of the Nauvoo Center. Yes, the rail line would be profitable, Young insisted; but that wasn't the larger point here: "We ought to take hold of it for the sake of building up the Kingdom of God, whether it pays or not." And when Utah Mormons evinced little enthusiasm for the financing scheme behind Young's pet project at the start, he let the divine mandate for the capital outlay be known in no uncertain terms: "It is the mind and will of God that the Elders of Israel should take the Utah Central Rail Road Bonds."[157] Thus was the Mormon Church launched as a railroad concern— in much the same way that Smith had earlier made it the first major religious movement in history to operate its own bank and circulate its own currency. However, Young's dalliances with the railroad and telegraph industries did not prove to be the canny end run around dreaded Gentile commercial influence within the territory that he had hoped for; indeed, they inevitably extended the reach of Gentile businesses in the Mormon kingdom. So Young ratcheted up his bid for Mormon economic self-determination another notch by founding a central mercantile cooperative run by the church. In 1868, he launched the Zion's Cooperative Mercantile Institution (ZCMI), which purchased goods wholesale from the eastern United States and sold them at low profit margins to the Mormon faithful. To remind patrons of the enterprise's holy provenance, ZCMI branches featured two symbols of the original Mormon temple in Nauvoo: a rendering of the all-seeing eye of Jehovah above the legend "Holiness unto the Lord."

As a business model, the ZCMI resembled nothing so much as the latter-day Christianized retail colossus of Wal-Mart, driving smaller independent merchants (Mormon and Gentile alike) out of business as it continued to spread its cartel-style control over the region's supply chains. Not long after the cooperative had opened for business, one influential rival merchant named William Godbe joined forces with Elias Harrison, who published the well-regarded *Utah Magazine* out of Salt Lake, to protest Young's tight grip over Mormon economic and theological affairs. (Like Young, these two opinion-makers recognized little functional difference between the two realms—but they had fallen under the heterodox spell of a renowned New York City spiritualist named Charles Foster, an affiliation that would later hamper the appeal of their breakaway movement.)

In decades past, Young had met the claims of commercial critics and rivals with thinly veiled threats of death and/or damnation. This time, however, he could repair to his own church infrastructure to enforce economic orthodoxy. When Harrison published a scathing attack on the church president's fixation on agriculture and "home manufacturers," and his neglect of the territory's lucrative mining prospects (which for Young represented the ultimate threat of Gentile economic domination), Young swiftly retaliated with a court proceeding against Harrison and Godbe at the School of Prophets. There he was able to magisterially wave away Harrison's case against his alleged commercial myopia and spiritual megalomania. "I do not pretend to be infallible," he said in response to Harrison's charges of prophetic overreach; "but the priesthood I have on me is infallible." Young also noted that his economic policies thus far had proven effective enough for Godbe and Harrison both to make handsome livings in the Mormon capital—and that even when his economic plans came up short financially, they usually served a higher spiritual end. The assembled council members, not surprisingly, sided with the patriarch; they voted to excommunicate the economic dissenters and hand them "over to the buffetings of Satan."[158] The two men continued to agitate against Young's heavy-handed management of the church and its affairs, but when they sought to found a breakaway Mormon movement called the Church of Zion—essentially a spiritualist reading society that still endorsed the original prophecies of Smith—they drifted into the backwaters of respectable Mormon society.

Young's comparatively genial handling of the so-called Godbeite rebellion spoke volumes about his newfound confidence as head of a world religion now firmly anchored within its own temporal empire. But as the Gentile world continued to burst in upon the economic and religious borders of a Mormon kingdom that Young sought to keep autonomous and pristine, the great Moses figure of the faith was finally driven, near the end of his life, to a curious cul de sac: He tried to review the long-latent Mormon ideal of wholly communitarian self-help, in the vein of the holy example set by the Primitive Church. In 1872, he founded the Order of Enoch—a gathering of saints within the Mormon kingdom that sought to recover the perfectionist worldly designs of the early phase of Mormon life.

Named for an obscure figure in the Book of Genesis who was so loved by God that he was instantly dispatched to Heaven, Young's experiment, in which members consecrated property and labor entirely to the Church's control, was well grounded in Mormon tradition. In a creative scriptural gloss of the Enoch episode, Joseph Smith had explained that the transported son of Heaven had left behind him the worldly city of Zion as his great historic legacy—a people of "one heart and one mind, and dwelt in righteousness, and there was no poor among them." In a similar vein, Smith's successor envisioned the Mormon scheme of individual salvation segueing naturally into potent new forms of collaborative effort and intentional community. When he announced the formation of the ZCMI in 1869, he remarked that it was "a stepping stone to what is called the Order of Enoch, but which is in reality the order of Heaven." In the more detailed model of Mormon communitarianism that Young promoted at the Mormon conference of 1872, the Mormon patriarch laid out plans to settle a city "after the order of Enoch." He envisioned communities of about 1,000 profit-sharing workers, pooling their belongings and meeting for meals in an enormous dining hall (in an apparent flight of quasi-utopian fancy, Young envisioned them being served via a miniature train-trolley, which would deliver meals and cart away dirty dishes). Not all working arrangements would be egalitarian, however; in the manner of most business barons of the American West, Young proposed that the drudge work of cleaning the dishes after communal meals fall to "a few Chinamen."[59]

When the Panic of 1873 crippled many smaller enterprises in the Utah territory, Young was all the more convinced that the Mormon community's

curious hybrid of large-scale economic cooperatives and family-scaled household production would preserve the Mormon world's prosperity and spiritual
identity in a seamlessly profitable business model. In the settlement of St.
George, founded in 1874, a group of Mormons officially launched the movement as they banded together under an ambitious charter, seeking once more
to plant the foundations of Mormon life in "self-sustaining . . . home manufactures" such as cotton and wool. Improvements in productive work would
secure more time for the "cultivation and training of our minds," the group
optimistically announced. While the aims of the community were utopian,
Young and his followers were no socialists; the community's wealth might be
held in common, but individuals would still earn dividends and wages based
on the work they contributed to the greater good. In what proved to be the
ultimate equivocal show of support for the experiment from on high, Young
also refrained from sharing his own vast holdings of wealth with the communal movement—now known simply as the United Order—after initially
pledging in 1874 that he was "going into the Order with all that I have."[160]

This apparent hypocrisy badly wounded both the project itself and
Young's reputation as a righteous leader. The anti-Mormon *Salt Lake Tribune* gleefully laid into "the Profit" Young, announcing that "if he don't
make the rich men fork over as well as the poor we shall think him an
unjust, discriminating Profit."[161] The *Tribune* and other detractors of
Young suggested that the United Order was little more than a get-rich-
quick scheme to defraud gullible believers of their hard-earned wealth.

In reality, though, the failure of Young's last bid for a truly harmonious
melding of the Mormon spiritual and temporal empires bespoke something
much more serious, and poignant. The dream of a self-sustaining yeoman
economy had, after all, harkened back to the day of Thomas Jefferson—and
farther back still, to John Winthrop's communitarian vision of redemptive
charity in the Puritan's New World errand. In seeking to enshrine it permanently at the center of his idiosyncratic vision of true civic worship in Utah,
Young was desperately trying to fortify the Mormon economy for a last
stand against debilitating Gentile influence—only much like the indifferent gentleman farmer Jefferson, Young was much better at prescribing the
ideal way of life for the agrarian masses than in living it himself.

In all events, the ideal proved unsustainable amid the mounting pressures of rival modes of enterprise, regardless of their tribal or religious provenance. Young's dream of an agrarian Utah was mooted by the emergence of California as the American West's farming powerhouse; and Utah's mining centers would become major hubs of development, in a seeming vindication of Joseph Smith's original obsession with precious metals. Even if outfits such as the ZMCI had weathered downturns such as the '73 Panic in better shape than their smaller competitors, that still didn't mean that Young's imagined empire of consecrated wealth and shared labor would hold any abiding interest when economic booms returned to the Utah frontier. Even the United Order's flagship community—a settlement of some 1,000 Mormons that went by the almost comically Youngian name of Orderville—finally succumbed to the familiar specter of fast profits as a mining boom took hold in southern Utah in the 1880s.

And in perhaps the most fitting irony of all, the ZMCI would shed its initial identity as a just-above-wholesale cooperative devoted to the Mormons' commercial and religious purity to become a major player in the Western retail world. It would later gain renown as "the world's first department store," anchoring much of the retail activity of Salt Lake City well into the twentieth century. The church finally sold off the chain in 1999, but it still operates today as a division of Macy's. The cooperative also lent its name to the ZCMI Center Mall, which opened in 1975 across from Temple Square in downtown Salt Lake City, and was the nation's largest downtown shopping mall—until it closed in 2007 to make way for the much larger LDS-owned City Creek Center, which opened in 2012 with a price tag of roughly $2 billion.

This is perhaps the respect in which the Mormon faith is most characteristically American. Begun as an outbreak of postmillennial enthusiasm on a largely unsettled Western frontier, the Mormon vision of cooperative enterprise overseen by the church hierarchy mutated into something very different, and far more characteristic of the new age of American enterprise: a spiritualized corporation. In touting his vision of the United Order at St. George, Young had announced that "to me all labors are spiritual" and "our labor is one eternal spiritual work."[162] Yet the epic story of the Mormons' settlement of the frontier produced something quite opposite to Young's republic of spiritualized labor—a centralized, top-down model of production and distribution that would perform its own strange kind of alchemy within the rapidly industrializing American economy of the next century. Working at the outer margins of the American frontier and the American religious mainstream, the Mormons had used the same materials that Joseph Smith had summoned out of his original revelation to craft their own proto-corporate vision of redeemed commerce, propelled by a powerful New World gospel—a veneration of wealth as both an object of grace in its right and as a virtual proof-text of the rewards of faith; a super-American confidence in the promise of frontier enterprise; and (not least by a long shot) the Gnostic theology of the self's eternal progression into Godhood. For Young, the last of the faith's pioneer prophets, Mormonism's organizational genius had finally outstripped its roots in the Primitive Church's fast-obsolescing model of communal self-help. Capitalism would soon be the LDS Church's principal agent of worldly redemption. The worldly corporation, much like the nuclear family that Joseph Smith had likewise initially scorned on grounds of a higher Gnostic revelation, would become the calling card of the modernized, Americanized Mormon patriarchs of the twentieth century and beyond.

5

THE BUSINESSMEN AWAKE

Steeped in the doctrine of continual prophecy and revelation, the Mormon experience was itself prophetic in one crucial respect: By fulfilling their own unique vision of primitivist faith and Gnostic communion—and by carving out their own prosperous empire from the American frontier—the Mormons proved to be spiritual homesteaders, staking out the lead trends in the modern money faith that would soon overrun the Protestant world at large. With the Mormons clearly in view as the apostles of the Money Cult's vanguard tradition, it's a far more straightforward proposition to chart the advance of the influential movements that ushered in the Protestant tradition's full passage into American modernity.

But the Protestant mainstream took a typically more measured and incremental path toward its own eventual absorption into the Money Cult, via two significant movements beginning in strikingly divergent settings. The revival of 1857–58—known colloquially as the "Businessman's Revival"—is remembered mainly in evangelical circles today, but it established the powerful template for the deeply individualist, materially unabashed, and confidently masculinized model of salvation on virtually universal offer in today's Protestant world. Meanwhile, the distinctly Gnostic (and distinctly feminized) New Thought movement that took root within the liberal heart of New England Protestantism permitted spiritual seekers on the frontiers of organized religion to make their peace with America's emerging consumer society. When these parallel movements eventually converged, in a bold and modern brand of money-preaching, the new synthesis would bear abundant fruit for the Money Cult's future—

especially as this nimble new structure of belief came to merge with the powerful social mythologies of American commercial culture.

The Businessman's Revival, like most religious movements of the frenetic, laissez-faire nineteenth-century religious scene, boasted an unlikely origin story. Instead of springing from the inspired pen of a fire-breathing prophet, or stealing over a congregation in a series of physical paroxysms, the revival originated in the efforts of a lonely missionary worker to motivate himself to continue on in the work of redemption. And as befits its name, the Businessman's Revival soon spread into an efficiently organized, tightly scheduled series of prayer meetings bent on demonstrating the material returns of a simple pietist faith in the face of the crippling Panic of 1857.

Like so many other pivotal figures in nineteenth-century Protestantism, Jeremiah Calvin Lanphier hailed from the provinces of upstate New York, in the Hudson Valley village of Coxsackie. He'd moved to New York City as a young man seeking to make his fortune, but after toiling for twenty years in various "mercantile pursuits," he decided to devote himself to full-time missionary work at the North Dutch Church. His new vocation didn't get off to an auspicious start; the immigrant, and heavily Catholic, neighborhood of Five Points, which Lanphier targeted as his recruiting ground, needed much more than a lone (and distinctly mild-mannered) door-to-door evangelist to induce them to embrace the dictates of middle-class Protestant faith.

Still, while Lanphier didn't win many converts among his prospective flock, he did realize that he could work a wondrous change within himself. After exhausting and frustrating daily bouts of failed missionizing, Lanphier had made a crucial religious discovery in the sanctum of his own apartment: a regular interval of nightly prayer promptly restored him to health and emotional equilibrium. And Lanphier soon grasped as well that the restorative and pragmatic benefits of prayer could be spread outward among his erstwhile colleagues in the financial and commercial world. Hence, by the sympathetic account of a contemporary chronicler of the revival, Talcott W. Chambers, the idea of the revival spread more as what we would today call a viral marketing appeal than out of any new theological insight into the condition of sin or the doctrine of substitutionary atonement. "Waiting upon the Lord," Chambers wrote, Lanphier renewed his strength; calling upon God, he was answered. His own soul was cheered and refreshed, and he was enabled to set forth on his daily rounds with a quickened sense of the Divine favour . . . This fresh, personal experience of blessedness and the power of prayer suggested to Mr. Lanphier's mind that there might be others, especially those engaged in business, to whom it would be equally pleasurable and profitable to retire for a short period from secular engagements and engage in devotional exercises.[163]

While no one could have apprehended it at the time, this simple idea— bringing a gospel of therapeutic personal renewal before an emerging public in the business world—would revolutionize the basic terms of Protestant worship over the next century. As the modern commercial era overtook the American spiritual scene, the odyssey of faith would be taken up less and less with the thorny dilemmas of social reform, and move increasingly in time with the placid reveries of personal rehabilitation undertaken for the sake of full deliverance within the consumer marketplace.

In the meantime, though, there were converts to be won. Lanphier set about distributing handbills in the financial district adjoining the North Dutch sanctuary on Fulton Street. And like everything else having to do with the 1857–58 revival, the language of these appeals was principally tailored to the exigencies of the marketplace: "This meeting is intended to give merchants, mechanics, clerks, strangers, and business men generally an opportunity to stop and call upon God amid the perplexities incident to their respective avocations," it read in part. "It will continue for one hour; but it is also designed for those who may find it inconvenient to remain more than five or ten minutes, as well as for those who can spare the whole hour."[164]

Within a few weeks, the prayer meetings had swollen into the hundreds, and were transferred from their original storefront site to the North Dutch Church's third floor—or, as biblically minded adherents called it, the "upper room." (That designation stems from a prayer command of Jesus in the opening verses of the Book of Acts—one of the revival's many echoes of the primitivist faith of the early Christian Church.)

This was one of the important differences that set the Businessman's

Revival apart from predecessor movements of Protestant renewal: It was in many ways a contrived and self-conscious media spectacle as much as it was a spontaneous outpouring of heightened religious observance. Lanphier and other revival leaders well understood the significance of placing their crusade at the center of the nation's financial industry, and reaped the rewards from the novel conversion of bankers, tradesmen, and merchants professing a new kind of public piety in the midst of their workdays.

Indeed, other area churches soon got swept up in the prayer revival, but since they still catered principally to traditional female and family-based congregations, they commanded less attention than Lanphier's congregations of faithful businessmen. While the spread of Reformed Church revivalism to the seat of financial power counted as news, the broader sweep of the crusade followed more familiar demographic lines. So it's scarcely remembered today that by some accounts, the 1857–58 revival didn't begin with Lanphier's meetings at all, but in a more traditional revival sponsored by the Methodist holiness preacher Phoebe Palmer and her husband, Walter, in the Canadian town of Hamilton, Ontario. Thanks to a steamship's misplacement of their luggage, the couple had been stranded in Hamilton during a family visit; Phoebe took advantage of the delay to hold a special prayer meeting. Once that gathering inspired a steady torrent of conversions and public prayer, she encouraged each person in attendance to turn out the following evening with a friend in tow.

Over the ensuing week or so, hundreds of Hamilton residents attended the meetings and pronounced themselves converted. Phoebe Palmer's published account of the Hamilton revival in two New York papers, the *Methodist Christian Advocate* and the *Journal of New York*, stirred great local interest in laity-led prayer gatherings. That, in turn, fed the attendance rolls at Lanphier's meetings, which had launched a few weeks prior to the Hamilton revival.[165]

De-feminizing Faith

Laid said by side, the Lanphier and Palmer origin stories of the 1857–58 revival highlight the distinctive ways in which gender roles shaped the course of the midcentury urban revival. Throughout its history in America, evangelical Christianity—i.e., the revivalist faith that hinges on a second birth in Christ, and a personal relationship with the savior—always had a

preponderance of male leaders presiding over predominantly female congregations. With the spread of the Businessman's Revival, however, it was
moving on to newly masculinized—and newly commercialized—ground.

Even as the revival shored up traditional notions of how gender roles
should play out in public worship, it also opened up new territory for
Protestants of both sexes. Young men whose public identities had been
beholden to the recently poleaxed financial sector were seeking new outlets
for their emotional and spiritual longings, while female revivalists were
seeking new public legitimation for their traditional religious concerns—
up to and including organized efforts to break down gender segregation at
revivals in the financial centers of New York, Boston, and elsewhere.

In this respect, the designation of "Businessman's Revival," which began
life as a hasty journalistic catchphrase, remains apt, despite its misleading
gender connotations for the broader movement in piety launched in 1857. The
important common thread is the "business" end of the coinage, as opposed
to the more restrictive "man." Both the male and female constituencies of
the revival had experienced, in spiritual terms, a crisis of personal identity
largely sparked by the world of business—and, in the rhetoric and practices
of the revival, they learned to express their inward spiritual longings in the
approved argot of the commercial sphere. In the pietist doctrines of the
revival, the Gnostic strands of the Second Awakening were now converging
on the male-dominated marketplace—even as men and women were still
largely consigned to quite divergent models of behavior within the revival.

Among other things, the business-minded conduct and content of the
revival help account for the absence of any dissenting or utopian message in a
revival that occurred in the immediate wake of an acute financial crisis. While
the apostles of prayer-meeting revival focused on worldly results, the revival's
call to inward spiritual order focused on tighter conformity to market-
approved conduct, such as workplace discipline and emotional self control.
As the religious historian John Corrigan notes in his perceptive study of the
Businessman's Revival in Boston, the prayer meetings' preoccupation with
emotional rectitude, across the spectrum of gender, reinforced the key cultural boundaries that preserved the high-functioning self-image of the white,
Protestant, and upwardly mobile middle class. In this urban context, the older

behavioral restrictions that fomented the key religious uprisings of the Market Revolution like the Finneyite class war in Rochester were transformed into important markers of status, as well as key points of racial and ethnic distinction. "The principle of control was one part of the set of guidelines for emotional expression for the Protestant middle class," Corrigan writes. "And it functioned together with other rules not only as a means of guiding persons through their socio-emotional lives, but as a means by which to draw boundaries between them and other groups"—notably, in Boston, the stereotyped "ill-tempered" Irish, and "impulsive" African-American communities.[166]

Still, much of the language that characterized the inward transformations wrought by the revival was also distinctly feminized, in the cultural terms of the day. As Corrigan notes, the frequent promise of ready divine assent to a propitiating prayer was conditioned by the believer's vow to "give my heart to God," and the testimony of male petitioners during the revival betrayed a certain fretful anxiety over the heart-for-prayers transaction that distinctly echoed the plights of ambivalently affianced women chronicled in Victorian fiction. In Herman Humphrey's 1858 work *Revival Sketches and Manual*, which presented a series of interview transcripts with converts-in-the-making, male congregants confess to such vacillating sentiments as "it seems as if I ought to repent and give my heart to God in less than a *week*"; "I did *intend* to repent and give my heart to God, and fixed the time"—and occasionally, in a far more serene register of feeling, they will report "I have fully resolved to give my heart to God."[167]

At the same time, adherents of the revival remained guarded against any strain of Protestant belief that threatened traditional male, and marketplace, prerogatives. This was especially the case when detractors of the revival's inward turn, such as William Lloyd Garrison's abolitionist newspaper *The Liberator*, insisted that the vouchsafed heart of a business professional was still a debased spiritual currency. "You hear a great deal said in the Revivalist meetings about stocks in the Bank of Heaven," the paper editorialized:

> Do you think men would so glibly employ these analogies with their business life if the *motive* were not essentially the same with their business motives? It is the same, on the whole. They are, on the whole,

after precisely what they say—*spiritual "Bank Stock."* It is a private speculation to secure them an "interest in the kingdom of heaven"— to secure them against punishment at death . . . Doubtless it is easy to "give the heart to Christ at just six o'clock last evening." But what was the consideration for this so generous a gift, a gift so important as to be a sign of inward regeneration, so important as to be worthy of a public announcement? Why, bank stock in the kingdom of heaven.[168]

Another well-known Boston reformer, the Unitarian minister and theologian Theodore Parker, likewise inveighed against the revival's pronounced social quietism—its failure to reckon with the "five great evils of mankind": "war, wicked government, slavery, selfish antagonism in society, the degradation of women." The evangelical leaders of the revival, far from meeting Parker's challenge on his own ground and promoting social-reform initiatives of their own, instead used the new rhetoric of the praying heart for a seemingly unchristian end indeed: petitioning the Lord for the incapacity, or death, of Theodore Parker. Since 1857, revivalists had been earnestly praying for Parker's conversion, but in the wake of his assaults, Boston evangelicals had amended their appeals, in the event that the reprobate preacher was beyond "saving influence," so that God might put him "out of the way, and let his influence die with him."[169]

The anti-Parker campaign was admittedly extreme, but it also represents a significant early sounding in what we now recognize as the absolutist rhetoric of contemporary culture warfare. We are by now so accustomed to interpreting religiously themed culture confrontations as outcomes of the rivalry between religious traditionalists and secular moderns that it's easy to overlook their roots in the political disputes between reformers and business-minded pietists of the mid-nineteenth century.

In reality, the revivalist tradition largely bid farewell to the cause of social reform after the Businessman's Revival—some sixty years before the evolution controversy would pit theological liberals against orthodox biblical literalists in the nation's pulpits and seminaries. Even more than the prayers for Parker's death, the stolid silence of the Businessman's Revival about all the "five evils" he cataloged spoke volumes about the badly fragmented state of New England's covenantal tradition of reform Protestantism. In significant measure, of course, the revival's social quietism stemmed from the threats that Parker and Garrison's abolitionism posed to both the union and to the commercial standing of Northern industrialists dependent on the Southern cotton trade. But even after the crucible of the Civil War, revivalist religion persistently stressed the primacy of individual piety over communal social improvement.

As a result, evangelical devotions in the century ahead would have less and less to do with the project of social reform. It's revealing to note in this vein that the last great revival-inspired push for reform—the twentieth-century Prohibition crusade—was aimed at eradicating the individual sin of drinking; amid all sorts of new social upheavals characterizing the maturation of America's industrial capitalist economy, evangelical activists elected to resurrect the poster vice of the Second Awakening. This shift in sensibility goes all the way back to the immediate run-up to the Civil War—and to the individualist legacy of the Businessman's Revival. A quarter-century after the deregulation of state religion in Massachusetts in 1833, revivalists well understood that the historic link between their cause and social reform was a liability in the cultural marketplace—and that, on balance, the champions of the old postmillennial dream of steady social improvement, such as Theodore Parker, were better off dead.

The Public Clamor for a Private Faith

It's a mistake, however, to confuse the political quietism of the Businessman's Revival with a retiring cultural outlook. Quite to the contrary: The extensive interplay between the nation's commercial culture and the practice of individual piety meant that the doctrines of the prayer-meeting revival would reverberate much further into American life than any legacy of the now-beleaguered tradition of postmillennial reform. The pietist vision of a private faith nested firmly within the marketplace had, by its very nature, to burst the confines of Protestant pews and pulpits. Since the business world was already in the process of dramatically reshaping most American institutions, from the workplace and the political order to family life, the new alignment of faith and commerce would likewise traverse almost every established sphere of middle-class American life.

By bringing the Victorian sentimentality of the Finneyite phase of the Second Awakening into more direct and robust conjunction with the world of urban commerce, the Businessman's Revival paved the way for the broader vision of pietist self-improvement that would define the rise of a mass consumer culture in the late-nineteenth and early-twentieth centuries. The very traits that made the Businessman's Revival a powerful influence among the upwardly mobile workforce in the nation's major financial centers also made its legacy especially compelling for a postbellum nation eager to bypass the traumas of the Civil War, and to go about celebrating the bounty of the country's rapidly industrializing economy. The Businessman's Revival, in short, looked ahead to a broad-based pietist retrenchment across the new American economic landscape. After the Second Awakening's enthusiasms for postmillennial reform, the 1857–58 revival marked a dramatic return to a form of worship confined largely to the personal sphere: a version of purely evangelical preaching that was profoundly depoliticized and class-bound.

And more than any of its predecessors did, the Businessman's Revival codified its preachments to comport with the routines of the nation's urban commercial life. It was, first of all, a media sensation on a scale that George Whitefield could only have dreamed of. Around the same time that the nation divested itself of its last religious establishment in the 1830s, a new commercial press was taking root in major American cities. The first New York tabloid paper aimed at a mass readership was Joseph Gordon Bennett's *New York Herald*. Bennett, a mostly nonpracticing Catholic, was keenly attuned to the wide appetite for both sanctimony and scandal in his paper's heavily Protestant and middle-class reading public. The *Tribune* debuted in 1836 with a series of reports stemming from Maria Monk's heavy-breathing, and almost certainly apocryphal, account of corruption and sexual license in a Catholic monastery. Bennett also devoted extensive coverage to the Mormons' sexual scandals and eventful westward trek, and regularly doted on tales of evangelical backbiting and hypocrisy.

Bennett's main competitor, the *New York Tribune*'s publisher Horace Greeley, was by contrast an earnest champion of revivalist reform, and an especially ardent opponent of slavery. When the Businessman's Revival caught their attention, each publisher sought to harness it to his own political agendas. The pro-slavery Bennett treated it as an encouraging sign that Protestant believers in the North had wearied of the abolitionist crusade and were returning en masse to a simpler, purely personal form of piety, while Greeley believed that the great urban revival would be the crowning blow to the slavery cause.

Bennett also used the noonday prayer meetings, as was his general wont, to tweak the pious sensibilities of the city's Protestant elite. He launched the *Herald's* coverage of the revival in a special Sunday edition, just as New York's revived Protestant leaders were seeking to suppress the publication of papers on Sundays in a burst of Sabbatarian fervor. Bennett clearly reveled in using his own paper to feed the vanity of his Sabbatarian antagonists—while also editorializing against their cause in the same edition. It was a typically unfeeling show of moral bullying, he thundered, "to drive the working classes to church on their only day of rest"—after all, Sunday was "the poor man's day for exercise, enjoyment, and fresh air." And if the point wasn't clear enough there, Bennett published an accompanying editorial on the Businessman's Revival in which he lambasted the pious spectacle of the city's great Protestant "merchants, bankers, politicians, financiers" stepping forward at the prayer meetings to make "oral confession that they have done things which they ought not to have done, and left undone things which they ought to have done."[170]

Greeley, for his part, provided much more exhaustive and enthusiastic accounts of the New York revival—so much so that excerpts from the *Tribune's* coverage made up the last 100 pages of the best known book-length account of the Businessman's Revival at the time, William Conant's 1858 *Narrative of Remarkable Conversions and Revival Incidents*. Where Bennett made skeptical sport of the business world's sudden penchant for public repentance, Greeley marveled at the scene of public prayer gatherings "held in the center of the business circles of the city, and sustained largely by the most prominent business men." This was, he confidently asserted, the overture to the righteous overthrow of the slaver's reign in the South: "Simultaneously with the deep interest felt and expressed by the great body of religious men of the North in the attempt to save Kansas from the evils and horrors of slavery . . . we see a revival breaking out and extending over the country quite unprecedented in its character."[171]

But all this public jousting over the revival's moral content was largely a side attraction. The controversy that Greeley and Bennett summoned out of the otherwise innocuous and apolitical prayer gatherings was feeding a great circulation war, and their rival political allegiances aside, the two antagonists were first and foremost mass-circulation newspapermen. The main import of the media's intensive coverage of the Businessman's Revival was, in short, to revive the business of newspapering in a new, sensation-fed marketplace for news.

What's more, as Bennett correctly surmised in his cynical blowout coverage of the event in the *Herald*'s Sunday edition, the secular press's lavish attention to the revival created a significant ripple effect among the nation's Protestant leaders and religious press. As attention to the prayer meetings continued to build, revival preachers were increasingly conscious of the role of the press in spreading the good news of the prayer meetings—and indeed, came readily to incorporate newspaper reports about them as proof of their divinely inspired power and efficacy. Writing in *The New York Observer*, a religious weekly, the evangelist Samuel Iraneus Prime announced that "with scarcely an exception, the daily and other papers make mention of the work in terms which indicate their wishes for its continuance. Such a state of things is altogether unprecedented, and we regard it as evidence of the all pervading power of the Holy Spirit."[172]

The logic of this appeal was repeated in many pulpits of the revival, up and down the Eastern seaboard. In a March 1858 revival gathering of some 1,000 souls in Louisville, Kentucky, the proceedings opened with a newspaper's chronicle of a conversion at a Philadelphia noonday prayer meeting—a homily for the crowd on hand to go and do likewise. The next preacher taking the podium likewise cited a newspaper "account of the glorious work now going on in New York." In a fittingly self-conscious addendum, the *Louisville Daily Courier* reporter who brought news of these appeals remarked to his readers that their city was not "the only place in which the work of religion is . . . going on. Our exchanges bring us the news of the same thing from different parts of the state." He wrapped up his dispatch with a long string of revival-related reports from the *Lebanon (Tenn.) Republican Banner*, the *Chicago Journal*, the *Philadelphia Bulletin*, and the *New York Express*.[173] In the home state of the Cane Ridge revival—an experiential display of revival faith unlike any other in American history—the upsurge of a far more restrained and measured brand of religious piety was being demonstrated almost solely on the second-hand authority of the newspaper. In perhaps the ultimate such testament to this new Protestant romance with the mass-circulation press, two newspapers aimed at the newly roused evangelical national readership were founded in New York—though they did not last much beyond the lifespan of the revival itself.

But the media-friendly character of the Businessman's Revival was just one of the features that rendered it a unique meeting of commerce and Protestant piety. As Greeley noted, the prayer meetings drew their sponsors and followers from the nation's new class of urban financiers. It was thus perhaps natural for the revival's champions to look to it as a means of infusing the workings of the marketplace with the mysteries of faith. "We trust that since prayer has once entered the counting house, it will never leave it; and that the ledger . . . , the blotting book, the pen and ink, will all be consecrated by a heavenly presence," the novelist Harriet Beecher Stowe announced in a newspaper column on the prayer meetings.

In reality, however, something close to the opposite of Stowe's fervid wish came to pass. Far from overseeing a righteous transformation of the business world, the Businessman's Revival showcased the growing "affinity between urban revivals and a nascent corporate culture," as the historian Kathryn A. Long observes:

> The structure, organization, and methods of the business world shaped the urban phase of the 1857–58 Revival. The noon meetings were viewed as an appointment with God. They were scheduled to fit into the business day and reflected the intense time consciousness of Victorian men. Prayer . . . was considered a productive activity. The uniform format for the proceedings resembled an agenda as much as a guide for worship. The direction stipulated that the opening hymn, Bible reading, and leader's prayer were not to occupy more than 12

minutes; in addition, at precisely 12 PM, the leader was to inter-
rupt the proceedings, and allowed those who desired prayer to stand
for 30 seconds; and finally, at 12:55 he should announce the closing
hymn, "any one having the floor yielding immediately." The newspapers commented on the "peculiar legislative ability" needed to direct
the proceedings. It was a businessman's job.[174]

And just as press attention came to function as evidence of the revival's
divine inspiration, so did the ever shorter, sweeter conduct of the prayer
meetings serve as ready confirmation of continued miraculous progress in
the work of deliverance. As the New York–based magazine *The Evangelist*
directed its readers in late 1858, prayers "should be short, and come to the
point at once"; in an earlier dispatch on the revival, the weekly cheerfully
noted that "the exhortations and prayers are of a different character than
they were a year ago. When the brethren rise to speak, they seem to have
an idea of what they wish to say, and when they have said it they sit down;
consequently, they are brief, pointed, and telling."[175] If Charles Finney
introduced new believers to a God who helped cement their social position in the anxious bench, the midcentury revival jumpstarted by Jeremiah
Lanphier brought converts in contact with a God who organized their
faith confessions in the idiom of an annual report.

The Heart Contract

The Businessman's Revival also marked an important shift in the relationship between evangelical religion and economic thought. Taking shape in
direct response to the Panic of 1857, the revival gained significant public
attention due to the businessmen who took part in it—and unlike past religious efforts to mount some sort of moral response to hard times, from the
land-bank controversies of the First Awakening to the scattered utopian
and communitarian enterprises of the Second, the 1857–58 revival brought
a singularly individualist message for those believers who wrestled with
the failure of the midcentury market economy: *Pray harder.*

Or, to evoke the fuller import of the revival's emotional thrust: *Feel
more deeply.* Supporters of the revival such as Phoebe Palmer and the

recently transplanted Charles Finney made the inward and private cultivation of perfectionist piety their calling card. And as was the case in Finney's
Rochester revival, they trained much of their efforts on spiritualizing the
workplace—but in Boston, the revival didn't focus mainly on the leisure
pursuits of a heavily Irish-Catholic working class; rather, it targeted the
upwardly mobile corps of young workers in the financial world. The leaders
of the Boston revival deliberately set out to temper and chasten the rougher
edges of the thrill-seeking "boy culture" that took root among the city's
rapidly expanding corps of displaced rural young men working as clerks and
office boys in the finance capital of New England. As Corrigan explains,
the signature innovation of the revival, the midday public prayer meeting,
proved crucial in regulating the public maturation of Boston office boys—
and in laying out a new model of personal prayer as an economic contract.

The brisk, results-oriented conduct of worship in the revival's prayer
meetings presented a modern solution to the age-old dilemma of American Protestantism: How to re-create among the believing community's
younger male members the sort of galvanizing and identity-forging belief
necessary to reenact the core doctrines of the Reformation faith in the
hearts of its future spiritual and secular leaders. The answer, clearly, lay
in the world of the marketplace—which by the time of the Businessman's
Revival had already emerged as America's chief arbiter of social peace and
public order, and could be entrusted to transform raw and uncertain youths
working in the bosom of commerce into mature and confident believers.

So the critical work of inculcating self-discipline in the next generation of spiritual and business leaders became largely a matter of indulging
controlled bursts of emotion in a closely regulated public forum, geared
explicitly to move in concert with the rhythms of the corporate workday.
The Great Awakening of the long nineteenth century had begun with the
strange new free-will Pentecost at Cane Ridge. It reached into the centers
of American commerce with Charles Finney's anxious bench. And now,
in a moment of triumph, it had alighted on a model of mass conversion
conducted at a glorified shareholder's meeting.

Nor was the business imagery of such gatherings simply a metaphor.
For the Northeastern middle class, Corrigan writes, "prayer was a business,"

and it helped to seal the many tacit emotional contracts instrumental to the maintenance of middle-class Victorian life. The obsessive focus on lapsed self-control that Finney had introduced in the Second Awakening's early days was now formalized as the central message of the young man's praying life—and not incidentally, it was also redefined as a manful show of inner strength. The practice of petitionary prayer—as the bold and direct appeal to God for material reward for one's piety was known—was earmarked from the revival's outset as a masculine trait. It was "a mixture of boldness and feeling," Corrigan notes, and anything less than the direct address it codified for ambitious male believers was unseemly: "Prayer was thought useless, even insulting to God, unless it openly and forthrightly beseeched divine favor in pursuit of a specific end, and not only for comfort and joy, but for health, domestic tranquility, employment, help with alcoholism, food, shelter, and clothing—whatever temporal wants stood at the top of a petitioner's list."[176]

Inevitably, the contractual rhetoric of the prayer meeting came to dictate private as well as public demonstrations of faith. In a quiet revolution in domestic mores that distinctly anticipates the later market-obsessed domestic counsel of contemporary evangelicalism, the Boston revival briskly transposed the results-oriented language of market life into the traditionally intimate domain of spiritual distress. In an 1850 address before the Mercantile Library Association, George S. Hillard anticipated this development by declaring that "all movement, whether in things spiritual or things material, may be traced back to inequality" in trade relations; likewise, a post-revival tract for young male spiritual seekers called *The Still Hour; or Communion with God*, published in 1867 by Congregationalist preacher Austin Phelps, describes the penitential act of prayer as a simple transactional proposition:

> The prospect of gaining an object will always affect this, the expression of intense desire. The feeling which will become spontaneous with a Christian, under the influence of such a trust, is this: "I come to my devotions this morning, on an errand of real life. This is no romance and no farce. I do not come here to go through a form of words. I have no hopeless desires to express. I have an object to gain. I have an end to accomplish. This is a *business* in which I am about to engage."[177]

With such directives and similes coming from area pulpits and lec-
terns, it's small wonder that the young men who would become the center
of the revival readily adopted the market's guiding rhetoric to characterize
the spiritual tumult in their hearts. "In the book of my life, these experiences are unerringly debited by the great Accountant," confided one such
Bostonian, Tracy Patch Cheever, to his journal in 1854:

> . . . and the thought that the balance may be against one, must needs
> arise. Yet I am cheered by the hope that so much of providential good
> has been vouchsafed to me, as to prevent the entire bankruptcy of
> that treasure which was confided to me to keep and increase. Happy
> is the man, and happy the world through him, of whom it can be said
> that he added even a farthing of worth to the capital of his soul.[178]

Clearly the promoters of the 1857–58 revival well knew their target
audience when, in a placard advertising an April 1858 prayer meeting in
Philadelphia, they announced the issuance of stock certificates vouchsaf-
ing to their bearers "mansions in the skies" and a path to the "celestial city,"
all in exchange for publicly professing their "love to Christ."[179]

The Piety of the Merchant Prince

The immediate impact of this city-oriented soul-saving creed on the country's
new industrial economy was brought home quite vividly in the life of one of
the revival's most successful adherents in the business world, the Philadelphia-
based department-store tycoon John Wanamaker. Like many northeastern
youths stirred into action by the Businessman's Revival, Wanamaker was an
energetic partisan of urban Christian mission work, and remained a revival
enthusiast throughout his long life. Among his many religious pursuits, he
served as the main Philadelphia sponsor of the urban evangelist Dwight
Moody's phenomenally successful run of revivals in the 1870s.

Moody and Wanamaker were in many ways mirror images of each
other. Moody was a former shoe salesman who elected as a young man to
devote himself solely to the work of evangelism: "I regard the world as a
wrecked vessel," he'd announced in one of his famous bursts of missionary

zeal. "God has given me a lifeboat and said, 'Moody, save all you can.'" But Wanamaker's life largely traversed the opposite professional arc. Beginning as a pious and ambitious young Presbyterian, he blazed a new career path as a merchant-prince of the industrial age—someone who both envisioned and embodied (albeit in measured and ambivalent form) the luxurious promise of America's emerging new consumer society. When both men were in their professional prime, Moody would regularly correspond with Wanamaker, pleading with the retail tycoon to forsake his worldly pursuits and join Moody in the great work of evangelizing the world. But Wanamaker never came close to the hands-on revival work of bailing sinners out of the wrecked vessel.

Instead, throughout his successful adult life, Wanamaker adopted the central gospel message of the Businessman's Revival: He sought to infuse his secular calling with a larger spiritual purpose. At the high-water mark of the revival, in 1858, he became caught up in two of the age's most import- ant urban campaigns of pietist outreach: the Sunday school movement, and the Young Men's Christian Association. Both of these national crusades set out to instill regular habits of Protestant self-scrutiny and self-control in the multi-ethnic working classes of America's cities—and the twenty-year-old Wanamaker was an eager recruit. He was appointed the first paid secretary of the YMCA in 1858, and in the same year he established Philadelphia's Bethany Mission Sunday School—his lifelong pet spiritual cause, which would become the largest Sunday school in the world by the 1890s. After he co-founded the allied Bethany Presbyterian Church in 1858, Wana- maker was installed as an elder and was one of the congregation's principal funders. He went on to found three other major churches in Philadelphia, all designed to cater to the new immigrant workers in the inner city. He was president of the Philadelphia Sabbath Association for most of his adult life, and acceded to the presidency of the World Sunday School Association in 1919. And throughout his life, he remained a fervent advocate of the urban missionizing agendas of both the Salvation Army and the YMCA. He hailed the latter group in particular as a critical source of moral tutelage for young men adrift amid the many temptations of urban life—and hence, an unrivaled kind of investment in the cultivation of a sound and reliable urban workforce. As he explained in an 1886 letter to a friend,

I consider a well-organized YMCA indispensable to the best welfare
of any City . . . The reason for my large investment of money in it
is because I do not know any other field which promises so good
a return for the money. As a businessmen, I believe the usefulness
of the Association to be beyond value in offering safeguards and
encouragement to the young men we employ.

When it came to promoting the YMCA movements on a global scale,
Wanamaker put his money where his mouth was, helping to fund fledgling
Association schools in Madras, Calcutta, Seoul, and Beijing.[180]

For all this missionizing ardor, however, Wanamaker exemplified the
retiring, pietist faith that was characteristic of his age and social class. The
closest he came to advancing a theological doctrine was his enthusiasm for
the French Lutheran pastor Charles Wagner, author of a sensational bestselling 1901 tract called *The Simple Life*, which contended that the many distractions and comforts of industrial civilization were diminishing the basic
moral sense of ordinary believers. The beneficiaries of consumer abundance,
Wagner complained, existed in a "general state of agitation . . . the more
needs, the more desires we have, the more quarrelsome we become." What's
more, Wagner argued, the rampant "love of advancement" characteristic of
the modern era's spirit of material striving meant that people had become
obsessed with the "wish to imitate the great" and thereby "have forgotten
how to be simple, authentic, self-sacrificing, and especially self-effacing."[181]

Wanamaker wholeheartedly embraced this vision of the Protestant faith's
saving simplicity. He was the chief sponsor, agent, and publicist for Wagner on
the pastor's 1904 tour of the United States, arranging for him to preach before
an audience of some 1,000 congregants at Bethany Church, and to travel to
Washington for an interview with President Theodore Roosevelt (who duly
incorporated Wagner's ideas about an invigorated, emotionally simplified
observance of faith into his own personal gospel of the strenuous life). Wagner
stayed on for two weeks at Wanamaker's anything-but-simple Philadelphia
estate, and the two men maintained a close friendship throughout their lives.

Wagner's simple message of heartfelt piety was, on the face of things,
a surpassingly strange gospel to win the enthusiastic endorsement of the

largest department-store titan of the new century. It was, after all, Wanamaker's commercial mission to create among the crowds thronging into
his consumer emporiums in Philadelphia and New York just that "general state of agitation" and confusion that Wagner so eloquently deplored.
Wanamaker's trademark store displays, indeed, sought to achieve the
sanctification of commerce on an unprecedented scale; they deliberately
mimicked cathedral-style architecture—complete with cornices and
swooping central arches and festive Christmas décor. But significantly for
the great sponsor of unadorned piety and functional behavioral reform,
Wanamaker studiously kept his store installations from indulging in any
specific religious displays. (The closest he came was the then-fashionable
motif of Islamic Orientalism—and even then, his stores' famed *Garden
of Allah* fashion shows traded on the exoticized image of Islam as a faith
steeped in royal luxury rather than prayerful devotion.) Wanamaker lovingly showcased not merely the retail stock and theatrical splendor of the
displays in his block-long department stores, but the store's own operational infrastructure; he would take shoppers on guided tours of the back-
room operations of his stores, pointing out all of the hulking machines
and technical wizardry that brought his grand bazaar of consumer goods
to life. He took special pride in the Wanamaker stores' up-to-the-minute
innovations. They were the first retail concerns to sell automobiles, radios,
and airplanes, and the first to be wired for electrical lights.

Clearly, none of this translated into a spiritually retiring version of
the simple life, and it would be the easiest thing in the world to dismiss
Wanamaker as a stuffed-shirt pious hypocrite of the old school, holding
forth a noble vision of humble piety for the clientele of the YMCA, the
Salvation Army, and the Bethany Sunday School, while touting an altogether different standard of living in the aisles and window displays of his
far more influential and profitable retail empire. But there is zero evidence
that Wanamaker was any sort of cynical opportunist. He clearly regarded
the cultivation of a Christian workforce and polity as an indispensable, if
not *the* indispensable, mission of his life.

The difference here has less to do with any seeming double standard in
Wanamaker's practice of pietist urban reform than with the larger retreat of

religion itself into the cloistered rites of American domesticity. When work moved away from the home in the initial phase of industrialization, the working class was largely dispatched into the nether regions of urban vice and temptation. The project for the reformers of the Second Awakening was to marshal these imperiled and/or lost souls into the charmed circle of the saved—and, not coincidentally, explicitly to tie their life prospects to the punctilious observance of middle-class Protestant morality. However, the next, pietist phase of revival pivoted on the clear expectation that aspiring members of the urban middle class needed, first and foremost, to regulate their behavior themselves: Reformers and sinners alike were encouraged to confine their most powerful convictions about their ultimate spiritual destinies within the circumscribed rites of private, prayerful worship.

There is some truth, to be sure, in William Leach's argument that Wanamaker was driven into monumental shows of piety in much the same way that his retail emporiums memorialized his business savvy and enthusiasm for all things modern. But the more salient point is that, by the time that merchant princes such as Wanamaker rose to power, they were seen as doing essentially the same missionary work that the worldwide spread of the gospel via the YMCA or the Sunday School movement was achieving. And in advancing the spread of consumer capitalism, the captains of retail commerce saw themselves as promoting the Christian betterment of the world at large. It wasn't just that tensions between the believing life and the buying life were relaxing and becoming less consequential for the conduct of a civic faith; for major business and spiritual leaders such as Wanamaker, such tensions were simply inconceivable. When one Protestant minister queried the retail titan on the baleful effect that "modern commercialism" might have wrought on the life of worship, Wanamaker's reply was unequivocal: There was no way that a "business properly conducted, unless it is a brewery, or a liquor saloon, or a gambling den, or something akin to the three of these things, [could] possibly interfere with a Christian profession. So far as my observation goes, I believe that the higher planes upon which mercantile life has been set in the past twenty years have been very favorable to a religious life."[182]

This placid outlook differentiated itself from past feints of Protestant reform mainly by virtue of asserting the tight identification of religious values with worldly endeavors that past reform movements had heroically struggled to achieve in their campaigns of reform. The end-point of the Businessman's Revival—a new market economy whose workers were conditioned at the most basic levels to infuse themselves with spiritual purpose—was the basic starting point for John Wanamaker's missionary work in both his Sunday schools and store displays. And this largely unearned sense of metaphysical serenity was plainly the legacy of the pietist retreat from social reform inaugurated by the Businessman's Revival. Leach's assessment of how this little-noted shift in sensibility played out in Wanamaker's believing life is so finely attuned to the shifting currents of faith within the Protestant mainstream that it bears quoting at length:

> From at least the 1850s onward, many Protestant Americans, perhaps the majority, believed in the compatibility of religion and commerce and that both were moving on a fast track toward progress . . . [thus] it really didn't matter . . . whether Wanamaker felt ill at ease over what he had created. For him, religion was not only nonjudgmental, it was extremely personal and private, as much unrelated to or removed from commerce as it was mixed up in it. Christianity's tenderheartedness and its pleas for sacrifice and service made Wanamaker feel good, virtuous, clean. He wasn't interested in religion as a body of critical ideas, as a prophetic light that might measure behavior by high standards of ethical probity and spiritual insight. This is not to say, of course, that he was indifferent to the social side of religion; all his missions and his schools were intended to aid the poor as well as to promote a moral middle-class morality, Christian paternalism, and orderly and polite behavior. But the piety, the personalism, stands out as the cardinal feature of his religious life. For him, as for countless others, religion brought him "closer," as he put it, to [God's] "strengthening touch," and "His love." . . . Wanamaker's use of religion illustrates what was and still is a trend in mainstream American Protestantism—its failure to sustain a strong critical, intellectual tradition. Wanamaker's religious institutions were important . . . but as religious "thought," they had minimal depth. They

promoted individual salvation, personal well-being, and harmony, not discontent, shame, or insight. Bethany Mission Sunday School and all the other institutions similar to it flourishing in America were wholly incapable of reflecting critically on the "other" world that Wanamaker and others had done so much to bring into being.[183]

In other words, the key distinguishing trait of Wanamaker's prosperity faith wasn't so much its monumental ambition as its underlying sensibility—the conviction that salvation was a business to be transacted off the main public stage where civic life and commerce held sway. Unlike preachers such as Charles Finney, Wanamaker saw no cause to directly mingle the disciplines of the workplace with the rigors of prayer and behavioral rectitude (for one thing, any such campaign would likely strike directly at the business model of Wanamaker's retail empire). And unlike Finney, Wanamaker felt no great compulsion to extend his perfectionist faith to the project of reforming the world at large—beyond, that is, the missionary outreach necessary to prod more of the world's laboring population to share in the restorative, therapeutic piety that Wanamaker championed in the YMCA and Sunday School movements.

This newly privatized piety no doubt functioned as something of a compensatory defensive crouch in an American public sphere where precious little hope was held out for the project of postmillennial reform. The Civil War years and their Gilded Age aftermath were, after all, the most divisive, violent, and corrupt chapter of modern American political history—and as Leach notes, the new world of consumer abundance that businessmen like Wanamaker were creating required a powerful sense of cultural uniformity to work its magic on a multi-ethnic, class-bound, and geographically dispersed buying public. To galvanize the producerist republic of the Jeffersonian yeoman ideal into a mass consumer society, it was necessary to develop a model of middle-class experience that could be readily distributed throughout outlets such as Wanamaker's stores, and the mail-order catalogs and print advertisements that stoked demand for mass-produced goods. And a key element of this process was the conviction that American believers could work out their own salvation in the consecrated privacy of their own chosen parlors, pews, and missions. In short, a purely private brand of Protestant

worship left ample room for the masters of the new consumer market to pro-
mulgate their own vision of the good life, and of duly redeemed commerce.

Indeed, Wanamaker's diffidence about the public applications of his
faith stands out in stark contrast to the public mission that he envisioned
for his commercial exploits. He spoke of his stores as citadels of learning;
places where the masses were inculcated with the masses the more refined
tastes associated with the new industrial civilization. His shopping emporiums provided an "education in what was new," as one Wanamaker's ad
campaign put it. In his correspondence, he described the marketing alchemy
that transformed "luxuries into commodities or into necessities," and waxed
rhapsodic about his store displays as "beautiful fields of necessities."[184] The
brand of spiritual uplift favored by Wanamaker and his pioneering cohort of
consumer prophets belonged to the massing empire of consumer goods; the
only conceivable place for formal professions of Christian faith in this context was to fortify the emerging sense of mission shared among the outsized
figures creating the nation's new commercial world. Put another way: While
the perfectionist revival of Charles Finney inspired rich merchants like the
Tappan brothers to bankroll his forays into the public realm of reform, the
Businessman's Revival at the cusp of the new consumer age dispatched John
Wanamaker to his drawing room, to dream of the magical, fast-multiplying
baubles of material abundance while nursing in his innermost heart the receding—but for that very reason, beguiling—vision of the simple Christian life.

But as with most visions of conflict-free faith, the most pious turn in
American religious life came with some punishing hidden costs of its own.
In the postbellum era, the reinvigorated national Protestant establishment
could reinterpret the drama of salvation as something forever separate and
from the fallen realm of politics—a process epitomized in many ways by
Wanamaker's impassioned gospel of strictly personal piety. In this way, the
devastating legacy of the Civil War could be sacralized for the disenchanted
old-line reformist believers of the North—who increasingly fell into line
with the nostalgic politics that Northern Republican campaign bosses
cynically dubbed the ritual quadrennial appeal to the "bloody shirt." And
meanwhile, southern Baptists, Presbyterians, and Methodists retreated
still further into the social myth of the vanquished white patriarchy's "lost

cause." These pietist retreats into either political nostalgia or social fantasy ensured that the pressing question of how best to curb the antidemocratic excesses of the Gilded Age's barons of finance and commerce—the Money Power, as the secular reformers of the age called it—was largely downplayed in favor of the campaign to spread piety more widely while stamping out personal vice, be it the old standby scourge of alcoholism, or the newer threats of urban decadence and neurasthenic collapse.

The Protestant piety of the postbellum world would also become fatally detached from the broader currents of cultural inquiry. Most famously, of course, the revived Protestant faith of the latter half of the nineteenth century steered clear of any historical controversies that contradicted the divine provenance of scripture, or complicated the narrow strictures of worship within the Primitive Church tradition. More than ever in the American context, Protestant heirs to the pietist legacy of the Businessman's Revival would feed off their growing sense of persecution at the hands of the secular modern culture of creeping unbelief—while staying firmly aligned with that culture's most conspicuous handmaidens in the world of capitalist enterprise. With ever greater fervor, postbellum Protestants staked their identity on a model of faith that insulated them from the corrosive features of modern skepticism—and for this state of spiritual self-quarantine to take hold, the basic terms of that faith had to be kept as simple, and as private, as possible.

This didactic embrace of cultural isolation as an affirmative ideal continues to serve as a central platform of evangelical belief in our own century—and indeed, has gone on to shape an alternative version of both the faith's and the nation's history. One central case in point: the contemporary movement of Christian Reconstructionism, which is founded on the jealously defended evangelical myth holding that the American nation was founded on Christian principles. Reconstructionist ideas are now firmly implanted throughout the nation's evangelical subcultures. Home-schooling curricula champion the Christian piety of the nation's founders—usually courtesy of apocryphal or fabricated quotes misattributed to many of them. Natural-law theories of the Constitution likewise elevate the founding document's hard-fought political provisions into the status of revealed truth. And prophecies of Armageddon, in both popular preaching and popular fiction, would seal the nation's sense of election and divine calling, even amid the imagined rubble of a civilization judged by God and ultimately found wanting.

In today's climate of culture-war melee, we tend to view this casual conscription of both history and prophecy to a present-minded political agenda as the result of an excess of ideological zeal. We assume that the determined propagandists of the evangelical right are seeking to reimagine not merely the American past, but the entire divine plan for the cosmos, in order to make it conform, letter by lumbering letter, to their own pre-ferred image of eternal punishment and reward. In reality, though, these revisionist undertakings aren't so much symptoms of Kulturkampf grandi-osity as they are important markers of the final enclosure of the mindset of pietist retreat. If the evidence of history won't cooperate with the project of promoting a wider brand of personal piety, then the obvious solution is to refuse to meet history even halfway, and invent a more accommodating set of facts to safeguard your faith. This is a species of hermetic belief in the most pejorative sense of the term—reflecting not simply the inexhaustible Gnostic faith in self-reinvention that Joseph Smith or Charles Finney pro-fessed, but the deeper, claustral urge to insulate believers from history, rea-soned political debate, and social conflict altogether—while also, of course, ensuring that God grants them the last word in the drama of history. The insulated, privatized worship of the Protestant pietist inevitably comes to depend on a vision of the surrounding world as unremittingly hostile to the practice of faith. But it would be the modern movement of New Thought, which took hold among disaffected Protestant liberals, that would draw out the full Gnostic implications of this world-denying posture.

The Breath of Money

If pietists were defecting in droves from the reform tradition of postmil-lennial Protestant faith, the heirs to New England's own reform tradi-tion were divorcing themselves from the energies of Protestant revival. In the process, they found themselves venturing into strange new byways of faith. When theological liberals found the public vocations associated with evangelical preaching now seemingly closed off to them, they charted their own inward path toward a private vision of redemption.

This quest took the shape of a much more intensive romance with the Gnostic spirit unloosed during the Second Awakening. The heterodox movements gathered under the late-nineteenth-century rubric of New Thought might be mistaken for John Wanamaker's embrace of the healing and restorative powers of the simple life—except that, when viewed through the lenses of traditional observance and doctrinal orthodoxy, New Thought was anything but simple. And just as the Businessman's Revival had represented—in public terms, anyway—a new upsurge in young male participation in revived Protestant religion, so did the rise of New Thought usher in a striking new role for theologically liberal and politically progressive women, as self-ministering spiritual healers.

Little about New Thought was conventionally Protestant—and as later historians of the movement have been forced to concede after many long hours squinting over its vitalist aphorisms, even less of it was philosophically coherent. Nevertheless, the movement represents an important stage of the Money Cult's modern guise: the moment when a restive cohort of middle-class reformers staked a decisive claim on the post-material promise of Gnostic redemption. From these unlikely roots, a bold new iteration of the consumer faith would take shape in the modern era, with the meliorist scheme of postmillennial redemption migrating inward, into what New Thought devotees perceived as the only abiding spiritual reality in a cosmically corrupt and error-ridden world: the reconstructed self.

In the confusing welter of New Thought speculation, therapeutic religion was anointed as a metaphysical brand of reform. The traditional revival project of bringing about the world's betterment one converted soul at a time became morbidly inverted among the adherents of New Thought, who typically viewed the project of reform as beginning and ending with the inward saga of the believing self. By virtue of this same resolute plunge inward, the idea of social reform was downgraded into an endless regime of calisthenic spiritual self-improvement. This uniquely American crusade of the spirit—envisioning a quasi-millennial transformation of public life based on the intensive self-scrutiny of enlightened individuals—forcefully continues to shape religious and social attitudes in contemporary America.

With a minimum of conscious design, the New Thought acolytes

of the late nineteenth century, much like their theological counterparts
from the pietist wing of conventional Protestant worship, soon found that
their devotions alighted on the marketplace as the primary theater of their
redemption. However, New Thought divines typically viewed success as a
metaphysical birthright rather than a medium for upward striving. They
hailed the hard-won spiritual insights permitting them to transcend the
travails of the merely created material world as signs of their own noble
spiritual birth—as the pathway to the enlightenment of the "Higher Self,"
in the movement's jargon. But this bold scheme of redemption concealed
a deeper enervation among the ranks of the New Thought faithful: As the
New Thought cult of the self gradually overtook popular religious sensibilities, the formulas of transcendent faith at its core preached little more than
a more refined and occult embrace of the status quo. In a revealing, and
entirely typical, excursis on the theology of industrial consumer abundance,
Elizabeth Towne, publisher of the New Thought magazine *Nautilus*, delivered a version of the Protestant ethic stripped of all its trademark ceaseless
striving—a much more inert and baldly pecuniary variation on Emerson's Gnostic gospel of individualism. For Towne, as for most other New
Thought adepts, material success was a simple matter of correctly adjusted
perception—or in this instance, proper meditative breathing practices:

> The only thing that prevents us from taking plenty of money or air is
> fear . . . We take in breath of money by expanding. We force out air
> or money by contracting. The trouble with us is that we are afraid to
> expand . . . Money is *really* as free as air. Take it in by knowing that
> it is yours . . . Wake up and stretch yourself. Yawn. Take long, full
> breaths of air and money and glory. All you desire is YOURS NOW.
> Take it in mentally and work it out physically.[185]

The serene certainties that New Thought apostles brought to the
strenuous world of capitalist enterprise were of a piece with the movement's complacent outlook on every other facet of physical and spiritual
being. Indeed, New Thought's popular appeal stemmed largely from the
conviction that physical and spiritual categories of existence were iden-

tical—or that, more precisely, the realm of matter could easily be made to do the bidding of the Higher Self. This core mind-over-matter faith had the unfortunate effect of reducing most of the central conflicts and dilemmas of the believing life into flat, mechanistic formulas—as though the central problem for spiritual pilgrims in the modern age was that they were operating from an outdated owner's manual. In this enlightened view of things, all the obstacles and upheavals of spiritual life that believers had formerly experienced as crushing blows to their sense of self and meaning-ful endeavor turn out, on closer inspection, to be mere perceptual illusions.

The emotion of fear, for example, was nothing more than "a self-imposed or self-permitted suggestion of inferiority," taught one Mind Cure prophet—the famous Theosophist Madame Helene Blavatsky; embracing the thought of success would, pari passu, banish such destructive thought formations, and make one a success. The creative principle known as God lurks behind all such ingrained patterns of thought, as a force that is "latent in all individuals."[186] In this can-do model of divinity as a virtual subset of achievement-minded psychology, the Higher Self also took on a crudely mechanistic character. As the popular New Thought apostle Orisen Swett Marden preached in a 1903 article in *Success* magazine, ascending to a state of personal happiness was a simple matter of feeding better data to the aspiring self, aka the "happiness machine":

> Just make up your mind that you were made to be happy, that you are
> a happiness-machine, as well as a work-machine. Cut off the past,
> and do not touch the morrow until it comes, but extract every possi-
> bility from the present. Think positive, creative, happy thoughts, and
> your harvest of good things will be abundant.[187]

Such tidy Mind Cure aphorisms commanded a wide following in early-twentieth-century America. High-profile adherents included Greenwich Village's great bohemian impresario Mabel Dodge, the philosopher William James, and the dour realist novelist Theodore Dreiser. The enor-mously popular *Wizard of Oz* franchise of children's books teems with New Thought themes and imagery; their author, L. Frank Baum, a former department-store window dresser, salesman, and aspiring musical theater composer, was a devoted Theosophist.

As Leach demonstrates, Baum's New Thought fairy tale made itself very much at home with the same sort of market nostrums that animated John Wanamaker's more orthodox odyssey into organized mass piety. Only where the main object of Wanamaker's diffidence was political, in Baum's case it was moral. Take, for example, the climax of the first volume in the Oz series: The exposure of the mighty wizard as a bumbling, garden-variety shyster—a pivotal return to the reality principle in the famous 1939 film adaptation of the series' initial installment—occasions no great moral chastisement in Baum's books; the wizard, clearly a stand-in for Baum in his career as a tireless Midwestern promoter of spiritual fads and commercial enthusiasms, is airily described as "a very bad Wizard" but "a very good man."

Similarly, every supporting character's journey toward self-realization is its own complacent Mind Cure fable, with the Scarecrow, the Tin Woodsman, and the Cowardly Lion all coming into full possession of the latent powers of self-transformation that they had within their souls all along. Perhaps most significantly, by the series' final installment, the Emerald City of Oz itself—the shrine that the phony wizard had constructed as an homage to his frightful make-believe power—loses its initial image as a capital of untrustworthy manipulation and trickery (i.e., the kind of morally treacherous playground of vice, wealth, and inauthenticity that rural Americans such as Dorothy, the series protagonist, had long equated with urban industrial life). Indeed, in *The Emerald City of Oz*, published in 1910, Dorothy—famously identified with the mantra "There's no place like home"—has moved her Uncle Henry and Auntie Em into their own lavish home in Oz and has set herself up in her own suite within the palace, replete with "four lovely rooms," a "big marble bathroom," and a row of closets stocked with custom-tailored dresses. Here, in Oz's house of latent spiritual abundance made pleasingly real, "everything that was dear to the little girl's heart was supplied, and nothing so rich and beautiful could be found in all the department stores of America," Baum wrote.[188]

One can, of course, protest that Baum's work is a mere child's fable—but in a way, that's precisely the point. The New Thought movement, for

all of its Orientalist eclecticism and labored forays into metaphysical speculation, isn't very far removed from fairy-tale theology. No other trend in
American religious history can be so purely identified with the practice of
magical thinking, and no other spiritually inflected social ethic has been so
relentlessly upbeat in the face of the notoriously daunting questions of faith
and right conduct in a complex and rapidly secularizing industrial economy.

Indeed, the best-known thinker within the movement is something of
a Dorothy figure in her own right—a frail daughter of the old village agrarian order transformed by her own system of magical thinking into a figure
of wealth and influence in the Oz-like frontiers of mental healing in the
name of Christ. Much as Jeremiah Lanphier had symbolized the underlying currents of market-minded faith that gave rise to the prayer revival of
1857–58, so had the life story of the revered founder of Christian Science,
Mary Baker Eddy, effectively distilled many of the cultural changes at work
in the rise of New Thought. Eddy had grown up in a New Hampshire village, married young, and was widowed at the age of twenty-three, while
still pregnant with her daughter. The ordeal had preyed on her already
sensitive nerves—so much so that, as she repaired to the family home for
care, one of her sisters fashioned a modified cradle, whose rocking motions
soothed the young woman's regular and debilitating nervous attacks.

Upon her remarriage in 1853 to a dentist named James Patterson, Eddy
fell into a still more restless state of invalidism—an early precursor of the
upper-middle-class malady that physicians would later diagnose as "neurasthenia." Eventually, Eddy fell into the care of an area mesmerist and healer
with the delightful echt–New England name of Phineas Parkhurst Quimby;
Eddy's husband had gotten wind of Quimby's reputed gifts for spiritual healing, and arranged for a referral visit. Quimby restored her to health, and after
he died in 1866, Eddy suffered a relapse into nervous exhaustion, but then
proceeded to cure herself based on what she called "the Science of divine
metaphysical healing." Her husband left her the same year that Quimby
died, but she married a man named Asa Gilbert Eddy in 1877—an adept,
as Donald Meyer writes, "not unlike Quimby, in being small and mild."
The unfortunate man died five years later, succumbing in Eddy's view to the
brand of purely mental contamination she called "mesmeric poisoning."

But by then, Eddy had transformed herself into the nation's best known apostle of New Thought, with the 1875 publication of *Science and Health, with Keys to the Scripture*. Shortly after the sensational reception of her tract laying out Jesus' true divine gospel of metaphysical healing, the First Christian Church of Christ, Scientist was launched, and with it an influential New England empire of New Thought preaching, headquartered in the old Puritan stronghold of Boston. Obituaries at the time of her death in 1910 reported that Christian Scientists numbered 85,000 congregants; the church that Eddy founded, which, like its progenitor, was impatient with the empirical strictures imposed on mere material life, was more apt to cite a worldwide following numbering in the hundreds of thousands or—why not?—a few million. In reality, the Christian Scientists appeared to hit a peak membership of around 270,000 in America during World War II; latter-day estimates place the church's worldwide membership shy of 100,000.[189]

Numbers aside, two things stand out about Eddy's new healing faith: the strain of sturdy primitivism conveyed in the confident announcement that this was indeed the "First" church of Christ to preserve his mystic teachings as a healer of the body as well as the spirit; and the deeply Gnostic character of a new Christian sect ultimately committed to demonstrating the unreality of all matter in the created world.

As Catherine Tumber, one of the most astute students of the New Thought movement, has observed, the Gnostic complexion of Christian Science and its many successor faiths presents itself initially as a paradox. Emerging at the same time that the allied late-nineteenth-century movement of Mind Cure was taking hold, Christian Science was the first great modern fount of the American faith of positive thinking. Gnosticism, on the other hand, is steeped in morose cosmic pessimism of the most distraught kind. "That human beings had the capacity to 'live out' the 'unity' of life was cause for 'optimism'—'cosmic optimism,' as the title of one New Thought periodical put it," Tumber writes. "Yet in spite of this language, which New Thoughters shared with the early Social Gospel movement, they rather sought knowledge of an acosmic God who inhabited a realm alien to human struggle."[190]

Indeed, both the Gnostic and the New Thought traditions share a relentless scorn for merely created life—and both sought to subsume the shameful fallen state of physical existence into the higher truths of the spirit the duly initiated cosmic self. Held confidently aloft in the rarefied meditations of the Higher Self, New Thought believers were, largely unbeknownst to themselves, mimicking the world-denying spiritual retreats of the first-century Gnostics.

The deeper Gnostic affinities of New Thought become especially clear when the movement is laid beside its nearest point of origin, in the embattled tradition of New England reform. During the Second Awakening heyday of this tradition, the postmillennial champions of reform had sought to affirm the public role of women as a key element of their moral crusades. By the time that New Thought had worked its way into the centers of separate-sphere New England worship, however, the notion of organizing a revival faith around an agenda of public activism was largely discredited in the old citadels of reform.

This shift in sensibility was especially striking, since the rise of New Thought was in many ways a direct expression of, and response to, the spiritual plight of middle-class women confined for too long within the private realm of separate-sphere domesticity. But unlike the great corps of Presbyterian, Methodist, and Baptist women mobilized to combat social ills via the improving faith of free-will awakening, the apostles of New Thought deliberately spurned any serious vision of social reform. If the political process had been too sullying a prospect for a comparatively mild proto-Gnostic perfectionist such as Charles Finney, it became exponentially more so for the socially insular devotees of New Thought. After all, if material life was itself a delusion, the effort to improve or redeem the fallen domain of matter could be nothing but a second-order kind of hallucination, piling error upon error. Both the Gnostic and New Thought traditions place the ideals of personal self-improvement (or the pursuit of spiritual "health and wealth," as the Mind Cure tradition would be called in its mid-twentieth-century incarnation) well beyond the perceived corruptions and defeats that attend any sustained participation in public life.

If distraught and suffering believers could be made medically whole by adopting the right verbal formulations, then the true power of mind, unleashed on a mass scale, could likewise work out the world's political salvation—provided, that is, that the world at large is also left to its own laissez-faire devices. An early Mind Cure doctrine—the notion of abundant supernatural "supply" available to be tapped virtually at will by New Thought adepts—drew out the complacent, and deeply upper-middle-class, drift of New Thought's economic and social outlook. "He who lives in the realization of his oneness with the infinite Power," the great Mind Cure thinker Ralph Waldo Trine wrote in 1898, "becomes a magnet to attract to himself a continual supply of whatsoever thing he desires"—a summation of a nominalist theology of worldly abundance that is entirely of a piece with the latter-day prosperity preachments of Joel Osteen or Rhonda Byrne's *The Secret* in the spiritual marketplace of our own new millennium.[191]

In this strategic inward retreat toward an imaginary world of infinite supply, New Thought divines were not merely following the lead of their Gnostic spiritual forefather Emerson, to whom Trine was indebted for much more than his name. They were moving in full concert with the leaders of the frantically industrializing American economy—figures such as John Wanamaker, who also saw the bounty of the material world as ready and unassailable confirmation of their higher personal virtues and spiritual calling. It's customary to interpret alternative or fringe spiritual movements such as New Thought in the light of latter-day bohemian social dissent. But that approach limits us from understanding them in the full context of their times—New Thought's true spiritual home was in the mainstream of American consumer culture.

This did not only mean that otherwise hard-bitten market empiricists such as the shipping baron Cornelius Vanderbilt might indulge a weakness for spiritualism (consulting, for instance, the departed shade of the financier Jim Fisk for business counsel); the robber barons and their popular apologists also gravitated intuitively to the notion that wealth emanated from the higher properties of the self. Tireless celebrants of material prosperity, the New Thought elite nevertheless imagined themselves to be prophets of a more enlightened, *post*-materialist conception of health, wealth, and personal redemption.

This dalliance with mysticism might seem out of character, at first glance, for a Gilded Age business elite allegedly in thrall to the fashionable secular philosophy of social Darwinism, which anointed their fortunes as the just reward in the human species' epic struggle for survival. But the business leaders of the nineteenth century never paid much more than lip service to social Darwinism. They recoiled, first of all, at the rigidly secular implications of natural selection; what's more, the image of successful captains of industry as nature's most accomplished predators was far less flattering than the impression that they were both the recipients and guardians of the ineluctable workings of divine favor. As the business historian Edward Chase Kirkland notes, when contemporary journals of business opinion sought to explain important events such as the crippling recession of 1873, they dismissed the Darwinist notion that such reckonings were necessary if brutal measures employed by the natural order of things to thin out the noncompetitive herd. Social Darwinism in such contexts was merely a "fashionable philosophy," sniffed the *Commercial and Financial Chronicle* in 1874, which can do little more than "to spin its shining web and to apply its specious theories where it can." At most, the weekly allowed, the newfangled theory of social evolution was simply directed to the established folk wisdom of the market: "Experience keeps a dear school, but she teaches well." As Kirkland observes, "Darwinism may have done no more for the business community than to furnish a new terminology for old ideas."[192] The new ideas destined to beguile the lords of commerce in the century ahead would come at the behest of the New Thought movement.

The Diamond Dogma

So while the British social Darwinist Herbert Spencer might have commanded the bulk of the age's elite intellectual attention on questions of economic achievement and cosmic design, the nation's new class of business titans found much more accommodating explanations of their right conduct and metaphysical dominance coming from the prophets of the popular religious mind. And perhaps no one was better suited to champion the abundant supply of, well, spiritual supply than the celebrated Mind Cure apostle and Baptist minister Russell Conwell, the author of the best-known sermon of the age, "Acres of Diamonds"—an undeniable foundation text of the modern Money Cult.

While it's always misleading to typecast a given thinker as the Zeitgeist on horseback (to borrow Hegel's famous—if apocryphal—characterization of Napoleon), one would be hard pressed to find a better spiritual candidate for the distinction than Conwell. The Baptist preacher was, first of all, heir to the rich postmillennial tradition of New England reform: Conwell was raised by a devout Methodist family in Lexington, Massachusetts; the family home was a stop on the Underground Railroad; and the young Conwell regularly encountered fugitive slaves en route to eventual freedom in Canada. John Brown and Frederick Douglass were also guests of the elder Conwell, who ran a country dry goods store; Russell Conwell told a magazine profiler that his family prayed nightly for the deliverance of the captured Brown before he was hanged, and that his father considered selling his store to help fund the abolitionist's defense.

At the urging of an area preacher, the overachieving young Conwell was enrolled in a preparatory boarding school, the Wilbraham Academy, and sold books door to door to help pay his tuition—an early tutelage in both the rigors of self-made young manhood and the art of salesmanship that would prove decisive in his later career. After the Civil War broke out, the nineteen-year-old Conwell, by then matriculating at Yale, enlisted in the Union Army in 1862, and his Berkshires regiment named him an officer in recognition of his precocious leadership skills. On furloughs home, the young officer would deliver rousing recruiting speeches; upon his discharge, he followed the example of his great provincial frontier hero Abraham Lincoln and was admitted to the bar, eventually launching a successful practice in Boston. He also was a well-known writer of popular biographies, including campaign-supported life studies of Republican presidential candidates James G. Blaine and James Garfield. In 1881, when an aging and shrinking Lexington Baptist congregation sought his legal assistance in liquidating their decrepit church, Conwell heard them out, but then quixotically proposed restoring the building instead. Finding this too great an undertaking, he set about demolishing the structure and raising money among Lexingtonians to erect a new one in its place.

Somewhere in the midst of this campaign, Conwell, who had felt an increasingly strong calling to the ministry after he'd abandoned his youthful Methodism for collegiate agnosticism, resolved to become a preacher.

It's revealing that, like other preachers and publicists in the emerging Money Cult tradition, he came to his vocation after an initial series of false starts toward worldly renown; as with Charles Finney, Jeremiah Lanphier, and Horatio Alger, Conwell was adapting the redemptive inward certainties of gospel faith to the more visible, and ultimately more manageable, dramas of commercial achievement.

It's also telling that Conwell should have come to his calling as he carried out a real-estate deal. As he rose to unprecedented global fame, he would continue to bring home the true force of his success gospel to his listeners by summoning the all-too-visible hand of commercial providence in his preaching career. Shortly after he'd restored Lexington's Tremont Baptist Church to a prosperous state of revived membership, Conwell was recruited to fill a newly vacated Baptist ministry in Philadelphia; indeed, the congregation had hired him sight unseen, on the authority of a single deacon—and of course, on the basis of what they'd heard of the miraculous church turnaround in Lexington. This Philadelphia congregation, too, had fallen on hard times, and Conwell soon revived its membership with his trademark brand of market-minded homilizing.

He also wound up dumping the old church building and erecting a huge new temple on a newly purchased lot in downtown Philadelphia—a move that Conwell effectively urged on the church's trustees with the heartrending tale of a sick young girl in the congregation who couldn't find room to attend Sunday school in the old building. After the girl died, her father gave Conwell the 57-cent bequest she'd begun saving toward a new-church fund the new minister had promised her that he would launch. In short order, the new home on Broad Street was erected, with the property's seller insisting that the 57 pennies serve as a down-payment, and a far-better-appointed Baptist congregation in town paying the $10,000 mortgage on the parcel outright. The final structure, known as the Temple Baptist Church, was arguably the country's first megachurch, with seating room for more than 4,000 congregants, and an adjoining Sunday school, and young-men's and young-women's auxiliaries. Nor was Conwell done: Prompted by the growing cohort of young men seeking further instruction in his flourishing gospel of success, he founded Temple College (today's Temple University) in 1884.[193]

For a minister wielding such outsized cultural influence, Conwell was notably thin on intellectual achievements—another trait that would be shared by later apostles of the Money Cult. No one would mistake him for an original thinker or theological innovator; his famous "Acres of Diamonds" oration was largely made up of what he called homespun "illustrations" of his version of the true faith—all largely delivering the same core message: Untold opportunities for success and wealth lay within your grasp, and it's your God-given duty to seize them. The sermon, which Conwell delivered as many as 6,000 times before a cumulative audience easily running into the millions, is nevertheless eloquent testimony to the full identification of Protestant faith with the dictates of industrial capitalism—and to how readily the New Thought precepts of health and wealth merged with the historically populist thrust of Baptist preaching.

The sermon's opening homily concerned the story of Golconda—the legendary Indian diamond mine that yielded some of the world's most valuable and best-known jewels. The owner of the Golconda mine, legend has it, was a prosperous farmer who had misinterpreted the counsel of a Buddhist monk who'd pronounced him destined to unearth a cache of the precious stones in a preserve of clear water and white sand. He sold his farmland to trek across the world in search of these riches, and wound up committing suicide, desperately poor and hopeless, in faraway Spain. And the whole time, of course, the prophesied diamond hoard had been right under his nose, on his Golconda estate.

It was a curiously downbeat sort of success parable: *Recognize the potential riches beneath your feet*, it seemed to preach, *lest you perish by your own hand, unmourned, in a strange land*. But the redoubtable Conwell kept hammering away at the same theme, with tales of casually relinquished coal and oil fortunes in Pennsylvania, a motherlode of Massachusetts silver ignored by a hapless farmer who set out prospecting for the precious metal in the West, and the saga of the poor sap who sold Sutter's Mill—which would become the epicenter of the California gold rush—to pursue a spectacularly ill-timed bum lead on a precious-metals motherlode in southern California.

The thrust of all this homilizing, Conwell stressed, was to awaken his listeners to the bounty and riches that beckoned to them directly in their paths: "if you do not have the actual diamond mines literally," he preached, "you have all that they would be good for to you." Nothing about this promise was figurative, Conwell emphasized; he did not mean that the riches abounding were spiritualized symbols, or the prizes of biblical allegory. No, his listeners were destined to be rich, as a sign that God favored them and blessed their worldly efforts:

> The men and women sitting here, who found it difficult perhaps to buy a ticket to this lecture or gathering to-night, have within their reach "acres of diamonds," opportunities to get largely wealthy . . . I say it is the truth, and I want you to accept it as such; for if you think I have come to simply recite something, then I would better not be here. I have no time to waste in any such talk, but to say the things I believe, and unless some of you get richer for what I am saying to-night my time is wasted.[194]

Yet such exhortations sat uncomfortably beside the substance of Conwell's treasured parables of "illustration." In reality, his stories contained a much more bleak and unsettling moral, one that likewise regularly undermined the plots of the cheery success novels churned out by Alger, Conwell's New England contemporary. For these illustrations were not so much reassuring fables of lushly abundant Supply as weirdly chilling testimony to the random and impersonal workings of blind fate. The sellers of these mineral reserves were not especially feckless or wastrel souls; indeed, if anything, they were all-too-vigilant seekers after the main chance for material improvement along the American frontier (or Spanish, as the case may be). Nor were the eventual reapers of these windfalls marked by any pronounced spiritual virtue or moral rectitude; rather, they just happened to be in the right place at the right time, when a posthole pointed to a silver lode or the sand in the creek at Sutter's Mill sparkled with gold dust. This was, indeed, the great destabilizing trait in New Thought theologies of abundance and Supply: As exhortations to *perceive* the universe, and its creative sources, in a more benign and abundant light, they are largely silent on how these newly enlightened perceivers ought best to live as responsible citizens of a republic.

Indeed, as Tumber has argued, the spiritual outlook of New Thought represents a decisive break with classical republicanism, which explicitly acknowledged the randomness of fate, or *Fortuna*, as a key counterpoint to, and crucible for, the formation of civic virtue. It was Fortuna that undermined the great civic republics of the past, by subjecting them to the inevitable cyclical coruscations of corruption and wealth. Only by affirming and overcoming such sources of civic disorder could republican religious thinkers preserve the ever-frail bulwarks of civic virtue; indeed, the preservation of such a civic character amid the familiar undertow of grasping human venality was the overt aim of the separation-of-powers doctrine articulated in the Constitution and the Federalist Papers.

Yet the blissful metaphysical unities of New Thought simply dissolved all this closely calibrated tension at the heart of republican politics. That's why thinkers such as Conwell took no real notice of the shuddering abyss that yawned just beneath their confident exhortations to embrace the mystic vocation of the capitalist go-getter. Far from apportioning fortune and distress on a random grid, completely detached from mere human conceptions of moral worth and civic virtue, the Fortuna envisioned by New Thought divines was an all-conquering life force—and as Conwell preached, money was in many respects its purest expression. Money was, indeed, a failsafe *marker* of what the preachers of New Thought took to be the higher virtue of the cosmos. Conwell summed up the core postulates of the faith nicely:

> Money is power, and you ought to be reasonably ambitious to have it. You ought because you can do more good with it than you could without it. Money printed your Bible, money builds your churches, money sends your missionaries, and money pays your preachers, and you would not have many of them, either, if you did not pay them. I am always willing that my church should raise my salary, because the church that pays the largest salary always raises it the easiest. You never knew an exception to it in your life. The man who gets the largest salary can do the most good with the power that is furnished to him. Of course he can if his spirit be right to use it for what it is given to him.[195]

And much as Emerson had a half-century earlier dismissed the errant impulses of reform as a bald intrusion on his hard-won state of Gnostic repose, so Conwell derided the specter of poverty in a land of unthinkable plenty. Since all wealth needed was to be named and claimed by enlightened aspirants after it, it therefore stood to reason that poverty *had* to arise from purely personal failings, and not as a byproduct of any divine or human injustice. Virtue was by no means threatened by wealth in Conwell's post-republican vision, but the lack of wealth was most assuredly the product of a perverse and deficient spirit. While Conwell did concede that he shared somewhat in the historic Christian injunction to sympathize with the poor, he stipulated with no small show of relief that

> the number of poor who are to be sympathized with is very small. To sympathize with a man whom God has punished for his sins, thus to help him when God would still continue a just punishment, is to do wrong, no doubt about it, and we do that more than we help those who are deserving. While we should sympathize with God's poor— that is, those who cannot help themselves—let us remember there is not a poor person in the United States who was not made poor by his own shortcomings, or by the shortcomings of some one else. It is all wrong to be poor, anyhow.[196]

Clearly, capitalism and religion have entered a new state of synergy when the age's most popular Christian preachers can declaim simply that the poor are the deserving objects of God's punishment—and that it is, in addition, "wrong" either to be poor, or to extend more than vaguely pro forma fellow-feeling to the souls whom God has chosen to afflict with material want. More than that, though, thinkers such as Trine and Conwell achieved the first major breakthrough in what might be called the American metaphysics of money. By eliminating the inward spiritual tensions involved with the conventional Christian trials of sin, conversion, and conscience, the apostles of New Thought also effectively abolished the rationales for traditional Protestant public activity, including the Second Awakening's postmillennial legacy of charity, philanthropy, and reform.

Having come of turbulent age in the company of John Brown and Frederick Douglass, and having fought for the Union side in the Civil War, Russell Conwell now casually superimposed the preferences of the market on his image of the Lord. And the Lord reciprocated this market-minded devotion with the most tangible covenantal graces that a New Thought vocation could yield—a series of favorable real-estate transactions, and a lucrative ministry as a motivational speaker. Like many pilgrims of the faith in the century ahead, Russell Conwell had followed his transfigured heart all the way to a palace of his own in the Emerald City.

6

LIBERALS AT THE END OF HISTORY

Pietism and New Thought, each in different ways, explored a growing fissure at the center of the Protestant encounter with industrial-age capitalism: The solitary inward character of experience, at once the source and proof-text of Protestant conversion, had now opened onto unsure metaphysical ground. Believers could no longer be confident that salvation resided in submission either to the communal covenants of the Puritans' political economy or to any other outward source of cultural authority. With the help of a Mary Baker Eddy or a Ralph Waldo Trine, the full crisis of modern authority could be deferred—or perhaps more accurately, sublimated—by aggrandizing the spiritual self, and identifying it with the benign will of the cosmos. Alternately, by heeding the success nostrums of a Russell Conwell, the newly homeless Protestant souls of the modern age could believe that God had singled them out for special worldly favor. But these were solutions by, for, and about the believing self; twentieth-century liberal Protestants were hard pressed to find any version of a beloved spiritual community, let alone an enlivened model of Christian charity, that effectively took them outside of their own consumerist malaise.

But liberal Protestants were more than simply adrift—they were at a loss to conjure any persuasive, non-secular framework that could accommodate the embattled traditions of postmillennial social reform. Where complaints against injustice or cosmic indifference once called down demands for redoubled faith and trust in spiritual discipline—as exhorted by the jeremiad preachers of the eighteenth century—the urban and upwardly mobile adherents of both the New Thought movement and the American gospel of success were well insulated from conditions that might evoke such primal reaffirmations of covenantal faith. The emerging cult of a new American nationalism—together with the allied fantasies of permanent cultural influence within a heroically progressive Protestant liberal consensus—had prompted the leading thinkers and activists within the Protestant mainline to effectively abandon the messy, equivocal world of serious theological conflict. The beguiling pietist dream of complete social harmony that first surfaced in the evangelical business establishment in the latter half of the nineteenth century was now largely a fait accompli, so far as most apostles of religious liberalism were concerned. Without any grander plan for collective salvation obviously at stake, there was no clear reason to bother with the scut work of religious controversy—particularly when religious conservatives seemed to be growing so stolidly fanatical and unreasonable.

Meanwhile, the defeats that conservative evangelicals faced in the culture wars of the 1920s would produce an outcome quite familiar to students of American politics circa 1964: By delving deep within their own subculture of theological purity, the fundamentalist right of the interwar years was able to move into unparalleled prominence. And like the premature revolutionaries of the Goldwater era who went on to mastermind the landmark political victories of the Reagan coalition, the conservative evangelical movement of the mid-twentieth century had emerged from its long hibernation phase primed to lead—not least because it had formed a bone-deep alliance with a self-conscious new conservative business elite.

But this is all to get somewhat ahead of things. In continuing to preach a deeply individualized version of faith against a doctrinal backdrop of bland and noncommittal ecumenicalism, many liberal Protestants of the early twentieth century largely ceded the central American narrative of revival faith to their evangelical and fundamentalist opponents. As a result, the course of twentieth-century Protestantism, long interpreted as an uninterrupted string of intellectual vindications for modernist liberals, placed American faith firmly on a new conservative footing.

This meant, among other things, that when the leaders of the Christian right ascended to their present-day cultural influence, the story that they were telling about the purview of public faith was one that theological liberals had given up on long ago. Pitted against a literal-minded evangelical movement in the initial bout of the twentieth-century culture wars, liberal Protestants surrendered a good deal of what made both faith and prophecy compelling for the apostles of nineteenth-century reform: the closely held conviction that history served an ultimate purpose, and the allied faith that human efforts to remedy injustice and enact social reform were important incremental steps to realizing God's plan for the world. As religious liberals quit the main fields of historical conflict, they retreated into their own bubble of intellectual privilege— turning many theological liberals into cultural conservatives along the way.

The Colonizing Creed

It wasn't that the liberals didn't try to reinvent their faith to address the social ills of the modern industrial age. Early apostles of the Social Gospel, such as Congregational pastor Josiah Strong and Baptist theologian Walter Rauschenbusch, sought to wed the intense evangelical conviction of sin to the challenges of industrial-age social reform. As Rauschenbusch argued, modern believers needed to extend their understanding of sin beyond individual behavior to include mass poverty, unemployment, and other modern social ills as "social sins."

Rauschenbusch's insistence on sin and divine judgment as the enduring central articles of Protestant faith furnished a strong corrective to the decadent transcendentalist soundings of the New Thought movement. At the same time, his social program remained steeped in the nineteenth-century quest for the Primitive Church. Against a rapidly consolidating corporate economy, Rauschenbusch preached a reclaimed personal conception of the Kingdom of God, as exemplified in the communal social relations of the first church of the Pentecost. Rauschenbusch seized upon what would be the great animating source of theological controversy over the next century or so—modern scholarship on the intensely millennialist (and thus historicized) complexion of the oldest portions of the New Testament and the early church—as he built out his own primitivist theology from a spiritual community that expected sudden deliverance into a model for worship in the industrial age:

The primitive Christian churches were not ecclesiastical organizations so much as fraternal communities. They withdrew their members from the social life outside and organized a complete social life within their circle. Their common meals expressed and created social solidarity. Their organization at first was executive, and was devised to meet social and moral, rather than religious and doctrinal, needs. Their income was completely devoted to fraternal help . . . This fraternal helpfulness was more than mere religious kindliness. It was animated by the consciousness of a creative social mission and accompanied by a spirit of social unrest which proves the existence of a powerful current of democratic feeling . . . This impulse proves that a reconstructive social dynamic inheres in Christianity and must find an outlet in some form, slow or swift.[197]

Rauschenbusch's appropriation of the Primitive Church tradition was an astute brand of leftist restorationism, and its insistence on the affective bonds of Christian fraternity served as a strong rebuke to the contractual social ethic that dominated the other religious movements of his age. Grounded as it was in the historical scholarship of the New Testament, Rauschenbusch's theology was a much more faithful account of the practices of the early church than were the invented traditions of other primitivist movements—including those within his own Baptist denomination—which read all scripture as literal revealed truth. While Rauschenbusch sought to create new democratic institutions and movements from the precedents bequeathed by the early church, the overall thrust of primitivist faith, in the American setting, was to radically de-institutionalize the social reach of Protestant teaching—another trend in modern evangelical thought that, like the broader retreat into pietism, made ample room for the sanctification of market prerogatives.

Though Rauschenbusch's scheme of social sin and primitive observance was intellectually compelling, the Social Gospel had little more than a rhetorical appeal for the restive heirs to the traditions of liberal Protestant reform. In large part, this is because the Social Gospel was the first major push toward postmillennial reform that was divorced from any broader revival movement; Rauschenbusch's insistence on a neo-Calvinist sin-based theology was thus unable to draw on the enthusiasm of freshly minted believers. As the theolo-

gian Philip J. Lee observes, "the Social Gospel movement . . . was short-lived
and had relatively little impact outside the seminaries and denominational
bureaucracies . . . for the average person of the pew, Protestantism remained
a very *private matter* between an individual and his God."[198]

This is not to say that all varieties of the Social Gospel failed to attract
significant followings. Cincinnati pastor Josiah Strong, Rauschenbusch's
predecessor in preaching a new socially minded Protestantism, produced in
his bestselling 1885 tract, *Our Country*, a sweeping vindication of the Protestant cult of the American nation as he made a case for a more equitable
distribution of wealth in the new industrial age. Like the apostles of New
Thought, Strong grounded his appeal in an extended portrait of divinely
sanctioned abundance. In the first chapters of the book, Strong presents a
litany of statistics to prove America's unique chosen status as demonstrated
in its unparalleled economic promise. But where the leaders of New Thought
studiously shunned political matters, Strong mapped out a fiercely activist—
and frankly imperialist—role for the Protestant republic as it emerged from
the crucible of the Civil War into global dominance. Indeed, Strong insisted
that the closing years of the nineteenth century would be recognized as a
key pivot point, not only for American prosperity, but for the course of world
history. The present epoch, Strong declared, is "second in importance only to
that which must always remain first; viz., the birth of Christ."[199]

In a curious compound of exceptionalist postmillennial faith and
Social Darwinist orthodoxy, Strong ticked off a long roster of threats to
the nation's Protestant and Anglo-Saxon purity—from Mormonism and
"Romanism" to immigration and urban corruption—but, in the tradition
of a good revival preacher, he ended his lamentations on a soul-saving,
millennial note. In spite of the many perils poised to unsettle America at
its foundations, the nation still remained the leading exponent of Anglo-
Saxon civilization, Strong argues, and that noble race was clearly emerging
as the world's most prosperous people: "Among the most striking features
of the Anglo-Saxon is his money-making power—a power of increasing
importance in the widening commerce of the world's future."

An allied trait of the ur-Protestant race, Strong wrote, was "what may be
called an instinct or a genius for colonizing": "He excels all others in pushing

his way into new countries. It was those in whom this tendency was strongest who came to America, and this inherited tendency has been further developed in the westward sweep of successive generations across the continent."[200]

Strong grounds his view of America's imperial destiny on a weirdly deterministic case for the American nation's evolutionary superiority, based on factors such as climate and environment. But while this might smack of Darwinian determinism, Strong also stressed that vitality and upward mobility were the ultimate arbiters of an individual's destiny in the United States:

> Again, nothing more manifestly distinguishes the Anglo-Saxon than his intense and persistent energy; and he is developing in the United States an energy which, in eager activity and effectiveness, is peculiarly American. This is due partly to the fact that Americans are much better fed than Europeans, and partly to the undeveloped resources of a new country, but more largely to our climate, which acts as a constant stimulus . . . Moreover, our social institutions are stimulating. In Europe the various ranks of society are, like the strata of the earth, fixed and fossilized . . . Here society is like the waters of the sea, mobile; as General Garfield said, and so signally illustrated in his own experience, that which is at the bottom to-day may one day flash on the crest of the highest wave. Every one is free to become whatever he can make of himself; free to transform himself from a rail-splitter or canal-boy, into the nation's President. Our aristocracy, unlike that of Europe, is open to all comers.[201]

At the heart of this wealth of material-cum-biological advantage is the simple logic of racial preservation. While Rauschenbusch made his case for the more equitable distribution of wealth in the precedents set by the early church, Strong chiefly urged social democracy as a means of consolidating the gains achieved by Anglo-Saxons in the competition for global dominance. In much the same way that the Progressive Theodore Roosevelt would hymn the challenges of imperial conquest as part of what Christopher Lasch called "the moral rehabilitation of the ruling class," Strong heralded the twin Gilded Age legacies of New World colonialism and economic inequality as important crucibles for the Anglo-Saxon character. The polarized economy and the pagan lands of the not-yet-converted each presented an important new field of conquest for a revitalized Christian faith. And in Strong's account, the struggle against enervating wealth and pagan unbelief was destined to draw on the same racialized spirit of mastery. However, in Strong's view, the spirit of racialized conquest was also inevitably a civilizing force. The white man's burden was therefore also a Christian calling to greater generosity and charity. In this delicate reckoning, wealth had to be accumulated along the lines of the country's racial destiny—but then disbursed in an exercise of national moral rehabilitation:

> The tendency of human nature, intensified by our commercial activity, is to make the life a whirlpool—a great maelstrom that draws everything into itself. What is needed to-day is a grand reversal of the movement, a transformation of the life into a fountain. And in an exceptional degree is this the need of Anglo-Saxons. Their strong love of liberty, and their acquisitiveness, afford a powerful substitute to offer some substitute for self-abnegation. We would call no man master. We would take Christ as master. We would possess all things; we must surrender all things.
>
> One of the grave problems before us is how to make great material prosperity conduce to individual advancement. The severest poverty is unfavorable to morality. Up to a certain point, increase of poverty serves to elevate man morally and intellectually, while it improves him physically. But, as nations grow rich, they are prone to become self-indulgent, effeminate, immoral. The physical nature becomes less robust, the intellectual nature less vigorous, the moral less pure. The pampered civilization of old had to be reinvigorated from time to time with barbaric blood—a remedy no longer available. If we cannot find in Christianity a remedy or preventive, our Christian civilization and the world itself is a failure; and our rapidly increasing wealth, like the "cankered heaps of strange-achieved gold," will curse us until our destruction . . . A hundred years ago poverty compelled men to endure hardness, and so served to make the nation great. Now that we are exposed to the pampering influence of riches, Christian principle must inspire the

spirit of self-denial for Christ's sake, and the world's sake, and so make
the nation greater.[202]

This is worldly asceticism on steroids. In Strong's remarkable perora-
tion, the challenges of industrial-age wealth and poverty have ceased to be a
social problem—or even a significant obstacle for the ranks of the working
poor themselves. Instead, they are part of the far more historic and vaster
quandary of racial self-definition for the nation's Protestant moral leaders.
Where divines such as Rauschenbusch counseled the direct identification of
Christian believers with the new industrial working class as an organic extension of the doctrines of primitive Christianity, Strong preached a vitalist and
distinctly imperialist version of the American success gospel, one that was
keenly attuned to the growing sense of spiritual enervation among the country's embattled WASP elites. Yes, the acquisitive Anglo-Saxon was going to
have to learn to accept that most of his wealth would be requisitioned by God
if he wished to continue prospering—but in this way, Strong preached, the
white man's burden would soon become the white man's blessing: "He who
is infinitely blessed is the Infinite Giver; and man, made in his likeness, was
intended to find his highest blessing in the completest self-giving."[203] This,
strangely enough, is one of the earliest formulations of the prosperity gospel's
influential "seed of faith" doctrine, which preaches that believers who tender
cash donations to their home congregations or favorite televangelists can see
that seed investment multiply as much as a hundredfold. It speaks volumes
about the confusion in the house of postmillennial liberal reform that one of
the founding preachers of the Social Gospel should also be an apostle of the
unique wealth-creating powers of the WASP race.

Strong's immensely popular tract—it logged reported sales of 170,000
within the first years of its publication—captured the discontent of traditional
Protestant leaders at the dawn of America's industrial revolution. On the one
hand, the tremendous new material fortune that marked the country's postbellum maturity clearly brought new millennial urgency to the Social Gospel's brand of Christian Americanism. But for the socially engaged Christian,
ethnic and social "perils" were multiplying on all fronts; indeed, Strong issued
a revised edition of *Our Country* in 1891 that incorporated figures from the

1890 census to prove how dramatically immigration had increased. Amid such specters, the self-made man's quest for self-control leached into the broader challenge of boldly navigating the course of the country. Strong's imperialist confidence in the mission of the Anglo-Saxon meant that the Social Gospel must reach into new fringes of the American nation. Settlers along the western frontier and the urban industrial working class were prime targets for missionary-style spiritual reclamation: *Other*-made men, as it were.

The Book Nobody Knows

But such poor and marginalized populations would ultimately remain aliens, so far as Strong's cohort of WASP missionizers were concerned. In trying to "Christianize" the American nation anew, amid the great demographic changes wrought by industrialization, many Social Gospelers inadvertently exposed their own anxieties about their waning cultural and social influence. Seeking to baptize a new generation of believers within the Primitive Church tradition, the nation's Protestant elite had to rely once again on the beleaguered resources of the self. Proponents of the Social Gospel wound up almost compulsively tending to the finer points of confident self-presentation, as though the lineaments of a new Christian commonwealth could be summoned up out of the recesses of the managerial will. Through figures such as the advertising executive-turned-exegete Bruce Barton—an ardent apostle of both the Social Gospel and the new century's WASP-branded Christianity of commerce—the Gnostic homilies of New Thought were winningly repackaged, and couched in the sloganeering of the booming ad industry.

Barton's 1925 study in popular Christology, *The Man Nobody Knows*, is in many ways the book nobody knows. It's routinely name-checked in cultural histories of the twenties as Exhibit A for the triumph of the decade's booster-minded business culture: a straight-faced religious tract—and, as it happens, one of the bestselling books of the twentieth century—it puts forward the figure of Jesus as a model business executive; the cultural-studies punch lines more or less write themselves. Students of the early-twentieth century's "muscular Christianity" have likewise made much of Barton's virile, sociable portrayal of the Savior as a wood-hewing, homily-reciting son of toil in the manner of Abraham Lincoln. (Lincoln,

too, was an exemplar of spiritual fortitude for Barton, as he was for Conwell and scores of others who extolled a character-based success gospel.)

It's true enough that Barton's portrait of the managerial Jesus veers
readily into the one-dimensional sloganeering that marked the author's rise
to the top of the advertising industry as a partner in the famed New York firm
Batten, Barton, Durstine and Osborne. Readers are reminded over and over
again that, by sheer force of his charismatic leadership, Jesus commanded a
ragtag group of a dozen disciples to eventually conquer the world. The great
personal magnetism of Jesus, his "consuming sincerity," emanates—not least
for readers of Barton's own liberal Protestant persuasion—from the savior's
"faith in himself."[204] For good measure, Barton deems the parables recorded
in the gospels "the most powerful advertisements of all time."[205]

But beyond this promiscuous mingling of the languages of faith and
commerce, *The Man Nobody Knows* conveys a curiously progressive-minded
message of renewed social engagement. Indeed, in reconfiguring the New
Testament as the saga of "the founder of modern business," Barton was at
least as determined to sanctify the operations of American commerce in the
benevolent image of the early ministry of Jesus as he was to reenvision the
life of Jesus as a study in executive forcefulness. Like many twentieth-century
prophets of liberal Christianity, Barton was steeped in the great pietist dream
of the Businessman's Revival—the notion that a faith organized on the model
of the counting room would introduce a permanent culture of moral reform
within the boardrooms and trading centers of the business world.

Barton didn't craft *The Man Nobody Knows* as a celebration of masculine business values—at least not as they were preached by the leaders of the
vast and deferential financial press of the 1920s. He hails the onset of Jesus'
true adult ministry with the eviction of the money-changers from the Jerusalem temple—an episode that showcases the physical strength of the savior
(in keeping with the book's complaint that high-Victorian rectitude in Christian worship left us with an image of Jesus as "effeminate," "pale" and "flab-
by-armed"). He also highlights how Jesus the angry prophet was animated
with "a flaming moral purpose; and greed and oppression have always shriv-
eled before such fire."[206] Amid all of Barton's paeans to Jesus' marketing genius
and the toastmaster-style pleasures he enjoyed at the homes of many of his

powerful and well-known hosts in Jerusalem, *The Man Nobody Knows* argues for the recovery of the original Protestant ethic that was deeply out of step with the new consumer society taking shape in the money culture of the twenties. "Great progress will be made in the world when we rid ourselves of the idea that there is a difference between *work* and *religious work*," Barton wrote:

> Ask any ten people what Jesus meant by his "Father's business," and nine of them will answer "preaching." To interpret the words in this narrow sense is to lose the real significance of his life . . . For if human life has any significance it is this—that God has set going here an experiment to which all His resources are committed. He seeks to develop perfect human beings, superior to circumstances, victorious over Fate. No single kind of human talent or effort can be spared if the experiment is to succeed. The race must be fed and clothed and housed and transported, as well as preached to, and taught and healed. Thus *all* business is his Father's business. All work is worship; all useful service prayer.[207]

Such sentiments anchored Barton's tract clearly within the liberal Protestant mainstream—a posture that the book's many fundamentalist detractors well understood. One evangelical pamphleteer denounced Barton as "a Modernist of a rank type," and another Scriptural literalist declared that the book's modernist message "is no more a gospel of salvation than is Buddhism or Mohammedism."[208]

The invective was typically overheated, but such antagonists knew their quarry. Barton, like so many other founding apostles of the gospel of business uplift, was a minister's son—the first son born to the circuit-riding preacher William E. Barton, a Tennessee Methodist who later graduated from Charles A. Finney's great citadel of Protestant reform, Oberlin College. In his own published sermons, the elder Barton adumbrated many of the themes that would later bring fame to his son, hymning both Jesus' physical prowess and his devotion to a "life of service."[209] (The elder Barton was also, significantly, a successful Lincoln biographer, whose popular life-study of the Great Emancipator, *The Soul of Abraham Lincoln*, was briefly on the bestseller list at the time that *The Man Nobody Knows* began its three-year reign in 1925.)

The younger Barton spent his first year of college at Kentucky's Berea College, where students effectively worked off their tuition by maintaining and administering the school's physical plant; the boy's father explained that he'd deliberately steered Bruce there with the aim of placing his "sympathies always . . . on the side of the boys and girls who have to struggle for an education."[210] The younger Barton had pondered entering the ministry, but decided his father's vocation wasn't for him; still, he hewed throughout his life to the ethic of Protestant service, helping to organize Christian relief efforts during World War I, and afterward spearheading the Salvation Army's successful urban public-relations campaigns.

Even as he ascended in business, Barton propounded the Progressive Era vision of expansive popular (or at least middle-class) sovereignty. Jesus' message of universal brotherhood under a benign heavenly Father, Barton wrote, "is the basis of all revolt, the basis of all democracy. For if God is the Father of all men, then *all* are his children, and the commonest is equally as precious as the king."[211] Thus the modern era's best-known propagandist for business Protestantism strangely subscribed to a version of the Social Gospel. He never abandoned his allegiance to progressive Republicanism, but in an exchange of letters with Socialist Party leader Norman Thomas toward the end of his life, he flirted, perhaps not altogether seriously, with the notion of mounting a Socialist candidacy for Congress.[212]

Barton also brought together many of the other key movements that marked American Protestantism's passage into modernity. The whole conception of *The Man Nobody Knows* is steeped in the primary method of the anti-theology of the Primitive Church—the enterprising reading of Scripture to penetrate its original meaning via a deeper intuitive communion with its message: "to wipe [the] mind clean of books and sermons," as Barton explains in his introduction.[213] The effect of centuries of theological speculation "has spoiled the thrill of life," Barton insists, echoing the pragmatic and experiential refrain sounded so frequently by the Second Awakening's primitivist prophets. Once we discard the accretions of "creed," Barton writes, we apprehend the true miracle of Jesus: a man whose influence was "building so solidly and so well that death was only the beginning of his influence! Stripped of all dogma this is the greatest achievement story of all! . . . Books and books and

books have been written about him as the Son of God; surely we have a reverent right to remember that his favorite title for himself was the Son of Man."[214]

In the vein of other preachers of the modern world's great achievement
sagas, Barton also professed allegiance to the health-and-wealth verities of
New Thought. In summing up the fatherly indulgence in the parable of the
Prodigal Son, Barton even tacitly name-checks one of the bestselling works
of New Thought, Ralph Waldo Trine's 1897 tract *In Tune With the Infinite*:
"God laughs in the sunshine and sings in the throats of birds. They who
neither laugh nor sing are out of tune with the infinite."[215] More broadly,
Barton accentuates the healing ministry of Jesus in much the same terms
that his New Thought forerunners did—stressing both the practical impact
of his healing miracles and the aura of health that attended him during his
itinerant ministry. The Son of Man, Barton wrote, "did not come to establish a theology but to lead a life. Living more healthfully than any of his
contemporaries, he spread health wherever he went . . . He healed a lame
man, gave sight to a blind man, fed the hungry, cheered the poor, and by
these works he was advertised much more than by his words."[216]

Most obviously, Barton's portrait of Jesus as a prophet of divine abundance overlapped strikingly with the key New Thought precept of Infinite
Supply. "We speak of the law of 'supply and demand,' but the words have
got turned around," he writes. "With anything which is not a basic necessity, the supply always precedes the demand." This was the case for a litany of modern conveniences that waited many years for their full popular
adoption in the market—from the sewing machine to the Fulton steam-
boat—and it was all the more the case for Jesus' ministry: "Assuredly there
was no demand for a new religion; the world was already oversupplied.
And Jesus proposed to send forth eleven men and expect them to substi-
tute his thinking for all existing religious thought!"[217]

The Great Commoner's Lost Communion

Barton's opus is a powerful reminder of just how congruent the many strands
of American Protestant belief remained—not merely across the otherwise
divided denominational landscape of the twenties, so riven (in our retro-
spective accounts of the era) with the formulaic controversies over funda-

mentalism and modernism, but also within the mind of one of the era's most influential religious figures. Indeed, one can discern much the same set of intellectual forces at play in the work of William Jennings Bryan, the most powerful symbol of the fundamentalist rebellion, thanks to his role in spearheading the prosecution's case in the 1925 Scopes "monkey trial." Bryan, too, was a son of the progressive Protestant interior, raised in Illinois by a family of Methodists and Baptists, though he converted to Presbyterianism in his teens during a revival. Bryan famously championed a version of the Social Gospel in his early political career, likening the travails of the exploited agrarian masses and urban workers to the crucifixion of Jesus in "The Cross of Gold," his famous speech at the Populist-Democratic convention in Chicago in 1896. After his three failed presidential runs in 1896, 1900, and 1908, Bryan threw himself into ecumenical work on a number of Social Gospel fronts, from campaigns promoting pacifism and anti-imperialism to the temperance crusade. Bryan also was clearly drawn to the ideals of primitivism, embracing both the communitarian vision of the early church advanced by Social Gospelers such as Rauschenbusch, and the growing anti-Darwinist lurch toward biblical literalism within his own Presbyterian faith.

We are now so accustomed to reading back into the past the clean and absolute cleavages of contemporary culture warfare that it's disorienting to ponder a pair of formative figures such as Bryan and Barton occupying the same divided space in the wars between evangelical certitude and secular modernity. But their spiritual odysseys are key exemplars of the divided mind of liberal Protestantism in the early twentieth century. Much as John Wanamaker longed for a simpler life of unmannered piety as he multiplied the consumer desires of a vast new national retail market, Barton and Bryan looked to purified versions of a Primitive Church gospel as the unlikely panacea for the ills of an industrializing mass society that they could only bring into partial alignment with their visions of social redemption.

Indeed, for all the gospel certitude that figures such as Barton and Bryan share, it's never quite clear just what kind of ideal society they're describing. Barton's evocation of Jesus' world-conquering managerial genius rests strangely—and uneasily—on his hero's credentials as a rural outcast. Jesus isn't so much a self-made man, in Barton's reverent telling, as he's a creature shaped to a striking degree by his environment. For all of Barton's eagerness to depict the Savior as a sought-after dinner guest and toastmaster, a pronounced antisocial streak still inheres in the gospel according to Barton. Just prior to the climactic meditation at Gethsemane—when Jesus renounces the idea of serving as merely a worldly Messiah, or a revolutionary leader for the disenfranchised Jews suffering under the oppressive rule of ancient Rome—Barton imagines this question-settling scene:

> Then he saw the other picture—the vast dumb multitudes of men, his brothers and sisters, squeezed dry of vision and hope by the machinery of formalism. He saw generations born and die in spiritual servitude which nothing could end except the Truth that he had come to declare. To put himself at the head of this army of fanatical patriots would be to risk his life and perhaps his message with it. But worse than the possibility of failure was the possibility of success. To be king of the Jews would mean a lifetime spent in the defense of his throne and title, a lifetime of bloodshed and intrigue, while his message remained unspoken.[218]

In spiritual servitude which nothing could end: In this ultra-confident business booster's account of Jesus' life, the prelude to the Savior's final passion is rendered in the starkest Gnostic terms imaginable. Engagement with the world and the sphere of historical conflict is rendered in this climactic moment of Jesus' ministry as an unthinkable spiritual degradation—an existential defeat, even if it resolves into success on its own terms. In this undercurrent of despair over any worldly prospects, Barton betrays a telltale metaphysical distrust of the ideal self created under the urban capitalism that he celebrated so effectively in his day job at BBDO.

In the wake of his third failed presidential run, William Jennings Bryan certainly harbored no such compunctions about getting and holding worldly power. But he was also, in significant ways, a figure adrift: a revivalist crusader in a new age of corporate-financed political campaigning; an agrarian populist scourge of "the money power" as the American frontier closed and urban commerce increasingly propelled the national economy; a producer's tribune in a fast-consolidating consumers' republic. And of course, there's the identity that has been bequeathed to him by secular culture scolds such as H. L. Mencken, and the authors of the 1950s Broadway hit *Inherit the Wind*: the diehard foe of the theory of evolution, witlessly expounding the principles of biblical literalism in the face of a modern scientific consensus that had long passed him by.

That Bryan is now known almost exclusively in this latter role, as the buffoonish whipping-boy for generations of smarty-pants secular liberals, again speaks volumes about the impoverishment of our moral imagination when it comes to the intersection of faith and public life. In political terms, the Bryan crusades of 1896, 1900, and 1908 were far more than a last-ditch ghost dance for the fading small-town barons of Protestant reform; they were arguably the last serious bid to shore up popular economic sovereignty in the history of our national politics. Yet the Bryan who manned the reactionary right flank of the science-and-religion wars has been largely divorced in the popular mind from the cause that mattered to him most: reclaiming the American republic and its political institutions for the people who actually produced the lion's share of the country's wealth.

When Bryan and other divided minds on the religious left failed to meet the fundamental challenges of modern thought, the closely calibrated balance between individual religious experience and broad-based social reform swung in a fateful new direction. In the emerging division of spiritual labor that Bryan's career presaged, the market was to become the unquestioned repository of the ideal Protestant self, while the urgent course-of-history concerns that so exercised previous generations of postmillennial Protestant reformers succumbed to the far more compelling and popular conservative movements of premillennialism and biblical literalism.

Bryan tailored his personal calling to these changed circumstances, dividing the time since his ouster from the Wilson administration over entry into World War I between well-remunerated duty as an inspirational lecturer and ill-advised speculation in the booming Florida real-estate market of the 1920s. In this embrace of the new modern gospel of self-engineered success, Bryan was only following the well-trodden path of public-minded divines into the great modern enterprise of Gnostic self-help. But his theological outlook, like that of many Americans in the wake of the debacle of the Great War, had taken a pronounced and sour turn to the right.

To appreciate the full trajectory of Bryan's shift, it's first necessary to consider the fate of economic democracy in the politics of the Gilded Age. In 1896, when Bryan, a boyish thirty-six-year-old former Nebraska congressman, first stormed to the top of the Democratic Party's presidential ticket, the national political scene was convulsed with the question of money and credit in a way that's completely unrecognizable to the post-meltdown, bailout-addled regime of economic management on both sides of today's partisan aisle. Smarting from long-standing grievances with banks and transportation trusts, the nation's farmers had mounted an effective third-party insurgency, with the cooperative movement spearheaded by the Southern and Western Farmers' Alliance moving into electoral politics under the rubric of the People's Party—or Populists, as they came to be known. In the face of a new set of economic depredations stemming from the American republic's rough passage into the industrial age, the Populists sought to revive the Jeffersonian founding spirit of the Democratic Party. At the center of their crusade was what might be called the physiocrats' view of the true nature of wealth: the idea that productive activity was measured in material commodities (i.e., crops, finished manufactures, and the handiwork of artisanal laborers), rather than by the subterfuges of monopoly or financial manipulation. Populists saw themselves as the true creators of wealth, and the nation's owning and financial classes as a conspiratorial ring of expropriators of that wealth. In some ways, this was an oversimplified account of the complexities of modern economic life—much as Jefferson's original vision of the yeoman farmer as the ultimate guarantor of political liberties made little ultimate allowance for the growth of a national market along the country's western frontier, largely endowed to the American republic by Jefferson himself.

Still, the Populists' account of the antidemocratic shift in America's economic life was in some ways a bracing clarification. In 1893, at the moment that the Democratic administration of Grover Cleveland suspended the redemption of silver specie in the nation's treasury in a misguided bid to revive the country's flagging commerce through "sound money"—i.e., a gold-backed currency—the country had suffered a crippling recession. In reality, any measure like the gold standard that tightens the circulation of currency always works to the advantage of creditors, who are repaid the

money they loan out to debtors in money that's more valuable than it was at
the time the loans were contracted. Since small farmers almost always have
to go into debt to cover the increased expenses of planting and harvesting—
to say nothing of making good on major shortfalls that arise from droughts
and other weather emergencies—the agrarian classes of the late nineteenth
century were plunged into deepening debt, a condition that looked to be
permanent with Cleveland's redoubled embrace of the gold standard. At a
minimum, Populists began demanding the remonetization of silver, to be
minted over gold at a ratio of 16 to 1; only by such an expansion of the
money supply, they argued, would desperately needed financial relief reach
the nation's debt-strapped producing classes. (The more ambitious policy
minds in the Populist movement—those affiliated with the original Farmers' Alliance cooperatives—contended that the agitation for "free silver" was
largely a distraction, and almost certainly a co-opting of more fundamental
guarantees of economic democracy, such as the creation of a whole currency
weighted to actual wealth production; a system known as the Subtreasury
Plan, which would go on to furnish the model for the Federal Reserve.)

Free silver was the fulcrum that permitted Bryan—merely a boy ora
tor by the standards of major-party presidential strategists, with but two
terms in the House of Representatives and a failed run for the Nebraska
senate on his résumé—to win the 1896 nomination during the fused Democratic and People's Party conventions in Chicago. Bryan's candidacy not
only lent the Populist insurgency the support of a major-party infrastructure; it also advanced an explicitly religious critique of the foundations
of industrial capitalism. And the failure of this first great Bryan crusade
foreshadowed the collapse of the prophetic Protestant creed of economic
justice. Bryan titled his memoir of the historic 1896 campaign *The First
Battle*, but in terms of the nation's shifting cultural and religious consensus, the first in this case truly was destined to be the last.

The causes of Bryan's 1896 electoral defeat were the same forces that
monotonously poleaxe most reform movements in our politics: unrestrained
campaign spending from big-ticket economic interests, the official media's
prostration before power, and the fragmenting of reform-minded coali-
tions into pet policy obsessions and general infighting. But at its deeper

levels, the landmark failures of Populist-Democratic fusion pointed up an unresolved tension at the heart of the Protestant encounter with modernity: Was salvation in this world ultimately consonant with the challenges of social reform? Or, to put things another way: Had Bryan's core audience of the faithful become sojourners in a strange new social order?

This dilemma came through powerfully in what was by far the best-known summation of the Bryanite producers' creed: his famed "Cross of Gold" oration at the 1896 Democratic convention. Prior to that speech's stirring, and baldly Protestant, climax—"You shall not press down upon the brow of labor this crown of thorns, you shall not crucify mankind on a cross of gold"—Bryan enumerated the ways in which the moneyed interests distorted the true character of the nation's productive life in their campaign for the gold standard. After all, he explained,

> The man who is employed for wages is as much a businessman as his employer, the attorney in a country town is as much a businessman as the corporation counsel in a great metropolis; the merchant at a crossroads store is as much a merchant as the merchant in New York; the farmer who goes forth in the morning and toils all day . . . and who by the application of brain and muscle to the natural resources of the country to create wealth, is as much a businessman as the man who goes upon the board of trade and bets upon the price of grain; the miners who go a thousand feet into the earth, or climb a thousand feet upon the cliffs, and bring forth from their hiding places the precious metals to be poured into the channels of trade are as much businessmen as the financial magnates who, in a backroom, corner all the money in the world.[219]

As Bryan's biographer Michael Kazin notes, Bryan's hymn to the humble industry of the nation's real producers of wealth conspicuously omitted the industrial working class. "The only wage earners he singled out for praise were miners," Kazin writes, "most of whom toiled in company towns quite dissimilar from the swelling metropolises where factory hands and building tradesmen lived and worked."[220] What's more, of course, Bryan suggests that the heroic efforts of the nation's miners ultimately *aren't* all that productive, in terms of the wider aims of economic equity. They yield the precious metals that unscrupulous urban "financial magnates" employ to prop up their monopolies of exchange—unless, that is, they happen to be mining silver.

More than Bryan's well-documented agrarian outlook, though, the Great Commoner disclosed in his three runs at the presidency a disabling penchant for sentimental individualism, entirely of a piece with the pietist turn of nineteenth-century Protestantism. Sizing up Bryan's quixotic and characteristically principled 1900 rematch against made-to-order GOP machine nominee William McKinley, Kazin observes that, in turning the election into a referendum on America's imperialist invasion of the Philippines, Bryan helped seal the new century's verdict on his own brand of Protestant reform. After McKinley had far outspent—and via his running-mate surrogate, the arch-imperialist Teddy Roosevelt, also out-campaigned—his righteous opponent to claim a decisive reelection victory, legions of faithful Bryanites soon modified their scriptural interpretations of the life and career of their spiritual hero. No longer poised to deliver rural and small-town Christian America from the snares of the money power and the burgeoning American empire, the Great Commoner was downgraded from savior to prophet. And Kazin further notes that the embattled Bryan crusade subtly shaded its substance into the stuff of Victorian melodrama:

> The notion of the unsuccessful politician as a prophetic hero was drenched in melodrama, a genre ubiquitous in American culture at the time. Men and women who wept at Dickens' novels and *Uncle Tom's Cabin* (the play as much as Stowe's book), who thrilled to the sermons of Henry Ward Beecher (whether or not they agreed with his liberal theology) and the temperance homilies of Frances Willard, and whose altruistic imagination was kindled by [Edward] Bellamy's *Looking Backward* could find in Bryan a sympathetic scourge of the privileged and the greedy.[221]

It's one thing, of course, for a political leader to suffer the scorn of his opponents—Bryan faced plenty of that in 1896, as the GOP faithful excoriated his insurgent Populist campaign as everything from the feckless propagation of a platform "made in hell" (in the estimation of Brooklyn Baptist minister Cortland Myers) to "fundamentally an attack on our civilization," as Roosevelt famously thundered from the stump that year.[222] But it's something else for his own supporters ultimately to condescend to his agenda—to treat him like the restive Zeitgeist of a dying age. Bryan's populism, so often assailed by later progressive-minded liberals as a terminally nostalgic bid to impose small-town Protestant moral probity on a national scale, was significantly hailed by many Bryanite voters themselves as a backward-looking movement, even in its own heyday: a sop to their own receding image of their more confident, halcyon days as the laborers, farmers, and merchants accorded due pride of place in the Jeffersonian republic. Even at the height of his popularity, in other words, Bryan was embraced as something close to a museum piece for a white Protestant electorate in the rural South and West that was hard pressed to come up with a vision of a beloved community or Christian commonwealth for the industrial age.

This failure to articulate a broad-based, post-yeoman-age vision of economic equality was a notorious shortcoming of all of Bryan's presidential campaigns, which hinged more on an appeal to individual conscience than on any direct challenge to entrenched economic interests. As Kazin observes about Bryan's most successful failed campaign—the 1908 challenge to William Howard Taft, in which both nominees ran on rhetoric-heavy platforms pledging to curb the abuses of large business trusts—Bryan's crusade was long on targeted speechifying and party discipline but tellingly short on policy detail:

> He had no grand solution to corporate malfeasance distinct from that espoused by TR and Taft. Each man would intervene, with the help of Congress and the courts, to force big business to heed the public's desire for a marketplace governed by rules of fairness and equity. None would attempt to destroy the oligopolies on which increasing numbers of Americans depended for goods, services, and jobs. Audiences cheered when Bryan vowed to humble the trusts and restore an economy where the little man could thrive. But neither he nor his allies had the vaguest idea of how best to bring that about.[223]

For Taft to be vague on the specifics of antitrust agitations was a tactical strength, since the Republicans were the party of business, and only interested in creating enough of the appearance of economic reform to quiet the policy elites in the party's Progressive wing. But Bryan's myopia on the question ran far deeper; his approach to political reform was, in its innermost parts, a species of revivalism. This outlook came across most clearly in the work that propelled Bryan to his most abiding mass following: his career as a lecturer on the Chautauqua circuit—the late nineteenth century's signature delivery system for Protestant cultural uplift. The annual summer Chautauquas in small or mid-sized communities across the Midwest offered a combination of earnest instruction, inoffensive middlebrow entertainment, and inspirational speaking. It was in this latter sphere that Bryan became the unexcelled master. His two best-known speeches on the circuit—"The Value of an Ideal" and "The Prince of Peace"—he delivered some three thousand times, before audiences that easily numbered in the millions.[224] In the former oration, Bryan gave the fullest account of his political philosophy; in structural terms, it was not much different from Conwell's famed "Acres of Diamonds" sermon, but its content was much more suited to Social Gospel–style reform. It was folly, Bryan announced, to suppose that successful men—or anyone else, for that matter—were self-made; their fortunes and fates sprang from the collective forces of their environment. (This environment-first message was, among other things, a curious disclaimer from a public figure who would become best-known, decades later, as a diehard foe of the teaching of evolution.)

If individuals were helpless to form themselves, so, too, were they helpless collectively, Bryan preached. Just look at the state of the nation's leading political institutions: "Men sell their votes, councilmen sell their influence, while State legislators and federal representatives turn the government from its legitimate channels and make it a private asset in business." Here the Protestant reformers' outlook truly verged on a critical breakthrough—the frank acknowledgment that the mediating forces of the American republic entrusted to embody a higher public good had been corrupted fatally from within. Tellingly, however, the practiced Democratic also-ran grounded his case for reform not in a call to group action, but rather in a roused individual passion for moral improvement. "We must appeal to the conscience," Bryan admonished his listeners, "not to a democratic or a republican conscience, but to an American and to a Christian conscience and place this awakened conscience against the onflowing tide of corruption in the United States."[225]

A similar call to postmillennial reform via individual, inward expressions of piety suffused Bryan's other great Chautauqua oration, "The Prince of Peace." In this two-hour performance, Bryan briefly cited, and dismissed, the brewing controversies over Darwinism and the biological origins of human life with the confident claim that the vast energetic activity of creation must evince "a Designer back of the design." But such speculations should take a backseat, Bryan stressed, to the practical wonders that Christian faith works in the lives of individual believers. In Bryan's account, belief in the social maxims of the Bible worked into a sort of calisthenics program for the perplexed individual soul. He predicted that "if we try to live up to what we do understand, we will be kept so busy doing good" that such speculative matters as the disposition of the Creator's role in the creation would fade into the background. The key, he argued, was to institute a "personal responsibility to God at the center of the faith," along with a regimen of right conduct based on Jesus' ethical teaching. The results, Bryan maintained, would speak splendidly for themselves: "What greater miracle than this, that converts a selfish, self-centered human being into a center from which good influences flow out in every direction!"[226]

As with Barton's spirited endorsement of the muscular, businesslike Christ, Bryan's vision of the salutary benefits of believing for the aspiring altruist/activist is clearly indebted to the therapeutic outlook of New Thought. Indeed, Bryan's bestselling chronicle of the 1896 campaign, *The Last Battle*, ended with an inspirational poem by popular New Thought poet Ella Wheeler Wilcox, in which she neatly evoked an intersection of social reform and sentimental individualism. Wilcox's oddly sunny anatomy of the '96 debacle proposed that the hard work of reform would be ultimately subsumed by a higher order of historical synthesis, in which conflicts would one day be "settled right," in a classic flourish of postmillennial optimism:

However the battle is ended
Though proudly the victor comes
With fluttering flags and prancing nags
And echoing roll of drums
Still truth proclaims this motto
In letters of living light,—
No question is ever settled
Until it is settled right.[227]

Paradoxically enough, this sort of faith is best sustained by limited exposure to the abrasive world of political engagement, as the later migration of New Thought into both the resurgent primitivism of the Pentecostal movement and the sprawling twentieth-century market in business-inspirational literature would soon make abundantly clear. The step from the conscience-driven precepts of Bryan's crusading Populism to the quiescent motivational jargon of the rising modern cult of business perfectionism proved to be a short one.

Ironically enough, in the latter phase of his career, Bryan himself anticipated the fastidious and deeply individualized course of the liberal Protestant. After his final presidential run in 1908, Bryan—a lifelong teetotaler who'd declined to take any stand on the liquor question in deference to the Democratic Party's immigrant and Catholic strongholds in northern cities—swiftly full-throated support to prohibition. Bryan's advocacy sparked broader Democratic support for the dry cause—so much so that by the time prohibitionists had mounted their successful press for approval of the Eighteenth Amendment in Congress, they were able to yoke it to the other utopian Progressive cause of the day: American entry into the Great War. The best-known national lobbyists for the liquor industry were recent German immigrants, so it was a simple enough matter to harness raging anti-German war hatreds to the moral crusade to purge the American republic of demon rum. (Even though Bryan himself famously dissented against American entry into World War I, and was forced to resign his post as Woodrow Wilson's secretary of state on the question, Progressive backers of the propaganda campaign against the rampaging Huns made the most of the country's growing wartime xenophobia: They also targeted the fledgling fundamentalist movement on the Christian right, with decidedly more mixed results, as we shall see in the next chapter.)

Populist Science

Bryan's ardent prohibitionism anticipated his no-less-ardent embrace of the anti-evolution cause. And in both cases, significantly, he continued to explore the question of how best to groom and cultivate the development of the individual moral self. Hailing a 1909 vote in his adopted hometown of Lincoln, Nebraska, to outlaw liquor traffic, Bryan exhorted the readers of his long-running political weekly *The Commoner* to greet the news as a critical breakthrough for "popular government"—but also as a vital step along the path of Christian perfectionism: "The moral awakening upon which the nation is entering is making both the individual and the public conscience more sensitive," he wrote in an editorial headlined "Let the People Rule."[228] In later press interviews he hailed the spread of prohibitionism as evidence of a "world-wide religious awakening" that was spurring "signs of uplift all along the line."[229]

That same focus on the optimal conditions of individual spiritual self-improvement propelled Bryan's later embrace, in the 1920s, of a preacher's vocation—albeit without a formal seminary degree or a fixed congregation. Bryan took up his bully revivalist pulpit in part because he was convinced that the scourge of modernist theology, abetted by Darwinist science, was leaching away at the foundations of the reformist faith he'd extolled from the campaign stump. It's crucial to grasp the continuities between Bryan's embrace of the anti-evolutionist cause and his political past, since the dominant image of Bryan in our popular culture is of the jowly, censorious fundamentalist bigot portrayed by Frederic March in the 1960 film adaptation of the Broadway dramatization of the Scopes trial, *Inherit the Wind*. (It's worth noting as well that this self-congratulatory liberal fable loosely based on the "trial of the century" is doubly misleading, since it not only depicts its fictionalized Bryan character as an arch-fundamentalist, but also seizes upon the trial as an allegory for the McCarthy-era Red Scare—the kind of anti-radical inquisition that Bryan had vigorously protested throughout his political career.)

In his bestselling 1923 tract, *In His Image*, based on a lecture series delivered to a Richmond, Virginia, Presbyterian seminary, Bryan laid out the ways in which Darwinian evolution was subverting the core principles of Christian nurture. Echoing critics of harsh pseudoscientific initiatives such as the eugenics movement, Bryan charged that introducing Darwinism into school curricula was tantamount to endorsing untrammeled social predation and exploitation—an empirically misguided, but entirely consistent, claim for someone who touted the Christian faith as the ideal remedy for selfishness. If American children were schooled in evolution, Bryan argued, they would cease altogether to sympathize with the plight of "the weak and the helpless," and must logically spurn belief in a divinity "ready to give at any moment the help that is needed." The only way to protect the beleaguered foundations of Bryan's Social Gospel was to bar these wicked doctrines from public schools. Bryan contended, not altogether ingenuously, that this stance was not censorious so much as it was an extension of the simple Bryanite principle of safeguarding the people's rule, in the electoral and cultural realms alike. Private schools could adopt any secular scientific curricula they chose, Bryan suggested. But it was plainly critical, in Bryan's view, to withhold public funding and sanction for "atheism, agnosticism, Darwinism, or any other hypothesis that links man in blood relationship with the brutes."[30] This portrait of democratic education as a direct expression of popular sovereignty—using public resources to fund only curricula that reflected popular religious sensibilities—was, among other things, a curious inversion of the principle of church-and-state separation that Bryan's hero Thomas Jefferson had famously advanced in his Virginia statute upholding religious freedom.

By the time Bryan and his allies had mounted their courtroom defense of the Tennessee law forbidding the teaching of evolution in the state's schoolrooms, Bryan's focus on the role of religious morality in the cultivation of broader civic virtues had predictably fallen altogether out of the public debate over evolution. Both the denominational schisms and the obsessive press coverage that stoked public controversy over the issue turned on the flattened-out, binary opposition of one oversimplified narrative (that of the biblically literalist account of the origin of the human species in Genesis) against another (that of the militantly secular appropriation of Darwin's teaching, as exemplified by Bryan's courtroom foe and longtime political ally, Clarence Darrow). This scripting of the conflict permitted partisans on all sides to maximize their sense of cultural superiority without ever approaching anything close to a reasoned accord. Thus the whole spectacle was primed to enter the national folklore of culture warfare long before the jeering anti-Bryan memorials penned by H. L. Mencken and the revived Cold War Broadway narrative of the conflict so successfully dramatized in *Inherit the Wind*. The trial's legal outcome was all but foreordained: The Dayton, Tennessee, jury upheld the state law, and convicted the defendant, John Scopes, of teaching Darwinian science to his high-school students. Given the shifting currents of the modernist-fundamentalist controversy, it was just as predictable that Darrow would triumph in the court of public opinion over the plainly aging and ailing Bryan, who died within a week of the Scopes verdict.

Lost in the hoopla surrounding the Scopes trial was the steady diminution of William Jennings Bryan's social vision—an odyssey that prefigured much of the course of politicized religion in the century ahead. Beginning firmly in the tradition of postmillennial social reform, Bryan understood political life as a natural extension of revivalist faith. "When you hear a good democratic speech," he announced in the pages of *The Commoner* on the eve of the 1904 election, "it is so much like a sermon that you can hardly tell the difference between them."[231] And Bryan's campaigns were indeed much like sermonizing tours of the nation; he basically pioneered the barnstorming modern presidential campaign, and his three runs at the presidency also effectively doubled as hortatory conversion crusades aimed at steering the people's will toward his reform issue of the hour: bimetallism in 1896, anti-imperialism in 1900, and trust-busting in 1908. In all these efforts, Bryan effectively depicted his campaign's defining issue as a pivotal moment of *self*-definition for Americans beholden to the one true faith of Christian self-rule. Would they permit shadowy moneyed elites to continue to extort the virtuous producing classes out of their right livelihood— via either the plutocracy's control of the White House, or its mastery of allied institutions of power such as the banking system, the military, and the courts? Or would they come together to invoke the sturdy protections of popular government, as crafted by their Jeffersonian forebears, and as vouchsafed to them in the preachings of the Social Gospel?

After the voting public rejected Bryan's successive appeals to their Christian conscience, the Great Commoner began to tinker with the broader forces that, in his view, had been leading the moral outlook of the individual American astray. Bryan the Populist was thus driven, by his own political logic, to become Bryan the anti-modernist. (As Kazin and his other biographers note, Bryan was never in any theological sense a fundamentalist; he neither owned, endorsed, nor, apparently, read *The Fundamentals*, the founding tracts of the fundamentalist movement, and was chiefly interested in promoting biblical literalism not for its own sake, but for what he saw as its practical efficacy in the formation of human character and virtue.) Bryan's long-professed and unqualified faith in the people as the obvious fount of both political and moral sovereignty thus wavered subtly as he endorsed the increasing use of the federal state and the legal system to collaborate in the cultural project of making a better people. It's true that Bryan still applied the yardstick of popular sovereignty to his newfound cultural crusade; in championing his failed proposal for his own Presbyterian denomination to withhold official approval from any educational institution that "seeks to establish a materialistic evolutionary philosophy of life," Bryan explained he was once again only advancing the principle of majority rule. "It is deplorable that there should be a division on matters so plain," he wrote in a letter to the editor of the *Christian Herald* in 1922, "but . . . the believers in evolution number less than ten per cent of the professing Christians . . . we cannot make a religion to suit only those who have a college education." After all, Bryan explained, Jesus himself "selected His followers from the common people—fishermen, tent makers, etc. . . . He himself worked in a carpenter shop."[232]

Bryan's sentimental apostrophe to Jesus the man of the people was, strikingly, much the same case that Bruce Barton—a far more theologically liberal and stridently pro-business prophet of a more modern version of the Christian faith—was mounting on behalf of Jesus the model manager. Yet in the climate of the 1920s, the new national sport of culture warfare blotted out the affinities that these rival thinkers plainly shared when it came to the challenge of recasting a primitive Christian faith in the face of strange new modes of modern thought and living. As it turns out, Bryan's invocation of the vox populi Christ was far more fundamentally misguided than Barton's. The findings of science actually *don't* hinge on plebiscite votes, and the Great Commoner's suggestion to the contrary was irresponsible at best and demagogic at worst. Nor did advances in knowledge map directly onto class distinctions, as Bryan's invidious mention of the college-educated cultural elite implied.

But of course this is the sort of drive-by dismissal of elite pretensions to social superiority that has since become the main artillery on the right flank of the American culture wars. And you can't help but discern a certain cunning historical genius at work as you behold its early manifestation in the rhetoric of a Populist devotee of the Social Gospel, who variously campaigned to revamp our currency to favor the debtor class, to nationalize the railroads and telephone industries, to institute strict regulations on bank deposits, and to purge corporate money from the American campaign system. It would be a far greater irony that anti-evolutionists who initially disowned Darwin's theory in the spirit of Bryan—holding that it modeled unseemly self-seeking, greed, and predation for the nation's young—would in future decades be replaced by the country's most ardent apologists for laissez-faire capitalism, i.e., the very economic system that Social Darwinists aggressively championed as foreordained by human genetic destiny.

Bryan's much-caricatured image as the ignorant tribune of hillbilly reaction (memorably summarized in Mencken's famous 1925 Bryan obituary, *In Memoriam*) now permits us to overlook the momentous transformation in cultural politics and religious thinking about the economy that his late career foreshadowed. That's because the Great Commoner's individualist focus on behavioral reform rendered him an inviting target for secular ridicule from Menckenite scoffers who eagerly embraced their elite status among what Mencken was pleased to call the "civilized minority." In a telling but little-noted reversal, the partisans in the struggle over the cultural fallout from Darwin's theory were now in the process of switching sides: Majoritarian liberals who had formerly endorsed an industrial-age version of the Christian commonwealth—what the utopian novelist Edward Bellamy, the New England–bred descendant of Jonathan Edwards's protégé, Joseph Bellamy, had famously dubbed "the religion of solidarity"—would opt more and more often for the competitive-minded outlook on nature and God that came with the Social Darwinist creed. And the debunking elitists of the twenties Kulturkampfs grew increasingly comfortable in the role of representing the improvers of society for the good of all—the position that had, in other words, been the fallback of several generations of postmillennial reformists.

Curiously enough, it was only the chief propagandists in the Dayton battle who would forever remain frozen in amber, in their assigned Victorian-age outlooks on cultural progress and political economy. The arch-secularist Mencken would become a bitter foe of New Deal liberalism, inveighing against the lumbering social engineering of the Washington bureaucracy—while Bryan, for all of his later renown as a backward and backwoods preacher of social reaction, would soon anchor much of his policy agenda in the New Deal reforms of the thirties, from the public ownership of utilities to the community regulation of banking and the forfeit of the gold standard. But both figures were increasingly irrelevant to an emerging popular religious landscape that counterposed the stark dictates of premillennial prophecy and the emollients of consumer capitalism—wherein the longstanding evangelical cult of the American nation would serve as the staging ground for history's climactic conflict with the Antichrist. And to confuse matters further, these anti-modern augurs of the millennium were, in terms of both their communications strategies and their economic philosophies, exemplars of modern innovation, preaching the verities of apostolic prophecy and free-market fundamentalism over the national airwaves and in gleaming new temples of celebrity. Just because the world was abruptly poised for the Final Judgment didn't mean that there weren't still money to be made and biblically sanctioned economic liberties to be defended.

Indeed, the entire pat staging of the Scopes trial, like so many other set pieces in the annals of American culture warfare, obscures and distorts the actual state of the era's religious and political consensus. Despite the public drubbing suffered by the anti-evolution cause in Dayton, overall church attendance was on the upswing throughout the twenties. And in contrast to the role of culturally chastened underdogs that many standard religious histories have carelessly scripted for the anti-modern wing of Protestantism in the wake of the Scopes debacle, the forces of religious primitivism and Gnostic redemption were actually poised to emerge in a powerful new capitalist synthesis—freshly aligned in a buoyant new incarnation of the American Money Cult.

7

HOLY ABUNDANCE

William Jennings Bryan died just days after the Scopes verdict in 1925—the same year that *The Man Nobody Knows* launched its three-year reign on the bestseller lists. Each event was in its own way a landmark in the breakup of the Protestant reform tradition—yet most standard accounts of Protestant faith in the wake of the Scopes trial treat the ensuing three decades as something of a golden age of religious liberalism. It's true enough that theological liberals had the better of the intellectual arguments dramatized in the Dayton show trial—but it's just as true that economic, religious, and political debate in America rarely hinge on intellectual consistency or reason. In reality, fundamentalists did strategically retreat from the public stage immediately after the Scopes debacle—but conservative evangelicals emerged from that period of self-imposed exile with a firmer sense of missionary purpose, and a determination to draw upon the saving truths of the old-time religion to revive not merely the embattled church, but the entire moral character of Christian America.

The sturdy narrative arc of contemporary culture warfare—pitting liberal modernists against fundamentalist conservatives in mediagenic controversies over science education, gender and sexuality issues, arts funding, foreign policy, and the like—has blinded many observers to the deeper realignment of Protestant belief in concert with the Money Cult. In this familiar saga, conservative evangelicals have been cast as staunch anti-modernists, determined to hold the line of fidelity to biblical literalism, traditional family life, and small-town civic piety against the corrosive forces of secular progress. Yet even in Bryan's day, this broad caricature was at best a half-truth. Evangelicals readily adapted to the leading messaging formats of the modern age by crowding into urban revivals and supporting far-flung radio ministries. Celebrity preachers such as Dwight Moody, Billy Sunday, and Aimee Semple McPherson attracted huge followings, and preached in well-appointed sanctuaries in major cities—not the backwoods tent-revival gatherings immortalized in Sinclair Lewis's 1927 satire of evangelical hypocrisy, *Elmer Gantry*.

In theology, too, conservative evangelicals adopted innovative models of scholarship and interpretation, however unwittingly. Indeed, the signature fundamentalist doctrine of premillennial dispensationalism—dividing up human history into distinctive segments following the recondite symbolism of the Book of Revelation—was itself a recent contrivance, the handiwork of the nineteenth-century British preacher John Nelson Darby. Darby's teaching—which held that Revelation not only recorded in veiled form the leading spiritual and political conflicts in the age of its author, John of Patmos, but also laid out the future course of human history, right up to the Last Judgment—became formalized for American believers in Cyrus Scofield's Reference Bible, published in 1909, and a mainstay in evangelical homes and seminaries ever since.

Yet for all the putative reverence fundamentalists hold for the inerrant, literal truth of the Bible, works such as Scofield's lean on wildly one-sided and selective interpretations of scripture. The famous red-type annotations of the Scofield Bible mingle closely with the original text—thereby achieving much the same idiosyncratic and didactic reading of scripture that Thomas Jefferson created with his Deist edition of the Bible, which the sage of Monticello had pared down to what he believed to be Jesus' unadulterated instruction, shorn of later orthodox teachings and priestly agendas. Each of these biblical interventions conveyed in its own way a message tailored to its age: Where Jefferson sought to enshrine the skeptical, reasoned inquiries of Enlightenment thought in scripture, Scofield instituted an alarmist slant on biblical teaching as a buildup to an imminent apocalypse. In a similar fashion, other key scholarly movements bound up with biblical literalism, such as the twentieth-century conservative doctrine of "presuppositionalism," sought to impose such a thoroughgoing cultural quarantine upon biblical scholarship that it became impossible, in this rigid school of literalist orthodoxy, for devout Christians even to communicate with non-believers. The presuppositions behind the religious and secular worldviews had grown too radically incommensurate for partisans of the two camps to refer to the same basic structure of reality. "If humanists wish to be completely consistent," the presuppositionalist theologian Gordon Clark curtly announced, "they ought to kill themselves."[233]

Such uncompromising visions of fundamentalist orthodoxy drew additional momentum from the rolling sense of crisis that scourged the secular modern world. When the great calamities of the first half of the twentieth century—two World Wars, the Great Depression, the Holocaust, and the Cold War—seemed to lend themselves to the dispensationalist scheme of prophecy, its adherents leapt forward to declare their all-too-close reading of scripture vindicated by the course of current events. This, too, was a distinctly modern and opportunistic bid to interpret biblical prophecy as a reliable oracle; the overwhelming thrust of Christian theology from St. Augustine onward had been to interpret the language of prophecy through the lenses of allegory and symbolic allusion. But American believers, long tutored to see the stuff of biblical deliverance in their own nation's founding, greeted the breakdown of modern conceptions of progress and world order as undeniable signs that the foreordained climax of world history was coming to literal fruition in their own lifetimes.

The growing popular conviction of premillennialist reckoning gained an altogether new kind of traction when the state of Israel was founded in 1948. This landmark moment—which set the stage, in the views of prophetic literalists, for the mass conversion of the Jews as foretold in the Book of Revelation—coincided with another important modern innovation in conservative bible theology: the novel doctrine of a pre-tribulation rapture, which directly fed into the long-brewing sense of special cultural election among American biblical literalists. Rapture theology offered literalist believers a crucial, saving interpretation of the cultural persecution that had dogged them throughout the twentieth century. Biblical literalists were already disposed to see their role in biblical history as that of a vital prophetic fragment of believers; indeed, the uniquely self-involved character of their inquiries into prophetic scripture all but guaranteed that they would wrest such an interpretation from the text. But now the rapture ideal had powerfully reinforced that conviction, with the good news that a devoted Savior had earmarked his most faithful followers for special treatment, and immediate transport into heaven, at the dawn of the end-times. This potent, if theologically unstable, combination of ripped-from-the-headlines prophecy-spotting and serene rapture certitude made for a wide audience among literalist believers the United States, who had been long conditioned to regard the nihilistic scholarship and vain power plays of secular liberals as the handiwork of Satan.

All the diehard certainty surrounding the modern American version of biblical literalism served to conceal, however, just how novel—and, indeed, how thoroughly modern—this strain of prophecy belief actually is. Far from an austere reversion to the one true ancient faith, modern fundamentalism is what historian Eric Hobsbawm calls "an invented tra-dition"—an appropriation of the past deliberately customized to the rhe-torical and social specifications of a no-less-imagined historical present. Indeed, the profound structural adaptiveness of the superficially rigid end-times faith proved to be, well, its saving grace in the twentieth century.

And its centrality in the modern brand of Money Cult belief springs from a related paradox: the repurposing of premillennial faith to appeal to comfortable members of the American middle class—right down to the founding of a free-standing, well-financed evangelical subculture dedicated to promulgating the message that the end might well be at hand. Unlike prior millennarians, who either stoked spiritual rebellion in the lower orders or preached fatalist resignation from all affairs of this world, modern fundamentalists did something exceedingly strange for a group anticipating the imminent destruction of civilization: They went on a binge of institution-building. This was a doubly curious development since, as we've seen, most theological innovation in America is predicated on a deep and abiding distrust of all worldly institutions, from the princi-palities of government to the vanities of higher learning. But the interwar renascence in plain-folk piety was very much a counter-establishment in the making—the hallmark coming-of-age moment for a new generation of spiritual entrepreneurs, steeped in the new saving creeds of a resurgent evangelical conservatism and a modern revival of laissez-faire capitalism.

The Anti-Social Gospel

Although most religious historians of the 1930s have chronicled a "religious depression" that followed in the wake of the decade's ruinous economic crisis, conservative evangelical leaders actually increased their followings as they branched out into the wider culture of American revivalism. No longer trusting the instruction that their children might get even in mainline religious educational institutions, they founded their own network of private schools. And with limited prophecy-minded instruction in universities and seminaries, fundamentalists launched their own Bible study groups—first as informal gatherings and summer camps, and later as full-fledged colleges, such as South Carolina's Bob Jones University (founded in 1927) and California's Pepperdine University (founded in 1937).

They also mastered the powerful new medium of radio. In the 1920s, radio broadcasts were the foundation of Aimee Semple McPherson's Pentecostal empire in Southern California, while a Chicago-based fundamentalist preacher named Paul Rader launched a phenomenally successful regional radio network under the aegis of the Chicago Gospel Tabernacle. (To again drive home how readily the fundamentalists could make selective peace with worldly power: Rader began his religious-broadcasting career on a station owned by Chicago's then-Mayor, William H. Thompson.)[234]

Meanwhile, name-brand fundamentalist colleges, such as the Bible Institute of Los Angeles and Chicago's Moody Bible Institute, operated their own radio stations. Mindful that they were losing a crucial entrepreneurial battle in a popular medium, leaders of mainline denominations lobbied both CBS and NBC to ban sales of time slots to religious programming—instead designating free slots to "nonsectarian" broadcasts from mainline-approved voices. But as movement historian Joel A. Carpenter notes, fundamentalist broadcasters were able to turn this restriction to their advantage, since it "forced them to work hard at producing popularly appealing programs and building loyal audiences." And sure enough, the flagship show of conservative evangelical broadcasting, Charles Fuller's *Old Fashioned Revival Hour,* commanded the largest audience in network radio in 1942 and 1943.[235] Liberals flummoxed by the way conservative talk-radio syndicates captured a dominant share in most AM radio markets from the 1990s onward would do well to recall that these modern-day radio entrepreneurs were simply capitalizing on the model launched and perfected by the fundamentalist subculture of the thirties and forties. (And they would do still better to note that our own era's signature right-wing talker, the gold-peddling Tea Party prophet Glenn Beck, is a zealous convert to the signature Money Cult faith of Mormonism.)

Likewise, the broader demographic trends that have overtaken today's American Protestantism—steady declines in mainline church membership and upsurges in market-friendly faiths stressing end-times belief and the salience of primitive-church worship—first took root in the thirties. "While fundamentalists' missions and ministries grew, Southern Baptists gained almost 1.5 million members between 1926 and 1940, and the Pentecostal denomination the Assemblies of God quadrupled during the same period to total some two hundred thousand members," Carpenter writes. "At the same time, almost every mainline Protestant denomination declined in membership, baptisms, Sunday School enrollments, total receipts, and foreign missions."[236]

Here, indeed, is a suggestive structural affinity. The thirties, like the second decade of the twenty-first century, should have been an opportune time for a resurgence of the Social Gospel. Social Gospelers had long lamented that the salvation of individual souls ultimately counted for little amid a social order that condemned large segments of the population to acute poverty and social stagnation; the only path forward to Christianizing modern society, they argued, was to redress these deeper social sins. Yet far from stoking a Social Gospel revival, the hard times of the thirties seemed to bring on the first great growth spurt of the Protestant denominations that endorsed an intensely fatalist brand of spiritual individualism—just as in the aftermath of our new millennium's Great Recession we have seen all the signature features of the Money Cult grow more entrenched amid crippling levels of joblessness, indebtedness, and wealth inequality. And each market collapse came, as we shall see, at a critical juncture of exhaustion in the liberal moral imagination.

The Self-Made Man Goes AWOL

The religious scene of the Depression era was, first, a study in liberal paralysis. As Donald Meyer has noted, the crisis of capitalism's near collapse in 1929 caught the nation's Protestant establishment entirely off guard. It's true that the Republican Party—the traditional bastion of Protestant rule—was all but certain to surrender control of the White House in the wake of the great market crash and incumbent President Herbert Hoover's anemic response to the crisis. But the massive political realignment of 1932 was much more than a verdict on Hoover's failed policy agenda; it transferred long-term power away from an ethnic and religious elite that was deeply invested—in much more than a metaphorical sense—in everything involved in the Protestant ethos of the self-made man.

Shortcomings in the social thought of the routed Protestant mainstream became unmistakable in the Protestant business community's efforts to resist the innovations of FDR's New Deal—a political and economic program that was, moreover, the product of a rising new coalition of urban Catholics, immigrant communities, and southern whites. The very existence of this strange New Deal coalition defied many of the social assumptions informing the old theologies of New Thought and the Social Gospel: It brought together the people whom earlier liberal prophets such as Josiah Strong saw as incorrigible obstacles to northern WASP progress and unified them behind a program of progressive economic reform.

The Protestant retreat from the New Deal, in short, embodied a very different sort of church-state separation—one that stressed the unabating rivalry of religious and secular forces in a struggle for this-worldly power and influence. Prophets of this growing split preached a vision of the competing spheres of sacred devotion and secular power that eclipsed the older notion of eternally separate "cities" in the Augustinian tradition. In place of that doctrine of mutual noninterference, the anti-modernists of the fundamentalist right embraced a fresh conception of the public sphere as a rival, and indeed menacing, scheme of power. To overcome its depredations, true believers would need not merely to vanquish godless science and socialism, but also to sanctify the American scene anew, employing the alluring new spiritual powers that were becoming available to true fundamentalist believers via the mass consumer marketplace.

Nor was this flight from un-moralized (if not, strictly speaking, *de*-moralized) collective life confined to the Protestant business world's rhetoric of reaction. The era's great self-styled "realist" theologian, Reinhold Niebuhr, as Donald Meyer notes, "found it necessary to reject the New Deal, not to support or even adequately interpret it, as proof of his own realism."[237] Indeed, Niebuhr's best-known work, *Moral Man and Immoral Society* (1932), pivoted on the stark insistence that social collectivities were, by definition, incapable of true moral action, and therefore only offered moral-minded reformers at most incremental opportunities to blunt their coercions and abuses.

But back of such formulations, Meyer contends, were telltale effacements of social reality—especially as it pertained to the non-Protestant, the non-self-made segments of the American population: "Niebuhr's implication that 'realism' was the realm of politics and economics"—i.e., to the exclusion of most religious thought—"neither he nor anyone else ever justified," Meyer writes:

> The social gospel always suffered, even in its own circles, from a severe dilution in the felt, experienced quality of its religious ideas. The holy phrases—"Fatherhood of God," "Brotherhood of Man," "the Kingdom," and above all "Love"—seemed more to becloud than penetrate the reality of steel strikes, assembly lines, labor unions.[238]

Faced with the new challenge of reimagining economics and politics for the mass consumer society of the 1920s, liberal Protestants instead gravitated that much closer to the orbit of the ordered self. This maneuver transcended the passing ideological postures of the New Deal era; indeed, if anything, the liberal Protestant retreat into still-more-elaborate schemes of depoliticized self-improvement was of a piece with the radical turn on the Protestant right toward de-institutionalized individualism. As liberal Protestants began to reckon with the challenges of modernity on more than a theological level, they withdrew into a merely therapeutic vision of individual action in the world. The apostles of liberal faith could do little more than to reassert the placid slogans of a divine kingdom that was plainly nowhere in sight amid the Depression's hulking industrial ruins. They believed that an enlivened social faith, like prosperity, was just around the corner.

This glorified theology of wishful thinking was, at bottom, a willed refusal to relinquish the old dogmas of heroic Protestant individualism.

When "the immense new system of the industrial economy arose," Meyer observes, "Protestants had no real bearings . . . Industrial economy was insusceptible to the Protestant strategy of dissolving rather than directing concentrated power."[239]

But Protestant belief hadn't been simply outgrown and discarded by its American adherents. The United States has always been the great outlier case for the dominant theory of modernization, which holds that religious belief will decline amid conditions of rapid industrial development and scientific research, and as ordinary citizens attain higher levels of education. Writing at the summit of Great Society liberalism in 1965, Meyer was clearly unable to foresee the degree to which both economic liberalism and the mainline Protestant variety would become a dead letter by the end of the century. But from our more chastened vantage, we can reconstruct the curious saga of how evangelical Protestantism remade itself in the image of capitalist modernity—via a newly revived theology of primitive Gnostic power, harnessed to an experiential scheme of personal redemption, and promulgated widely by an explosion of premillennial social prophecy.

Where Meyer and other critics of Protestant individualism took its ill-timed retreat from New Deal politics to be an enervating defeat, a new cohort of believers on the right—many of them anchored in the fast-growing and influential Pentecostal faith—found exhilaration in the post-historic, post-reform turn of Protestant belief. And they wasted little time in broadcasting their new gospel to America's newly revival-minded consumer republic.

Laissez-Faire and the Latter Rain

The twentieth-century Pentecostal revival shares many striking affinities with the Mormon Church's earlier evolution into a founding pillar of the American Money Cult. Like the LDS church, the modern Pentecostal movement began as a heterodox mode of worship among poor and disenfranchised believers. Both traditions adopted egalitarian models of church organization, bypassing the authority of a learned clergy in favor of the experiential traditions of prophecy and divine intercession; followers referred to each other as saints, and they adopted the democratic-cum-apostolic honorifics of "Brother" and "Sister" for their spiritual brethren and leaders. Like the Mormon patriarchs Smith and

Young, Pentecostals believed in the living traditions of the one true Primitive Church—uncorrupted by the accretions of moribund dogma and misguided clergy, and evinced in latter day signs and wonders. And like the early Mormons, the Pentecostal leaders of the new century laid claim to an experiential communion with the divine that promised dramatic and ongoing spiritual and material self-improvement—a vision of perennially uptending personal success.

But there were obvious and significant differences between these two foundational faiths of the modern Money Cult. As we've seen, Mormons have hewed to an alternate and continually evolving version of scripture, one that's set almost entirely in the New World, and tailored to the strongly felt spiritual needs of clan-based solidarity, frontier expansion, and market conquest. By contrast, Pentecostals combine a strict biblical literalism with the immediate visitations of the Holy Spirit, triggering in believers a profound *personal* transformation, manifested by wonders such as speaking in tongues (or glossolalia, as the experience is known in clinical terms), faith healing, and vastly improved material fortune. And while both Mormonism and Pentecostalism are steeped in millennial expectation, they pursue strikingly divergent approaches to the end-times faith. Mormons stalwartly lay in provisions for an afterlife that promises to be a cosmic extension of their existing earthly bonds of family, clan, and work; Pentecostals interpret at a close literalist remove the millennial forecasts enunciated in Revelation and Old Testament prophecy.

As was the case with the other preachers caught up in the land rush of twentieth-century premillennialism, Pentecostals preached that they could confidently trust the returning savior to right the balance of history in exactly the way that Revelation prophesied. As J. Vernon McGee, the transplanted Texan Pentecostal preacher who commandeered Southern California's enormous Church of the Open Door, counseled amid the ideological tumult of the Cold War, "When the plain sense of Scripture makes common sense, seek no other sense."[240]

Over time, however, Pentecostalism's potent fusion of imminent millennial expectation and the personalized experience of the divine would become fully superimposed on the broader Protestant experience of consumer capitalism. The Pentecostal sensibility would become a trans-denominational idiom that defined much of the latter-day Money Cult, from the megachurch pastors preaching the Prosperity Gospel to the pop chiliasm of the *Left Behind* fiction series.

That Old-Time Religion

The modernized, mainstreamed Pentecostal movement is all the more striking for its humble social origins. Like most of the major denominations in America, Pentecostalism is rooted in the early tumult of the Second Awakening. Its theological origins stem from the holiness movements in Methodism and Baptism—and the key holiness doctrine of perfectionism found powerful platforms in the ministries of Charles Finney and Phoebe Palmer. John Wesley's famous teaching of "entire sanctification" of the believer, premised on the continual inward cleansing of the self from sin, unleashed a strong tide of experiential encounters with the Holy Ghost in the New World. In England, meanwhile, divines inspired by the doctrines of American holiness preachers launched the Keswick Higher Life movement, which taught that the sanctification that accompanied a new believer's second birth should be attended by manifestations of grace and wonders—an "embuement of power," in the movement's phrasing.[241]

It wasn't until the beginning of the twentieth century that these disparate strands of holiness belief were bound together in a new understanding of inner sanctification, based yet again on the practices of the Primitive Church. Tapping into the culture-wide mood of enhanced millennialism at century's end, a Methodist preacher named Charles Fox Parham met with a Topeka, Kansas, Bible school class to review the famous accounts in the Book of Acts of the miraculous happenings within the early church—healings, handlings of poisonous serpents, and speaking in tongues. Parham and his class concluded not merely that such divine visitations of grace were accessible to present-day believers, but that, indeed, glossolalia was a defining demonstration of a believer's second birth in Christ. No other Christian denomination had hit upon this reclaimed practice of the Primitive Church as a proof of conversion, and significantly, the Pentecostals would go on to employ this core experiential doctrine as an entry into their uniquely Gnostic and protean encounter with spiritual modernity.

Parham's insight soon caught fire among African-American believers

in the South and West. William H. Seymour, an itinerant black Methodist preacher, attended a Parham-led revival in Houston, and imported the
experiential tongues speaking faith to Los Angeles in 1906, sparking the
famous Azusa Street revival that brought thousands of African-American
believers into the Apostolic Church, as it was then known.

The drama of Pentecostal worship held an especially strong appeal
for the outcast communities of southern whites and urban African Americans who first embraced the faith. Most obviously, feeling oneself placed
in direct contact with divinity—and speaking a kind of language only
intelligible to the Lord—produced a bracing sense of self-worth and living
purpose. As the Pentecostal movement has gained a vast global following,
contends Grant Wacker, the leading historian of the faith, it has oscillated
between the poles of primitivism and pragmatism. But these impulses are
more twinned than contradictory, he writes, since they're both so firmly
anchored in the experiential quality of Pentecostal worship:

> Pentecostals' primitivist conviction that the Holy Spirit did every-
> thing, and that they themselves did nothing, bore grandly pragmatic
> results. It freed them from self-doubt, legitimated reasonable accom-
> modations to modern culture, and released boundless energy for feats
> of worldly enterprise. At the same time, this vigorous engagement
> with everyday life stabilized the primitive and kept it from consum-
> ing itself in a fury of charismatic fire."

The doctrine of the Pentecostals' absolute dependence on the Holy
Spirit—as well as the copious application of that Spirit's counsel to the rigors
of daily living—calls vividly to mind Weber's characterization of the original
Protestant ethic and its vision of worldly asceticism. To the Pentecostal, the
principle of entire sanctification encouraged the ready conflation of material
and spiritual realms: If everything in a believer's life was sanctified, there
was no special opprobrium attached to worldly riches. The Pentecostal leader
Elizabeth V. Baker, who founded a complex of spiritual centers in Rochester,
New York, declared bluntly that "to be poorly clothed or fed is *a lack of faith*"
and that "a religion that does not unlock our pocket books as well as our

hearts is not the religion of the Christ who gave himself to poverty so that we might be rich."[243] When the New York City physician-cum-Pentecostal-missionary Arthur L. Slocum was preparing to board an ocean liner for an extended stay in India, he heard the Lord tell him to spring for first-class tickets for himself and his wife—and for good measure, God offered this disclaimer: "He died for the well-to-do just as much as for the poor."[244]

Such assurances contrast quite sharply with the socioeconomic profile of the early Pentecostal movement. Yet Mormonism, too, had begun seven decades earlier as a radical evangelical movement among poor white farmers in the Northeast and the Midwest. And in both the Mormon and Pentecostal founding moments, close proximity to the godhead translated into dramatically rejuvenated economic activity—and the habits of personal prosperity were institutionalized in the tithing practices of each faith. Mormons set about erecting cities and temples on the U.S. frontier, and eventually presiding over their own desert kingdom, which matured over time into a vast array of corporate and real-estate holdings. Pentecostals, meanwhile, focused on the more individualist goals of health-and-wealth miracle-working. In both cases, though, economic and spiritual outsiders were able to reinvent themselves by closely mapping their salvation along the coordinates of capitalist enterprise. Both faiths regarded the accumulation of wealth as a sign of divine favor, and both endorsed strenuous personal regimens to help believers better conform their lives to the expectations of an intimately indwelling God. For Pentecostals, the born-again believer was especially mindful of the divine mandate to make the most of one's time here on Earth. "Laziness is one of the most lamentable diseases one can be afflicted with," the L.A.-based Pentecostal newspaper *Good Report* editorialized. "Nothing but the grace of God is sufficient to deliver one from this dreadful malady."[245]

Maybe so, but that didn't prevent other Pentecostal leaders from providing close-on counsel for the most efficient and prosperous ways for believers to run their lives—in the great tradition of Protestant self-help instruction harking back to the Second Awakening. The healing evangelist Raymond T. Richard published a popular 1922 manual of self-improvement titled *Helps to Young and Old* that, according to Wacker, "might have passed for an updated version of Benjamin Franklin's *Poor Richard's*

Almanack. Rise early. Never be unemployed. Never trifle. Never allow your thoughts to wander. Never speak without thinking. Stay busy."[246]

Much the same logic extended to Pentecostal preachments on the individual believer's moral probity; strictures against tobacco, alcohol, gambling, self-indulgent diets, and allegedly salacious trends in fashion and self-presentation all advertised the straitlaced conduct of a good Pentecostal believer, but they also helped establish exemplary habits of work and thrift among congregations otherwise short on material resources. (In the same vein, it bears noting that the famous Mormon injunctions against caffeine and alcohol were only codified into the faith's formal teachings in the twentieth century; prior to that, the "Words of Wisdom" in which Joseph Smith counseled against these indulgences were informal admonitions. Mormons later embraced them as orthodox teaching both to impress their own probity on an American Protestant majority still keen to identify the faith with outlaw practices such as plural marriage—but also to formalize abstemious habits in the already hardworking and provident Mormon rank-and-file.)

The early Pentecostal gospel of sanctified self-help also coincided with a landmark shift in the interpretation of biblical prophecy: the rise of premillennial dispensationalism. That mouthful of scholarly jargon actually conveyed a fairly simple idea in the interpretation of end times scripture, such as the Books of Revelation and Daniel: the assignment of a specific symbolic designation—or "dispensation"—to a segment of biblical history, so that the course of human history more closely mapped the archetypes featured in biblical prophecy. In the readings of prophecy favored among American Pentecostals and fundamentalists, the Abrahamic span of Old Testament history, for example, corresponded to the era of Promise; the time of Jesus and the Primitive Church represented the era of Grace. But Pentecostals introduced one important variation to the dispensational system. Much of Christian history, in this prophetic scheme, was an outlier phase—the "Great Parenthesis," so-called in part because it was delaying the final acts of the millennial (or Kingdom) age by the manifest failure to bring about the conversion of the Jews to Christianity, as foretold in Revelation. Pentecostal believers saw their own movement as an important augur of the climactic dispensation, the so-called Kingdom Age, reasoning that Scripture pointedly notes the advent of signs and wonders at both the outset and the closure of a dispensational era. Thus latter-day signs and wonders, such as speaking in tongues—the experiential sine qua non of Pentecostal belief—were clearly book-ending the church's Great Parenthesis, and betokening the rapid approach of the Final Judgment.

The logic here issued directly from the hallowed pioneers of the primitivist tradition in America, dramatically fusing the ancient and contemporary modes of purified Christian worship: "The relative absence of miraculous gifts between the second and the twentieth centuries did not mean that God had withdrawn them, as other dispensationalists contended," Wacker observes. "Rather, it only meant that the church's apostasy and disobedience had rendered them unusable for those who were spiritually unfit."[247]

The crucial proof of unshakable continuity with the early Christian church, in other words, was the Pentecostal movement itself. Drawing on the imagery employed in Scripture, Pentecostalists dubbed the miracle of speaking in tongues at the cusp of the Kingdom Age the "latter rain." The experience of glossolalia attributed to the original Pentecost (aka "the Upper Room") was, suitably enough, the "former rain"—i.e., a divine foreshadowing of how prophecy would be fulfilled, in its full glory, some eighteen centuries on.

Publicists of the Pentecostal revival consistently played up the experiential fulfillment of prophecy as a key theme of the movement; the Azusa revival's influential newsletter *The Apostolic Faith* announced that God "gave the former rain moderately at Pentecost, and He is going to send upon us in these last days the former and latter rain." Bennett F. Lawrence, who wrote the first book-length history of the movement from within its ranks in 1916, flatly announced that the Pentecostal church did not need to demonstrate any historical bona fides leading back to the biblical Pentecost, for the simple reason that the twentieth-century revival was already mystically bound up with the original Primitive Church: "The Pentecostal movement has no such history; it leaps the intervening years, crying "BACK TO THE PENTECOST!"[248] In the conviction that their own battery of codified, self-administered experiences of divinity were bringing forth the Last Days, twentieth-century Pentecostals had closed the circle on the Primitivist-Gnostic synthesis begun at Cane Ridge a century earlier. What had started out as an ecstatic display of the powers of free-will faith was now maturing into a full prophetic scheme of mass redemption.

Prophet Centers

And in this innovation, the Pentecostals shared yet another important affinity with Mormonism, which produced its own parallel account of prophecy's fulfillment in the New World, culminating with the Mormon faith's restoration of the purified conventions of Primitive Church worship. In both Pentecostal and Mormon circles, prophetic interpretation significantly downplayed the traditional middle term of postmillennial social observance of the nineteenth century: the gradual progress of the American nation as a vital means of realizing the millennium on Earth.

The Mormons, naturally, had ample reason to look askance at American civic institutions from a divine perspective—elected officials routinely conspired in, and often directly perpetrated, the oppression and disenfranchisement that Mormon pioneers suffered along the interior frontier of the United States. The most important—if still widely disputed—piece of prophecy concerning the destiny of the American nation ascribed to Joseph Smith is the "White Horse" pronouncement, wherein Smith declared at the funeral of a founding Saint in Nauvoo that Mormons would ride to the rescue of the American republic at a moment of crisis when its Constitution and (by implication, at least), its leading civic institutions would be "hanging by a thread."

Early Pentecostals didn't so much foresee grave peril for the American republic so much as they insisted upon its scriptural irrelevance. Imbued with the direct experience of apostolic salvation, Pentecostal founders swept up the pitiable delusions of American exceptionalism into a sweeping biblical denunciation of the world and its many sins and errors. "Though pentecostals did not see *themselves* standing in the path of divine judgment (since they expected to be physically raptured from the earth), they saw their own country deservedly falling into the maw of God's awful retribution," Wacker writes. Shortly after the historic outbreak of tongues speaking in Parham's Topeka classroom, the preacher convened "special services" on July 4, 1901— but also went out of his way to tell the local media that neither the date nor the spiritual gathering had any patriotic significance. In the preparedness debate running up to the United States' entry into World War I, Parham fiercely denounced the idea of fighting for his country, both because of the New Testament's traditional pacifist preaching, and because the United States held no special merit on the global stage; the country would soon enough "end with a dictator and a final fall," he preached ". . . in which the government, the rich and the churches will be on one side and the masses on the other."

Such apocalyptic social visions could easily be mistaken for residual hardcore populism in the Bryanite vein, but the notion of popular sovereignty in politics or economic affairs was anathema to the early Pentecostals—as indeed was the hallowed American ideal of democracy itself. For ardent Pentecostals, "democracy represented just another political scheme cooked up by humans to serve their prideful interests," Wacker writes, "no worse perhaps but certainly no better than any other political scheme." As Rochester Bible Institute co-founder Susan Duncan archly summed things up, "democracy will not save the world. Republicanism will not bring the Millen[n]ium."[249]

Of course, in their later careers, both Mormonism and Pentecostalism came to fervidly embrace the icons and symbols of American civic religion, so that each faith now embodies a kind of plus-perfect spiritual Americanism. The moment of ultra-American assimilation arrived most plainly in the house of Mormonism during the 2012 presidential candidacy of Mitt Romney; for Pentecostals, the reckoning came much sooner. As America formally joined the Allied forces of the Great War in 1917, the Wilson administration launched a vicious crackdown on antiwar dissent; both these developments triggered a dramatic about-face among Pentecostal leaders on the question of placing God's dictates far above the nation's demands. E. N. Bell, the Pentecostal divine who edited the Assembly of God's national newspaper, *The Weekly Evangel*, modified the hardcore pacifism preached by Parham and others by stressing, quite absurdly, that the question of participating in military killing was purely a matter for the individual conscience, and that religious pacifists should not "push" their faith on others. Bell was also inspired to urge his Assembly of God readers to purchase war bonds, while reminding them of their Christian duties to pay taxes and to recognize the ultimately divine provenance of all civil government. He even went so far as to order the pulping of a blistering antiwar broadside that the Assembly of God had published, first in installments in *The Weekly Evangel* and then as a separate tract, back in 1915, during the prewar-preparedness debate.[250]

However expediently it may have been abandoned, the foundational skepticism that Mormons and Pentecostals originally displayed toward the civic cult of the nation is still important to flag, however. These are, after all, the most popular and powerful faiths spawned within America's borders— and both are today experiencing explosive growth through their aggressive mission outreach programs. Most comparable religious movements in other Western countries have emerged from a fairly explicit nationalist sensibility, even if formed in opposition to existing governments—e.g., the obdurate Anglicanism of John Wesley's nineteenth-century working-class Methodism. But a deeper animus toward the principalities of worldly power suffused the Mormon and Pentecostal movements in America—a posture that seems very much of a piece with their shared experiential Gnosticism, which could not help but starkly portray the path toward individual salvation as a scornful retreat from the broader course of fallen worldly history.

The unique, overlapping prophetic outlook that the two faiths share marks another crucial pivot point in the elaboration of the modern-day Money Cult. Freed of the mediating institution of the American state— and the tradition of social reform that usually accompanied its appearance in postmillennial prophecy—Mormons and Pentecostals burrowed that much deeper into the realm of sanctified this-worldly materialism. With the nation, the Social Gospel, and related matters of civil religion all consigned safely to "the world," Mormons and Pentecostals could focus all the more deliberately on the most immediate demonstrations of the efficacy of their faith, in the culture of the market.

Primitive Moderns

Perhaps one of the most misleading legacies of the battle over biblical literalism in the 1920s is the notion that fundamentalist and evangelical believers are implacably hostile to modernity and modern culture. In fact, Pentecostals in particular have turned their primitivist faith to uniquely modern ends—and in this way, they fell into line with the other conservative evangelical insurgencies stirring to life at the outset of the modern age. A more apt characterization of the conservative evangelical quarrel with modernity in the first third of the twentieth century doesn't hinge on a flat-out rejection of the modern; rather, it would begin with the question, "Modernity for what?"

Fundamentalism is, in its own way, a mirror-image reflection of the mainline Protestant encounter with modernity—except that where modernist liberals sought early to recast Protestant faith to accommodate new discoveries in science and biblical history, conservative evangelicals sought to separate out those dogmatic elements of the true faith that must remain untainted by skeptical inquiry and the forces of historical change. If there is no version of Christianity that can transcend the created world, the defenders of Protestant orthodoxy sensibly asked, then what purpose is served in worshiping a risen Christ? The exercise of isolating these non-negotiable features of the true faith—"The Fundamentals" in the famous twelve-volume series of orthodox tracts published between 1910 and 1915—was itself a paradoxically modern method of interpreting Scripture, selecting out the articles of faith best suited to advance an anti-modernist theological agenda.

As historian George Marsden argues, the interpretive scheme favored by fundamentalists and other conservative evangelicals was an unstable fusion of the romantic individualism of nineteenth-century revivalism and the inductive "common sense" view of revealed scripture as scientific fact, famously articulated by the sixteenth-century British philosopher Francis Bacon. Thus it was chiefly when modernist and evolution-minded thought penetrated the sanctums of mainline Protestantism in America that fundamentalism sought to pull up the drawbridge between earnest believers and the modern world.[251]

Apart from such well-established intellectual influences, there's a much more immediate sense in which the conservative evangelicals of the early twentieth century typified a modern sensibility: In virtually every new innovation of modern communications technology, they proved to be exceptionally nimble early adopters. As Joel Carpenter writes,

> Evangelicals have responded readily to modernity's compartmentalization of life because theirs is an intensely personal religious experience. Modern society is structured to favor voluntarism and choice mak-

ing . . . and evangelicals have responded with aggressive recruiting and creative institution-making while more established faiths have tended to take the church's place in life for granted . . . By offering authoritative religious knowledge and intense religious experience to "whosoever will" rather than reserving them for scholars and mystics, evangelicals have provided an accessible faith for millions of modern people, including at least a quarter of today's American adult population.[252]

This deeply individualist outlook was, in turn, part and parcel of the growing Protestant infatuation with the dispensationalist reading of end-times scripture: If the Final Judgment was fast approaching, dallying with any institutional forms of social reform was an idle humanist reverie at best, and at worst a mockery of the grander divine plan of history. It seems apt that a drastically telescoped account of the Last Days (and the dogmatic turn away from social reform that accompanies it) would arrive at a moment when modernist scholarship in both theology and the life sciences was adopting a far more expansive temporal framework to account for the beginnings of life. In much the same way that the pressures of a relativized and contingent modernity prompted conservative evangelicals to redouble their commitment to the Scripture as inerrant and literal truth, the allied forces of unfathomable evolutionary and archeological time heightened the sense of imminent crisis for the prophecy-watchers who scoured both the sky and the calamitous currents of world news for signs of the imminent Apocalypse.

Viewed in the compass of the country's inherited Puritan philosophies of history and the millennium, this abrupt shift in American belief from a socially engaged brand of evangelical faith to the more recent, starkly individualist variety was also a distinctly modernist departure. Recall that the postmillennial preachments of the eighteenth and nineteenth centuries anointed the collective notion of the American redeemer nation as the vessel of history's gospel redemption. This vision of the country's unique prophetic mission, in turn, had licensed a wide array of reform movements, which were viewed as augurs of the millennium's progress. Now, however, the emphasis was shifting. For all their interest in hastening the millennium's advance, Puritan divines stood aloof from any forecast of its actual imminence in history; they held that the figures and recondite symbols of prophecy were recurring historical types, modeled on Scripture's ideal accounts of right human conduct. Fundamentalist and premillennialist believers had reversed the polarity of this founding faith, by seeking to torture a literal account of past and future human events from the pages of scripture.

Apocalypse Now

But the vogue for fundamentalist literalism was also, in its own way, a triumph of fortuitous timing—another key defining trait that made it very much a signature product of the modern age. The twentieth century proved tailor-made for a theology of imminent apocalyptic reckoning, bringing in rapid train the Great War, the atheist Communist takeover in Russia, the Great Depression, World War II, the advent of nuclear weaponry, the founding of Israel, another atheist Communist uprising in China, and the protracted Cold War, during which the United States put itself aggressively forward as the standard-bearer of the civilization of Christian individualism. Small wonder that the adherents of prophecy's literal fulfillment would seek their most sensational proof-texts in the international news cycle.

Small wonder, as well, that the holiness movement (as the more broad-ranging expressions of the Pentecostal spirit came to be known) emerged as a chief vessel of the gathering mood of millennial fatalism. In the closing decades of the nineteenth century, plenty of holiness preachers still followed in the footsteps of Charles Finney, and saw the perfectionist pursuit of personal holiness as something wholly of a piece with the postmillennial improvement of the social order. But, as Marsden notes, the traumas of early-twentieth-century social conflict—particularly the crucible of the Great War, and the intellectual ascendance of the Social Gospel, which many holiness thinkers viewed as an entering wedge for an entire battery of modernist betrayals of the one true faith—had decisively driven the holiness movement away from any program of economic or political activism. For the rising holiness wing of the fundamentalist movement, Marsden writes,

> The result was almost as if the positive aspects of the progressive
> political movement had not only been rejected but even obliterated

from memory . . . [F]undamentalists emerged from the experience not so much without social or political views as fixated on a set of views that had been characteristic of middle-class Americans in the last years before the crisis [i.e., the Great War] occurred. Their social views were frozen at a point that had been the prevailing American political opinion around 1890, save that the fundamentalists of the 1920s had forgotten the degree to which their predecessors—and even they themselves—had earlier espoused rather progressive social concerns.[253]

The doctrine of imminent judgment worked wonders in perpetuating this state of self-inflicted social amnesia—and no one preached it with greater force that the holiness apostles of Pentecostalism, who knew the rapid advance of the final reckoning from their own firsthand experience of the latter rain. But some Pentecostals took the logic of premillennial expectation one striking, Gnostic step further, and invested the believing self with new powers of creation. Under the Word of Faith teaching pioneered by holiness preacher F.W. Kenyon in the early twentieth century, the Pentecostal theology of "Oneness"—which held that Jesus, via his atoning sacrifice, had achieved full identity with the universe's creator—became refined into a stark Gnostic dualism separating matter and spirit. Kenyon posited that as believers experienced the gifts of the Pentecost, they became sanctified vessels in a healing progression that approached godhood. As Kate Bowler writes, Kenyon's theology

held that [the] profound ontological shift from sinner to saint signaled only the first phase of redemption. To explain, Kenyon appropriated New Thought's focus on mind, spirit, and universal laws to show that Christians could look to the cross not as a promise of things to come, but as a guarantee of benefits *already* granted . . . In language reminiscent of New Thought, God was a spirit who created a spiritual universe. The physical world was a shallow reflection of this preeminent and preexisting spiritual universe. Though clothed in the "temporary dwelling place" of flesh and bones, humans too were *primarily* spirit.[254]

From this spirit-imbued progression, it proved a short step to the corollary point that sanctified believers were imbued with divine power the same way that divine gifts marked their spiritual election. "Clear-eyed believers henceforth possessed God's ability and authority to rule over the material world," Bowler observes:

> Christians, now unburdened by sin, hovered only a little lower than angels . . . Jesus' death and resurrection had shifted believers' onto-logical status, making them legal shareholders of certain rights and privileges. At times, Kenyon's Holy Spirit-filled Christians hardly could be identified as human at all, as their total identification with God approached deification. "The World has not known that there is a superman in their midst today," Kenyon marveled. "They don't know that every new creation is a superman in the embryo."[255]

Referencing the opening of the gospel of John (far and away the most Gnostic book of the New Testament), Kenyon preached that believers had access to the same force that had actuated the Creator: the power of the spoken holy word. Just as New Thought Gnostics had banished all man-ner of delusive wrong thinking from their regimens of spiritual self-im-provement, healers and prosperity preachers in the Word of Faith tradition would later underline the central importance of intoning the right phrases of divine-sanctioned spiritual growth. John G. Lake—a Pentecostal con-temporary of Kenyon's who founded a breakaway holiness congregation from a New Thought church he'd co-led with the well-known mind-cure writer Arthur C. Grier—freely cited Kenyon's groundbreaking theology in his own transformative spiritual teaching. "God intends us to be gods," Lake preached. "There is a God-power and a soul-force in the nature of man that God is endeavoring to bring forth . . . The man within is a real man. The inner man is the real governor, the true man that Jesus said was a God."[256] (Lake was citing John 10:34, where Jesus says to the disciples, "Is it not written in your law, that I have said ye are 'gods'?")

Here Pentecostal thought pivots on the same crucial insight that fueled Joseph Smith's later revelations in Nauvoo: the principle of eternal progression, or, as it would be phrased in the Word of Faith tradition, entire sanctification. In both visions of Gnostic transcendence, the extreme bifurcation of spirit and matter permits the spiritual adept to master common material adversities—and to ascend to new heights of godhood. For Word of Faith believers, the pietist and prayerful gospel of self-advancement that had been the great legacy of the Businessman's Revival acquired an unprecedented metaphysical significance. In the teachings of Word of Faith, words addressed to divine power became the principal means of material advancement—and (when abused or neglected) the telltale cause of backsliding into poverty and illness. Such "pentecostalists relied on prevailing prayer to transmit their pleas not as requests but as contracts, guaranteeing miraculous results," Bowler notes:

> Believers ferreted out the meanings of God's many names for personal use. To the sick, for instance, God revealed himself as *Jehovah-Rapha* ("I am the Lord that healeth thee"). To the fearful God's redemptive name was *Jehovah-Nissi* ("The Lord Our Banner of Protection"). In each name adherents found a key to personal power . . . In pulpits and prayer closets alike, believers intoned [the name of Jesus] with a sweet reverence, expecting it to bring their petition, praise, or deliverance to completion.[257]

This was, of course, the same pietist breakthrough behind the Businessman's Revival—only under the influence of Word of Faith preaching, it was being elevated into a first principle of Protestant metaphysics. What's more, the social reach of the doctrine of materially minded petitionary prayer had expanded considerably. It had now trickled down to a predominantly poor and marginal community of believers fervidly calling down the material comforts that the Lord personally approved as rewards for their faith, while also urging on the signs and wonders of the endtimes. With the Pentecostal revolution, American Protestants were formalizing the premillennialist revision of traditional prophecy—and into the bargain, erecting an entirely new theology of sanctified capitalism from the bottom up.

The Gnostic Cash Nexus

It's worth noting again how far this version of personal Christian deliverance has traversed from the more austere, covenantal Calvinist precepts of the original Puritan errand into the wilderness. How exactly had this transformation come to pass? Like the New England Puritans, Pentecostals administered a gospel of complete dependence on otherworldly grace—yet in their hands, an annealing and demanding covenant with the divine is transformed into a bald worldly contract, guaranteeing ongoing supernatural service in the material realm in exchange for a shared partnership in the Gnostic godhead. As the great student of historical Gnosticism Hans Jonas has argued, the Gnostic theology of self is preeminently a theology of power: "For the Gnostics . . . man's alienation from the world is to be deepened and brought to a head, for the extrication of the inner self which only thus can gain itself. The world (not the alienation from it) must be overcome; and a world degraded to a power system can only be overcome through power."[258]

But this individualist evocation of otherwordly power cuts, most uncomfortably, in two directions. As the Gnostic strain of belief has steadily overtaken the older social forms of Protestant worship in America, it has suffused the culture of the capitalist market with the agency of divine intervention. From the founding theology of Word of Faith has sprouted the lavish self-imbuements of the latter-day Prosperity Gospel, as preached by the well-known televangelists Joel Osteen, Creflo Dollar, and T. D. Jakes. The faith-healing megapastor Benny Hinn likewise plies a Word of Faith message strictly conditioned on the repetition of healing words and phrases—while urging the same hopeful rote remedies on believers coping with the material afflictions of poverty and thwarted ambition.

In all these settings, the divine will is made plainly manifest as the will of the market: Where God is well pleased, the blessings of health and wealth flow naturally in concert with his bidding; when God punishes— or worse, perhaps, merely withdraws his abundant support—the market shrivels, and the believer is economically punished.

This synthesis of premillennial certainty and Gnostic self-culture has produced plenty of crass offenses against a long-standing official reticence about money matters in Protestant institutions—but that's really not the most noteworthy thing about this spirit-infused version of the Money Cult. The caricature of the Prosperity Gospel as a grasping hustle is no more illuminating than the twenties-era caricatures of evangelicalism as a rube-swindling con game. In both cases, the focus on the motivations of the movement's spiritual leaders pointedly overlooks the obvious: The problem isn't so much the shallow celebration of material wealth or the fear-based invocation of a vengeful deity commanding literalist fealty; it is, rather, the appeal of the money faith's theological reach.

Now Will You Go?

In this regard, it's also worth noting that the Pentecostal Word of Faith movement, while an extreme instance of the Gnostic self's close calibration to the market's values, is by no means an outlier. Indeed, the original Pentecostal revival of the early twentieth century, and its later expansion into the theological mainstream, were striking in their resonance across rival denominations—especially since, like all apostles of Primitive Church restoration, Pentecostalists had virtually no tolerance for either doctrinally suspect ecumenical affiliations or the truth claims of competing faiths.

The impact of the holiness movement stretched far beyond the rural churches and storefront ministries that bred a new sense of spiritual election among humble-born believers in the West and South. The appeal of the Pentecostal message was vastly multiplied, for one thing, by the pioneering radio ministry of Sister Aimee Semple MacPherson. It is no exaggeration to call McPherson, a Canadian émigrée who experienced a dramatic divine call to the ministry during her first marriage to the itinerant Pentecostal preacher Robert Semple, a walking advertisement for the holiness way of life. In the first vision adumbrating her eventual calling—which occurred during a 1910 missionary trip to China from which Robert would not return alive—MacPherson beheld a clutch of puffed up divines who symbolized the baleful excesses of modernist faith. They were "clad in priestly robes and ministerial attire," she recalled in a later written account; armed with mistaken "thoughts and theories," they crowded out the real and true Scripture, the "Book of light and wisdom." Their legacy was to be "the dark and foolish sayings and theories of the unbelieving and false church." But God announced to McPherson that she was anointed to do holy battle with the dark forces of theological modernism: "Even so have I chosen and ordained thee," the divine voice assured her, "that thou shouldst go forth, and clear away the debris and contamination, with which they have covered and obscured the light of My Word."[259]

It's easy to recognize by now the classic call to arms of a primitive restorationist ministry. Minus the golden tablets, MacPherson's galvanizing encounter with the divine was, indeed, nearly identical in structure and content to the initial vision Joseph Smith received from God almost a century earlier. Like Smith's angelic visitation, McPherson's call to ministry featured a Babel-like confusion among self-styled Christian divines over the nature of the true Church's message; a firm assurance from on high that mere denominational bickering conceals the gospel's truth from humanity; and, far from least, the investiture of the chosen beholder of the vision with a charismatic charge to restore the true faith of the Primitive Church to its world-conquering glory—to "clear away the debris and contamination, with which they have covered and obscured the light of My Word."

Like Smith, the young McPherson was delayed by several years in executing her charge; she became enmeshed in an unhappy second marriage to a Canadian businessman, which gave her a son and a disabling bout of seeming neurasthenia, punctuated by occasional urgent messages from the divine: "Preach the word!" an inner voice insisted repeatedly to the ailing prophet. "Will you go? Will you go?" Physicians sought to treat McPherson's depression with the clumsy measures of the age; after she had suffered through both a hysterectomy and an appendectomy, she appeared to be on the verge of death. In this precarious state, she received a still more forceful call to preach: "NOW—WILL—YOU—GO?"

McPherson reported that when she finally assented, she experienced the miraculous healing of her symptoms—just like the one that Mary Baker Eddy had undergone at the moment of her New Thought conversion several decades earlier. Fully recovered and newly secure in her mission, McPherson abandoned her husband in their Chicago home and lit out to preach the Pentecostal message while spreading the healing gift of the redeemed word in the West.[260] Eventually, she constructed the block-long, 5,300-seat Angelus

Temple as the home of her landmark Four Square Gospel ministry, which soon exploded into a worldwide Pentecostal denomination in its own right.

Like the Pentecostal movement at large, the Angelus Temple bore a Janus-faced relation to the modern and traditional components of holiness worship. As McPherson's recent biographer Matthew Avery Sutton notes, "[T]he temple provided a space where newcomers could simultaneously hear the glories of the old-time religion, experience the emotional thrill of a revival in the old tent tradition, and participate in a distinctively Hollywood-style church that was in touch with the latest California trends."[261]

McPherson's preaching was likewise theologically conservative in content and bracingly modern in form. For the mass audience on her radio network, she would act out didactic "illustrations" of modern applications of gospel principle, frequently based on the mishaps of her own life as a media celebrity—a famous episode involving the near explosion of a passenger plane she had contracted to transport her back to Angelus from a media appearance in San Francisco, and a widely reported run-in with the Los Angeles police over a speeding ticket. She offered a defense of her novel approach, clearly steeped in the sanctified view of the culture of the mass American market. "If Christ were alive today, I think he'd preach modern parables about oil wells and airplanes, the things that you and I understand. Things like being arrested for speeding."[262] Anyone seeking out the origins of Joel Osteen's God of optimal parking and exquisitely timed house-flipping need look no further.

McPherson also was a pioneer in the less savory spheres of evangelical celebrity. She effectively set the template for later Pentecostal preachers plying mediagenic pulpits by touching off a months-long tabloid scandal in 1926, concerning her alleged kidnapping from Venice Beach and eventual transport to a safe house in Mexico. After national news outlets breathlessly reported on her case for weeks on end, McPherson abruptly turned up in the Mexican border town of Agua Prieta, claiming to have fled her captors on foot. No perpetrators were ever found, and the Los Angeles district attorney favored an alternate account of the preacher's disappearance—that she had absconded for a romantic getaway with Kenneth Anniston, the married producer of her radio show. But efforts to bring McPherson to trial went nowhere, leaving the lurid unsolved mystery to overshadow much of the remainder of her ministry.

Despite its sensational and scandal-ridden latter phase, McPherson's career was nearly an ideal-type study in the ways that Protestant experience was now being seamlessly mediated in America's market culture. McPherson was the first major evangelical figure to harness the power of radio, and media celebrity more generally, to propagate her holiness gospel; in the process, she was able to make the otherwise exotic and strange protocols of Pentecostal worship seem familiar and comforting to a mass audience. McPherson's odyssey through the politics of early-twentieth-century social reform also importantly prefigures the modern coming-of-age of the evangelical right. McPherson started out as something close to a Social Gospel figure in the liberal-leaning cultural scene of Southern California. Angelus Temple offered free meals to the unemployed in the early years of the Depression, and McPherson personally assisted unwed mothers in the congregation in their searches for jobs and housing. On a visit to India, she lauded the anticolonial populist crusade of Mahatma Gandhi, and she sent a congratulatory telegram to Franklin and Eleanor Roosevelt after FDR's successful 1936 reelection campaign.[263]

But McPherson's political views soured shortly afterward, and she became an early exponent of the new breed of Christian nationalism that would take serious root during the Cold War. As Sutton writes, as McPherson "no longer concentrated on rooting out theological subversives, who were most often elite white men, but instead began to focus on non-Protestant immigrants, many of whom were darker-skinned Catholics and Jews, as potential agents of the Antichrist."[264] This turn from the confident liberalism of the New Deal would soon become a standard trope among California's evangelical believers—it was also, famously, the story of Ronald Reagan's later political career—but as Sutton notes, the simple fact that McPherson possessed a public political profile was as significant as its lurch from left to right:

> Politics became one of the mechanisms by which pentecostals moved from the margins to the mainstream of American culture, in defiance of the common perception that theologically conservative Protestants abandoned the public sphere after the Scopes trial. Far from

withdrawing, McPherson kept pentecostals active and involved in contemporary culture, thus helping lay the foundation for evangelicalism's reemergence after World War II. And most important, she linked Pentecostal theology with American nationalism, establishing new precedents for action at both the local and national levels.[265]

In the cultural broadsides of a Sinclair Lewis or an H. L. Mencken, a figure like McPherson was little more than an inviting figure of satirical fun—yet one more illustration of the gullibility, sentimentality, and fairy-tale superstitions long in favor among America's backward-looking small-town booboisie. But everything about McPherson's ministry looked ahead, not backward. In creating a series of flamboyant set pieces about her own celebrity antics, Sister Aimee encouraged her followers to imbue their own worldly trials—and more important, their worldly successes—with divine meaning. In building an international ministry out of the new medium of radio, McPherson also looked ahead to the long, influential, and ongoing emergence of televangelism as the dominant preaching and revival idiom in the American Protestant world. And most important of all, the political trajectory of her career traced the same economic and ideological conversion that would await legions of Protestants coming into full cultural power in the Golden State and across the country. Secular liberals could laugh at Sister Aimee all they liked, but she understood all too well that God would make her a model of a robust, market-conscious, and thoroughly modern brand of world-transforming worship.

As the Market Bids

In two key respects, though, McPherson failed to symbolize the spirit of Southern California's great evangelical revival: She wasn't a man, and she wasn't a transplant from the American South. While the Pentecostals, like every other Protestant denomination, skewed strongly toward female membership, Southern California's boom in what Darren Dochuk calls "plain-folk" religion—chiefly Southern Baptist and Methodist congregations in addition to the homegrown Pentecostal movement—was spearheaded by a new generation of aggressive male preachers, delivering a new free-market gospel of cultural confrontation. The Methodist preacher "Battling" Bob Shuler typified this new preaching style, even as he set himself up as the nation's most prominent theological critic of McPherson. A onetime candidate for the U.S. Senate on the Prohibition Party ticket, Shuler looked to the explosion of smaller conservative congregations out West as a crucial sign of life in an otherwise sclerotic Protestant establishment. Derogating his own denomination's dalliance with "high-brow Methodist preachers with . . . university degrees and a new social gospel," Shuler went on to note that the real balance of spiritual power was shifting to self-organized southern congregations harking back to the prophetic traditions of the Primitive Church:

> The great Methodist Church, once the burning evangel of two centuries, is now barren and without spiritual fruit. Her altars are empty. Many of them have been destroyed . . . The same thing has happened to the Northern Baptists, the Presbyterians and the other great ecclesiastical bodies. They are engaged in large enterprises looking to world movements. The fires have gone out of their altars. They are cold, lifeless, formal, dead.

Very much by contrast, Shuler descried a strong revival spirit among "Pentecostals and others like them," who were "building little churches everywhere," led by "fiery prophets" raised from among the "poor and lowly."[266]

Marshalling the scattered troops of the fundamentalist faithful behind a potent new fusion of the anticommunist and free-market crusades, figures such as Shuler adumbrated a new ecumenicalism of growth among the long-divided ranks of evangelical faith. The new entrepreneurs of conservative religion in Southern California recognized many deep cultural affinities lurking beneath their doctrinal differences. And with the advent of the Cold War, they soon found common cause in both the global crusade against communism and the moral defense of the free enterprise system. Upon the elder preacher's retirement, Shuler's son Patrick took over his rock-ribbed empire of Methodist fundamentalism and steered it into a

soft-spoken but ardently anticommunist mission that was rivaled only by
Billy Graham's postwar ministry in terms of mass appeal.

J. Vernon McGee, a Texas-raised Presbyterian who in 1949 took over
the pulpit in downtown Los Angeles's mammoth Church of the Open
Door (which boasted two thirty-foot "Jesus Saves" neon signs on its exte-
rior walls, and what were reputedly the "largest set of chimes on the Pacific
Coast") preached a simple message of impending premillennial judgment
to a mass radio audience on the pioneering Los Angeles religious flagship
station KGER. As Dochuk observes, McGee's broadcasts were a crucial
turn in the mainstreaming of the dispensationalist message: Where premillennial prophecy faith had formerly been "a complex doctrine that encouraged intellectualizing, McGee and his cohort helped turn it into an impetus
for local action, cultural engagement, and American global intervention."[267]

McGee also propagated an aggressively anticommunist interpretation
of end-times scripture, very much attuned to the conspiratorial outlook
of the Golden State's right-wing business elite. Indeed, it's impossible to
review Dochuk's account of McGee's exhaustive pulpit anatomies of the
wide-ranging Red menace without thinking of the similar sweeping inventories of liberal conspiracy also delivered in a softly spiritualized register
by Glenn Beck. "Echoing the likes of J. Edgar Hoover, whom he lauded,
McGee believed that communism was 'religion's mortal foe' and a tool
used by Satan to eradicate Christian democratic values," Dochuk writes:

> Working from this totalizing worldview, he was always willing to
> entertain even the most fantastic theories of internal subversion and
> conquest by fifth columnists, including those advanced by Joseph
> McCarthy. One of his favorite sermons, for instance, titled "Ori-
> gins of Communism," offered a history lesson laden with conspira-
> torial charges that began in the late twelfth century and continued
> through Jean-Jacques Rousseau and Adam Weisshaupt, ending with
> wild condemnations of Karl Marx, Friedrich Engels, and Vladimir
> Lenin, and praise for [red-baiting Texas GOP Rep.] Martin Dies.
> This historical foray into radical philosophy was "scheduled to pro-
> voke serious minded Christians to recognize the menace."[268]

And like his twenty-first century successor Beck, McGee located the ultimate seat of spiritual betrayal in a Democratic White House:

> Agitated by an "intrusive" state, McGee became convinced that "only an immediate and continuous uprising of conservative thought [could] halt our nation's plunge into socialism"—this, and the final destruction of Franklin Roosevelt's legacy. Like other southern plain-folk preachers, McGee had welcomed the New Deal as a temporary correction to the excesses and failings of capitalism, but now it was obvious, in his mind, that New Deal liberalism was actually a halfway house to communism. In one telling sermon that called for a "New Age, Not a New Deal," McGee elaborated on a catalog of political failings: from the abandonment of Christian economics to the continuation of the Fair Deal, from rampant moral degeneracy to the disappearance of traditional education. Animated by the very same impulse that commanded communism, each of these developments, McGee ventured, could be traced to the New Deal.[269]

As they marshaled vast cross-denominational followings, popular broadcast preachers such as McGee and McPherson quickly became instrumental in the Golden State conservative establishment's postwar embrace of libertarian economics. This alliance was, at first, anything but simple or intuitive. The migrant Southern transplants who furnished much of the base for the early phase of California's evangelical revival also tended to cleave to their inherited Southern New Deal political sympathies—or worse, from the point of view of the state's conservative business elite, they revered Louisiana's late populist kingpin Huey Long, who had launched a nationwide Share the Wealth campaign calling for a $1 million cap on individual incomes. In the teeth of the Depression, California's large Southern migrant population gravitated toward similar populist crusades, such as the novelist Upton Sinclair's nearly successful 1936 campaign for governor on the End Poverty in California platform, and the postwar "Ham and Eggs" ballot initiative to secure a minimum income credit for unemployed and fixed-income citizens of the state. (This latter crusade, significantly, was originally the brainchild of a self-styled Pentecostal prophet in Los Angeles named Jonathan Perkins, who'd been defrocked from a senior position in the Assemblies of God for publishing allegedly slanderous material about Sister Aimee Semple McPherson and her staff; like many another evangelical populist who'd fallen out of public favor, Perkins descended into bigoted and conspiratorial delusion, forging alliances with Long's onetime aide de camp and raging anti-Semite Gerald L. K. Smith, as well as with the resurgent Ku Klux Klan of the 1920s.)

It was, in other words, no mean thing to bring white Southern evangelicals on board with a tax-slashing pro-business platform—but the leaders of the business wing of the postwar Golden State GOP desperately needed an engaged grassroots movement to propel their political allies into statewide office. And the hyper-American ideology beamed from the pulpits of McPherson, McGee, and their influential Southland colleagues provided an ideal pretext for what proved to be a historic marriage of political convenience. Once the Ham and Eggs insurgency was defeated in 1946, adherents of the plain-folk revival increasingly endorsed the prerogatives of the market—a shift fueled in large part by the changed political climate of the Cold War.

Protestant free-market propagandists such as George Benson, the popular opinion columnist and director of the benignly titled National Economic Program, an enormously influential (and corporate-funded) public-school curriculum extolling laissez-faire economics, found an especially strong following among the Southern transplants in and around Los Angeles. By the late 1950s, some 750,000 Los Angeles schoolchildren had been exposed to NEP programs such as the cartoon series *Adventures in Economics* and an allied film series stressing the triumph of free-market principles over various sinister and wrong-headed forms of collective endeavor.[270] Meanwhile, preachers such as McGee continued to loudly trumpet the preservation of free-market virtue as the key to both personal and civilizational redemption.

Younger divines such as the transplanted Dallas preacher Bob Wells, who presided over Orange County's thriving Central Baptist congregation, likewise took up the cause of "Evangelism and Patriotism." In Wells's case, that slogan translated into congregation-rousing appeals to defeat a pending ballot initiative to increase taxes on private religious schools—and to support another ballot initiative endorsing so-called right-to-work policies in the state. Meanwhile, the evangelical patriot's cause also eagerly embraced the fledgling John Birch Society, named for a missionary martyred in China who'd been the protégé of another plain-folk Texas preacher, J. Frank Norris. The Birch group had been conjured into existence during the speaking tour of still another rabid anticommunist evangelical businessman named Robert Welch. And while the 1958 right-to-work initiative was defeated, the effort midwifed another influential statewide business lobby, the California Free Enterprise Association, funded mainly by the reactionary agriculture baron–cum–amusement park titan Walter Knott.

All these political alliances were formed amid California's historic postwar suburban boom of the 1950s—a time of unprecedented middle-class prosperity, largely underwritten by regional defense contracts and federal agriculture subsidies, but also an era of fiercely anti-government sentiment among the region's newly prosperous evangelicals. The Golden State's political culture, now regarded as a hotbed of lifestyle liberalism, was in this crucial takeoff phase of Southern California's welfare economy seized by a curious kind of existential self-hatred. Protestant ideologues of the McGee, Welch, and Knott persuasion devoted much of their air-time and organizational prowess to fervidly denouncing the basis of the miraculous abundance blooming all around them. Once again, revivalist religious sentiment was running counter to the strict logic of economic determinism: It was almost as if California's aerospace-and-defense boom itself were unconsciously apprehended as an economic original sin, as a new cohort of evangelical believers dependent on the latest applied innovations of modern science sensed dimly that they must be defying both the Genesis myth of creation and the sainted dictates of the free market. Their response was to embrace the enabling mythologies of the laissez-faire faith all the more tightly—and in the newly confident ranks of the region's resurgent conservative movement, that mission was easily accomplished. Not merely in the region's thriving plain-folk pulpits, but across its political and economic

spectrum, a robust new free-market faith was stirring to life, heavily subsidized by the federal government, and yet fiercely dedicated to the ideal of
an ultra-American brand of laissez-faire ideology, unmolested by the state
and sanctioned by the will of God.

The libertarian future, in other words, was being imagineered right
before the eyes of California's new cohort of upwardly mobile postwar
evangelicals. Previous iterations of the Money Cult hinged on the notion
of private inward contracts, sealed by prayer, and solemnized before the
Creator to effectuate a better life—be it in the spheres of courtship, self-reform, or career advancement. Now, however, the imbuing spirit of Pentecost—scattered throughout the kindred Southern denominations now
basking in the prosperity of the Golden State—was forging a new social
contract. The far-flung aerospace suburbs of the Southlands were repurposing the gospel message in their image: spawning nondenominational para-
churches, hosting revival efforts targeting college youth and businessmen,
and most of all, advancing a stalwart vision of what Dochuk dubs a new
gospel of wealth, one that "identified threats to pristine capitalism in big
government" and "urged [parishioners] to protest a political order whose
bureaucratic tendencies and Keynesian initiatives undermined" the just
and godly imperatives of laissez-faire capitalism.[47] And in this instance, at
least, it's quite evident that as California goes, so goes the nation.

8

A NEW SPIRIT OF CAPITALISM

The man who would become the most influential public face of Golden State piety—and postwar Protestant faith in America—was, fittingly enough, a charismatic Southern transplant. When the North Carolina–bred Baptist preacher Billy Graham had burst onto the national scene with a stunning seven-week revival in Los Angeles in 1949, he was at a career crossroads, having sacrificed a comfortable post as a Midwestern Bible College president to pursue a far more risky career as an international youth revivalist. His fiery L.A. performance—fortuitously launched two days after the USSR successfully tested its first atomic bomb—forecast a coming apocalyptic battle with godless Communism ("a religion that is inspired, directed, and motivated by the Devil himself") that would all too likely claim greater Los Angeles as a deserving casualty, since "the Fifth Columnists, called Communists, are more rampant in Los Angeles than any other American city."[272] After netting a series of celebrity converts—thereby proving out, yet again, the Charles Finney strategy of targeting local elites to win over major metropolitan followings for Christ—Graham was launched as the great biblical statesman of twentieth-century America.

But Graham's breakout revival performance wasn't the bolt from the heavens that dumbstruck media coverage of the event made it appear to be. Graham was sponsored by a consortium of fire-breathing evangelical groups, massed under the banner of the Christ for Greater Los Angeles Campaign. This quiet organizational push was just as significant as the fire-and-brimstone clamor of Graham's Cold War revivalism; it marked the first major stirring of the modern "parachurch" movement—i.e., a cross-denominational initiative to bring evangelical influence to bear on major issues of the day. As one of the group's chief organizers, the hard-core anticommunist preacher "Battling" Bob Shuler noted, the Graham crusade's major sponsors were the Southland's demotic Bible-first faiths—"the Assemblies of God, the Church of the Foursquare Gospel, the Pentecostals, the Southern Baptists," and other adherents of the plain-folks fundamentalist gospel.[273] These would also, of course, be the lead denominations of the Christian right, as that enormous political confluence of pararchurches would rally behind the successful 1980 presidential campaign of the great California-bred (and parachuch-converted) backlash leader Ronald Reagan.

But Graham, like Reagan, would prove to be a curiously equivocal bearer of the galvanizing free-market faith thundering down from the plain folks pulpits of the Southland. To be sure, Graham proved to be a phenomenally accomplished revival preacher, and his active career far outstripped those of the great apostles of past Awakenings, such as Charles Finney and Jonathan Edwards. Yet for all the attention that Graham has won in the wider culture, and in spite of his carefully tended portfolio of private spiritual counseling sessions with presidents and world statesmen, Graham's legacy is notably thin on theological and historic weight. In a sense, the fundamentalist activists who so fervently prayed, organized, and fundraised in the hopes of witnessing a wonder-working divine transformation of the worldly order got both more and less than they bargained for. In the ministry of a prophet like Graham, they won something that had seemed completely unthinkable for the evangelical movement just a generation before—unparalleled cultural respectability, and a global platform for the movement's core message: to win the individual salvation of as many believers as possible ahead of the advancing millennium.

Somehow, though, all this did not add up to an awakening—nor even, in spite of the huge turnouts and the vast new (and overwhelmingly complimentary) media attention, much of a revival. In part, of course, this was a simple function of Graham's own renunciation of a more intellectually demanding version of the faith. No fundamental reorientation of the believer's life was pronounced or expected at a Graham crusade, and so the institutional half-life of his urban revivals proved much shorter than the upheavals in observance wrought by evangelical forerunners such as George Whitefield and Finney.

Hundreds or even thousands would line up at the end of Graham's rallies to pronounce themselves born again—to declare that they, like Graham, had surrendered their own will to God's. But then—well, then the inner sanctification of life under capitalism took hold. Without any clear sense of where their revived spiritual energies might be channeled, the crowds awakened by Graham's preaching largely went about their business as usual—which was, in many ways, precisely the gospel message that Graham was bringing to them in the first place.

Though Graham would later temper his public views on economic affairs in line with his heightened profile as a spiritual statesman, he initially opposed any social reform bearing even the faintest whiff of collectivist thinking. He commonly referred, for instance, to the Garden of Eden as a joyful place afflicted with "no union dues, no labor leaders, no snakes, no diseases."[274] On a 1949 crusade in England, he inveighed more directly against the perils of collectivism in the guise of the country's postwar Labour government. Labour leaders were stoking a sinister "Communist advance," he warned, and in the process of "killing all initiative and free enterprise"; England's new welfare state "has not solved one of Britain's economic ills," he said. "Instead, it has created a thousand economic problems."[275]

To be sure, such sentiments won wide support on the American evangelical scene in the early years of the Cold War. More fundamentally, however, this social myopia and economic quietism were themselves signs that Graham, for all his fundamentalist ardor, had accommodated all too smoothly to the temper of modern times. The prayers of the fundamentalist movement for a second businessman's revival had been answered—but because the revivalists in question were ill disposed to challenge any aspect of America's business civilization, the great postwar mobilization of evangelicals was not any sort of reformist crusade. Instead, it resembled nothing so much as the inevitable coming of age of a potent new consumer demographic.

The temptation is always great to interpret the postwar rise of a newly politicized evangelical right as a crude propagandistic power move—something conjured into being by plutocratic fiat or canny propaganda appeals playing up a coming secular humanist coup d'état. That, indeed, is a frequent refrain among leftist adversaries of the religious right, who tend to view religious activism, like religion itself, as an elaborate put-on job, designed to distract a downwardly mobile corps of middle- and working-class believers whose visions of relentless cultural persecution are punctuated by the occasional cruelly manipulative promise of eternal bliss that will redeem their worldly suffering.[276]

But pleasing as such reveries may be to secular-left critics, there's no dark saga of stage-managed mass religious sentiment or marionette-style manipulations of outrage in the inner history of modern evangelical conservatism. For one thing, as we've seen, the rising wave of Protestant apostles of nationalist prosperity were far too media-savvy to attempt anything so crude as a leveraged takeover of the American religious imagination. And for another, any such ploy would be readily recognized for what it was among their no-less-media-savvy parishioners, viewers, and listeners.

No, the millennial fears and worldly promises of modern evangelical religion share much deeper roots in the underlying civic faith of twentieth-century Americanism. What we're accustomed to viewing from the top as a triumphalist seizure of political influence by an aggrieved cadre of high-profile culture warriors turns out on closer examination to be a self-organized revolt among believers seeking to redraft the troubled means of success in an American social order on the fast track to post-Keynesian austerity.

One key force behind this shift was structural; the organizational momentum of the rising evangelical insurgency had moved deeper into the parachurch movement that had helped launch Graham's phenomenally successful career on the national stage. Freed by Graham's example of avoiding anything more than a notional commitment to social reform, the new breed of parachurch believers also hunkered down into a sunny new variation of the old American cult of the Gnostic self. And for the first time in recent American memory, the evangelical scourges of a secular modern culture became downright cheerful.

In a little-appreciated irony, the premillennial believers of the revived evangelical movement were becoming enthusiastic purveyors of a strikingly psychologized account of the Christian life. And this trend was firmly aligned with an outward push to institutionalize the substantial gains of the parachurch movement into a new cult of church growth. Evangelical ministries thus became bigger in their popular reach, while becoming stalwartly miniaturized in their social and theological vision. "I remain convinced," wrote the prominent church-growth advocate C. Peter Wagner in 1976, "that without faith, it is impossible for churches to grow. Empirical evidence also validates the necessity of faith or whatever else you want to call it—possibility thinking or goal setting—as a prerequisite for church growth."[277]

Within that "whatever else you want to call it" lay a world of pragmatic, self-improving enterprise. Linked up with the mania for church growth, the parachurch uprising turned itself into a bona fide subculture. Conservative believers, no less than their mainline Protestant counterparts, had grown impatient with the routinized outward forms of devotional piety and denominational division; they conceptualized a new brand of "seeker-friendly" worship that packaged socially and theologically conservative doctrines in the familiar and accommodating popular messaging formats that have since been institutionalized in the megachurch. In highlighting the central experience of the readily replicated mediagenic revival, postwar evangelicals embraced all the things that went with orchestrating religious sentiment on a mass scale—modes of proselytizing, personal testimony, and fund-raising that place a premium on media spectacle; a related new focus on ripped-from-the-headlines interpretations of biblical prophecy; and, most crucially, the propagation of a new gospel of prosperity, which endowed believers with an otherwise elusive sense of personal control over their economic fortunes as the old foundations of Keynesian affluence started to erode from within.

It's worth pausing a moment here to take stock of this unlikely cultural convergence. The restless countercultural experimentation of the hippie age is usually credited—and fairly enough—with spurring in its wake an enormous growth market in therapeutic religion, tailored to individualist, antinomian visions of faith as a personal quest of self-discovery. But conservative evangelical believers were no strangers to America's sprawling experience-based consumer culture; as they developed new modes of worship and cultural and political outreach, conservative postwar believers took to their own brand of the "almost lascivious preoccupation with self" that sociologist Will Herberg found to be corroding the substance of suburban America's mainline piety.[278]

This curious new fusion of prophetic and therapeutic faiths hinged on many superficially conflicting impulses. The adherents of the post-war evangelical revival were at once materially comfortable and cultur-ally aggrieved, deeply pessimistic about the immediate course of human history but expansively committed to the sturdy American gospel of self-improvement. Perhaps most of all, they were distrustful of any theological or intellectual approach to religious observance—even as they promoted the functional expansion of evangelical faith into every reach of the inti-mate and carefully ordered life of the believer.

Rank Positivity

"Experience" was the byword of the strangely confident Gnostic evangel-icals of the postwar suburbs—and the range of experiential problems that the new gospel set out to solve multiplied with the steady advance of post-war American prosperity. Philosophic pragmatists such as William James (who, it bears reminding, had been an early and enthusiastic adherent of the Mind Cure wing of the New Thought movement) had largely justified the value of religious ideas based on the measurable, positive outcomes that they generated in the life of the believer. And in the latter half of the twentieth century, this liberal and pragmatic account of the benefits of belief burrowed, improbably enough, into a modern faith tradition steeped in the expectation of the imminent end of the world. This meant, among other things, that therapeutic faith had somehow to be squared with the profoundly *other*worldly, nonhumanist, and dubiously pragmatic arrival of the Last Judgment and the Second Coming. The life-enhancement veri-ties of the suburban end-times gospel are, in other words, the very sort of bewildering welter of faith-based contradictions that the expression "only in America" could have been coined to describe.

The first major phase of this transformation came from outside the evangelical world, courtesy of the blockbuster classic of modern self-help, Norman Vincent Peale's *The Power of Positive Thinking*. Like Russell Con-well before him, Peale was something of an avatar for his distinct chapter in the modern history of the Money Cult. Peale prefigured many of the radical transformations that lay ahead for American Protestant faith, fus-

ing a hard-line conservative political outlook with an enthusiastic embrace
of modern therapeutic technique. Heedless of traditional doctrine-based
divides, he toggled effortlessly between the liberal Methodist faith that
decisively influenced his youth and seminary training and the adopted
Reform Calvinist teachings of his famous home in New York, the Marble
Collegiate Church. To this denominational alloy he added the metaphysical speculations of the New Thought movement—again, much as Russell
Conwell had before. In the unlikely person of a squat bespectacled pastor
from a midtown Manhattan congregation, postwar America became initiated into the mysteries of an occult brand of New Thought piety, and for
the next half-century the New Thought movement's once-fringe healing
science of the Mind acquired a vast new global following.

Meanwhile, as Peale ascended to unprecedented cultural renown and
political influence, he parted company with the deferential niceties of life
in the Protestant mainline establishment. He promoted the postwar launch
of the breakaway conservative ecumenical group the National Association
of Evangelicals, and in concert with the conservative theologians behind
that project, he regularly denounced the relativist theological leanings and
communist-appeasing political views of liberal Protestantism's leadership
class as the bitter harvest of a fallen, decadent culture.

The trajectory of Peale's career is thus a jarring one for anyone who
expects spiritual and cultural allegiances of schools of thought to be confined in place, strictly obeying the conventional liberal-conservative divide
demarcating evangelical insurgency and its mainline establishment opposition. At times, Peale's success surprised even him. Throughout his career,
for example, Peale was an eager minister to anxious American business
leaders—his flagship Christian self-help magazine *Guideposts* was conceived as homiletic reading for "the businessman alone in a hotel room,"
and in its formative years relied heavily on bulk purchases from major corporate clients such as General Motors, who sought to tamp down union
militancy among its huge workforce with Peale's trademark tales of fantastic self-healing and indomitable success for ordinary Americans. But the
magazine, and Peale's books, won a far wider readership among anxious
female spiritual seekers trapped in the postwar domestic sphere.[279]

Peale's message of overweening personal and industrial harmony may have been an awkward fit within the heavily unionized and conflict-prone workplaces of the 1950s, but it would carry a great deal of prophetic portent for the future shape of industrial relations and Protestant belief as the old New Deal social contract frayed and faltered in the decades ahead. What's more, the heavily feminized character of Peale's following would point the way toward a much more self-consciously domestic and evangelical approach to management theory in the many post-Keynesian traumas facing the American economy from the 1970s onward.

But this is all to anticipate the later triumph of Peale's outlook, across the porous boundaries of secular, economic, and religious life. Peale's career was a remarkable sojourn, in no small part because of its roots in what had by now become classic middle-American spiritual ambitions. Like many of the Money Cult's most important acolytes, Peale grew up the son of a preacher—in his case, the Methodist minister Charles Clifford Peale, who traded in his first professional calling as a doctor for the pulpit when he was cured of a bout of smallpox by what he felt was divine intervention. Norman grew up along the Methodist circuit in Ohio adulating his father and developing an interest in politics via his family's ardent support of prohibition in the early twentieth century. He committed himself to the ministry as a young man after his father assured him that God would help him to conquer his chronic feelings of inferiority and his crippling fear of public speaking. And like many Midwestern Protestants of his day, the young Peale drew additional inspiration from the region's great culture hero William Jennings Bryan; Peale's biographer Carol V.B. George reports that Bryan's example initially spurred Peale to embrace what he felt was his first calling, as a politician.[280]

In his first tour of pastoral duty, Peale served a relatively new congregation in Brooklyn; after he transformed that church into a thriving communion, he was called to serve a struggling church in Syracuse. There he used his personal and folksy pulpit style to great effect, doubling the church's membership rolls to more than 1,600 congregants over his six-year tenure.[281] His next and last appointment was at the pulpit of the Marble Collegiate Church in Manhattan, which he oversaw from 1932 until he retired in

1984. The Reformed Marble Congregation was a shabby-genteel institution harking back to the colonial settlement of New York; the congregation was started in 1628, and at the time it took Peale on as pastor, it was rumored to be among the city's largest real estate owners. Now, however, it was struggling to combat the flight of believers from mainline Protestant pews in the teeth of the Depression, and it prevailed upon Peale, despite his ordination from a rival denomination, to work the wonders of church growth that had already earned the young pastor the nickname "the Methodist marvel."

It was in the service of the Marble Church's conservative and elite board of elders that Peale cultivated his self-conscious cross-denominational appeal—pulling the minister's lectern away from the center of the altar, for example, so he could address the audience directly as he preached without notes. It was rough going at first; the stuffy Marble congregation wasn't initially receptive to Peale's unbuckled brand of "practical Christianity," which took many of its conceptual cues and much of its language from the New Thought gospel of infinite Supply, personal power, and the all-conquering (capital-M) Mind. But Peale continued to preach his distinctive homilies of personal success, and he eventually found an audience beyond the sanctum of the Marble Church; in 1934, he began a weekly national radio broadcast on the NBC network called "The Art of Living."

His pastoral calling likewise expanded to take in the more workaday, practical dilemmas of his modern congregants. Together with a psychotherapist who was all-too aptly named Smiley Blanton, Peale started the Marble Collegiate Church Clinic (later the Religio-Psychiatric Institute) in the church's Fifth Avenue basement in 1937. The joint project drew on both Blanton's background in Freudian technique—he had been among the analysands in the master's Vienna practice—and Peale's sunnier New Thought counsel to address the inner anxieties that tended to wear away at the church's following during the balance of the work week: addiction, marital troubles, blocked family communications, feelings of inferiority and unworthiness, and the like. In his pastoral work, Peale discovered a special affinity for luring "rising New York executives" into religious life, as he explained to a gathering at New York's Harvard club. He would later tell his biographer George that he saw himself as "a missionary to American business," and began booking weekly addresses to business groups across the country via a professional speaker's bureau.[282] By the end of the thirties, Peale was a name-brand success preacher with a national audience; he published his first two self-help books, *The Art of Living* (1937) and *You Can Win* (1938), to wide acclaim, and in 1941, he began to publish a syndicated newspaper column, "The American Way."

Subduing Pagan Stateism

But what set Peale's message apart from standard New Thought invocations of the Higher Self and its abundant earthly reward was his clear allegiance to a reactionary brand of business conservatism. Past New Thought preachers of prosperity were still notionally aligned with New England tradition of postmillennial social reform. Not so in Peale's case: He was a harsh and early spiritual critic of FDR's New Deal, on the grounds that it sapped the individual's work ethic and obstructed the divinely ordained operations of the free market. "A sinister shadow is being thrown over our liberties," he preached from his Marble pulpit in 1936—an unmistakable reference to FDR's runaway executive power at the time of the president's notorious court-packing scheme to strong-arm the Supreme Court into following the party line on the New Deal. In sounding such alarms, Peale was merely picking up the broader pro-business themes he'd already trumpeted from his Syracuse pulpit after the 1929 market crash: "The supreme test of [Christianity's] influence is to be found in the business and commercial life of our great urban centers," he proclaimed.

Indeed, for Peale, the question of Christianity's power in the economic sphere and its impact upon the lives of striving individuals were all of a piece. It all began with the believer's invitation to Jesus to enter into their innermost hearts, and from there, Peale explained, the faith was set on a course of "world conquest":

> Emotion breeds enthusiasm, and enthusiasm is that which is necessary to Christian world conquest. The need of the church today is for mystic or emotional contact with Jesus. This will create enthusiasm for world conquest . . . The real need is a consciousness that Jesus is a living personality in the twentieth century.[283]

Peale's own enthusiastic path of conquest involved a slew of political partnerships on the economic right. He was on the advisory board of Spiritual Mobilization, a lobbying group founded by a fellow positive-thinking Protestant divine in Southern California with another successful radio ministry, the Congregationalist pastor James Fifield. The group was dedicated to the defeat of "pagan stateism" as practiced by the brain trust in FDR's Washington, and was closely aligned with ambitious libertarian initiatives such as Leonard Read's Economic Freedom Forum, which would later oversee the widespread disbursal of libertarian textbooks and teaching curricula in California public schools. Peale also briefly chaired the Christian Freedom Foundation, a sister group founded by Fifield and largely underwritten by the evangelical oil tycoon J. Howard Pew, which published a laissez-faire journal called *Christian Economics*. Both of these groups had galvanized much of their support on the right behind efforts to beat back the New Deal's steady expansion of the public sector's influence in the American economy.

But Peale also lent his pulpit to right-wing causes pursuing far more ambitious agendas. From 1942 to 1945, he chaired the Committee on Constitutional Government, a controversial group that came under frequent congressional investigation thanks to the far-right political sympathies of its lead organizer Edward Rumely, a deputy of the conservative newspaper mogul Frank Gannett and a close political adviser to Henry Ford. Rumely had been convicted in 1918 on charges of using money from an agent of the German government—America's wartime enemy—to purchase a daily newspaper called the *New York Mail*. (Calvin Coolidge issued a full pardon for Rumely in 1925, reportedly at Ford's request.) Rumely had faced similar charges of trading with the Nazis during World War II, but they had resulted in acquittal. During Congress's investigations into the Constitutional Government Committee's standing as a nonpartisan tax-deductible nonprofit, Rumely repeatedly refused to disclose the names of the group's major donors. This resulted in another criminal conviction, this time for contempt, which was remitted on grounds of ill health.[284]

Whatever the sources of the committee's funding, it got expended in a burst of raw right-wing propaganda. From the moment of its inception, the committee embarked on an ambitious public-relations initiative to promote robustly libertarian and anticommunist talking points in American political discourse. In reviewing the group's expenses, Congress found that it spent $10 million to distribute 82 million pieces of literature, including vast numbers of books; advertisements in 536 daily newspapers with a combined circulation topping 20 million readers; 10,000 radio transcriptions; and some 350,000 personal telegrams. The committee's book-distribution network was especially aggressive. In a move that clearly presaged the bulk purchase of ideological books within the contemporary conservative movement, the committee contracted with politically sympathetic business leaders to buy preselected titles on a mass scale, and distribute them among their employees. In a total rejection of the group's laissez-faire ideology, these titles were marked up more than 100 percent above production costs, with books that cost the committee, say, 20 cents a copy to issue being sold at a price between 50 cents and a dollar. The tiles on offer were some of the day's most hard-line reactionary fare, such as John T. Flynn's red-scare manifesto *The Road Ahead*, Monsanto CEO Edgar Queeny's libertarian broadside *The Spirit of Enterprise*, and former Democratic Congressman Franklin Pettengill's anti–New Deal jeremiad *Jefferson the Forgotten Man*. The committee distributed a staggering 760,000 books on this lucrative basis.[285] The same rock-ribbed, markets-first, communism-everywhere outlook informed the group's main legislative goal a constitutional amendment to cap the federal income tax at 25 percent. In the words of Texas Democratic Congressman Wright Patman—who had launched the congressional inquiry into the committee's activities after he'd been led to suspect that it was funneling money to his Republican opponent—the measure would transform America into "a paradise for millionaires."[286]

Not surprisingly, Congress's review of its activities resulted in the stripping of the Committee on Constitutional Government's tax-exempt status. Rumely—who had already scrubbed his own name from the group's letterhead and stationery in anticipation of the congressional investigation—swiftly reorganized the committee as an educational trust, and named his daughter as the new group's sales manager.[287]

Peale, for his part, resigned from the group just ahead of its reorganization. He was immersed at the time in promoting *Guideposts*, which began publication in 1945. He apologized to Rumely in his resignation letter, explaining that if he kept up his affiliation with the committee, "I might as well drop *Guideposts*."

But the break with Rumely and the committee's activities was anything but definitive. It's true that *Guideposts* was aimed squarely at the same audience that thronged to Peale's burgeoning radio, publishing, and therapeutic ministries, and that it favored the same reassuringly personalized, live-life-fully apothegms of his resolutely practical, New Thought–inflected version of the Christian message. At the same time, however, Peale clearly envisioned the publication as an extension of the same laissez-faire propaganda work that he oversaw at the Committee on Constitutional Government. He leaned heavily on the committee's mailing lists and donor roster, and continued to consult Rumely on how best to shape the magazine's content and marketing stratagems; Rumely's best-known catchphrase, "Freedom is the child of religion," was a frequent refrain in Peale's fund-raising rounds. And Peale initially built up the circulation base for *Guideposts* by enlisting major business donors to take out bulk subscriptions and distribute copies among their workforce—the same model, in other words, that had turned the Committee on Constitutional Government into such an effective clearinghouse of propaganda for the economic right. The magazine's initial group of major donors read like a Who's Who of postwar business reaction, from the old Peale stalwarts J. Howard Pew and Frank Gannett to investment banker E. F. Hutton, retail mogul S. S. Kresge, and Eastern Airlines president Eddie Rickenbacker.[288]

Still, Peale was presumably still mindful of all the trouble that the Committee on Constitutional Government had weathered on his watch, and so took pains to reiterate to his liberal detractors in the Protestant world that "there is absolutely nothing political about *Guideposts*." In communiqués with his funders and right-wing allies, however, Peale sounded a very different, and much more urgent, note of political engagement. *Guideposts* could be counted on to "refertilize the soil of American life by widely spreading religious ideas, [so] we can counteract the communistic virus . . . and defeat left-wing influences such as communism," he wrote to George E. Stringfellow, grand potentate of the Shriners. In correspondence with one of his chief financial angels, Frank Gannett, Peale stressed that the Protestant clergy in America was being undermined by "left-wing CIO-PAC forces," which made it especially critical "to get our project [*Guideposts*] under way [so] we can exert a constant and widening influence in the right direction."[289]

Peale's remarkable ideological fealty to the business right was, it bears reminding, not particularly exceptional among the ranks of American clergy, despite his complaints about their rapidly spreading left-wing indoctrination. One 1936 poll of more than 20,000 Protestant and Catholic clergy found that more than 70 percent of respondents opposed the New Deal; among national religious publications, only the liberal *Christian Century* was a consistent backer of FDR. Even at the height of Roosevelt's wartime popularity, this general trend held; in 1944, Thomas E. Dewey won a plurality of the Protestant vote despite FDR's comfortable overall winning margin. This background consensus within the Protestant establishment helps explain how, even in the aftermath of the Committee on Constitutional Freedom debacle, Peale's popularity as a spiritual therapist and generic champion of American individualism continued to grow—right up through the release of the great self-help tract that both reinvented the genre and launched him into a global celebrity that in many ways surpassed that of his great spiritual and ideological ally Billy Graham.[290]

The Power of Open-Shop Thinking

Among the many things that distinguish Peale's blockbuster self-help manual, *The Power of Positive Thinking*, were the circumstances surrounding its composition. Alone among the vast American literature of spiritualized self-help, it was written on a union-busting junket. By the time he had conceived of the idea of a general manual of the self-administered success faith, Peale had become manically overscheduled. His Marble Church ministry, his pastoral work at the Religio-Psychiatric Clinic, his weekly radio broadcasts, and his frequent addresses to business groups had left him with little enough time to breathe, let alone to draft another book. So at the suggestion of his old friend James Fifield, the founder of the Spiritual Mobilization and the Christian Freedom Foundation, Peale lit out for Hawaii in 1951, with the dual purpose of conducting a speaking tour to gauge the spread of labor militancy in the American territory and carving out an undisturbed block of time on his schedule to write the manuscript that would become one of the bestselling self-help books of all time. Under the aegis of his pet advocacy groups, Fifield aggressively promoted anti-union right-to-work laws, and recent labor unrest in California, under the leadership of the socialist longshoremen leader Harry Bridges, had roused Fifield into suspecting that employers in Hawaii might need to act more deliberately to head off similar outbreaks of union activism there.

Not surprisingly, Peale's visit quickly confirmed the casual alarm of his sponsor; he wrote to friends that the labor climate on the islands was "sinister," and that the unions' "communistic leadership" was sowing a mood of confrontation among the rank-and-file membership. But as he spoke with area business leaders, and addressed an overflow Chamber of Commerce gathering, Peale also argued that this sinister process could be reversed. As he enthusiastically reported to Fifield on the results of his efforts, Peale wrote that labor peace could be won by force of the bosses' organized will: "If we can get these people to be aggressive and to equal in aggressiveness that of the [longshoremen's union]," he wrote to Fifield, "it is my judgment that the common people over here, the workers, will respond." To a local clergyman, Peale explained that in order to bring about lasting concord between workers and owners, it was first necessary "to change the communistic people" and "to bring everybody into harmony with the spirit and ideals of Christ."[291] Here again was the defining trait of the Money Cult: American Protestantism's core commitment to radically reconfigure the self so that divine deliverance and market prosperity were indistinguishable. In Peale's hands, however, the returns of this alliance were rendered in refreshingly direct and ideological terms: Jesus could be counted on to revive the hearts of communists, and that spirit of revival would, in turn, be the surest guarantor of peace and harmony within the industrial workplace.

Peale's industrial witness in Hawaii was so valuable to Fifield and his business allies precisely because Peale radiated the conviction of his beliefs. It's important to stress that Peale, like other chief apostles of the Money Cult, never envisioned religion as a crude means of social control—something to keep workers in line and beguiled by glittering reveries of pie in the sky while the barons of capital praised a very different sort of God (the one who recognized kindred spirits of creative destruction in the pious hearts of the mogul class) in their uptown Manhattan or suburban Connecticut pews. No, the God of Peale's distinctive brand of success faith was effective as a corrosive force in the dispelling of labor and social tensions precisely because he bore no class affiliation for any particular group of worshipers— be they the Chamber of Commerce executives who were responsible for so much of Peale's personal inspiration and livelihood or "the common people over here, the workers," who could be expected to fall spontaneously into line with business prophets of a pristine capitalism, once these natural leaders summoned the strength to call out and expel the unclean "communistic" spirits of labor unrest in their midst. The genius of the Peale gospel is that, in its modernized, therapeutic gloss on New Thought, it managed to package a reactionary economic outlook within an expansive theological one.

Because Pealeism was above all a self-administered technique—like Mormonism, it required no interceding church hierarchy, relying instead on the believer's own powers of auto-suggestion—it also enjoyed a superficial cachet of democratic worship. In his self-help preachments, Peale made all the conditions of personal prosperity seem within as easy reach as a success mantra or a creatively visualized career breakthrough. Under the simple formulas of Peale's positivity creed—to "picturize, praycrize, and actualize" positive life outcomes, as Peale described the process—all believers could divine the preordained destinies of their Higher Selves, in a fashion that made their present social station but a layover en route to a far more fortunate and uplifting spiritual destination. Much as Russell Conwell had divined the workings of a benevolent, harmonious, and orderly cosmos concealed within the winning of worldly fortunes during the brazenly amoral Gilded Age, Peale was winningly repackaging the mystic truisms of the New Thought movement as seemingly self-evident teachings of a primitive Christian revival, aimed squarely at the struggles and ambitions of the striving American self-improver and professional man-on-the-make.

The Power of God Within You

It was a vision that was at once abidingly Gnostic and beguilingly ecumenical. Peale's career pivoted upon an inward version of the same vision of piety as an all-purpose social fixative that figures such as Eisenhower and Henry Luce had preached from their own bully pulpits of midcentury Americanism. But where the apostles of patriotic Protestant uplift were largely indifferent to the theological content of civic faith, Peale thrived on a confident determination to get under the hood of Christianity as a system of personal motivation; Pealeism tirelessly incanted a personalized vision of infinite possibility and achievement, in which all good things flowed spontaneously from the act of believing. At bottom, Peale's theology was an updated ultra-pragmatic variation on Bruce Barton's Christology—with the significant caveat that it was studiously stripped of anything resembling a social ethic. If Barton's Christ was a muscular son of toil, Peale's was a model middle manager, focused much more intently on the inner hydraulics of the Christian mindset than on any more demanding expression of the faith in the form of a social ethic.

The mechanical image is especially apt in Peale's case. Peale's accounts of the mental process of spiritual inspiration were steeped in the breezy, reassuring rhetoric of product improvement, readily recognized as the lingua franca of progress in postwar America. As such, it ultimately trumped Blanton's more conventionally dour, Freud-influenced understanding of the unconscious; the two colleagues would eventually fall out, ironically enough, over their disparate readings of how much importance should be attached to the specter of psychic conflict. For Peale, the unconscious was not a site of unresolved inner struggles, thwarted longings, or the irresolvable tension between the civilized superego and the savage id. No, it was the old New Thought repository of infinite (and therefore materially abundant) Supply. "In the subconscious God presides with his illimitable Power," Peale pronounced in a world-class flourish of spiritual confidence in his 1957 bestseller *Stay Alive All Your Life*. "If you are allowing yourself to be defeated, practice thinking confidently and focus your thoughts on God. This inward power, this power of God within you, is so tremendous that under stress and in crisis people can perform the most incredible feats."[292]

This casual annexation of God's "illimitable power" to the striving human psyche was indeed the principal achievement of *The Power of Positive Thinking*, which in most other respects is the standard assemblage of homespun anecdotage and exhortations to individual morale-boosting that had characterized spiritual success literature since the mid nineteenth century. Peale's central contribution was to reduce these sweeping and well-worn formulas—*Envision your best life now* or *Become in tune with the Infinite*—to a series of self-administered techniques tailored to the success gospel of the consumer society of postwar America. Like Graham's saving eschatological gospel, the logic of Peale's success preachments was short-circuited in many ways by a strange formalist circularity; it was a call for the embrace of a world-conquering faith premised chiefly on . . . the need to embrace a world-conquering faith. "Simply accept faith," he'd preached in classic prag-matist fashion in the pages of *You Can Win*. "Believe you have it, and you will have it. That, you see, is itself faith." In Peale's work, as Donald Meyer observes, "it was not so much that philosophy and theology were absent; they were assumed and swallowed into technique, dissolving silently."[293]

Peale's scheme likewise assumed that the entire social background for Protestant success was not to be tampered with—any whiff of a social-re-form mentality clearly flirted with godless communism. With spiritual and social reform out of the picture, technique was indeed all.

As a result, in *Positive Thinking*, Peale chiefly invoked the functional utility of Christian faith—its wondrous capacity to restore energy, infuse grand ambitions, and, most important, to condition individuals to refrain from entertaining any negative thoughts or worldviews. The result was a brisk fusion of crude scientism and strictly results-oriented faith. "It is my conviction that the principles of Christianity scientifically utilized can develop an uninterrupted and continuous flow of energy into the human mind and body," Peale writes at one point, in a sort of pseudoscientific visionary transport. He goes on to cite the case of an energetic business-man whose physician, charged with closely monitoring the man's workload and stress levels, pronounces that he's able to take on stupendous amounts of new work and responsibility because he's a paragon of industrial effi-ciency: "He is a thoroughly well-organized individual with no energy leaks in his make-up," this doctor exclaims in the manner of a draftsman por-ing over an industrial blueprint—and what's more, he notes, the man's prodigious reserves of energy can be chalked up almost exclusively to his advanced piety: "From his religion he has learned how to avoid drainage of power. His religion is a workable and useful mechanism for preventing energy leaks."[294]

This oddly schematic account of the benefits of religious belief runs throughout the pragmatist-cum-Gnostic gospel of Pealeism.[295] As Peale dilates on the physical and emotional benefits of prayer, for example, he notes that "prayer power is a manifestation of energy. Just as there exist scientific techniques for the release of atomic energy, so are there scientific procedures for the release of spiritual energy through the mechanism of prayer."[296] (Of course, the great irony here was that the "release of atomic energy" directly accounted for a great deal of the cultural and existential anxieties that Peale was everywhere diagnosing and correcting in the nation's vast cohort of blocked and negative-thinking men of power—a reflection that Peale himself would likely disown as impermissibly unbiblical and incorrigibly negative.)

It also bears noting that amid the many positive homilies that prophets such as Peale carefully extract from the pages of Scripture, the not-inconsiderable darker stretches of the Bible always escape mention. The church-building aphorisms of Paul and the Book of Acts always claim pride of place, as do the sunnier, meritocratic parables of Jesus, such as the story of the servants and the talents. But the Book of Job and Ecclesiastes almost never come up, nor, naturally, do the bleaker moments of the Passion narrative, or Jesus' famed camel-through-a-needle's-eye simile about the rich man's chances of entering the Kingdom of Heaven.

More commonly, though, Peale divines metaphors for achieving the state of true grace from outside the domain of scripture entirely. In packaging positive-thinking as a bona fide science, he took great care in adopting the rhetoric and mundane imagery of the consumer market. "On a roadside billboard I saw an advertisement for a certain brand of motor oil," he says, launching into one of his typical homilies:

> The slogan read, "A clean engine always delivers power." So will a mind free of negatives produce positives, that is to say, a clean mind will deliver power. Therefore flush out your thoughts, give yourself a clean mental engine, remembering that a clean mind, even as a clean engine, always delivers power.[297]

It's hard to imagine a more apt metaphor for the Peale brand of New Thought—or one that reveals more about the drift of the mid-twentieth-century Protestant business gospel. The image of the mind as car engine neatly distills the Gnostic obsession with spiritual power—the only means by which the believer can realize deliverance from the fallen world of matter. The simile also resonates, much as the ad slogan that inspires it, with the midcentury cult of pseudoscientific industrial efficiency. The mind not only lays claim to new transformative power; it also does so in a satisfying, streamlined fashion, by simple force of incantation: "a mind free of negatives produces positives." Finally, the image of a clean mind, which is unnervingly close to that of an empty one, evokes a spiritual world that, much like its mass-consumer counterpart, requires no real effort or sacrifice from adherents beyond pledging faith to a catchy slogan: "a clean mind, even as a clean engine, always delivers power."

Peale's persistent adherence to this bare Gnostic functionalism produces a distinctly flattened-out version of Christian faith. Take, for example, the only passage in *Positive Thinking* that really comes close to a conversion narrative—a procedure that is, once again, tellingly recounted in the tone and language of an industrial-era instruction manual. Nowhere can readers fasten onto the Protestant revivalist's historic appeals to a soul in crisis and teetering on the brink of eternal damnation. Nor is there any hint of the subjective anguish and emotion that had historically preceded the moment at which Protestant believers crossed from the threshold of sin into the second birth. Instead, Peale recommends that a troubled seeker—someone who has "not been doing so well in the game of life"—follow a simple regimen of Bible-approved thought-cleansing:

> Start reading the New Testament and notice the number of times it
> refers to faith. Select a dozen of the strongest statements about faith,
> the ones that you like the best. Then memorize each one. Let these
> faith concepts drop into your conscious mind. Say them over and
> over again, especially just before going to sleep at night. By a process
> of spiritual osmosis they will sink from your conscious mind into
> your subconscious mind and in time will modify and reslant your

basic thought pattern. This process will change you into a believer, an
expecter, and when you become such, you will in due course become
an achiever. You will have new power to get what God and you decide
you really want from life. The most powerful force in human nature
is the spiritual-power technique taught in the Bible.[298]

This is a fairly crisp summation of the Peale faith—and, tellingly,
the terms "process" and "power" are more frequent touchstones, here and
throughout Peale's work, than the Bible or the gospel. Even in a self-
consciously religious setting, Peale depicts the benefits of faith almost
exclusively in terms of its instrumental value; indeed, in this account, the
demands of religious observance are reduced to rote memorization and
motivational incantations. If faith was now deemed central to the challenges of living as a better American by the lords of Washington and Time,
Inc., the chief function of religious thought seemed to be to demonstrate to
believers how best to make incremental progress toward the main event in
American life: maximum personal and material success.

The Gospel of Tomorrowland

It's worth noting how Peale's midcentury mantras of personal success,
delivered from the heart of the Protestant mainline, overlap with Graham's
urgent message of millennial preparedness. Both versions of the gospel are
strikingly functionalist—that is, they proffer a strictly schematic view of
world history and personal salvation, demanding very little in the way of
social action on the part of the redeemed. Both strains of midcentury faith
are, moreover, steeped in an overt celebration of the values of the consumer
market, even as they occasionally vent distress over the moral license of
latter-day capitalism. What's more, the Graham message of grateful surrender to the gathering signs of the millennium's imminent arrival, and
Peale's patient exposition of the carefully ordered qualities of the redeemed
Gnostic self converged in the great proving ground of postwar evangelical
self-organization: the bedroom suburbs of Southern California.

Not surprisingly, Peale found a staunch following among the promoters
of California's booming libertarian business culture. In addition to the long-

standing alliance with James Fifield, Peale and Pealeism drew other acolytes out West who soon joined Peale in the fruitful intersection of evangelical conservatism and American popular culture. Little more than a knockoff of *Positive Thinking*, Robert Schuller's mid-1960s bestseller, *The Art of Possibility Thinking*, boasted an introduction by Peale—a close friend and confidant of Schuller's—pivoting largely around Schuller's own ministerial success story. In the early 1960s, the young Reformed minister resolved to leave his home congregation in Chicago for the booming Los Angeles suburb of Orange County; he famously launched his first California ministry at a drive-in theater, and then went on to erect the all-glass Crystal Cathedral, designed by the great modernist architect Phillip Johnson, in Garden Grove, California. Schuller launched his historic televangelical ministry, "Hour of Power" in 1970, heeding the advice of his other close ministerial ally, Billy Graham. (The Crystal Cathedral facility was bankrupted in the wake of the 2008 financial collapse, and was sold off to the Roman Catholic diocese of Los Angeles in 2012, and Schuller's grandson Bobby now helms the pastorate as it repatriates to a smaller home at the site of a former Catholic church.)

Other key Californian ministers helped expand and refine the nexus between prophecy belief and success psychology. By far the best known of these figures today is Tim LaHaye, who launched his career as an enterprising right-wing leader of San Diego's Scott Memorial Baptist Church, and has gone on to found a series of influential evangelical lobbying groups, from the Carter-era Californians for Biblical Morality to the influential and secretive Council for National Policy, which coordinated closely with the Reagan White House on several fiscal and cultural policy cultural fronts.[299] Along the way, LaHaye and his wife Beverly have published many psychological primers for evangelicals, ranging from marriage advice handbooks to modern updates of the medieval psychology of the four temperaments—all once again steeped in the self-enabled theologies of scripture-based positive thinking. Today, of course, LaHaye's central claim to fame is as a popularizer of end-times prophecy—the series of *Left Behind* novels co-authored with Jerry Jenkins stands as one of the bestselling fiction franchises in history, amassing global sales of more than 65 million. Indeed, LaHaye's readily interchanged, and hugely successful, preoccupations with personal therapy and end-times belief neatly gloss the paradoxical impulses at the heart of today's Money Cult: closely heeding the Peale-approved battery of therapeutic formulas of self-improvement while anticipating the divinely sanctioned destruction of civilization.

Another tireless Californian purveyor of midcentury therapy-cum-prophecy faith was Bill Bright, the founder of the phenomenally success-ful parachurch group Campus Crusade for Christ. Bright, a Presbyterian preacher, started out as an entrepreneur in the conventional secular mold, distributing a successful line of high-end candies called Bright's California Confections. On the side, he was an evangelical youth recruiter, minis-tering to college students at UCLA together with his wife, Vonette. The couple soon realized that their evangelical outreach program—dubbed the Campus Crusade for Christ—represented a winning formula; unham-pered by the quasi-paternal authority of traditional denominational groups on campus, the Brights' effort yielded 250 faith commitments from UCLA students over its first few months. (One high-profile recruit was the school's star quarterback, Donn Moomaw, who would go on to a pastoral career of his own, and most famously prompted the evangelical conversion of onetime actor and aspiring statewide politician Ronald Reagan in the early 1960s.) Before long, the Brights expanded the Crusade to other Golden State campuses, and then on to the rest of the country; the group now boasts more than 27,000 full-time employees, affiliates in 190 countries, and a volunteer corps of some 225,000 lay activists.[300]

Bill Bright, who died in 2003, had more than 100 books to his credit—most of them marketed in the sprawling niche of Christian self-help. His nine-part "Joy" series, featuring such titles as *The Joy of Dynamic Giving: Investing for Eternal Blessings*, culminates with the Peale-esque title *The Joy of Supernatural Thinking*; its audiobook version is narrated by recidi-vist hopeful and erstwhile Fox News commentator Mike Huckabee. Like LaHaye, Bright also was an avid student of end-times prophecy, and pub-lished his own series of historical novels (co-authored with Jack Cavanaugh) dramatizing America's apocalyptic redemption, *Great Awakenings*. And like Schuller, Bright was a close compatriot of Billy Graham, who frequently preached at Campus Crusade revivals—indeed, Graham's breakthrough moment of holiness conversion occurred on the grounds of a Campus Crusade mountain retreat—and contributed the foreword to Bright's authorized biography.

Like the formative political-cum-theological alliance that first took hold between Peale and Graham, these successor ministries of therapeutic evangelism based in the Golden State all underlined the degree to which the sojourning spirit of American Protestantism had morphed into an all-purpose doctrine of life enhancement for the saved. The Pealeist worship of pure Gnostic technique proved adaptable to a seemingly boundless array of mediagenic pulpits and parachurch movements preaching a thoroughgoing spiritual accommodation to the dictates of self-maintenance under a new postwar spirit of capitalism. In all of these success-themed ministries to the striving American soul, the core dogmas of Pealeism—the broad incantations of Christian achievement across the porous divisions of denomination and doctrine, the repurposing of the generic Americanist civic faith of the postwar world into a hard-line business conservatism, and the mechanistic success formulas of faith for faith's sake—proved readily adaptable to the political and cultural agendas of the insurgent evangelical right.

There was no need any longer, though, to shield the political and economic aims of this new faith behind an armada of business-funded interest groups seeking to overthrow the liberalism of the New Deal. Thanks to the broader slowdown of the American jobs economy from the seventies onward, what had formerly been a fairly narrow lobbying agenda on the economic right had blossomed into a populist political crusade. As the Keynesian momentum of the New Deal stalled out amid the stagflation of the seventies, a robust brand of market fundamentalism overtook the American centers of power and policy-making. Therefore, all that the modern evangelical faith of the Peale dispensation needed in order to better tailor its ministry to the displaced economic souls of the seventies and beyond was to reinvent itself as a management theory.

9

NEW GOSPELS OF THE
PROTEAN SELF

The 1970s were, on paper, among the most unpropitious periods for self-advancement to claim pride of place in America's spiritual odyssey. Conventional measures of American economic attainment such as income gains, union membership, and job security were stalling out; meanwhile, inflation—to date, a theoretically unheard-of accompaniment to soaring unemployment—was unloosing many traditional footholds in the postwar vision of mass prosperity, such as affordable credit to purchase homes and finance a college education. Spikes in energy prices exacerbated all these dismal trends, while rampant political corruption and war-making seemed to turn the promise of any responsible political response to the mounting crisis in the nation's political economy (like the original New Deal itself) into a bitter joke.

Yet in the face of this forbidding cul-de-sac, the American religious imagination did what it had always done best. It turned resolutely inward, mining the frontiers of Gnostic experience for still greater promises of personal self-fulfillment. The myth of success might now look more threadbare than ever, but in the interregnum famously hymned as the Me Decade, a new stage of Gnostic reformation lay in wait.

The old Protestant mission of self-improvement was again at the center of this reconfiguration of enterprising faith. But this venerable ideal pivoted now on a far more protean and adaptable vision of how best to reengineer the self for success, in keeping with the chastened tenor of the times. The pressures of competition within a postindustrial service economy meant that achievement-minded workers relied more than ever on the finer points of marketing themselves as just-in-time people-pleasers.

Without any clear sense of how or whether they might be thrust into gnawing economic insecurity, workers of the seventies and eighties hedged their diminishing life prospects. The traditional model of workplace confrontation—the strike—went underground, not surprisingly, in these years of slack labor demand; fighting off wage concessions that the leadership of many international unions agreed to, aggrieved workers turned to wildcat actions, with minimal strategic and organization gains to show for them. By the time Ronald Reagan had broken the famed air-traffic controllers' strike in 1981 with a battery of replacement workers, the action, significant though it was, felt in many ways like the rushed epilogue to a decade of lost labor activism.

Deprived of any sure public means of redressing their workplace privations and anxieties, Protestant workers responded with a renewed determination to master the elements of a successful life that they felt were still most firmly under their control—namely, their own psychic dispositions. The fabled land rush in self-help and human-potential literature over these two decades relied to a remarkable degree on the fundamental project of making the narrowing demands of the age's labor market seem as though they were, in fact, the full flowering of each American's journey toward inward liberation.

Even as the Gnostic gospel of self-elevation overtook the evangelical world in the seventies, the diminished economic expectations of the stagflation era produced a boomlet in soul-supervision among career counselors and management gurus, who contracted out their spiritual wisdom in a flailing postindustrial work regime that was failing to deliver broad-based prosperity. As a result, the basic terms and conditions of Gnostic expression came to be the controlling vision of how things got done in the service-economy workplace. This is, among other things, why the dismal labor market of the seventies midwifed America's all-time bestselling job-seeking manual, Robert Bolles's *What Color Is Your Parachute?* While this colorful and chipper guidebook still festoons many a recent college graduate's makeshift library, its gospel of bottomless self-reinvention speaks volumes about the you're-on-your-own-now sensibility of the 1970s workplace—and about the reserves of individual spiritual power that it sought to impart to the hapless new class of striving job seekers in a strange new postindustrial world.

It may seem odd to count this warhorse of the business self-help back catalog as a spiritual text, but Bolles was in fact a former Episcopal priest, and a veteran of the Intervarsity Christian Fellowship parachurch. Throughout the book's practical litany of job tips and career research, Bolles took pains to clarify that he was offering much more than merely material counsel. In just the same way that the postwar Gnostic God wanted His children to be happy, and their appetites to be fulfilled, so did He intend for them to find jobs granting their fullest capacities of self-expression. Thus the hedonic gospel of Bolles:

> Enjoyment, in human life, isn't a fluke. It's part of God's plan. He wants us to eat; therefore He designs us so that eating is enjoyable. He wants to have us procreate, love, and make love; therefore He designs us so that sex is enjoyable, and love even more so. *He gives us unique (or at least unusual) skills and talents; therefore He designs us so that, when we use these, they are enjoyable.*[301]

In lieu of the grim and dutiful search for the fast-receding mirage of a long-term social contract with one's employers, Bolles was advising job aspirants to follow the trails blazed by the "creative minority" of career counselors—in sum, to reinterpret the plight of joblessness as an opportunity to uncover an inviting preappointed personal destiny. In this fashion, the *What Color* gospel functioned as a critical way to institutionalize the near-permanent instability of the job market, and to condition employees to think of their work as the transient, ever-shifting scaffolding of an expansive self always on the verge of a great moment of inward transformation. At the same time, though, *What Color* was able to persuade them that they were being let in on a crucial life-changing secret: the way that the corporate "creative minority" in American *really* thought, and how it regarded the prospects of the modern Protestant's crusade of self-reinvention.

Such was the familiar-but-skittish liberal vision of spiritualized harmony and communion in the workplace; it offered all the Gnostic wonderment of Pealeism without the right-wing union-busting agenda. Indeed, the specter of workplace conflict is quite conspicuously wished away in such period documents of the stagflation age: There is, quite serenely, no hint of the old industrial-age notion of labor strife disrupting the spiritual odysseys of the 1970s-era aspiring middle manager.

Under the Bollesian self-help gospel of maximum expressivity, one's career can only be a property of the conquering Gnostic self. To admit unseemly material conflict into the picture is to grant entirely too much ground to a fallen, exasperating, and merely human creation; the liberal God, and the Gnostic cosmos enfolding Him, had far greater things in mind for His sojourners on the job market.

A Mission to Serve

This ideal was made even more plain in the spiritualized business manuals that explicitly targeted the managerial class. Here, too, the doctrine that would become the central organizing conceit of evangelical management— the scriptural principle known as servant leadership—actually originated from well outside the subculture of American business evangelicalism. In management circles, the notion of the servant leader began with a 1970 essay, *The Servant as Leader*, published by a human-relations consultant named Robert K. Greenleaf, who worked with a wide range of clients, including his longtime employer AT&T, and the influential trade association of large employers, the Business Roundtable. Like Bolles, Greenleaf was a stolid theological liberal. A lifelong Quaker, he'd hit upon the idea of servant leadership as he read Hermann Hesse's New Age novel, *Journey to the East*. Given this lineage, the theory behind the servant leadership movement is appropriately tinged with lotus-eating insight, stressing the front-office cultivation of a workforce made up of "holistic individuals," who are motivated by managerial shows of empathy and attention to strategic deployment of decision-making, nonhierarchical command structures, and other forms of "empowerment." The servant-leadership model, in other words, was grounded in the spiritual outlook of the sixties counterculture, privileging the personal values of authenticity, community, and accountability over the traditional, quasi-military model of workplace discipline that stressed impersonal character traits such as deference to authority and seniority as the keys to advancement on the job.

Greenleaf's vision soon proved to be a natural fit with the overall trend of labor relations in the de-industrializing U.S. economy of the 1970s. As Bethany Moreton notes, servant leadership also exerted an unexpectedly strong appeal among the burgeoning new class of personnel managers who were charged with administering discipline in the workplace. Greenleaf's model obviously flattered the spiritual vanity of company managers, since it offered a softer, more humane variation on the messianism that lurked in all-too-plain sight in the American managerial class's psychic profile. What's more, similar seventies-era schools of management theory were more broadly advancing a new consensus on workplace relations that pivoted on the development of a new "humane" and harmonious business culture. Douglas MacGregor's immensely influential "Theory Y" of corporate management, for example, stressed the quest for meaning in the workplace as it instructed managers in obtaining a commitment from their workforces that ran deeper than the simple allotments of time represented on their paychecks. Likewise, the "managerial grid" theory pioneered by the industrial psychologists Robert Blake and Jane Mouton bemoaned the traditional mores of impersonal production while advocating a more person-centered approach to producing labor value in the workplace. Meanwhile, more conventionally secular and modern apostles of office design sought to reenvision the postindustrial workplace as a humming foundry of ideas and "serendipitous encounters" engineered to produce new forms of creativity and innovation within the once-stuffy. Bold experiments such as Herman Miller's "action office" grid sought to spur erstwhile office drones into new feats of entrepreneurial invention.[302]

The trend rolled on into the 1980s and beyond, with Greenleaf's protégé Kenneth Blanchard scoring a series of servant-leadership bestsellers with his *One-Minute Manager* franchise, and the more sweeping vogue for W. E. Deming's Total Quality Management, which preached extensive worker-management cooperation in the enforcement of basic production standards. (Blanchard, by the way, went on to experience an evangelical conversion in the 1990s; he now presides over a Christian management consulting firm called the FaithWalk Institute and publishes far more overtly spiritual servant-leader manuals such as *Lead Like Jesus*.)[303] The explicitly spiritual vision of upward mobility as redemption-by-other-means fueled successive faddish cults of management theory, starting with evangelical servant leadership up through to the Mad Lib–style congeries of New Age nostrums that Tom Peters launched in his wildly successful 1980s "excellence" franchise.

But there was a conspicuously brittle quality to all the energetic efforts to enhance the morale of Protestant strivers during the age of stagflation— as though the apostles of the tirelessly reorganizing Protestant self were at last facing the sort of crisis that their storehouse of relentlessly sunny motivational slogans could not alter, at least not for the better. To make matters worse, the age's prominent social critics were starting to take aim at the very project of Protestant self-regeneration as a shallow and suspect perversion of America's nobler visions of success and self-advancement—symptoms of mounting cultural exhaustion, at best, or a rampant "culture of narcissism" at worst.

Still, the history of the Protestant success ethic militated against even a qualified posture of defeatism. While the broader currents of social thought in America were becoming suffused with dread, the evangelical outlook of the 1970s stalwartly resisted such tendencies. Still intoxicated by the great inward promise of the Peale dispensation, evangelical moderns reinvented themselves and their visions of worldly enterprise in a whole new spiritual register. They seemed intuitively to grasp that, if the problem were not strictly in the unaligned stars of the Keynesian heavens, the solution certainly lay in a bold new therapeutic realignment of the evangelical household.

All in the Family

As they turned their attention to troubles on the home front, the evangelicals of the seventies were able to turn the Americanist civic faith of the early postwar years to very different ends. The first Businessman's Revival of the nineteenth century helped believers make their peace with the precarious rounds of impression management in the new industrial workplace via new modes of emotional release and self-control; now, the seventies boom in therapeutic self-help turned increasingly on what evangelicals viewed as the last bastions of their spiritual autonomy—and by force of their own millennial vanguardist convictions, civilization itself: the sacred preserves of the home and the patriarchal family.

This intensive new focus on family life helped to point the Protestant self's way out of the dilemma posed by the rise of the liberal state and the New Deal social contract that underwrote it. No longer were the spiritual exertions of individual strivers after success an outmoded relic of the old, accumulative stage of industrial capitalism; now, within the Protestant visions unloosed by the seeming collapse of the certainties of liberal economic planning, a much more powerful gospel message was taking shape. Rather than affixing their life chances to the hulking gray dictates of the liberal state, the believers of the seventies and beyond could indict the existing order of labor relations and economic planning as moral and cultural failures—affronts to the distinctive, overlapping ideals of servant leadership and the patriarchal order. In order to be reclaimed as part of the saving remnant now stirring to life in the ruins of the Keynesian dream, American business had to be made to function more like the family.

Indeed, this bold and emerging vision of the realigned evangelical hearth suggested that American evangelicals were, in economic terms, *already saved*. They merely had to pronounce their salvation in bold and unwavering certainty, and the rest would be up to a providential God to work out in the due course of history. Ardent premillennialists had never before been very persuasive optimists; nor were the more lurid and vengeful passages of Revelation very close to the anodyne and progressive brand of liberal faith favored by the likes of Dwight D. Eisenhower and Henry Luce. But these conflicting theological impulses were fused into a powerful, if unlikely synthesis, thanks to the alchemical forces of Money Cult piety—and thanks to a powerful new constituency for Greenleaf's core message stirring along the frontiers of the great gender struggles of the 1970s.

Like Pealeism, servant leadership had originated with what its first corporate following had to regard as a reassuringly masculinist stamp of

approval, courtesy of Greenleaf's impeccable resume as a managerial lifer
at AT&T. But like Pealeism, the servant-leader ideal acquired very different gender connotations as it fanned out into the wider culture.

There was eminently good reason why this should be so. The service
economy's new dominance signaled, among other things, a crisis in spiritual masculinity. The republic of producers that William Jennings Bryan
sought to revive was also quite clearly a commonwealth of patriarchal pro-
viders, and well into the twentieth century, the gender politics of organized labor remained rigidly masculinist, with skilled workers making up
a supposed "aristocracy of labor" that commanded deference from their
domestic dependents. The value of their labor was explicitly vindicated
by the ability to earn a family wage—i.e., an income to ensure that the
worker's spouse and offspring remained fully reliant on his economic contributions. Likewise, as we've seen, a great deal of Protestant thought in
the industrial age was taken up with the challenge of preserving a robust
vision of spiritual manhood, from the initial stirrings of the Businessman's
Revival to the boardroom Christology of Bruce Barton.

But ever since the early nineteenth century, the main run of Protestant believers in America were women—a demographic trend that, if anything, made it all the more incumbent on the traditionally male leaders of
the mainline Protestant world to defend and vindicate their own elevated
standing. In other words, to be a faithful Protestant believer in America's
industrial age usually meant to embrace the spiritual authority of accomplished male leaders in the traditional alpha mode. (The exceptions to this
trend, such as the early Pentecostal Aimee MacPherson, were very much
exceptions that proved the rule; especially in the scandal surrounding her
alleged kidnapping, MacPherson was the object of nonstop sexualized
innuendo in the press and the popular mind—i.e., she was a woman in the
upper reaches of Protestant influence who *simply did not know her place*.)

This all began to change during the seventies and eighties. As Bethany Moreton shows in her incisive study *To Serve God and Wal-Mart*, the
overlapping economic crises of the seventies triggered a core reevaluation
of the innermost productive logic of the Protestant work ethic—and this
revision would recast the gendered ideals of American labor in a new,

evangelically tinged light. Moreton lays out the gender significance of this shift in sharp and suggestive terms:

> During the 1970s and 1980s, the eclipse of production by the service economy heightened Christian fears that the wellsprings of American virility were drying up: where would real men develop if work came to look too much like home? How could male authority survive the ascendance of service work and the mobilization of women as wage earners? The experience of service labor itself offered the basis for a new ideology that met these challenges. Christened "servant leadership" by its formal adherents, this new ethic glorified the formerly humble, feminine reproductive labor against which the old manly producerism had defined itself. Taken up by Christian opinion-makers and embraced by many families in the pews, servant leadership offered something to everyone. Service workers found a measure of respect denied them by the heroic narratives of industry. Managers gained a new claim to authority just as their older ones came to look increasingly implausible. Christian husbands enhanced their status at home despite the loss of the bread-winner's mantle. And many evangelical women found wifely "submission" a small price to pay for men's reinvestment in the domestic sphere.[304]

In this new dispensation, evangelical women were to benefit rhetorically from Second Wave feminist calls for greater recognition of their labor and selfless service, while also claiming for themselves a notional equality of parental authority. But it was also taken for granted in the servant-led household that all the adult parties must cleave to the traditional biblical teaching of wifely submission within the power dynamics of married life. Self-help books such as Marabel Morgan's *The Total Woman*—which clocked in as the bestselling nonfiction book of 1974 with more than 10 million copies sold—brimmed with modern tips for reviving a marriage's flagging sexual momentum. (Morgan won a great deal of titillated media renown for advising women to surprise their husbands as they returned at the end of the workday by greeting them at the door clad in nothing but

Saran Wrap.) But Morgan's sunny celebration of the erotic charges to be won from the surrendered wife's confinement in the domestic sphere was not merely an exhortation for her readers to take traditional male authority at face value. In her alliterative four-point scheme of successful marital submission—"Accept Him," "Admire Him," "Adapt to Him," and "Appreciate Him"—Morgan seamlessly takes up the rhetoric of service management in the context of the more intimate marital challenges of optimizing sexual and emotional self-expression and shoring up a partner's self-esteem.

For all the heavy-breathing attention it won in the mainstream press for its sexual counsel, *The Total Woman* was at bottom a domestic business manual. Its first chapter, "The Organization Woman," directed unhappy wives to conquer their sense of creeping marital stagnation and malaise with a battery of to-do lists, prioritizing undone domestic chores while also freeing up time for self-pampering ahead of the vanity and dramatic seduction scenes at the end of a frazzled husband's workday. Morgan dubbed this regimen "Your $25,000 Plan," since it stemmed from a piece of managerial folklore in which steel-and-investment titan Charles Schwab rewarded a female management consultant with that sum for presenting him with a simple system for prioritizing the tasks of his workday. "If it works in a steel factory," Morgan wrote, "it will work for you in your house factory."[305] Morgan also readily employed management jargon to rationalize her controversial preachments of wifely submission: "Man and woman, although equal in status, are different in function. God ordained man to be the head of the family, its president, and his wife to be the executive vice-president . . . Allowing your husband to be family president is just good business."[306]

To judge by Morgan's wildly successful counsel, enterprising and ambitious women were finding that the challenge of navigating a traditionally patriarchal marriage had turned out to be a lot like the challenge of preserving one's self-worth and dignity in the far more impersonal realm of the market. And much like the bureaucracy of the postindustrial workplace, the family unit usually relies to an inordinate degree on the junior executive's superior initiative to jump-start the more constitutionally sluggish energies of company leadership. It's true, Morgan conceded, that it can be exasperating for the wife in a traditional marriage to be continually initiating the rituals of emotional appreciation and admiration demanded by the breadwinner spouse. But that outlook changes once women can "see they have certain strengths that a man doesn't have. It's a great strength, not a weakness, to give for the sake of giving. It is in your nature to give."[307]

Such dictums highlighted the limits of Morgan's difference-based interpretation of gender roles—and more broadly, they delineated clear cultural boundaries separating the evangelical vision of surrendered womanhood from the more blunt power politics of seventies feminism. But Morgan's tireless counsel to support the household's embattled husband at all costs also drew inadvertent attention to the frail condition of the partner requiring all this appreciation, admiration, joyful submission, and sexual instruction.

The Total Woman abounds with reminders that the female partner in marriage, while subordinate in executive authority, possesses the greater hands-on qualities of servant leadership. While their rigid, achievement-minded spouses are often emotionally inaccessible or unable to adopt more flexible views of their roles in the home and workplace, women are able to make marriages and the men in them "come alive"—as the book's subtitle had it—with the power of their faith. As Morgan explains, you, the emotional manager of the domestic sphere, "have the power to lift your family's spirit or bring it down to rock bottom." Citing the spiritual authority of Norman Vincent Peale, she dismisses the restlessly nagging stereotype of the dissatisfied housewife to argue that true change comes from within: "You can decide now on what level you are going to live, regardless of your husband's attitude . . . A great marriage is not so much about finding the right person as *being* the right person."[308]

And like any service-minded superhero, the Total Woman is charged ultimately with using her powers for good: When the nominal family president's self-esteem appears to be waning, the task is simple: "put his tattered ego back together with compliments."[309] Very much in contrast to the self-improving spirit of the nineteenth century's evangelical revolution, the Total Woman gospel is largely a great project of emotional and sexual reclamation—to undo, with the miraculous power of emotionally engaged female faith, the abrasive damage wrought upon the fragile male ego by the impersonal rounds of market competition and its drastically diminishing returns.

As the historian Jennifer Heller notes, the husbands in Morgan's vision of the gender division of labor come off as figures of near-pathos—and certainly as victims of a chronic and gnawing economic anxiety. In Morgan's schematic account of how marriages work, men "must live and work in a world of high-stakes pressures where their authority is often undermined and always uncertain," and so, under the dogmas of both market reward and scriptural wifely submission, they "deserve a comfortable domestic atmosphere and a loving, accepting wife."[310]

Tellingly, however, the payoff for all this conscientious servant-leadership programming of the domestic sphere is not simply an enlivened sex life or a more emotionally demonstrative husband; it is, rather, a vision of Gnostic evangelical redemption on a cosmic scale. Speaking in her closing chapter of her own conversion experience, and her consecration to her "forever family," Morgan finishes her book in an odd flourish of otherworldly triumph:

> Lastly, I have power. His power. He is not dead. He arose from the dead . . . He said that His resurrection power can be mine. I have the power to live the abundant life—power to love—power to transform my natural love for my husband and my children into a super love, a divine love, flowing out of me.[311]

The tremendous success of Morgan's self-help tract launched a thriving cottage industry in marriage and intimacy manuals for evangelical readers. In 1976, Tim and Beverly LaHaye issued *The Act of Marriage*, a sex-advice guide for Christian couples, which also teemed with surprisingly straightforward, informative, and quasi-clinical discussions of the act in question; it sold more than 2.5 million copies—and unlike Morgan's book, remains in print today. Beverly LaHaye followed soon thereafter with *The Spirit-Controlled Woman*, her own tract laying out the many dynamic and erotic charges that women can bring to conventionally patriarchal unions. In *Fascinating Womanhood*, meanwhile—originally published in 1964, but reissued in 1975 to capitalize on the exploding evangelical market for marriage-advice books—Helen Andelin made the demands of the market-wounded vanity of men even more explicit, in a list of the typical husband's essential "needs":

1. His need to be accepted at face value;
2. His need for admiration;
3. His sensitive masculine pride;
4. His need for sympathetic understanding;
5. His need to be No. 1;
6. His need to serve as the guide, protector, and provider[;] to feel needed in this role, and to excel women in doing so.[312]

In the wake of the Total Woman craze, media commentators and religious figures alike spent a great deal of time debating the ongoing challenge of squaring conventional evangelical piety with the more unvarnished demands for gender equality, in the domestic sphere and the workforce alike, coming from the women's-liberation movement. In this way, the pat and formulaic terms of culture-war debate over the nature and legacy of second-wave feminism were already congealing within the mold set by the skilled choreographers of mediagenic culture warfare. In this vapid pseudo–morality play, feminist critics of patriarchal family life were cast as arch-secular individualists, and issues like abortion rights were transformed into scripts of expressive self-assertion for a new breed of cultural radical who was determined above all to wield her rhetorical power to exercise individual choice in defiance of the biological and procreative tyrannies of conventional, patriarchal family life. Meanwhile, the women on the evangelical side of the divide in this foundational moment in American cultural warfare were, of course, hardy tribunes of "family values"—i.e., *counter*individualist celebrants of an organic, mutual set of informal obligations at the heart of domestic life. In this fanciful set piece, the traditionalist rebels against feminism were loudly insisting on the alleged essentialist limits of female experience, imposed both by the biological strictures of childbearing and the cultural ones of child-rearing, wifely submission, and housekeeping. In this script, confusingly enough, defenders of the traditional family come off as communitarian critics of rampant liberal individualism, preaching the features of family life that stubbornly refuse to bend before the sovereignty of personal choice—the fetus, the family, and the largely undercompensated domestic labor of caregiving.

But to dwell obsessively on this familiar pitched battle over feminist right and family obligation—choice versus submission, self-assertion over caregiving, career in opposition to "family"—as our culture has now for nearly half a century, is to miss at least half the picture. For as the testimony of Marabel Morgan and her cohort of defenders of evangelical womanhood made abundantly clear, they didn't see any contradictions between liberal individualist choice and the more mutual obligations of family life. If anything, their vision of the family was cribbed to a strikingly self-conscious degree from the psychological mandates of advancement within corporate America. In reorganizing evangelical families, the insurgent Total Women of the seventies were cannily spiritualizing the routines of a domestic sphere already groaning under the logic of market domination—just as the good reverend Mr. Bolles was retooling the stigmatized and shame-inducing experience of unemployment along softer-focus lines of a divinely sanctioned moment of redemption in the career-long unfolding of the job seeker's human potential.

A new chapter was beginning in the odyssey of the Protestant ethic—and its posture toward the world of capitalist enterprise was now paradoxically suffused in joy. The accumulation-minded outlook of the worldly ascetic could obviously no longer reign over a bewildering postwar economic regime of consumer abundance and beleaguered job security; the straight lines of causation that formerly seemed to bind personal virtue with productive enterprise had been severed, apparently for good. What lay ahead for the earnest Protestant striver was a deceptively empowering regimen of endless self-reinvention. Far from transforming working and professional life into a vast, edifying spiritual quest, along the lines proposed by Richard Bolles, the revolution in the seventies and eighties political economy of the spirit turned the formerly market-resistant preserves of personal life into a long succession of jobs that one had to apply for over and over again.

Selling the Evangelical Self

For the hardier breed of seventies evangelical seekers, the inner quest for fulfillment was a good deal of work: a thing of obsessive list-making, slogan-chanting, and careful emotional watchfulness—and of course, extensive prayer. These were all mental constructs and motivational devices cribbed from the mechanically minded prosperity teachings of their spiritual forefather Norman Vincent Peale. The result, as sociologist James Davison Hunter notes in an exhaustive study of the evangelical self-help literature of the seventies and eighties, was a highly ritualized cult of inward "hedonism" for the convicted evangelical believer. Under this modernist, pleasure-loving incarnation of the popular gospel, the austerity and pessimism of past Protestant versions of the self have at last been surrendered to a consumerist dispensation of faith. As a consequence of this shift, the specters of damnation and brimstone were relegated to the dour margins of the Puritan past; the new expectation among modern evangelicals, Hunter notes, is that

> human experience should be characterized by unfathomable inner joy and happiness and the unquenchable expectancy of good things . . . Within American Evangelicalism, if one is spiritual, one is happy and contented. Life is full and rich. Conversely, the routine mediocrity of everyday life, commonplace to most, is often considered a measure of the lack of spirituality . . . Even in the faces of extreme difficulties, the Evangelical often feels constrained to exhibit, not just perseverance and fortitude, but happiness and joy. This can foster a public dramaturgy unsupported by subjective conviction. Hedonism in this context . . . entails the public and subjective denial of inner suffering, dread, and boredom as essential features of human existence . . . In mainstream contemporary Evangelicalism, an austere instrumentalism has been replaced by a malleable expressivity.[313]

Yes, evangelical believers were becoming pleasure-lovers, in droves—and weirdly, at the very moment that the rest of American culture appeared to washed out, exhausted, and hungover from its long binge of postwar affluence. On the verge of the supply-side revolution in economic policy, and amid a widening pro-management political consensus on the open shop and the "right to work," evangelical workers and families were proving to be masters of mood enhancement.

To be sure, the age's dramatic shift in policy assumptions took place far over the heads of most Americans—but it created profound consequences

for the way they conceived of the elusive qualities of individual achievement and mass prosperity in a political economy increasingly hostile to
workers' interests. As the state and the labor movement continued ceding
economic power to private-sector business interests, ordinary American
workers found themselves left with the forbidding challenge of seeking to
imagine the conditions of a better life in a growing policy vacuum. This
was an act of faith, in much more than the metaphoric sense of the term.
In plotting out a newly joyful, self-engineered vision of individual material
reward, the seventies boom in spiritual success manuals ensured that the
manager's brain was placed more firmly than ever beneath the workman's
cap—especially after the worker had punched out for the day and returned
home, to what was still supposed to be a sentimental bastion of Christian
patriarchy. As they traced the work of their own salvation further out into
the sphere of political action, the Money Cult's postwar apostles assumed a
confident new role in instructing the believing self and the faithful American family to move in studious new concert with the market's fickle moods.

The portfolio of therapeutic home improvement has become so commonplace on today's conservative evangelical scene that we don't really see
it. Half a century after Peale preached his New Thought nostrums from
the bestseller lists, and forty years after the heyday of Marabel Morgan,
virtually every significant leader on the evangelical right routinely boasts a
sideline as a purveyor of faith-based popular psychology—from Focus on
the Family's James Dobson to Beverly LaHaye, a popular marriage counselor who doubles as the founder and chair of the culture-war lobbying
group Concerned Women of America.

And because we don't really see this evangelical-therapeutic outlook,
it never really sinks in just how strange it is. If it's the hallmark of mental
maturity to hold two utterly contradictory propositions in one's mind simultaneously, then today's prophetic phase of the Money Cult has truly come of
age: A resurgent evangelical movement that instructed believers in how to
manage their working lives, their marriages, their finances, and their overall psychological well-being also glories in prophesying the rapid approach
of the end of the world. Evangelical believers, at once charged with marking
the Apocalypse's approach and monitoring the effectiveness of interfamil-

ial communication, might well be forgiven for wondering just what all the domestic fuss was about. Why not just consign the trials of the suburban hearth to the consuming fire of the end-times, along with everything else?

Cash and Charisma

The answer lay largely within the dramatic seventies revival that launched much of the latter-day religious right on its colorful public career: the cross-denominational explosion of charismatic piety. From its original outcast roots in the poor white and African American congregations in the South and West, the Pentecostal movement had, by the 1970s, matured into a successful mainstay of the urban revival circuit, and soon moved into the vanguard of that era's pioneering boom in televangelism.

Like the allied managerial embrace of the inward Gnostic faith, the surge in an unvarnished and experiential prosperity faith seems at first blush a strange response to hard economic times. But within the larger logic of the Money Cult piety the charismatic movement was an entirely suitable religious accommodation to hard times; the original Business-man's Revival of the mid-nineteenth century had also, after all, been a direct response to a crippling recession.

So was it now that the stagflation age was calling forth broader, more ambitious, and infinitely more reactionary gifts of the spirit. The intensive spiritual individualism of the Pentecostal faith had been instrumental, after all, in propelling the displaced Southern populists in postwar Southern California into the heart of the small-government conservative revolution. Now, with a renewed urgency, and a far larger national following, the char-ismatic pioneers of Pentecostal faith had, in another great demonstration of the Holy Spirit's byways, set the stage for the reinvigorated interlock-ing American gospels of self-improvement, household management, and business redemption. As other brands of political and economic certainty were in conspicuous ideological free-fall, the charismatic revival was able to rebrand an attractive spiritual commodity that modern American Protes-tants had always craved: a species of reassuring individualist magical think-ing in the face of unexplained and systemic economic decline.

This shift had been under way for some time. The great postwar boom in Protestant piety, long identified with the heyday of theological liberalism, had been, in reality, a sustained growth spurt for the nation's most conservative, experiential, and money-aligned denominations. From 1952 to 1971, one of the leading Pentecostal denominations, the Church of God (Cleveland) reported a 120.9 percent growth in membership. For the Mormons, the comparable figure over the same period was 98 percent, while Graham's home denomination, the Southern Baptists, grew by 45.5 percent. By contrast, mainline denominations logged almost no significant gains over the long postwar "church boom": Methodists grew just by 5.2 percent, Presbyterians by 8.8 percent, and Episcopalians (the most well-heeled of the mainline denominations) by 19.2 percent.[314]

Nevertheless, the seventies were undeniably the great mainstreaming moment for the upsurge in apostolic holiness preaching that began with the early twentieth century's outpourings of the spirit in the South and West. But this boom in charismatic faith was a significant departure from its forerunner revival in a couple of important respects. It successfully shunned the founding Pentecostal penchant for divisive sectarian controversy; and, not coincidentally, it was grounded more than ever on the explicit promise of enhanced personal prosperity for its new recruits. As a result, the seventies explosion of charismatic faith was, like the parachurch land rush of the postwar years, a cross-denominational affair: Leading preachers even in staid established denominations within the Protestant mainline were experiencing the traditional Pentecostal manifestations of piety, such as tongues worship and faith healing; the revival even spread to some Catholic denominations.

The seventies holiness revival, in other words, was largely picking up where Graham's urban crusades of the late forties and early fifties left off: It sought to sanctify the inner workings of prophecy and experiential faith for a confident new following among the affluent American middle class. And as its reach extended into mainline denominations, this follow-on movement was itself aggressively launched as a parachurch enterprise, drawing heavily on the resources and institutional support of a new group of California-based Pentecostal businessmen, the Full Gospel Business Men's Fellowship International (FGBMFI).

This group took off in the wake of a fund-raising dinner that a prosperous Pentecostal dairy farmer named Demos Shakarian convened in 1945. A veteran of the landmark 1906 Azusa Street revival, Shakarian had sponsored a series of tent revivals with his wife, Rose. Emboldened by the success of that initiative, he summoned a group of Angeleno Christian executives to support a big-ticket revival meeting at the 20,000-seat Hollywood Bowl. The gathering soon turned into a kind of revival meeting of its own, with the assembled company bewailing the struggles involved in squaring their business practices with the message of the gospel. Drawing on that spontaneous outpouring to continue expanding the region's Pentecostal awakening, Shakarian in 1951 summoned the successful Pentecostal minister Oral Roberts to L.A.'s Clifton Cafeteria to formally launch the FBGMFI.[315]

Roberts was then riding high. He'd converted to the Pentecostal faith in 1947, after wrestling with his worldly ambitions as an itinerant Baptist preacher in Oklahoma. In his reminiscence, the moment of conversion came about after a dark night of the soul, when his eye fell randomly on a passage from the Third Epistle of John, which read "I wish above all things that thou mayest prosper and be in health, even as they soul prospereth." Thus assured, the young man of God went out and bought a new Buick and experienced a divine vision, in which God instructed him to go forth and heal the sick.[316]

Well before he'd agreed to help captain the FGBMI, Roberts's healing ministry had evolved into an ardent business faith. One of his early benefactors was a North Carolina banker named S. Lee Braxton—and Braxton was evidently the figure who introduced Roberts to the vast midcentury spiritual literature of positive thinking, loaning him one book in particular, Frank Bettger's *How I Raised Myself from Failure to Success in Selling*, that Roberts deemed the most influential title he'd ever read.[317] Roberts's distinctive theology, which he christened "seed-faith," was an early articulation of the prosperity gospel, drawing on the language of scripture to elicit donations from believers with the vague promise of returns on their faith investment of 30-, 60-, or a hundredfold, at some unspecified point in the future.

Roberts also pioneered a simple materialist appeal to place struggling believers directly in the path of divine power based on what he called "points of contact"—i.e., devotional everyday objects sanctified through prayer to "release your faith toward God."[318] His headquarters in Tulsa, Oklahoma, did a brisk business in "anointed handkerchiefs" to effectuate mass healing, advertised via Roberts's fledgling TV ministry.[319] Like Peale's casual appropriation of advertising imagery and sloganeering into a new divine psychology of the marketplace, Roberts's bluntly materialist gospel converted the culture of consumer capitalism into a readymade, yet individually customized, system of deliverance of the spirit. The seed-faith message, indeed, resembled nothing so much as salvation purchased on a layaway plan.

Under Roberts's firm guidance, the FGBMI sprouted into something of a model seed-of-faith miracle of its own. In the mid-1960s, the group boasted more than 300 chapters and a membership of 100,000. By the early 1970s, it claimed more than 300,000 members, and its monthly magazine, *Voices*, enjoyed a circulation of 250,000; its annual operating budget was by then more than $1,000,000.[320] Emerging preachers in the Roberts vein, such as John Copeland, Word of Faith founder Kenneth Hagin, Hagin's protégé John Osteen (father of contemporary Word of Faith megapastor Joel Osteen) all came up through FGMBI chapters, helping to seal the group's standing as "one of the most important outlets for charismatic renewal as a whole and a perpetual theology of prosperity in action," in the estimation of Prosperity Gospel historian Kate Bowler.[321] The group did more than simply promote charismatic revival, however; it also emerged as an early forerunner of evangelical activism in the economic world, especially as mainline Protestant congregations continued tilting toward charismatic practice.

In 1960, the popular Episcopal pastor Dennis J. Bennett shocked his staid Van Nuys, California, congregation with the announcement that he had been baptized in the Holy Spirit and was able to speak in tongues. In little more than a decade's time, virtually every major Protestant denomination—together with American dioceses of the Catholic and Eastern Orthodox faiths—had undergone their own version of a charismatic revival: "By 1975, the charismatic revival claimed more than five million souls belonging to Catholic, mainline and pentecostal churches," Bowler writes. As one revival adherent observed, "It was not unusual to see a Catholic priest, an Episcopal pastor, and a pentecostal evangelist sharing the same platform at Full Gospel Business Men's dinners, or the thousands of other conferences, revivals, crusades, and missions, sponsored by a multitude of churches and para-church organizations."[322]

In the post-1960s marketplace of experiential faith, the charismatic revival that began at the turn of the twentieth century had overtaken the Protestant mainstream. Roberts himself had foreshadowed this shift with his surprise conversion to Methodism in 1968; he retained all the same doctrinal principles of the Pentecostal seed faith, but by now the televangelist was shifting into full institution-building mode, having opened his sprawling, modernist eponymous religious college in 1963. He defended his conversion, which initially sparked a one-third decline in donations to his Tulsa empire, by claiming that, in essence, the Holy Spirit ministry was too large to be contained by any one denomination—and that therefore he felt more at home preaching it from within America's largest Protestant denomination. Throughout his career, he explained, "my concern was to follow the leadership of the Holy Spirit and to be true to the calling of God upon my life. I felt led to share this ministry of healing and to escape the tendency to denominationalize my full-gospel experience of the baptism with the Holy Spirit."[323]

These charisma-filled dramas of evangelical certitude seemed surpassingly strange to the established authorities of the American civic faith. But in another sense—the sense that guides the entire, perennially curious switchbacking career of the modern Money Cult—it's not very strange at all. The gifts of the spirit seemed newly accessible to Protestant believers in a way that their forbiddingly corrupt institutions of public accountability no longer were. When Vietnam, Watergate, and stagflation became everyday watchwords for the flagging American faith in public institutions, the overwhelming thrust of revived Protestant belief was to direct believers to delve deeper into their accustomed Gnostic routines of self-redemption.

How Shall We Then Live?

As the principles of the Pentecost spun outward into the American mainstream, the spirit listeth in some singularly strange places—and found a new breed of modern champion. Protestant believers sought out more comprehensive solutions to the quandaries facing them not merely in an allegedly hostile secular political order, but also amid rapidly shifting work and gender relations. A new class of what Molly Worthen calls "evangelical gurus" rose up to fill this new demand. These thinkers were crucial in the eventual rise of the evangelical right as a revived political force, but in many ways, their more enduring contribution was their effort to supply a comprehensive theory of the inner life of the modern evangelical believer. They were ideologues, in the fullest sense of the term—supplying a comprehensive theory of the evangelical self's encounter with the hostile modern world that reaffirmed the basic coordinates of a populist evangelical outlook while charting a resolute inward path of Gnostic redemption.[324]

Hal Lindsey, author of the decade's bestselling nonfiction book, *The Late Great Planet Earth*, reassured readers that, in spite of all the many fast-approaching blood-soaked crucibles of the Tribulation as foretold in Revelation, the coming rapture of humanity would be "the ultimate trip"—and as the first Christians were assured in Titus 2:13–15, a "blessed hope" for eternal deliverance. In spite of the fast-multiplying evidence that the end of days was approaching, Lindsey insisted that

> this hope gets more blessed all the time. This is the reason we are optimistic about the future. This is the reason that in spite of the headlines, in spite of crisis after crisis in America and throughout the world, in spite of the dark days which strike terror into the hearts of many, every Christian has the right to be optimistic! . . . According to the Scriptures, we are told that the place [God] is preparing for us will be utterly fantastic. Eternal life will surpass the greatest pleasures we have known on earth.[325]

Lindsey's odd premillennial ebullience was perhaps the most extreme expression of the evangelical ethos of therapeutic hedonism: *Let the world burn, for our place in heaven is assured.* But it was entirely in line with the broader upswing of the evangelical temperament. In part, it seems, this sensibility was rooted in the conviction that the world's coming crack-up would seal once and for all the deterioration of the old liberal American theology of adaptation to modernity. But Lindsey's smiling prophecies of doom partook more deeply in a wide-ranging movement among evangelical conservatives to claim the general course of Western history as their own.

Lindsey was by far the best-known figure among these DIY culture prophets, but he was far from alone. The seventies also saw the rise of such free-ranging activists and thinkers such as Franklin Schaeffer—the great theorist of the late twentieth century culture wars *avant la lettre*—and the Calvinist theologian Rousas John Rushdoony, who pioneered the "reconstructionist" school of thought that divined America's millennial origins and purpose in a strict (and largely mythical) body of orthodox Christian theology.

The emergence of the gurus signaled, among other things, a coming-of-age moment for evangelicalism as a public faith and social movement alike. It was a small step, for instance, for a figure like Rushdoony to harness his critique of secular American history to the nascent home-schooling movement. As more right-leaning Protestants followed Rushdoony's lead in disparaging the public schools as a hostile and militant breeding ground of heresy, sedition, and cultural decadence, they likewise rallied to his separatist remedy: to take charge of their children's curricula themselves. But there was a new purist ardor in this brand of cultural secession. While past fundamentalist crusaders withdrew from mainstream American culture to nourish their own rival faith traditions and institutions, Rushdoony and his followers repaired to the margins of on the grounds that they were defending the true, imperiled traditions of American patriotism.

The confident sweep of the gurus' analysis betokened a newly aggressive outlook for a conservative faith that had earlier settled for a self-insulating posture of retreat from the modern secular world. And when this quietist impulse was retired, so was the ambivalence among movement leaders that sometimes went with it. The lead thinkers of the resurgent evangelical right of the seventies had little patience for social or theological introspection; instead, they derived a new certainty in the millennialist conviction that God was directing the course of history to their ultimate benefit. So in a rare departure from the worldly pessimism that usually attends premillennial doctrine, they elected to retrofit their prophecy-driven faith to meet the more mundane challenges of securing prosperity and political clout on the American scene. They roused from their decades-long policy of cultural quarantine to pursue a bold and deeply politicized agenda of cultural conquest.

The sudden popular demand for guruship came from a wide range of sources—the breakdown of traditional liberal and ecumenical models of religious authority, the roiling political disenchantments of the age. But in a more immediate sense, charismatic gurus spoke to believers moved by charismatic religious experience.

The seventies political insurgency of the Christian right is far better known, but in the annals of inward-looking Protestant piety, the Holy Spirit's simultaneous rise to cultural prominence was just as institutionally significant and enduring. The seventies upsurge in charismatic piety is usually seen as a straitlaced (but still trendy) corrective to the countercultural excesses of the 1960s, with representative specimens ranging from the "Jesus People" movement, to the proliferation of multiday outdoor Christian rock festivals, to the vogue for Broadway vehicles of hippie-tinged piety such as *Godspell* and *Jesus Christ, Superstar.*[326] But this view of the revival as a kind of counterreformation of Middle American Hip overlooks the broader sweep of changes afoot in the nation's political and economic order. For believers in the seventies and beyond, the Pentecostal gifts of the spirit were far more important as an idiom of economic self-assertion than cultural style. The charismatic upheavals in all the major denominations gave earthbound shape to a far more sweeping sensibility taking shape within the evangelical world, one that distilled and refined many of the Gnostic preoccupations of past Protestant awakenings. Unloosed from the conventional structures of denominational discipline and theological doctrine, the experience of the indwelling Holy Spirit helped believers outside the comparatively narrow confines of Pentecostal piety achieve the central Gnostic payoff of this revived primitive faith: to lift their sanctified souls out of the disappointing, ugly, and perilous sphere of mere matter and history.

For ready confirmation of this important shift, one need only consult the other main expression of post-1960s charismatic faith: the boom in televangelism. Following on the pioneering TV ministries of the Reformed positive thinker Robert Schuller and seed-faith preacher Oral Roberts, popular Pentecostal ministers of the seventies revolutionized religious broadcasting. The signature televangelists of the 1970s and '80s—Jimmy Swaggart and the husband-and-wife team of Jim and Tammy Faye Bakker—all preached within the Assemblies of God faith tradition, while another Pentecostal power couple, Paul and Jan Crouch, founded the Trinity Broadcasting Network, a pioneering cable news empire for evangelicals, in 1973. (The other great impresario of evangelical broadcasting in the seventies was, of course, Christian Broadcasting Network founder Pat Robertson, an ordained Southern Baptist, but an avowed charismatic who speaks in tongues and endorses a strict literalist interpretation of end-times prophecy.)

The Swaggart and Bakker ministries also were vital proving grounds for what would eventually become the full-blown Prosperity Gospel of the Osteen age. The movement's theological epicenter was Kenneth Hagin's Word of Faith preaching, which reduced many past Pentecostal dalliances with faith's material rewards to a simple "name and claim it" formula. This was Peale's positive-thinking business gospel refashioned in the image of the Primitive Church. Under Word of Faith, believers learned they could summon wealth and prosperity through incantations of scripture, mixed with standard-issue motivational mantras; Hagin's Rhema Bible Training Center, across town in Tulsa from Oral Roberts's sprawling university-and-hospital complex, became one of the central training centers for prosperity preachers. Certified Word of Faith apostles also put a more decisive stamp on the American scene in what was now the standard modus operandi for serious religious organizing in the modern age: via a cavalcade of parachurch organizations. The Association of Faith Churches and Ministries launched in 1978 to coordinate global outreach efforts among Word of Faith preachers. The following year, Hagin's son-in-law, Buddy Harrison, launched the International Convention of Faith Ministries with much the same end in mind. Rhema alums banded into the Rhema Ministerial Association in 1985, and in the following year, Oral Roberts launched his influential International Charismatic Bible Ministries.

The message emerging out of all this hectic organizing was a straightforward (and then some) equation of piety and prosperity. Right observance of the Lord's sovereignty would naturally produce wealth, since God's word to his followers in both testaments clearly vouchsafed material reward to his chosen followers. "In the Old Testament, according to Deuteronomy," Hagin counseled, "poverty was to come upon God's people if they disobeyed them"—a striking Pentecostal echo of one of the central messages of *The Book of Mormon*.[327] As the Texas televangelist Kenneth Copeland—

one of Hagin's many successful protégés—put it, "The gospel to the poor is that Jesus has come and they don't have to be poor anymore!"[328]

Hagin himself would later seek to rein in the prosperity enthusiasms of figures such as Copeland and Copeland's own phenomenally successful protégé Creflo Dollar. But the tight convergence of untrammeled prosperity preaching and Word of Faith doctrine proved too potent for even Word of Faith's own progenitor to tamp down. Believers simply needed to cleave to the conviction that God would deliver them into abundance when all else had failed.

Indeed, what's most striking in this formative stage of prosperity preaching is that Word of Faith preachers were calling down divine favor to get God to perform the very wonders that were plainly well beyond the competence of the American economy to perform in the Nixon, Ford, and Carter years. Credit may have been unaffordable to ordinary working Americans, and inflation may have eaten steadily away at their faltering nest eggs, but Pentecostals in the Word of Faith tradition sought to counteract such worldly setbacks with faith-based financial appeals. In a practice that Oral Roberts called "naming the seed," donors to Roberts's Tulsa headquarters, for example, would commonly denote tithing payments and so-called "first fruit offerings"—which consigned the first installment, say, of a wage increase or a stock dividend entirely to God in the expectation that its value will be returned to the believer manifold. The mundane, and poignant, directives that cropped up in such donations included pleas "for a new car," "for a promotion," and "for new school clothes."[329]

As the overall economy came to pivot on the explosion of consumer debt, such incantations didn't seem any more outlandish than, say, Gerald Ford's efforts to contain inflation with his own disastrous executive-branch foray into positive-thinking preaching, via the "Whip Inflation Now" campaign. Indeed, with credit-card holders vying to reduce their debt obligations by repaying them in inflation-depreciated currency (much as the original Populists of the nineteenth century proposed to shore up the nation's faltering productive farm economy by loosening the strictures on credit imposed by the gold standard), Bowler notes that money itself held a value that was "increasingly theoretical, as the connection between the value of one's labor and the value of one's income grew increasingly unpredictable . . . These economic conditions boosted consumer confidence in unseen multipliers. For many, faith in supernatural hundredfold returns appeared a reasonable economic strategy. [Word of Faith prosperity preaching] was a movement that treasured the God of checks and balances, whose financial formulas and principles ensured that, when all was tallied, God was more than fair."[330]

Not surprisingly, the nascent prosperity faith was prey to many excesses and abuses—much like the debt-leveraged consumer republic on which it was consciously modeled. The ironclad promise of eventual financial well-being combined with the power of new mass-communication ministries to produce an extremely robust stream of tax-deductible donations for nationwide prosperity ministries. This proved all too often to be an open invitation to ministerial graft, as the televisual ministry of the Bakkers was to make abundantly clear. Jim Bakker was plunged into infamy by his extramarital affair with church secretary Jessica Hahn, but the true scandal of the Praise the Lord TV-and-theme-park empire he'd erected with his deliriously acquisitive New South wife, Tammy Faye, was financial. Bakker had fraudulently marketed tens of thousands of high-end lifetime "memberships" to Heritage USA, the ministry's gaudy Ozarks theme park, and pocketed some $3.4 million in unearned bonuses from the proceeds. (The memberships all promised donors complimentary three-day stays at the park's ostensible complex of luxury hotels, but there was only one such facility on site, with just a 500-room booking capacity.) Bakker was eventually imprisoned on federal fraud and conspiracy charges, and some $6 million in IRS liens on the Bakkers' former operations are still outstanding.

But to focus on the familiar, glum interplay of fast-talking spiritual hucksters and credulous believers is to miss the broader cultural and economic transformations that figures such as Bakker were capitalizing on. It's not so much that the Bakkers and the Swaggarts were hypocrites and mountebanks in the Elmer Gantry vein—though of course, that is what they turned out to be. Rather, it's that the gospel merchandised over the cable airwaves of the seventies and eighties was tailor-made for a postindustrial service economy, where labor was steadily casualized, and credit-based consumption was ascribed with its own magical, soul-transforming properties.

Prosperous Souls

For the spirit-imbued apostles of the charismatic age, their new faith dispensation offered the best of both worlds, even if it teetered on the brink of Apocalypse: American believers could both save Christian civilization, and get rich while doing so. An early and influential text of the prosperity faith, A. A. Allen's 1968 *Send Now Prosperity* vividly depicted the intimate work of salvation that God has in store for the faithful, in a personalized gloss on the Sermon of the Mount that confidently elides the bit about the meek inheriting the Earth:

> God promises you a prosperous soul if you obey Him and do what He
> wants. God wants you to have equal portions of health, wealth, and
> salvation . . . God promised it because He has it, and HE WANTS
> YOU TO HAVE IT! YOU ARE ONE OF HIS CHILDREN, and
> He is your Father. YOU are heirs of God and joint heirs with Christ.
> You are the rightful owners of all HIS WEALTH! Any Father
> that loves his child wants that child to be comfortable, well-fed and
> clothed . . . He loves you more than He loves the birds and the lilies
> of the field. Birds do not fall to the ground without His knowledge.[331]

In this urgent and magical account of the spiritualized economy, God is giving prosperity to individual believers directly, and their gifts to the church are, in reality, a glorified sort of personal investment, yielding enhanced returns in their spiritual lives—making them "prosperous souls," in Allen's phrasing—as well as far more direct material bounty. With everything else about material life in the seventies growing more precarious, the evangelical outlook of the age navigated a quasi-millennial enclosure of the economic question, as it migrated from the older improvement-minded project of self-culture to the promise of immediate abundance, miraculous prosperity, and managerial-style therapeutic self-care.

Sometimes this impulse found expression in subtler ways. The most influential intellectual text on the evangelical right, for instance, was Francis Schaeffer's Baedeker-style survey of the humanist follies of Western civilization, *How Should We Then Live?* This tract, which grew out of a wildly popular accompanying film project of the same name, did more than any other single work of the seventies to align evangelicals firmly against the bogey of "secular humanism"—the materialist and decadent assault on Christian orthodoxy that Schaeffer saw at the bottom of the modern world's many political, moral, and economic ills. But Schaeffer—a youth preacher who had founded a Protestant communal retreat in Switzerland called L'Abri—also castigated the material complacency within Christian orthodoxy in terms reminiscent of the more radical advocates of the Social Gospel. Writing of the Protestant world's complacency before the exploitation of the industrial age, Schaeffer noted that "all too often in England and other countries the church was silent about the Old and New Testament's emphasis on a compassionate use of wealth. Individual acts of charity did not excuse this silence. Following industrialization, the noncompassionate use of wealth was especially glaring." And in sizing up the ills of contemporary American society, Schaffer again singled out the false lure of the accumulation of wealth for its own sake, even going so far as to salute the campus rebels of the sixties for refusing to settle for the "impoverished values" of "personal peace and affluence."[332]

But when Schaeffer's ballyhooed lecture tours of the United States in the seventies distilled the message of his book and film for a newly activist evangelical audience, his critique of Protestant wealth-mongering dropped out of the picture entirely. Instead, Schaeffer galvanized crowds behind his attack on abortion rights as the logical end point of a godless humanism; in 1979, he went on to produce a follow-up movie on the subject with future U.S. Surgeon General C. Everett Koop, *Whatever Happened to the Human Race?* Schaeffer's broadsides against abortion rights—which at the time was principally a cause among Catholic believers and drew no significant opposition from evangelicals—would prove instrumental in persuading the Baptist televangelist Jerry Falwell to embark on his successful career in political organizing, as the founder of the Moral Majority. But Falwell—who made *How Should We Then Live?* mandatory reading for the incoming freshman classes at his Liberty University—and his other evangelical allies in the eighties New Right were strident enthusiasts of supply-side Reaganism. The political mobilization of the religious right, in other words, ensured that the rising mood of

evangelical militancy remained confined to the overlapping crusades of the
Cold War and the culture wars, leaving the agendas of the economic right
serenely intact—and indeed, scripturally anointed. "Ownership of property is
biblical," Falwell thundered in his bestselling 1981 call-to-arms *Listen America!* "Competition in business is biblical. Ambitious and successful business
management is clearly outlined as part of God's plan for His people."[333]

Falwell's fellow Baptist New Right preacher Tim LaHaye reproduced
long stretches of Schaeffer's *How Should We Then Live?* argument in his
own 1980 culture-war primer *The Battle for the Mind*—but likewise toed the
hard line of the supply-side right in economic matters, inveighing against a
prospective Communist putsch in America via the humanist infiltration of
public schools, and lamenting the academically engineered "socialist takeover" of formerly hardy Protestant free-market polities such as Sweden.[334]

Much more was at stake in such pronouncements than the casual mis-
reading or selective quotation of Schaffer's opus. The alliance of family-
values culture warriors and economic conservatives formed the heart of the
emerging Reagan coalition, which deftly exploited the cultural resentments
of white working-class Americans in order to discredit economic liberalism as yet another elite subterfuge aimed at marginalizing and de-funding
"real" Americans and their beliefs. But the cynicism of presidential political
strategists is, at best, only half of the story of the new Protestant consensus
on free-market magical thinking. Rather than serving as obliging stooges
for the architects of the new Republican majority, religious Americans had
already quite self-consciously staked out their own brand of sanctified capitalism. At the level of popular psychology and political leadership alike,
evangelicals of the post-Keynesian age had deliberately elected to transform
questions of economic fairness and equity into an unlikely but powerful
alloy of family-values self-help and laissez-faire opportunism.

In clearing a path for supply-side dogmas in the pews of Protestant
America, the leaders of the new evangelical right were also retooling the core
economic bargain at the heart of American Protestantism. The old bonds of
striving self-restraint, bequeathed to believers by the Second Awakening, were
dissolving. In their place was emerging a new Protestant economic consensus
that translated the experiential sensibility of the new charismatic age into a

straightforward dogma of libertarian entitlement. One of the critically unexamined articles of this postindustrial moment held, much as Mormonism had from the nineteenth century onward, that a well-stocked larder and an expectation of personal affluence were simply Protestant American birthrights.

We tend to see the trademark shifts of this crucial transitional phase of American capitalism—which took most Americans out of the orbit of manufacturing work and into the complex of service professions known as FIRE (i.e., finance, insurance and real estate)—from the vantage point of the policy elite who struggled to fully define and implement the transition. But the charismatic revival allows us to better understand how the historic emergence of the low-wage American service economy looked from the ground—and how it played out in the redemptive visions of a rapidly expanding charismatic Protestantism.

The Wal-Mart Way

Of all the legacies of seventies-era social change, the managerial model of the evangelical family had the greatest, and most unexpected half-life, as the helpmeets of the embattled corporate spouse of the seventies fanned out into the wider service economy. The Total Woman was well on her way to serving as the model middle manager.

The domestic and commercial versions of servant leadership were poised to converge at Wal-Mart, the retail chain destined to become both the largest company and the largest private employer in the United States. Wal-Mart is also a cultural icon nearly as significant for evangelical believers as a matrix of public piety as it is a source of private family bargain-hunting. As Moreton shows, the Wal-Mart Corporation has come to be the most enthusiastic exemplar of the servant-leader idea—so much so that the customer experience at the store's thousands of outlets serves as a kind of cultural shorthand for how Protestant citizens are to treat each other in the marketplace: with familial dignity, folksy personal concern, and hierarchical deference. "If you want to reach the Christian population on Sunday, you do it from the church pulpit," Ralph Reed has famously pronounced. "If you want to reach them on Saturday, you do it from Wal-Mart."[335]

As Moreton explains, Sam Walton's network of discount shopping outlets, which became incorporated in 1969, occupied a pivotal niche in the socioeconomic geography of the New American South. Nestled in the heart of the Ozarks, Wal-Mart's center of operations in Bentonville, Arkansas, neatly distills many elements of the postindustrial service economy. The region's former productive landscape of smaller farms, cultivating diversified crops, has largely given way to enormous agribusiness concerns such as Tyson Chicken; the displaced midcentury farm population now clusters in exurbs and small towns precariously knitted into the services-and-tech sectors of the information economy. Thanks in no small part to Wal-Mart's presence, Northwest Arkansas has also emerged as leading trucking hub, with large firms such as J.B. Hunt Transport poised at the northern and eastern portal of the American Sunbelt.

Like the ideological center of Sunbelt conservatism in Southern California, northwest Arkansas owes much of its service-economy infrastructure to massive federal spending; the all-year tourist and retirement settlements that fueled an eye-popping 80 percent increase in the Ozarks' population from 1960 to 1998 exist only thanks to the Army Corps of Engineers. Under the 1938 Flood Control Act, the corps was able to divert water from the White River into what are now a half-dozen manmade lakes, which form a picturesque mountains-and-water chain of southern vacation and retirement retreats. In an all-too-suitable historical irony, one of these Corps-created bodies of water, called Beaver Lake, flooded a resort camp that formerly belonged to the Gilded Age Populist economist William "Coin" Harvey—so nicknamed for his ardent advocacy of the free coinage of silver as a central means of debt relief to the nation's small farmers. Now Beaver Lake furnishes most of the water supply for Wal-Mart's Benton County.[336]

Wal-Mart, in short, was made for—and by—the service-based, federally subsidized world of Ozarks capitalism. But in the person of Sam Walton and his corporation's class of senior executives, the company was initially an awkward fit for its consumer base of heavily evangelical, budget-conscious family shoppers. Like other midcentury retail chains, Wal-Mart followed a strict gender-based division of labor, reserving most senior-, mid-, and store-level management spots for men not yet attuned to the niceties of servant-leader management theory; they were, rather, patriarchal individualists of the old school, expecting automatic deference in both the marketplace and the domestic sphere. This was an especially charged legacy culture of senior management, since the new titans of Ozarks retail were overseeing a heavily feminized workforce of cashiers and floor assistants: Wal-Mart in the early years actually had very generous health benefits for its Arkansas stores, which meant that it became an especially desirable workplace for working-class dual-income households and single mothers alike—an irony that sheds a harsh light on the company's later dismal record of keeping many workers on a work schedule just shy of full-time in order to avoid granting them health benefits. Wal-Mart's first managers tended to overlook the rapport that their employees shared with the women across the register from them—and to this day, Wal-Mart has a well-documented, and heavily litigated, record of sexual discrimination in terms of pay equity, promotions, and management hires.

In terms of the company's brand identity, however, Wal-Mart is all but synonymous with evangelical "family values"—so much so that GOP pollsters have discovered that regular patronage of Wal-Mart stores is a more sturdy measure of conservative voting habits than church attendance is. And as Moreton notes, this invaluable, softer perception of Wal-Mart's community profile is owed almost entirely to the company's managers attentively appropriating the ethos of servant leadership from their own female workers. Noticing an intense family-style customer loyalty taking shape in the store's client base, Wal-Mart's old-school managers started looking to mass-produce an in-store corporate culture that mimicked the mores of mutual care and servant-leadership that had historically been the province of the small-farm family—with the women of the household overseeing the bulk of its affective labor. "The genius of Wal-Mart and its imitators was to mobilize the very resource that had been devalued by the earlier rise of industry," Moreton writes:

> The ruling myth of labor enshrined a chain of association between masculinity, autonomy, and skill. This suite of concerns was given institutional form in the New Deal social provisions, in most unions, and in firms themselves. The burgeoning service economy then capitalized on this broad social agreement that women weren't really

workers, that their skills weren't really skills. The domestic economies
of farm families provided a model and a vehicle for this appropriation,
and companies in the Ozarks were working overtime to support the
direct transition from farm to service corporation . . . Much of the
economic substance had been drained from the farm. But for the generations raised there, the form remained, with all its ideological power
and all its resources of skill and social relations. Ozarks industry leaders in trucking and chicken capitalized on the area's historically late
transition from farming by mobilizing the yeoman himself. Wal-
Mart wanted the yeoman's wife as both a customer and an employee.
To get her, it had to model itself on her family relationships.[337]

And those relationships, in turn, were firmly grounded in an evangelical
vision of the managed self that was bubbling up at the same time in the works
of Marabel Morgan and company. The servant leader and the surrendered
wife occupied the same delicate point of self-definition in the new postindustrial realignment of American life: They were expected to demonstrate their
strength through their capacity to submit. They were also, curiously enough,
expected to exhibit the same basic omnicompetent emotional skill set of relentlessly positive spiritual affirmation, as the demands of managing evangelical
family life and Wal-Mart commerce have quietly blurred into each other.

None of which is to say, however, that Wal-Mart has in any way
diluted or discarded its own distinctly muscular Christianity as it trains
its resources on the wider world. In all sorts of institutional and educational settings, the company has emerged as an aggressive champion of the
influential strain of civic free-market faith that might be called open-shop
Christianity. Wal-Mart is of course mindful enough about its global market reach to refrain from defining itself overtly in religious terms; when
former CEO Don Soderquist was asked in 2005 whether the retail giant
was a Christian corporation, he denied it—but then delivered a measured
disclaimer that "the basis of our decisions was the values of Scripture."[338]
But regardless of his qualified public statements, Soderquist's resume bore
its own witness to how deeply an evangelical sensibility was embedded in
Wal-Mart's corporate culture: A graduate of Illinois's evangelical Whea-

ton College, he was both colleague and close friend to servant-leader management consultant Kenneth Blanchard, of *One-Minute Manager* fame. He's also helped to endow a center for Christian business ethics named for him at the Arkansas evangelical school John Brown University. (Company founder Sam Walton was, for his part, not an evangelical, but a staid mainline Presbyterian, and his wife, Helen, was quietly pro-choice—traits that were both out of line with the store's strong branding in the evangelical South and West, and therefore muffled by the founding couple's far more public profile as generically pious and service-minded corporate leaders and generous donors to Christian institutions of higher learning.)

More telling accommodations to the evangelical temper of Wal-Mart's host culture came in Sam Walton's fiercely pro–free trade and anti-labor philanthropic outlays. The company founder had been moved to greater political advocacy in 1978, during a Senate debate over proposed reforms to the National Labor Relations Board, which Walton saw as a direct assault on the open-shop hiring practices that prevailed in right-to-work states such as Arkansas. Writing in the company magazine *Wal-Mart World*, Walton sounded a dire alarm: "We need everyone's help to put down this labor law that is now being debated by the Senate. In my opinion, such a [*sic*] legislation could wreck our Company and largely negate the future for us all . . . It may be too late, but I'd like to enroll all of us in all our stores, our general offices and the distribution centers in the fight to preserve our free enterprise system." Walton also lobbied Congress personally to scotch the reform bill, and GOP senators successfully filibustered it into oblivion later in the year.[339]

Newly awakened to the state's designs on the sacred prerogatives of the free market, Walton set about bankrolling an astonishing regional empire of laissez-faire initiatives in education and professional training, mainly via a select group of evangelical colleges: The College of the Ozarks, a pet charity of his wife, Helen; John Brown University; Harding College, the home institution of the famed scourge of the New Deal, George S. Benson; and Harding's sister school, Oklahoma Christian University. Walton also helped fund and launch Students In Free Enterprise (SIFE)—a nationwide campaign to promote free-market initiatives in the nation's colleges that by 2003 was supplying Wal-Mart with 35 percent of the company's manager trainees. SIFE encouraged students to organize and lobby around pet industry causes, such as reining in the federal deficit, enacting steeper cuts in business taxes, and capping class action liability in court (aka "tort reform"). Faculty advisers to chapters are known as Sam M. Walton Free Enterprise Fellows, and participating students compete for cash prizes. After SIFE acquired its own free-standing communications arm in Springfield, Missouri, it would go on to serve as a model of sorts for Newt Gingrich's influential GOPAC—another New South dispenser of free-market verities, aimed at repurposing the nation's educational and political institutions in its ideological image. One of GOPAC's charter members was Gay Hart Gaines, the wife of former SIFE chairman Stanley N. Gaines, CEO of an auto parts distributor that was also a key vendor for Wal-Mart.[340]

Still another Walton-funded pedagogical initiative of the 1980s was the Walton International Scholarship Program. Launched in 1985 with a private endowment of $3.6 million, it brought a global scope to the promotion of free-market ideals. Concerned with the spread of socialist ideas among the intellectual leaders of Central American hot-spots such as Nicaragua, Guatemala, and El Salvador, Walton sought to fund the business education of 10,000 college students from the region, on condition that they return to their home countries for at least four years post-graduation to spread the free-market gospel. The program was administered mainly through the University of the Ozarks and Harding, even though larger state schools such as the nearby University of Arkansas were far better situated to handle such a large influx of foreign students. As Walton explained, these smaller Christian colleges fit the program's needs because "we thought we could stay close to them . . . we know what they teach and how they think."[341]

Serving on the Leading Edge

Wal-Mart's rise to market dominance in the 1990s did more than turn the Walton clan into billionaires: It elevated the company's wage-slashing business model and its allied management ideology of servant leadership to the front ranks of American business culture. The restless online retail mogul Jeff Bezos had early on adopted the Wal-Mart way as his own company's mantra for increasing market share across entire new retail sectors and technological

platforms. Amazon.com, like Walton's heartland retail empire, systemati-
cally identified and routed its market rivals through the simple practice of
bigfooting them out of existence. Bezos, like Walton, relentlessly centralized
and rationalized all phases of his global model of commerce, and bulked up
his market reach by the systematic undercutting of the pricing models of
competitors. And both companies consciously maintain their profit margins
via a low-wage, high-service model of casualized, postindustrial labor.

In the precincts of management theory, meanwhile, the servant-leader
ideal became near-omnipresent thanks to Wal-Mart's success—and much
more overtly evangelical in its substance. Indeed, the most successful servant-
leadership tract of the Wal-Mart age, James C. Hunter's 1998 management
parable *The Servant*, is striking for presenting its management advice almost
purely as a program for religious self-fulfillment. There's no longer even a
remote suggestion of the subcultural ghettos of evangelical publishing or
management consultancy, even though Hunter dedicates the book "to the
Glory of God" and studs its simple managerial dictums with unselfconscious
and unapologetic theological appeals. The Crown Business imprint acquired
The Servant from a smaller independent publisher, and outfitted it with a battery of enthusiastic blurbs from a wide range of alpha business and political
leaders, from Nestle CEO Joe Weller, ITT executive Robert M. Davie, and
then-leader of the Republican Party Conference in the U.S. House of Representatives, John Boehner. The book has sold nearly 4 million copies, and
spawned an ongoing consultancy and seminar franchise for Hunter, catering
to more than 20 Fortune 500 firms, and every branch of the U.S. military.[342]

Hunter frames *The Servant*'s baby-simple instruction to service-
minded managers within the deeply implausible setting of a leadership
seminar held in a Benedictine monastic retreat by a former airline CEO-
turned-monk. (That the didactic messages here are delivered by a Catholic adept is a further indication of the ever-widening post-denominational
character of the evangelical ethos, as well as a not-altogether uncynical
bid on Hunter's part to cash in on the unlikely burst of monk chic in
the pop culture of the late 1990s, from the "Chant" CD franchise to the
heavy-breathing Catholic conspiracy novels of Dan Brown.)

Hunter is also gratifyingly frank in demonstrating how the principles of servant leadership are designed to undermine union activity in the service-sector workplace. The narrator of the parable, "John," is a customer services executive for a successful glass-installation firm in the Midwest; his local Lutheran minister arranges for him to spend a weeklong leadership retreat at a southern-Michigan monastery after a series of personal and professional setbacks—chief among them an abortive organizing drive among disaffected wage workers at John's company. Once the vote to certify union representation failed by a narrow margin, John recounts, "I was elated but my boss was upset that the vote had taken place and suggested that it was a management problem, which was *my* responsibility." More irksome still, the "corporate human resources manager" at the firm also contended that John's hierarchical, task-and-results mode of management was the culprit here; "she was a liberal, touchy-feely, cause-oriented gal and what did she know about running a large business anyway?"[343]

John catalogs other symptoms of his spiritual distress, from dissatisfaction with his work routine and the blandishments of his suburban home life to mounting friction in his day-to-day interactions with his wife and children. But it's clearly this close brush with collective bargaining that strikes most deeply at his personal and professional sense of self-worth. And in the plodding weeklong instruction in the verities of servant leadership that make up the balance of the book, the far-from subtle prime directive is the repurposing of labor tensions as the occasion for shared spiritual edification—always midwifed, however, by an evangelically enlightened management caste.

This message is hammered home during the Scripture-quoting rounds of the seminar, whose ludicrously overcredentialed guiding light is a Benedictine monk named Brother Simeon, better known in his spiritual civilian life as "the legendary Len Hoffman" the erstwhile no-nonsense CEO of Southeastern Airlines, which he ran as part of a hostile wage- and cost-cutting hedge-fund takeover. Now serenely installed in post-retirement monkhood, Brother Simeon is something of a Thomas Merton for the neoliberal corporate age: a spiritual pilgrim preaching the higher wisdom of a spiritually self-regarding regime of high profit margins and low wages, delivered in a creepily condescending register of therapeutic and religious omniscience.

The seminars predictably throw the mildly angry white guy John in with a sassy multicultural coterie made up of a maternity nurse, a women's basketball coach, a high-school principal, a drill sergeant, and a Protestant minister who is, like Brother Simeon, a former corporate manager. (Hunter is anything but subtle in mapping out what he sees as the overlapping skill sets of the clerical and corporate managerial class, and as a good evangelical, it seems, he can't let it appear that the Catholics have a monopoly on servant-leadership wisdom.)

As the proceedings unfold, Brother Simeon continually stresses that labor unrest is really a spiritual cry for help from misunderstood workers. What these childlike souls are really seeking in strikes and organizing drives, Brother Simeon sagely counsels, is the affirmation of their deeper spiritual worth. And that messianic calling inevitably falls to the patrician servant-leader of the postindustrial corporation. The watchword of servant leadership, the market-savvy monk pronounces, is ensuring that the needs of all interested parties get met. "If our customers are leaving and going to the competition, we have a relationship problem" stemming from the neglect of the prime directive of "meeting the customer's *needs*," Brother Simeon explains in his unaffected CEO argot. "The same principle is true with employees. Labor unrest, turnover, strikes, low morale, low trust and low commitment are merely symptoms of a relationship problem. The legitimate needs of the employees are not being met."[344] Likewise, the monk stresses, "if we are not meeting the needs of the owners or stockholders, the organization will also be in serious trouble. The stockholders have a legitimate need to get a fair return on their investment—and if we are not meeting that need as an organization, then our relationship with the stockholders will not be very good."[345]

Lost in all this reassuring corporate feelspeak, of course, is the notion that the "legitimate needs" of workers and stockholders are frequently in fundamental conflict with each other—that stockholders' demands for higher profit margins cut directly into worker demands for a fair wage. As the example of Wal-Mart makes painfully clear, servant leadership, like the many patrician managerial schemes that preceded it through the industrial age, isn't at all designed to guarantee genuine job security, benefits, or decent wages to the service-economy workforce. It is, rather, carefully crafted to make it appear as though they are taking workers' needs into account when they are fact engaged in wage theft, benefits-starving, and casualized sub-contracting in order to pad the shareholders' bottom line. This point is, once more, made thankfully explicit, in one of John's pained self-conscious asides about his close call with his own company's union activities: "During a recent union drive at our plant," John tells his seminar-mates, "everyone kept telling me that the main issue was money until I became convinced that it was. But the union-buster consultant we hired to help us get through the union campaign kept telling us that the issue was *not* money. He insisted it was a relationship problem but I didn't believe him. Perhaps he was right."[346]

Not surprisingly, *The Servant*'s author James C. Hunter *is* that union-busting consultant in real life; his dossier as a "labor consultant" involves actively persuading corporate clients to pay lip service to worker self-esteem and spiritualized notions of therapeutic fulfillment precisely in order to bypass the all-too-genuine and urgent threat of institutionalizing conflicts about the main issue of money within the corporate workplace.

In this regard, Hunter is no different from the legions of other labor consultants diligently picking off union drives in service industries ranging from health care to information technologies. But what's valuable about the clumsy and didactic spiritual testimony assembled in *The Servant* is that it dramatizes the complete enclosure of contemporary management theory by the evangelical outlook of the Money Cult. Viewed in terms of simple agit-prop, the main action in *The Servant* is identical to the gospel of Pealeism. In both of these reactionary traditions, Christianity dogmatically urges devotees on to greater feats of inward spiritual Gnosis and worldly achievement, while militantly preventing the formation of anything resembling solidarity in the ranks of the working class. The only significant difference here is that Norman Vincent Peale had compartmentalized his self-help ministry, in organizational terms, apart from his union-busting campaigns and his various lobbying initiatives to unseat the New Deal. So Peale would use revenues from his books and radio ministry to campaign against labor-friendly social policy—and, when these two worlds came too close to converging, as when the contretemps on the Committee for Constitutional Freedom threatened to impair the launching of *Guideposts*, Peale was forced to intervene in order to separate them further.

In our own market-addled age, no such cosmetic measures are called for. The language of the evangelical gospel and the management consultancy have merged indistinguishably into one another—to the point that a long series of neoliberal workplace nostrums delivered in the pious voice of an enlightened monk is an affirmative marketing boon for the anti-labor message of the servant-leader movement. Monks, after all, are selfless souls who are themselves obedient model workers. In so conspicuously plying his management bona fides in pursuit of his own spiritual calling, Brother Simeon-né-Hoffman embodies the strange, but spiritually taken-for-granted priorities of servant-leader management in the American service economy. Managers are to be nimble people pleasers, keen to place their skills at the disposal of their stockholders—but to wash over the baser implications of this particular relationship with the agreeable fiction that like Christ himself, they can be all things to all people.

That fiction is creaking, however, in the aftermath of the 2008 economic meltdown—and especially as wealth inequality is the most enduring legacy of the past generation's worth of top-heavy, labor-soaking, counter-productive economic growth. And once again, Wal-Mart appears to be ground zero of the slow retrenchment of tougher economic truths. Walton's keen interest in expanding the open-shop Wal-Mart regime on a global scale was, of course, in line with the company's strategy of continued international expansion—but the recent economic downturn has pointed up the limitations of the Wal-Mart way amid sluggish overall economic growth and mounting wealth and income inequality. As experienced retail workers abandon the store brand for better-paying rivals, and as the firm's senior management remains dogmatically committed to containing costs with a casualized, low-wage workforce, Wal-Mart's stores are increasingly hard-pressed to move stock.

For all the lip service that the brand's managers give to ideals of Christian service and community, Wal-Mart is ultimately a corporate avatar of the Gnostic gospel of unchecked consumer growth—and now that such growth can no longer can be taken for granted, its masculinized management gospel of free-market expansion appears to be at war with the "softer," sentimentalized image of the store as a surrogate family of faith-based helpmeets. During the first quarter of 2013, the store placed dead last among retail and discount stores in the American Customer Satisfaction Index, according to a report by Bloomberg News—the sixth straight year that the Wal-Mart either claimed or tied for that dubious distinction. Earnings have flatlined, and the company has continued to cut costs by shrinking its workforce—leading to what Bloomberg writer Renee Dudley describes as a vicious circle: "Too few workers leads to operational problems. Those problems lead to poor store sales, which lead to lower labor budgets."[347]

In one way, the company's current plight is an all-too-appropriate gloss on the tacit social contract that fueled its successful expansion. The traditional evangelical conception of family values, hinging as it does on biblical notions of patriarchal headship, relies on vast amounts of undercompensated and invisible labor—and it makes little difference, in the ultimate scheme of things, if one chooses to infuse them with the kind of spiritual power that arises from incanting select words of faith. Or to put things another way: The New Thought–cum–Gnostic gospel of Infinite Supply serves no real purpose if it can't guarantee workers a living wage.

10

SECRET HISTORIES

The neoliberal apostles of servant leadership made it all too plain that work-ers could only rely on their own waning individual reserves of faith, pluck, and ingenuity to wrest any measure of just reward from the postindustrial rites of economic production. But that didn't prevent the American evan-gelical scene from the seventies onward from coalescing around a far more grandiose sense of purpose and redemption. Americans, in the mundane order of things, might no longer be justified in expecting reliable increases in their living standards, job security, pensions, or benefits; but America, in the collective spiritual sense, would be able to realize an infinitely greater payoff. A saving remnant of its evangelical faithful was destined to be on the vanguard of the final deliverance of the late, great planet Earth.

More than most of the mainstay issues of culture warfare, which have lately lost their once-sure pride of place on the conservative Protestant cul-tural agenda, the sense of the imminent end of history continues to loom in the revisionist popular theology of conservative evangelical believers—and together with it, their own corollary ascension into their blessed other-worldly reward. As of 2010, the Pew Center for People and the Press found that roughly half of all American Christians believed that Jesus would return to bring the curtain down on human history within the next forty years; 58 percent of white evangelicals assented to that view.[348]

Lest this strong plurality be chalked up to the cataclysmic events such as the September 11, 2001, attacks on the World Trade Center and the Pentagon or the ensuing War on Terror, Pew also found roughly the same proportion—44 percent—of American Christians held the same view of

Christ's imminent return 11 years earlier, in 1999. Clearly, the expectation of imminent apocalypse had settled into a permanent feature of the American worshiping life.

What's harder to explain is why. It's far from self-evident that the citizens of a frenetically future-oriented consumer republic, governed by ever-accelerating traffic in information, technological change, and commerce, should be going about their daily business with the background certainty that the whole world will collapse into grim, prophesied oblivion within a matter of decades. More curious still is the demographic profile of our own latter-day cohort of prophecy believers: They are, for the most part, comfortably well off, very much at home in the sensorium of contemporary consumer capitalism—and very, very American. Their brand of the end-times faith arises from a curiously inward, chauvinistic interpretation of biblical prophecy, projected across the vast stage of global history.

One clue to this shift lay, once again, in the robust Americanist drift of Protestant observance during the Cold War. As part of the great mid-twentieth-century upsurge in prophecy belief, the annealing vision of the Final Judgment—which had once been advanced to vindicate divine schemes of justice and eternal conceptions of history's inner logic—had become quietly conscripted into the Cold War crusade of world-conquering Americanism. Put another way, American Protestants increasingly came to believe that the business of the apocalypse in the twentieth century was to make eternity more distinctly American.

It took some patient trial-and-error to get Protestant believers to incorporate the new end-times faith into the otherwise sunny and postmillennial American outlook on the ultimate direction of world history and God's plans for humanity's mass deliverance. Among other things, the conviction of an imminent Apocalypse seemed to rub profoundly against the grain of the cherished American myth of progress—the old civic-religious certainty that the steady material expansion of America's market society all-but-automatically betokened the eventual salvation of all humanity, and (almost as an afterthought, it seemed) the second coming of Jesus. After nearly a century of steadily waxing premillennial sentiment in the United States, it's still not entirely clear why the relatively new conviction that the Apocalypse is running well ahead of all prospects for incremental social reform should mesh so completely with the postmillennialist tenor of the progress myth.

Nor was the consumer society of mid-twentieth century America a natural fit with the broader sweep of millennial tradition. Early sects devoted to the looming apocalypse, such as the Diggers, Levellers, and Ranters of the British reformation, were distinctly radical and communitarian: They wanted history to end so that it could be *fixed*—and the more perfect scheme of divine justice substituted at last for the flawed and sinful human one. They staked their believing lives on the old dictum from Matthew 20:16 that the last shall be first, and the first shall be last.

The American apocalypse cult of the twentieth century took root under drastically different social and economic conditions, to put things mildly. Indeed, the peak of the Protestant American dalliance with the Last Days emerged at the very moment that the American middle class was reaching the height of prosperity—when median income and union membership were both at historic highs, suburban homeownership was exploding, full employment was on the horizon, and social critics were starting to wonder out loud about how citizens might grapple with the "leisure problem" or otherwise stave off ennui in the affluent society.

Waiting for the End of the World

So what was it that compelled so many comfortable American Protestants, living in unparalleled postwar abundance, to endorse the notion that the Last Judgment was imminent—that all their hectic ambitions and hard-won wealth would soon be gathered up in the whirlwind? It was a bit as though they had been laying up a lifetime's worth of vacation capital for first-class passage on the *Titanic*.

Their own reply, of course, would be that they were merely heeding the scriptural writing on the wall—that world events had taken a sudden lurch in the direction of prophecy's literal fulfillment in their own life-times. In many cases, the founding of the modern state of Israel is the argument clincher: The ingathering of the world's Jews in the original chosen land *was* a key event foretold in Revelation, and Israel's status as a premier American client state has permitted American Protestants to assert their own credentials of chosenness by Old World proxy, as it were. Of course, the next phase of the Jewish state's predestined role in end-times prophecy—the mass conversion of the Jews to Christianity—has proven a far more elusive goal, but part of the genius of premillennial prophecy is that it confidently outsources all the miracle-working exploits in human history back to the God, for whom all things are possible.

Still, the faraway fortunes of the Jewish state—or the American occupation of Babylon (aka Iraq) in 2003—were not really the main events in the rescripting of modern prophecy belief. For Americans, the historical particulars of prophecy faith have proven less compelling than the simple fact of its method: Poring over the march of current events for telltale signs of the Last Days has proven a surprisingly durable pastime since the dispensationalist doctrine moved into the center of Protestant worship over the last century. Americans are notoriously amnesiac when it comes to their own history, but they seem to take great forensic pleasure in reading the scriptural arrangement of world affairs forward.

This obsessive dalliance with Last Days symbolism also represents a significant continuity with the postmillennial past. Just as confident and optimistic divines could find immense millennial significance in the battery of nineteenth-century improvements that incorporated the far-flung nodes of production along the American interior into a single national market, so have latter-day prophetic believers in the United States latched on to the fragmenting, disaster-prone course of recent world history as evidence that the end-times are near. The object in each exercise is to make the dramas of Revelation a lived, present-day vindication of the rigors of evangelical faith—and in so doing, to choreograph an unanswerable, real-time "I told you so" from on high.

Thankfully, the empirical particulars of the modern end-times faith are not our concern; if they were, we'd be conducting a long detour through the frenetic recasting of the final dramas of Scripture in the image of passing geopolitical conflict—whereby world powers from Nazi Germany to the Soviet Union have vied for the role of Gog, the empire from the north launching the great climactic assault on the Holy Land, and a wide array of global leaders, from Hitler and Stalin to the Ayatollah Khomeini and

Mikhail Gorbachev, to Saddam Hussein and Barack Obama, have auditioned for the role of Antichrist, and just as inevitably have washed out.

The obsessively serial nature of such opportunistic casting calls for the Last Days might prompt a bit of introspective caution among the end-times faithful—and, in turn, a lot less heavy breathing over the eschaton's imminent arrival. But once again, fidelity to actual historical developments has never been the point for this intensely presentist brand of prophecy. What matters instead is the structural confidence that prophecy faith has bred among believers—the hard-won realization that they are, in fact, on the right side of divinely scripted history. By their lights, prophecy offered a full-blown philosophy of history at a time when the battle lines of global conflict hinged more directly than ever on competing interpretations of the world system's inner spiritual meaning. Postwar prophetic belief posited an intelligible, divinely sanctioned reading of historical developments that otherwise struck casual inquirers as both definitively ruinous and terrifyingly contingent. The Cold War specter of nuclear annihilation propelled both unprecedented outlays for military spending and the routine acceptance of doomsday scenarios as the basis of American civil preparedness regimens and international policy debates—and promised, in the bargain, to upend all existing systematic bids to extract sense from history.

Cold War hostilities also lent fresh urgency to the always-crucial sense of divine election in the plotting out of millennial conflict: Besides doing battle with various secular and liberal enemies within their own society, American believers would also confront in the Soviet Empire an avowedly godless system of economic coercion. It was thus a straightforward matter to baptize the American scheme of prosperity—already infused with spiritual properties of self-advancement courtesy of the holiness and New Thought movements—in the image of the divine plan for history. And when new enemies needed to be summoned to evoke the specter of a future battle for the planet's future in a post-Soviet order of things, why, that was largely a straightforward matter of plugging them into the same basic Cold War script, pitting global Communist perfidy against American capitalist virtue. In straining to make the case that China ("The Yellow Peril") represented the enormous army to be massed along the eastern border of the Euphrates in Revelation 9:16, Hal Lindsey announced that China was squarely aiming at the global defeat of capitalism. "Without the total destruction of the capitalist system," Lindsey wrote in *The Late Great Planet Earth*, "the basic promise and goal of Communism could not be attained, that is, the changing of man's nature by the complete changing of his environment."[349]

Beyond this sense of geopolitical election, the whole thrust of books like Lindsey's, which crowded into the forefront of the religious bestseller lists from the 1950s onward, was to inculcate among believers a privileged sense of inward redemption—the knowledge that the *true* design of human history lay beneath the surface, accessible only to initiated followers.

In just this fashion, the substance of faith—the thorny questions of personal ethics and the paradoxes of theology—also tends to serve as a rushed postscript to the modern infatuation with the end-times. This tic, indeed, may well account for a good deal of the belief system's enduring appeal long after the lapse of Cold War hostilities, when at least the more dramatic brands of nuclear doomsday-forecasts had become blessedly more hypothetical. The relentless determinism implicit in the strict and literal foreordainment of world events makes for a faith that's pointedly impatient with anything that may resemble intellectual complexity: The proof of divine providence is, after all, right there in the day's headlines, so dark nights of the soul and efforts to plumb the non-oracular messages of Scripture come off as irrelevant byways as the world careens toward the end of human history. For several decades now, evangelical critics have bemoaned the absence of any serious theology in a worship culture that's besotted with consumer gratification and the undeviating conviction that the Last Judgment has already settled the major questions of faith for ordinary believers well in advance.[350]

History for the History-less

We are back, in other words, in the subversive byways of the Gnostic transvaluation of history—albeit via the unlikely back door of rigid prophetic literalism. In history's final act, the great mysteries of the divine will become oddly schematic and one-dimensional—a Gnostic theology elevating the believing self over the darker powers that have come rapidly to infuse the cosmic order. Consider in this regard one of the most common metaphors for historical exegesis among the popular expositors of prophecy: the image of the jigsaw puzzle—an analogy that, as historian Paul Boyer notes, reinforces the anti-intellectual outlook of this tradition. As Boyer writes, the idea of the puzzle suggests "both prophecy's universal accessibility and the certainty that, rightly assembled, the texts will yield a single meaning apparent to all."[351]

The curious thing about this intensely present-minded approach to prophecy is that it endures well beyond the continual, inevitable moments when the particular claims mounted by its enthusiasts are discredited. Over and over again, such empirical setbacks prove to be no serious obstacle to the overall appeal of prophecy belief. "Living off the intellectual capital of the past," Boyer writes,

> the interchangeable parade of popularizers continued, as though in a time warp, to expound a system of belief wholly cut off from the larger world of ideas and scholarship. Yet the paucity of intellectual substance and cultural depth proved to be no great liability, as premillennialism remained vastly popular at the grassroots level . . . Prophecy writing's popular appeal arose, too, from its vigorous, if selective and superficial, engagement with contemporary issues. Continually mining the headlines for end-time signs, the promulgators of this belief system addressed subjects of widespread concern, from communism and nuclear war to family disruption and the computer. Readers of these prophecy popularizations could recognize their own world and confront their own fears and anxieties, spread upon a vast canvas of eschatological meaning.[352]

The refusal to think in any depth about either theology or history is no monopoly of evangelical prophecy, as any quick canvas of the spiritual temper of our popular culture will quickly confirm. The explosion of popular conspiracy theories in the latter half of the twentieth century is clearly of a piece with the favored methods of literalist prophecy interpretation. Indeed, when a trio of excitable British researchers set about to demonstrate the

Gnostic myth that Jesus had taken a wife and fathered a bloodline prior to his death, the free-associative secret history that followed, *Holy Blood, Holy Grail* (1982), went on to become the basis for Dan Brown's blockbuster 2003 novel *The Da Vinci Code*, which has done at least as much to propagate pop Gnosticism as Lindsey's book has done to promote pop prophecy belief.

Everything about Brown's fictionalized secret history of the real Jesus and his family was steeped in the selective mythologizing of the biblical past commonly associated with prophecy. All of the novel's drama revolves around a Gnostic saving knowledge contained at the margins of orthodox worship and passed down through the arcane iconography of Western art and church architecture. The central revelations of the plot hinge on a tortured, decontextualized, and deeply implausible tally of self-reinforcing hidden messages concealed in the symbolic language of Scripture—just as Hal Lindsey's close literalist readings of the latter-day meaning of biblical prophecy do. Other subcultural and countercultural treatments of civilizational conspiracy trade in much the same brand of fetishized "secret histories" of everything from Gnostic punk-rock rebellion to various Gnostic celebrations of digital culture to the Gnostic science fiction and fantasy writing of Philip K. Dick, Phillip Pullman, and John Crowley.

The larger point here is that pop prophecy, like most other features of the Money Cult, is a consumer's vision of the path to eternity, one that works to radically insulate believers from the broader social demands of Protestant faith—or indeed, from any mature spiritual understanding of history at all. Just as the initial Victorian version of the Money Cult, in the hands of prophets such as Russell Conwell or John Wanamaker, whispered seductive success gospels to American followers who believed in their hearts of hearts that they were destined to become millionaires, so has the bewildering twentieth-century fusion of prophecy and Gnostic consumerism inspired a deeply consoling gospel assuring believers that they are, in a primordial, metaphysical sense, *already saved*, with no need to dally in the sullied, unreconciled matter at the grubby heart of humankind's historical endeavors. Like the early apostles of Mary Baker Eddy and the allied New Thought movement, these believers have surveyed the sad and fallen course of human endeavor, the folly-ridden schemes of human justice pursued under the aegis of merely human institutions, and declared themselves *pure spirit*—i.e., redeemed souls with access to the true interpretation of Scripture.

For all the surface populism of intellectual method that prevails among these diehard literalist interpreters of prophecy, the scheme of salvation they endorse is as austere, world-denying, and elitist as anything found in the Gnostic scriptures of antiquity. As Doug Clark, author of the bestselling 1982 prophecy tract *Shockwaves of Armageddon* reassures his readers, "It is such a marvelous comfort to Christians to know that Jesus Christ is coming and that He will snatch us up and out of this mundane sphere of living." Hilton Sutton, who wrote the 1983 survey of prophecy *He's Coming!*, is as terse as his book's title in his celebrations of the Gnostic benefits of rightly grasped prophecy; citing an admonition from Jesus to the disciples to be alert to signs of prophecy's fulfillment "that ye may be accounted worthy to escape all these things that shall come to pass," Sutton stresses that "the key word here is *escape*."[353]

The strict prophetic interpretation of world history is, in other words, a studied Gnostic flight *from* history. Among other things, this ethos of retreat has produced the singular paradox that the most militant self-appointed guardians of Western civilization, in their encounter with not merely modern culture, but also with the similarly prophecy-minded apostles of Islamic fundamentalism, are also pointedly incurious about the institutions and practices that actually sustain our civilization. Under the unwavering certainties of end-times faith, modern science, modern biblical scholarship, modern economics, and certainly modern liberal politics, all amount to so much vain and prideful chaff, destined to be consumed in the fast-approaching apocalyptic firestorm. The only stalwart defense that believers can count on in the Last Days is the properly interpreted literalist revelations pronounced by Jesus, Paul, John of Patmos, and the Old Testament prophets.

This is not to say, however, that adherents of modern prophecy are forswearing the conveniences and emollients of capitalist consumerism—far from it. Indeed, the most influential visions of the Last Days match up quite curiously with the fundamentalism of the free market. The ardent contemporary prophecy writer Joel C. Rosenberg embodies many of the culture-defining trends of end-times faith: He has authored a bestselling series of evangelical political thrillers, served as a political consultant to conservative political leaders in the United States and Israel, and he publishes a column in the influential evangelical newsmagazine *Word*. Sizing up the spiritual fallout from the 2008 financial crisis, Rosenberg—a one-time liberal Democrat who veered right after his conversion from Judaism to Christianity in the 1980s—writes that laissez-faire small government is the key to the economic and religious revival of America:

> Nowhere does Scripture indicate that government can save us or solve all our problems or take care of all our needs, and we shouldn't expect it to. Other divinely ordained institutions—including marriage, the family, the church, and even business—have specific roles to play in our society. The government isn't supposed to do their jobs; nor should it make their jobs more difficult. Instead, government is supposed to protect these other essential institutions and create a climate of safety and liberty where these institutions can flourish and thrive.[354]

Rosenberg's preferred policy remedies come, not surprisingly, direct from the playbook of the Tea Party right: drastically curtail expenditures on Social Security and Medicare, repeal the 2010 health-care reform law, and slash the federal deficit—the full battery of short-term austerity measures, in other words, that are guaranteed to exacerbate, rather than remedy, a steep downturn in the business cycle. But policy outcomes aren't Rosenberg's chief concern—he writes that the only way forward from the country's fiscal crisis is the voluntarist call to pray for a Third Great Awakening, in an appeal that once again fluently combines the flat therapeutic jargon of the Gnostic self with the apocalyptic rhetoric of the Last Judgment:

> At this point, nothing less than a Third Great Awakening will save us. These are not normal times. We are not facing normal problems. We cannot keep tinkering around the edges and procrastinating and living in denial. We are in mortal danger as a nation. We are on the verge of seeing God's hand of favor removed from us forever. We are

on the brink of facing God's terrifying but fair judgment. Yet some deny God even exists. Others concede God exists but deny that we really need him. Some give lip service to being a "Christian nation," but deny Christ's power, refusing to live holy, faithful, fruitful lives . . . God certainly can save America. He has the power, and he has done it in the past, but he has made us no promises—and we dare not assume that because America has been such an exceptional nation in the past, she will forever remain so.[355]

Rosenberg's plea makes perfect sense for a Protestant culture of money that has long regarded the comfortable American way of life as a self-evident sign of divine favor: Return to the true, undeviating principles of revived religion, and God shall likewise renew the material bounty he has reserved for prosperous, true-believing Americans. But in taking a more conditional view of American exceptionalism, Rosenberg also reminds us how far inward the recent course of the Money Cult has tacked. It would never have occurred to Charles Finney or other postmillennialist preachers of the Second Awakening to view God's providential designs for the American republic to be seriously in jeopardy; God's clear favor for the New World and its reformed piety was, indeed, the operating premise of the ambitious missionary activities and social reform movements undertaken under the aegis of the Benevolent Empire.

But where thinkers such as Rosenberg at least allow for the notion of America's central prophetic role to be qualified (he is also in the minority of speculative end-times writers who flatly deny, amid no small amount of personal perplexity, that biblical prophecy designates any clear role for the United States in the Last Judgment), the general run of end-times prophesying goes to great lengths to ensure that the final act of biblical history will redeem both America proper and the broader ethno-cultural profile of American consumer capitalism.

The Raptured Lifestyle

Today, the last word—as it were—in end-times writing belongs to the *Left Behind* series of evangelical thrillers, by Baptist preacher-turned-culture-warrior Tim LaHaye and evangelical sports and comics writer Jerry Jenkins. The sixteen-novel series, which debuted in 1995 and concluded in 2007 (not counting the raft of prequels, children's adaptations, study guides, and audiobooks that have come in its wake), has sold more than 65 million copies. It's a safe bet that it will be at least as influential a text in the annals of latter-day prophecy belief as the Book of Revelation—which, of course, furnishes source material for the series' intensively literalist accounting of the Rapture, the Tribulation, and the Final Judgment.

Much has been made of the ways in which *Left Behind* distorts the actual course of prophetic events in its labored effort to bring scripture's great otherworldly cataclysm to pass as a series of action-movie set pieces. For starters, the central precipitating event in the series, the rapture, is a recent innovation of dispensational premillennialism—and comes down to us, once again, from the British dispensationalist preacher John N. Darby. Until the mid-nineteenth century, no student of Christian prophecy professed the idea of a "secret rapture" of the faithful in any sustained way. That notion was first popularized by Darby, who told friends that he'd experienced it as a "new truth" as he reviewed the work of Old Testament prophets.

Darby's conception of an effective "second" second coming, brought on in advance of the grisly dramas of the tribulation and rendered duly spiritualized and carnage-free for the secret and elect cohort of true believers, had enormous appeal for fundamentalist Americans in the twentieth century. During a visit to the United States, Darby brought the doctrine to the attention of the great fundamentalist annotator of the Bible, C. I. Scofield, who promptly adopted it to his biblical thinking. As you'll recall, Scofield's 1909 reference bible—a standard fixture in most fundamentalist libraries—interpolates present-minded literalist readings of prophetic history alongside the main text, encouraging casual readers to conflate a highly idiosyncratic and largely unsupported theory of end-times prophecy with the approved language of the Bible. In other words, the rapture, like many another Protestant import to the New World, became bowdlerized and customized to the predilections of American believers who enjoyed equal assurance of both their own salvation and the pending damnation of the decadent, sinful, and secularized Old World.

The Darbyite revision hinges chiefly on differentiating the prophetic destiny of Israel from that of the Church, and on closely tracking the political fortunes of the former power along the spiritual coordinates established by the latter. In the hands of American believers, however, this exercise tends to collapse into a muddle; already armed with the conviction that they had revived the early church's devotional life, fundamentalists could casually annex the currents of contemporary history and global politics to their preferred version of history's divine plan. American Protestants might have hewed to a division of church and state in their civic lives, but they gleefully abolished it in their prophetic fantasies.

The *Left Behind* novels bear abundant testimony to this curious fusion of premillennial certainty and America-centric convenience. In fashioning their optimal account of the Last Days, Messrs. LaHaye and Jenkins have taken copious care to leave all the trappings of the American culture of abundance intact. Not for them the end-times preachments of figures such as Savonarola, the great Florentine monk of the Renaissance who summoned the followers of his millennial visions to conduct the original bonfires of the vanities—mass burnings of luxury goods. Nor would these prophets of the Last Days pick up where the Ranters and Diggers at the fringes of Cromwell's New Model Army left off—or even dally briefly with incremental feints at social reform as Aimee McPherson and the first generation of California Pentecostals did. Rather, the *Left Behind* series lays out, in carefully wrought detail, a fully wired, upwardly mobile, and incorrigibly flush account of post-Rapture life on earth. The LaHaye-Jenkins vision of the Apocalypse isn't about the final scourging of materialist America's excesses so much as it's about their apotheosis.

Far from reducing its protagonists to a post- (or, strictly speaking, pre-) apocalyptic Malthusian struggle to survive, the divine reckoning chronicled in *Left Behind* restores the book's protagonists—a ragtag band of pre-rapture skeptics, now hastily conducted into the second birth and primed to do battle with the Antichrist and his bumbling crew of bureaucratic evildoers—to still greater material largesse. Even as the plagues multiply and the cosmic forces of good and evil mass for the final confrontation, the members of the Tribulation Force, as they come to be known, absurdly continue to prosper and pile up high-end possessions.

The de facto leader of the Force, a steely, rational airline pilot named, appropriately enough, Rayford Steele, is promoted from his civil aviation job to captain the private flight team of the rising Antichrist, Nicolae Carpathia—a shifty Eastern European enthusiast of one-world government who murders his way to the head of the UN general assembly, and from there, inevitably, a dictatorial new perch as a potentate of a global cult of satanic power. Buck Williams, the hot-headed but brilliant features writer for a major newsweekly, likewise gets recruited to work in Carpathia's communications empire. (Both of these tersely named alpha-heroes begin working for Carpathia before it occurred to them who he was, but it's the fact of their overweening professional diligence, rather than its initial misdirection, that's the principal selling point here; *Left Behind* readers need at all turns in the series' counterscriptural plot to apprehend just how resourceful, talented, and relentlessly high-achieving the leaders of the Tribulation Force are.)

The Steele-Williams alliance even produces an evangelical version of the upper-class tradition known as assortative mating—i.e., the careful, class-bound tradition of securing life partnerships from the same socioeconomic-cum-genetic pool—when Buck romances and marries Rayford's much-younger college-age daughter, Chloe. (The implausible, forensically detailed passages designed to demonstrate that Buck and Chloe enter their union as virgins have to rank as some of the most off-putting and ideologically plodding evocations of human mating since the rape scenes in *The Fountainhead*.)

Even when Buck is outed as a devout Christian and Carpathia's sworn mortal foe—and is thus ejected out of the elite reaches of the new one-world government and into the underground evangelical resistance—he *still* manages to succeed. He sets himself up as the editor and publisher of *The Truth*, the online samizdat publication for evangelical pariahs that ferrets out the real news beneath the slick liberal secular propaganda put out by Carpathia's loyal minions.

How Internet connectivity continues to endure amid all the disasters of the tribulation—from the planet's sustained plunges into complete darkness to devastating earthquakes and the supernatural slaughter of much of the world's human population—is a miracle never spelled out in the exhaustive pages of the novels.

Souled American

It's tempting, Lord knows, to dismiss such clumsy contrivances as mere lousy writing and slipshod plotting and character development, all of which abound across the sequence's several thousand pages—Jenkins, the actual writer of the series, spent many years composing the hilariously flat dialog in the wholesome teen-jock comic strip *Gil Thorpe*, and the high-stakes cosmic drama of *Left Behind* never really rises above the intrigues of a high-school locker room. But there are plenty of cues in the dramatic foreground of the novels that make it very plain that the plan of deliverance on offer is just as much a socioeconomic vision of upward mobility as it is a prophetic depiction of worldly conceit and iniquity laid low by God's holy wrath.

For one thing, there's the simple question of why so much of the action occurs in the prophetically inconsequential United States. Early on, the members of the Tribulation Force are clued into the many ways in which they are living out the laboriously literal fulfillment of the prophecies of Revelation—yet even when Steele and Williams are bivouacked in the very heart of Carpathia's empire in the Middle Eastern desert kingdom of New Babylon, they compulsively continue to coordinate the Tribulation Force's activities by *commuting back to the United States*—a habit that, among other things, exposes them to all sorts of needless personal and tactical risk.

It's idle, on one level, to complain of shoddy verisimilitude in a fictional franchise, but the America-centric course of events in *Left Behind* is both bizarre plotting and poor Tribulation Force strategy. Tremendous amounts of time—and hundreds upon hundreds of pages—are eaten up by the minutiae of air travel, and the simple logistics of ferrying this or that Tribulation warrior from New World Point A to Promised Land Point B and then back again. (The creaking plot contrivance of the U.S.–based Tribulation Force also mandates that at key moments of travel urgency, elite professional pilots and/or the proprietors of under-the-radar private airports have to undergo a timely conversion to end-times faith, just to keep all the pertinent aerospace hardware humming.)

In a sense, though, even the physical American geography is fairly redundant, since the lead characters and the plot developments in the series are already saturated with the chipper ethos of soulful American self-help. All the major characters in *Left Behind* speak fluent English, even when they're outfitted with names and ethnic backgrounds that Jenkins and LaHaye clearly regard as suspiciously alien and exotic—and all quickly adapt the dictums of free-market success to the unprecedented challenges of ushering humanity through the final stage of divinely scripted human history. (It's worth noting here that the character-naming conventions of the franchise, which seem just quaint and comic-strippy when applied to the white Yank protagonists, become absurdly stereotyped and more than a little offensive when they're conscripted into the authors' blinkered effort to imagine the world beyond white suburban Protestants. The main Jewish characters—all of whom go on to become zealous Christian converts, per the letter of prophecy in Revelation—are named Chaim Rosenzweig, Tsion Ben Judah, and David Hassid; a slight improvement over simply styling them "Jews 1, 2, and 3," but not by much. A pair of Arab pilots are named Abdullah Ababneh—whom Rayford winningly nicknames "Smitty" because he finds "Abdullah" too much of a mouthful—and another is simply known as "Al B." for his hometown of Al Basrah, since once again, his full name is just too difficult for folksy Yank evangelicals to pronounce. A reformed African American streetwalker and drug addict at an inner city mission is known simply as Shaniqua; one of her sisters in the new birth is a former Latin American prostitute named Carmella. And so on.)

Just as important, from the franchise's aggressively success-minded standpoint, nearly all the leaders of the Tribulation Force are affluent, highly regarded professionals. The original band of Christian apostles may have been despised, marginal figures in the Judean social order, including fishermen and tax collectors, but that sort of dispensation doesn't cut it in the eschatology of the digital age. Among the supernatural wonders it produces, the Jenkins-LaHaye version of the end times summons a class of military-cum-spiritual warriors who are servant-leaders on steroids. Even an early blue-collar ally of the group, a church IT consultant named Donny Moore, turns out to be a world-class computer wizard, who upon his martyrdom bequeaths an ultra-secure wireless network to the hardy underground band of evangelical rebels.

And these achievements are nothing compared to those of figures such as Chang Wong, the hotshot teenaged evangelical double agent who's promoted to manage all the computer systems in the revived Roman Empire that Nicolae Carpathia runs under the anodyne liberal-secularist moniker of the Global Community. Chang make extensive use of his elite access to sensitive information in the Carpathian empire, passing along crucial financial and scheduling information to Tribulation Force leaders, and leaking damning intelligence to *The Truth*. More than that, though, he's able to use his computer genius to securely hack into the broadcast signals beamed out under Carpathia's authority, and subvert them with interpretations of the Scripture advanced by the revered Jewish convert (himself a copiously credentialed academic genius), Tsion ben Judah. As Judgment Day draws nigh, the young tech genius is exiled from the Antichrist's lair and sets up shop in the red-stone caves of the ancient Jordanian city of Petra—and on the verge of the climactic battle of Armageddon, he still has time for a managerial epiphany. Here he is closely monitoring via the Global Community's newsfeeds the pending martyrdom of a key founding member of the Tribulation Force, Buck Williams's wife (and Rayford Steele's daughter) Chloe, when God showers manna on the faithful, just as prophecy foretold:

> Chang glanced over to where the elders sat before a big screen, and beyond them, hundreds of computer keyboarders awaited instructions. The fading late-afternoon sun cast slanted rays through the door a hundred feet from Chang, and he was moved nearly to tears by the gently falling manna. Providing food for his chosen, protecting and thrilling Chang, comforting Chloe, and sending messengers with the everlasting gospel . . . God was the ultimate multitasker.[356]

It is, of course, jarring to see an omnipotent Creator characterized in language usually reserved for employee-of-the-month honors, but even more curious is the setting: Exiled in an ancient biblical holy city, the final faithful remnant have instinctively *recreated a giant data-processing facility*, replete with a wall-sized video screen and a bank of computers.

Indeed, the many volumes of *Left Behind* abound with this sort of inapposite conflation of prophetic faith with the rewards, work rituals, and rhetoric of the capitalist marketplace. Early into the third volume of the series, as the Antichrist is preparing to rain nuclear devastation down on Chicago in the name of preserving the post-Rapture One World social order, Buck Williams resolves to buy a tricked-out SUV. "I need a new car," he tells his new wife, Chloe. "Something tells me it's going to be our only chance to survive."[357] And given the stakes, he spares no expense, purchasing a hulking Range Rover for "just under six figures."[358]

As is the case in most of the many horrifying catastrophes that beset our heroes across the series, Williams's high-flying sense of entitlement pays instant dividends: As the great Midwestern metropolis suffers nuclear attack, he's able to elude a hopeless tangle of cars bearing panicked evacuees on the expressway by taking the mighty new purchase off road, expertly gunning it through the howling chaos of Chicago. As Buck explains to the skeptical Chloe on their maiden tour in the road-conquering behemoth, "the Antichrist"—i.e., Carpathia—"has never spent a better dollar for the cause of God." He then delivers one of countless smug perorations that will try Chloe's patience throughout the prophecy-shortened course of their marriage, sounding for all the world like the voice-over in a Ford TV spot:

> "Chloe," Buck said carefully. "Look at this rig. It has everything. It will go everywhere. It's indestructible. It comes with a phone. It comes with a citizen's-band radio. It comes with a fire extinguisher, a survival kit, flares, you name it. It has four-wheel drive, all-wheel drive, independent suspension, a CD player that plays those new two-inch jobs, electrical outlets on the dashboard that allow you to connect whatever you want directly to the battery."[359]

This salivating technophilia is a persistent motif throughout the series. In the prior volume, *Tribulation Force*, Rayford Steele is wooed into the

heart of the sinister Carpathian global cabal with the promise of pilot-
ing a bona fide Boeing 757, which he judges first as the Porsche, and then
the Jaguar, of commercial air vehicles.[360] In the series' eighth volume, Buck
and Chloe's hard-driven Range Rover finally gives out, and after a reverent
moment of gratitude—"No man could have done that," Chloe says after
Buck ticks off its record of miraculous service to the Tribulation Force—
Ms. Williams, a former SUV skeptic, announces that "I think a Humvee is
the way to go this time." The couple then adjourns to the basement garage
of the luxury Chicago high-rise in which the Force has taken refuge to find
two of the goliath trucks on offer. As Buck looks out across the armada of
vehicles abandoned in the wake of Chicago's nuclear devastation, he "let
out a low whistle. 'When God blesses, he blesses.'" Chloe responds in kind:

> This is the most fun I've had in ages. It's like we're in a free car deal-
> ership and it's our turn to pick . . . [A]ll we have to do is decide what
> model and color car we want.[361]

It's true that there's not a playbook for Christian ethics that spells out
the proper comportment and mood for appropriating the goods of fellow
creatures slaughtered by the remorseless advance of the ultimate enemy—
though then again, Albert Schweitzer and other historicist scholars of the
New Testament have long argued that the radical spirit of communion
and grace exemplified in teachings such as the Sermon on the Mount
stems from the conviction of primitive believers that the Second Coming
was imminent during *their* lifetime. In all events, it's exceedingly hard to
work out just how the material windfall from nuclear annihilation can be
summed up with the confident pronouncement that "When God blesses,
he blesses," let alone that the ghoulish pastime of combing over the discarded belongings of the dead can be "the most fun I've had in ages."

True heirs to the modernist dispensation of the Money Cult, the protagonists of *Left Behind* recognize no fundamental distinction between the
hand of God guiding the endgame of history and the invisible hand of
the capitalist market. If cities are annihilated for the sake of expediting
the timely delivery of a new all-terrain luxury vehicle, well, God works in

mysterious ways.

Divine Firepower and the Gold Solution

This is all to say nothing, of course, of the Tribulation Force's extended romance with military hardware, which makes for an extremely awkward tour as ambassadors for the Prince of Peace. As they decamp for their Armageddon HQ in Petra, most high-level members of the Tribulation Force tote an exceedingly powerful "directed energy weapon," which heats up the skin of any human target to an intolerable level. It's technically a non-lethal gun, which permits its Christian users to sustain the fig-leaf conceit that they are not actually taking human lives.

Meanwhile, Rayford Steele, guided by his trademark technophilia and macho can-do spirit, procures a decidedly lethal, massive force weapon known as "Saber" to be brandished in the assassination of the Antichrist. Though the mission is ultimately aborted, Steele gives it a trial run over a rapt, eleven-page passage that revels in the particulars of the enormous weapon's capacity for just-in-time gore delivery. Here is Rayford's supplier, exulting over its awesome power:

> As I told you on the phone, a man *missed* by the projectile by two inches from thirty feet away suffered a deep laceration from the air displacement alone. Should you hit someone from between ten feet and two hundred feet, the bullet will leave an exit wound of nearly six inches in diameter, depending on what body part is expelled with it. The thin, jagged, spinning bullet bores through anything in its path, gathers the gore around it like grass in a power motor blade, and turns itself into a larger object of destruction.[362]

Lest there be any doubt whether God would, all in all, prefer that such artillery be forged into ploughshares, a divine messenger lays it definitively to rest. After Rayford fires the Saber on two soldiers of the Antichrist's army, he is rendered deaf by the overwhelming force of the shot. On the inevitable return flight to the United States, he experiences a supernatural visitation of the Archangel Michael, who miraculously restores his hearing.

There is, of course, a set of background economic assumptions that undergirds the frenetic worship of testosterone-driven technology in *Left Behind*, and not surprisingly, it comes straight from the hard-money metal-hoarder's playbook. Even in the early phases of the tribulation drama, the always-enterprising Buck Williams realizes that "he needed to start investing in gold. Cash would soon be meaningless." His formal break from the new Global Community looming, Buck knows that it's only a matter of time until "his income would dry up. He would not be able to buy or sell without the mark of the beast anyway, and the new world order Carpathia was so proud of would starve him out."[363]

Like the occasional callouts that crop up in the *Left Behind* series hailing the paramilitary contributions that the former American militia movement have lent to the Tribulation Force's cause, this paranoid paean to the saving properties of gold in a civilization-wide crisis is an admiring nod to the thought leaders of hard-right conservatism. It is a cosmic upgrade of the hard-money gospel propagated by Mormon financier Howard Ruff in his 1970s gold-bug tract *How to Prosper During the Coming Bad Years*—or, for that matter, by Joseph Smith in the 1840s: True Americans will have the foresight to plan ahead, and to preserve the real value of their labor and property holdings against the ruinous manipulations of the money supply carried out by a scheming and sinister welfare state—which is, in turn, knitted into a still more sinister and scheming world financial system, one that's enmeshed in the empire of the Antichrist.

Once again, Buck's acquisitive instincts are abundantly borne out by the onrushing tide of millennial events. The principal benefactor of the Tribulation Force proves out to be Ken Ritz, a gold-hoarding pilot colleague of Rayford Steele, who cheerfully explains how God has led him to follow the one true economic faith of hard money:

> I'm 90 percent precious metal. As soon as we went to three currencies, I saw what was coming. Now we're down to one, and no matter what happens, I've got a tradable commodity. I got absolutely obsessed with saving when I turned forty. Don't even know why. Well, I mean, I do now. Tsion believes God works in our lives even before we acknowl-

edge him. For almost twenty years I've been living alone and running
charters. I've been a miser. Never owned a new car. Made clothes last
for years. Wore a cheap watch. Still do. I don't mind telling you, I've
made millions and saved almost 80 percent of it.[364]

Here, too, LaHaye and Jenkins take care to point out that resource
hoarding enjoys the supernatural favor of the Creator. One of the plagues
foretold in Revelation—the otherworldly apparition of some 200 million
mounted horsemen descending to Earth from the skies—occurs as Rayford Steele is rescuing a new Tribulation Force recruit, a nurse named
Leah Rose, as Global Community security forces prepare to ransack her
home. The ethereal horsemen are all too real for the jackbooted thugs of
Carpathia's global peacekeeping forces, who combust on contact with the
specters. But Steele is able to walk in their midst unharmed—nor is he
afflicted by burns or smoke inhalation when the supernatural riders, too,
start to burst into flames. As a result, he calmly and confidently returns
from the sturdy Range Rover, where he's stowed the new recruit, in order
to retrieve an enormous bag of cash that Leah has hoarded in a metal safe:
"Walking through smoke and flames he neither smelled nor felt, he pushed
the bag into the back of the Rover and slid behind the wheel. 'Welcome to
the Trib Force,' he said."[365] After the pair safely returned to the Tribulation
Force's suburban headquarters, they ensured that the group had convened
and "thanked God for the provision of the money."[366]

The tight equation of God and money is made most explicit, however, in one of the strangest subplots in the series, which involves Chloe
Williams stumbling on a poor congregation of believers marooned in the
post-attack wasteland of downtown Chicago. This group goes by the name
The Place—once again showcasing LaHaye and Jenkins' chronic inability
to imagine the lives of other-than-white and other-than-comfortably-well-
off characters in anything other than the most generic, broad-brush terms.
When Chloe sizes them up—"a wide-eyed mix of cross-cultural people in
their twenties and their thirties"—she thinks to herself that "these people . . . looked like they had raided a Salvation Army barrel."[367] As if in
fulfillment of the early prophesying of Buck Williams and Ken Ritz, the

seedily clad members of The Place have taken up refuge in an abandoned currency exchange; they'd originally been drawn there by a charitable mission, which proselytized them with an unsubtle come-on from a brochure: "Jesus loves pimps, whores, crack heads, drunks, players, hustlers, mothers with no husbands, and children with no fathers."[368]

And such, indeed, is the demographic profile of the group. They represent the criminal class of the nonwhite inner city—even though The Place's pastoral leader, Enoch Dumas, is incongruously described as a "Spaniard," since, one can't help but suspect, the more European an ethnic group is, the more LaHaye and Jenkins are able to identify with it.[369]

It's significant that Chloe should be the team member to establish contact with this outcast group of believers, since she is the omnicompetent servant-leader figure in the Tribulation Force directorate. Instinctively she reaches out to these straggling believers, and entrusts them with sensitive information—even though giving in to the same impulses under similar circumstances will later cost her her life. But she is the moderating, maternalist manager as the alpha egos of her husband, Buck, and her father, Rayford, rage across the globe, becoming enmeshed in prophesied crisis after prophesied crisis. When the mark of the Beast prevents Christian believers from buying and selling, Chloe takes it upon herself to organize a vast underground cooperative that transports black-market items to evangelical rebels throughout the world. She is also, naturally enough, a doting mother to her toddler son, Kenny (who is named in honor of the martyred goldbug Ken Ritz), and a loyal helpmeet to her man, Buck—so long, as she patiently explains to him, that he meets her halfway. In a monologue clearly repurposed from Tim and Beverly LaHaye's successful franchise of marital self-help manuals, she spells out her doctrine of qualified submission:

> Don't parent me, Buck. Seriously, I don't have a problem submitting to you, because I know how much you love me. I'm willing to obey you even when you're wrong. But don't be unreasonable. And don't be wrong if you don't have to be. You know I'm going to do what you say, and I'll get over it if you make me miss out on one of the greatest events in history. But don't do it out of some old-fashioned, macho

sense of protecting the little woman. I'll take this pity and help for
just so long, and then I'll want back in the game full-time.[370]

Small wonder that when the spiritual counselor of the Tribulation
Force, the converted rabbi Tsion ben Judah, wants to praise Chloe in
the most fulsome terms, he declares, "That girl could run any size corporation."[371] And in taking the followers of The Place under her wing,
Chloe effects a wondrous post-Rapture transformation of her own: This
former wastrel contingent first lends a hand in the decisive repatriation of
believers to their Petra fortress-cum-back-office compound, and then, in
an ill-specified sequence of events, they're transported on their inevitably
stateside return (one that is, indeed, exceptionally puzzling, since the battle of Armageddon is now on schedule to begin in the Holy Land) to the
well-heeled suburbs of Chicago.

Suburbanizing the Eschaton

Stranger still is that LaHaye and Jenkins go out of the way to have the
parishioners of The Place adjourn to the parking lot of a suburban shopping mall to await the pending return of Christ. It's risky, our authors
remind us, for The Place's flock to venture out in public at all, since they do
not bear the mark of the Beast, and even in the plague-battered, recession-
ary order of post-Rapture life, the congregation could instantly become
quarry for freelance bounty hunters or the reliably evil Global Community
security personnel. So Enoch Dumas and his crowd of about 100 followers move into the mall's interior—"to an inner court, where it was obvious they all felt safer." And as the anxious crowd awaits Dumas's sermon
on the fast-approaching timetable for Jesus' Glorious Appearing, one in
their number calls out, in typically stilted and stereotyped black-person
dialogue:

> "Ho'd on!" a woman shouted from the back. She was peering into
> a tiny TV. "Look like someone done took over the GC's airwaves
> again."[372]

It turns out that the pirated broadcast is from Tribulation Force leader Chaim Rosenzweig, the onetime ardent Israeli ally of Carpathia now converted with so many other of his fellow Jews into the evangelical fold—and also, in the miraculous dispensation of the Last Days, infused with the spirit of the Hebrew Bible prophet Micah. As the assembled Place congregants all pull out the miniature battery-driven TVs that they must have acquired as standard-issue perks of their suburban exodus, the scene spontaneously becomes a study in self-administered megachurch worship, facilitated by the pooling of personal electronic devices:

> Others pulled mini-TVs from their pockets and bags. "Should we listen, Brother Enoch? Will you be offended?"
>
> "Hardly," Enoch said, digging out his own TV. "What could be better than this? Dr. Rosenzweig is a scholar's scholar. Let's have church."
>
> The assembled put their tiny screens together on a concrete bench and turned them up so the combined volume reached everyone.[373]

That's right: The reformed sinners of The Place congregation have graduated to the signature form of worship in the new suburban landscape of piety that's been laid before them. They are experiencing the climax of history as a spectacle, beamed across a series of customized personal screens.

With its battery of cheap electronic gadgetry and air of total abandonment by the culture of commerce, this set piece also speaks volumes about the socioeconomic order that *Left Behind* takes great pains to superimpose even on the pending Last Judgment. As is the case with other prophecy-minded literature, there's not much in the way of theology in *Left Behind*—the series typically follows the evangelical warning that critical or systematic thinking about religion is the sort of prideful trick of the mind that works out, in practical terms, into deviltry. "Don't think yourself into Hell," one character counsels.[374] Significantly, though, one of the few snatches of theology that impinges on all the end-times action is a practice that LaHaye and Jenkins flag as the Pentecostal notion of intercessionary prayer by proxy—i.e., the doctrine holding that a prayerful brother or sister in the faith should be prepared to undergo the distresses that afflict the person they pray for. When Tsion employs this device in praying for God to tamp down the wayward and destructive displays of anger and machismo that torment Steele, for instance, he undergoes a convulsive, dramatic communion with the divine presence, a show of fierce "compassion" and "empathy" for his troubled friend that triggers a startling "lack of equilibrium" as he feels "a physical proximity to the creator God."[375]

None of this method, or anything close to it, colors the Tribulation Force's alliance with the members of The Place's communion of faith, however. Even though the golden rule of the Beatitudes is a central doctrine not only of Christianity but all major world religions, the parishioners of The Place are not treated as remotely equal in station or spiritual progression with their winning and well-spoken betters who manage the Tribulation Force, its aerospace and military resources, its mass media syndicate, and the International Cooperative that furnishes the backbone of the believers' underground economy. No, the poor and historically excluded recruits to the post-Rapture crusade are very much treated as *objects*, their ethnicity and personal histories an anonymous wash. They worship in racially stereotyped and emotionally demonstrative fashion; theirs is a primitive Christianity in the strictly pejorative sense.

As the last of the plagues preliminary to Jesus' return sets in—a dense rain of hundred-pound hailstones, or meteorites, sent to chasten the last remnants of unbelief on earth—Enoch returns to The Place's new worship site at the mall, even though his parishioners have fled in terror. There he simply "sat on a concrete bench and watched the show."[376] As the atmosphere turns ever more destructive and violent—"when the lightning seemed to lose all sense of proportion"—Enoch automatically assumes the mien of the complacent spectator: "What a show! The awful and terrible wrath of the Lord on display for the whole world!"[377] Eventually, the one-time minister to the outcasts of the inner city resolves to do what any suburban mall shopper would do in anticipation of a major sports broadcast or fireworks display: "He drove toward home, planning to drag a chaise lounge out of the cellar and enjoy the rest of the show from the yard." He then falls into a personal reverie:

> Somehow Enoch had to find a way to get to the Holy Land as soon as possible after Jesus returned . . . He and the people from The Place would have to start raising money to finance this trip.[378]

This idle reflection is, in a sense, the perfect gloss on this whole fathomlessly surreal set piece. Recall, after all, that in the Antichrist's reign, there *no longer is a money economy in which Christians participate.* So just what sort of money is Enoch imagining that he'll be raising to finance his return to the Holy Land, and from whom exactly, his parishioners having gone into hiding to avoid detection by the armed Global Community personnel? Stranger still, Enoch doesn't recur instantly to yet another airlift operation at the behest of the Tribulation Force's tireless battery of pilots: This is, after all, how all the travel business among senior Christian agents in the Force has transpired since the Rapture, and thanks to their service in the Petra airlift, Enoch and his Place flock would be more than entitled to call in a favor in these extraordinarily unprecedented circumstances.

But instead of these obviously reasonable travel strategies, the inspired pastor of this plucky inner-city flock is planning to *raise money*, even with no actually existing money economy yet in place either to generate revenue on the supply side, or to process his church's prospective payments at the point of ticket purchase. All this being the case, simple logic suggests that the millennial reign of Christ, as envisioned by the most popular prophecy writers in American history, will also entail the metaphysical triumph of sanctified capitalism. At a minimum, this final dispensation of the redeemed market demands that the flock of The Place, who largely sat out the character-building discipline of American capitalism prior to the millennium's onset, must demonstrate their worth in Christ's new global market by showing Jesus the money.

Enoch and his following even return to the prospect in the immediate aftermath of Jesus' first magnificent cosmic apparition. "Will we see Him again?" one Place parishioner asks:

> "Or do we have to go over there for that?"
>
> "I believe we *will* see Him again," Enoch said. "Even today. He is probably fighting one of the battles that precede the fall of Jerusalem and His delivering of the Jews there. But the prophecies say that when He delivers Jerusalem and ascends the Mount of Olives, every eye shall see Him. Obviously, that includes us."
>
> "But pretty soon, like after today, we're going to have to get ourselves over there, right?"
>
> "I sure want to," Enoch said. "But it won't be cheap."
>
> "Well, look at it this way: we got us a thousand years to raise the money."
>
> "I don't want to wait that long."
>
> "Me either. How about a car wash?"[379]

It's only when Enoch, gazing out on the ruins of Chicago, ravaged by a fresh round of divinely sanctioned earthquakes, starts to piece together the fearsome logistics of reviving a functioning economic order in the depopulated American interior that he's rewarded with a personalized guarantee of divine redemption. Jesus—who has indeed been reincarnated as the great multitasker—comes to him in a saving vision:

> Enoch had to talk with God about what to do. If only believers would be left in the United States, with scriptural prophecy seeming to ignore America, it was going to be one sparsely populated country. The various groups of believers might find each other, but what were they to do? Would there be enough of them to start rebuilding the country as, finally for real, a Christian nation? Was this why God was going to purge it of the unredeemed and had already leveled it, making the entire planet as flat as the state of Illinois? None of the believers had worked in public for years. Anyone responsible for any public service or utility would soon be dead. Maybe this was God's way of drawing all His people to be with Je-

sus in Israel.

As Enoch slowly drove through Chicago, Jesus spoke to him. "Fear not, Enoch, for you have rightly deduced that you and your flock are to be with Me."

"But, Lord, we—"

"I will transport you. You need not trouble yourselves."[380]

Enoch's gratuitous meditation on the prospects of Christians subsisting in a near-permanent state of scarcity, right down to his appraisal of the likely tenures of Christian public sector employees, affords a striking contrast to how the Tribulation Force's leaders experience their own saving visions of Jesus—through the usual filter of professional First World entitlement. A surviving trio of fighters in the Force behold their first vision of the returned Messiah not from the courtyard of an abandoned mall but from the side of a sturdy Humvee—and indeed, are able, under the protective gaze of Jesus and the returned saints, to drive the Hummer through the Antichrist's enemy lines unmolested.[381] Chaim Rosenzweig, the spiritual guide mystically infused with Micah's spirit, is returned to his body with the full energy of a young man, "virtually flying over the terrain," a vitally restored being who "had neither grown weary nor suffered from joint pain."[382]

Another Force leader likens his airborne vantage on the Glorious Appearing to being "in one of those blimps that used to hover over the football stadiums at night."[383] They are even pleased to discover that the return of the risen Christ hasn't interfered with their cell-phone reception.[384] Rayford Steele, the series' chief protagonist, finds that he is simply "having the time of his life" as Christ deals out vengeance to the Antichrist and his vast corps of unbelievers;[385] he has a fond burst of nostalgia for his days in a college fraternity, and receives a fully personalized blessing from Jesus' hand—a full-scale recapitulation of his life narrative, capped by the pleasing prospect of eternal Gnostic repose in the Godhead:

"I have loved you with an everlasting love. I am the lover of your soul. You were meant to be with Me for eternity."

Rayford had so many questions, so many things he wanted to say. But he could not. Looking into Jesus' face transported him to his childhood and he felt as if he could stay kneeling there, childlike, letting his Savior love and comfort him forever . . .

Jesus breaks off the session, suitably enough, with a scriptural directive straight from the Prosperity Gospel playbook: "Now to Him who is able to do exceedingly abundantly above all that you ask or think, according to the power that works in you, to Him be glory in the church to all generations."[386]

This envoi goes well beyond the simple confirmation of cosmic travel plans vouchsafed to Enoch Dumas and his stranded Illinois flock—and serves once more to confirm that the millennial Christ in this most detailed and influential account of the Americanized Parousia lavishes preferential treatment on confirmed and fully proven disciples of the market. As Jesus says in direct response to a prayer of thanksgiving when Rayford discovers that Rosenzweig's house, a former Tribulation Force hideaway that had been occupied and trashed by Carpathia's minions, has been miraculously swept clean: "You're welcome, Rayford. It is My delight to shower you with love in tangible ways."[387]

What's especially striking about this clumsily choreographed bid to ensure that the returning Christ follows the broad dictums bequeathed to him by the capitalist consumer market is that *Left Behind*'s creators, LaHaye and Jenkins, seem blissfully unaware of what they're doing. It would be simpler, and in some interpretive sense even a bit comforting, to conclude that they've consigned Enoch and his flock to the back of the Armageddon bus out of some overt racial animus. But, if anything, the whole awkward subplot thrusting The Place's parishioners into the drama of the Last Days seems like a deliberate ploy to tamp down the obvious discomfort that LaHaye and Jenkins feel with all characters of an other-than-white, other-than-wealthy lineage. They're committed to the proposition that Jesus can work the salvation of absolutely everyone, so, by God, that means they should show him tending to the material distress of the forgotten urban underclass as well as the supremely competent and well-heeled masters of the Tribulation Force. The thrust of the whole subplot appears to be to demonstrate that Christ will avail where no other worldly remedy can—yet if that's the case, why not have him deliver the Illinois parish to the Holy Land outright? Or why not have the born-again leaders of the Tribulation Force at least *remember* that they have close allies stranded in the suburban wilds of Chicago, far from the main action of the Second Coming? Why bother to dally at all with the nonsensical question of the congregation's limited mobility due to lack of funds?

New Market, New Earth

The logic of this bizarre byway in the redemptive saga of the Second Coming is far more disquieting than run-of-the-mill unselfconscious racism—though, as we've seen, LaHaye and Jenkins provide plenty of that along the way in their account of the Last Days, as well. What LaHaye and Jenkins are preaching, at the end of history, is evangelical market utopianism. After all, much of the point of end-of-the-world fiction, regardless of its particular spiritual rooting interests, is utopian—to deliver a fully realized portrait of how the cosmic drama of history can and should be redeemed. No less than *The Book of Mormon*'s account of the New World setting for the Garden of Eden and Christ's eventual return, *Left Behind* betrays a reflexive identification of the cosmic order of divine justice and the way that America's market culture orders life outcomes. (It bears reminding in this connection that *The Book of Mormon* also endorses a racialized hierarchy of divine favor—albeit a much more explicitly racist one, in which God punishes sinners for their trespasses by denying them a white pigmentation.)

But in this distinctly hierarchical vision of the freshly restored cosmic spiritual order, the meritocratic protocols of the old market regime quietly endure. The global information elite known as the Tribulation Force is settling into its privileged birthright—its members will quietly (and perhaps a bit ruefully) retire their Directed Energy Weapons and fighter planes. They anticipate they will neither age nor suffer pain during Jesus' thousand-year reign on Earth. (Conversely, as they see the final cohort of millions of their fellow humans banished to eternal torment in the pits of Hell, one in their number offers a deeply complacent one-word summation of the scene: "Sad"—conjuring much the same blasé social fatalism that a distracted CEO might volunteer if an unkempt squeegee man were to set about furiously wiping down the windshield of his Porsche in the expectation of a tip.)[100] The fortunate veterans of the Tribulation Force can even count upon the diligent handiwork of a concierge Christ who cleans out their abodes so that "not a speck of dust" remains[389]—and then graciously professes his pleasure in their domestic service.

In the besetting glow of a redeemed planet—New Heaven, New Earth— the smooth, shiny surfaces of the comfortable market order hum onward, with no rough beast slouching in its way. In the wake of great cosmic tumult and unspeakably bloody distress among the ever-sinning human race, the millennium has dawned, and it betokens the final enclosure of faith by the Money Cult. Jesus is restored to his true worshipers, and all, at last, is right in God's universe.

CONCLUSION

Particularly as matters of economic fairness and the underlying issue of systemic wealth inequality have come to loom with new urgency over the American scene, the world of Protestant faith has grown weirdly complacent. A sustained aura of puzzlement has come to envelop the once-charged encounter of Protestant faith and economic equity. As the Republican-controlled state legislatures of the South and Sunbelt—the modern American "Bible Belt"—spurned the expansion of Medicare coverage for poor Americans under the 2010 Affordable Care Act, some observers noted something strange: a deafening silence from the region's famously influential pulpits.

This was by no means a purely symbolic issue. The fourteen-state Bible Belt accounted for the preponderance of the 5 million poor Americans losing coverage under this last-ditch show of conservative resistance to universal health care, and all but two of the states within the Bible Belt had made the economically predatory decision to bypass increased Medicare funding for their poor citizens. Yet when CNN correspondent John Blake set out in 2013 to canvas the region's best known preachers for their reactions to this deliberate blow to the most needy members of their flocks, a torrent of non-replies ensued. "Virtually no prominent pastor wanted to talk about the uninsured poor in their midst," Blake found. "Joel Osteen, pastor of the largest church in the nation, declined to be interviewed on the subject. So did Bishop T. D. Jakes. Their megachurches are both in Texas, the state with the nation's highest number of people without health insurance. Max Lucado, the bestselling Christian author who is a minister at a church in Texas, declined to speak; Charles Stanley, the Georgia Baptist minister whose In Touch ministry reaches millions around the globe, declined to speak; Ed Young Sr. and Ed Young Jr., a father and son in Texas who pastor two of the fastest-growing churches in the nation, also declined to speak."[390]

And so on. On one level, of course, these megapastors knew all too well that taking a position on this issue would have pitched them headlong into the bitter and long running controversy over the implementation of the ACA law; far better to give the whole matter a pass, and preserve some civil peace and quiet within their pastorates. Yet that reasoning is hardly exculpatory. History has made it painfully clear that the decision to shun divisive social questions was far from a sufficient alibi for, say, southern pastors who remained silent, or complicit, with Jim Crow during the civil rights revolution. And this is all to say nothing of the familiar evangelical refrain "What Would Jesus Do?" It's an awkward business, to put things mildly, to meekly accede to the denial of health care coverage to the population that needs it most desperately while also claiming to represent the teachings of a biblical prophet who'd devoted a significant portion of his own ministry to healing the poor.

These basic breakdowns of the Protestant moral imagination stand out in especially stark relief, however, when laid aside the confident nostrums of the prosperity faith at the height of the mid-aughts real-estate bubble. Most of these same preachers, and hundreds upon hundreds like them, were nowhere near so reticent on the miraculous blessings that the Lord was furnishing to His poor worshipers through easy mortgage terms.

And just as it's important not to absolve the current corps of prosperity-minded megapastors of their silence before the unconscionable spectacle of the American right's so-far successful effort to create socially engineered suffering for the poor in order to realize short-term ideological gains, it's also fair to stipulate that our recent boom in prosperity preaching has not occurred in anything close to a cultural vacuum. Prosperity thinking, after all, wasn't just the obsession of especially impressionable Pentecostal believers, desperate for a foothold in the booming mortgage market; it was the all-but-official American civic religion in all manner of institutional and cultural settings. One scarcely had to trek into the pews of name-it-and-claim-it congregations in order to encounter the many no-less-crude articles of the broader market faith that also fed the 2008 catastrophe. Boosters of the housing boom incanted the classic bubble-stoking presumption that housing prices would soar indefinitely upward and praised the heroism of the elite class of market analysts who (so the superstition went) had eliminated severe market risk by carving it up into a comfortingly long regress of hedged and multi-leveraged "tranches" of securitized debt.

Such assumptions were the standard intellectual currency of the boom years, cropping up in speech after speech by Alan Greenspan, regularly programmed in the editorial pages of the *Wall Street Journal*, and routinely studding the analysis delivered by any given commentator on any given day on CNBC. One reason why financial manias are called bubbles, after all, is that they're all-encasing. In the worlds of finance, journalism, popular culture, and national politics alike, our boom culture was atmospheric, breathed in by most Americans regardless of their faith persuasion, age demographic, or class background. We emerged from the crisis knowing not only that certain financial titans were "too big to fail," but also—and more fundamentally—that the devastating consequences of the collapse were too ugly to contemplate.

But this background explanation of the Money Cult's recent prominence is also not an alibi. In the perennially fearful crouch of market consensus, it becomes imperative for some credible moral authority to summon the idea of a higher justice that transcends the impersonal, randomized verdicts delivered by the market. But it is here, much more than in the magical thinking of the prosperity-minded believers, that American religion has failed colossally to marshal any critical resources. The problem isn't so much that people are drawn into market-based delusions due to religious motivations. It's that religion no longer affords a sturdy vantage for persuasively criticizing the dominance of market values.

Religion for the Rentiers

This marks a spiritual loss as much as a material or political one, a distemper almost certain to outlast the grinding passage of the American economy out of its post-crash doldrums. It's nearly impossible to get at the deeper dissatisfactions of life under purely transactional conceptions of human relations without adopting some scheme of values that precedes and transcends the ideal of the market. In a host of morally charged questions of public import, from the nation's expansive multi-front war economy to the debates over gun rights to the core issues of wealth inequality that lurk just beneath the surface of political debate, religious values have been shut out.

Usually, the reasons offered for this conspicuous spiritual silence are the pet preoccupations of the religious right—the debates over abortion, school prayer, arts funding, gay marriage, and the display of traditional symbols of Christian piety in the public sphere. But many of these warhorses of the Kulturkampf have by now been flogged past the point of endurance, and younger evangelicals have begun simply quitting the field in droves on once-reliable culture-war flashpoints such as gay marriage.

Even as the traditional armature of the culture wars starts to rust away, the comparative Protestant silence endures on wealth inequality, the crisis of mass indebtedness, and the financial industry's predatory business model. That's because, *pace* the sensational headlines of the *Atlantic*—which asked in a goggle-eyed 2009 feature story on prosperity preaching, "Did Christianity Cause the Crash?"—and other outlets of respectable opinion, the prosperity gospel is much more than a passing symptom of materialist-minded religiosity gone wild at the height of a market bubble. As we've seen, there's nothing at all novel about prosperity preaching, or in the booming evangelical market in self-help and positive-thinking manuals, or in the vast reach of spiritualized management theories in the heavily financialized service economy of the early twenty-first century. These are all movements and trends that have taken shape across the last three centuries of American life, as the nimble and resourceful prophets of the Protestant gospel of the Gnostic self have gamely repurposed its account of individual redemption and its vision of the redeemed millennium.

It's simple enough to mock the crassness and the poignant wishful thinking mantras of the prosperity faith—but in that easy sport we claim an unearned critical distance from the main run of magical thinking (churched and otherwise) about the American socioeconomic order. In reality, the broad spiritual outlines of prosperity worship represent the logical outcome of a centuries-long accord between the Gnostic self and the capitalist market. The twenty-first-century prosperity worshiper is not very different from the early-nineteenth-century Cane Ridge revivalist, or the Mormon paterfamilias on the late-nineteenth-century Utah frontier. The prototypically American devotees of the Money Cult have projected themselves into a vision of salvation largely devoid of the traditional mediations of churchly life and bereft of the sense of communal and historical continuity produced in non-primitivist traditions of Protestant worship. Prompted by megachurch preachers and televangelical broadcasters, Money Cult believers recapture that primal American faith famously summoned by Thomas Paine: the ever-renewable power to make the world anew. To borrow the reelection slogan of one of the Money Cult's de facto household saints, Ronald Reagan, the Protestant gospel of success assures a sufficiently disciplined believer that it is, once more and forever still, morning in America.

What *is* different, of course, is the brand of capitalist enterprise that now governs most of America. While the core tenets of the Money Cult worship took root amid the expansion of a national market economy, and its subsequent ripening into a corporate oligarchy in the mid-twentieth century, the signature economic activity of the digital age is fee-collecting rentiership: the functional cornering of markets trafficking in private access to formerly public goods, such as education, housing, and information. By far the most widespread and influential brand of rentiership is the credit racket run by Wall Street itself: Following the 2008 crash, the Federal Reserve has ensured that financial institutions could obtain credit from the central bank at essentially zero interest—which they then, of course, proceeded to package as interest-bearing financial instruments in a tight credit market. Small wonder that 2011 and 2012 marked record-setting years for profits in the financial sector; the real wonder would be to figure out a way *not* to book enormous profits by loaning free money out at nominal interest.

And weirdly, in response to this explosion in nonproductive fee-gathering, our political culture and economic consensus have veered sharply into a hollowed-out mythology of producerism. At least the original Gilded Age Populist revolt and the insurgencies of retirees and organized labor in the 1930s involved constituencies of producers who actually *produced* things; by contrast, much of the official American discourse of conservative economic dissent in our own age pivots around the risible notion that the fee-collecting members of our financial elite are heroic job creators—bold and entrepreneurial hewers of steel and concrete, like the literary protagonists who haunted Ayn Rand's fevered imaginings. When the 2012 Republican Convention adopted the official slogan "We Built That" in response to a thoroughly anodyne set of remarks from Barack Obama concerning the role of public-sector investment in generating wealth, party leaders were informally placing the core tenets of Tea Party libertarianism—*Business makes, the government takes*—at the center of an otherwise incoherent economic platform.

For chapter and verse on how American Protestantism's old social contract has been discarded in favor of a Gnostic spiritual one, it's crucial to return to the success theology of Joel Osteen—the man who, both before and after the crash, remains the nation's most popular, beloved, and successful pulpit orator. Like most preachers of today's prosperity gospel, Osteen comes out of the "Word of Faith" branch of Pentecostalism—steeped in the high-capitalist Gnostic vision of material reward and individual transcendence. Word of Faith preachers teach that the words that individual believers think and speak actually have the power to shape their personal destinies—and in this vein, Osteen's phenomenally successful ministry largely consists of tailoring snatches of Scripture and personal anecdotes of adversity met and overcome to the simple mantras of upwardly striving self-help. A favorite homily concerns his family's rise out of hardscrabble Southern poverty—and the determination of his father, John (also a Word of Faith preacher who bequeathed to Joel his thriving Lakewood congregation) to forsake his roots and baptize himself in the fundaments of spiritualized success. In revealingly Gnostic terms, Joel Osteen recounts his dad's spiritual ascent in his breakout bestselling tract, *Your Best Life Now*: "In the natural, he had no future, no hope. But God is not limited by environment, family background or present circumstances . . . He didn't get stuck in the rut of defeat and mediocrity. He refused to limit God. He believed that God had more in store for him. And because he stayed focused on that dream and was willing to step out in faith, because he was willing to go beyond the barriers of the past, he broke the curse of poverty for our family."[391]

Such homilies strike many broad and familiar chords of recognition for Bible readers: the notion of an unlimited God (a creator for whom "all things are possible," as Jesus said in Matthew 19:26) and the rejection of the family as any ultimate source of spiritual authority ("If any man come to me and not hate his own mother and father, his wife and children, his brethren and his sisters, yea, even his own life, he may not be my disciple," Jesus announces in Luke 14:26—a verse designed to give fits to the contemporary Christian right). But also note that Osteen groups all these factors under the curious heading of "the natural"—i.e., the merely created obstacles to his father's success—and places God emphatically beyond the reach of all such social determinism: "God is not limited by environment, family background, or present circumstances." In striking contrast to the collective portrait of the divine patriarch that emerges in the Hebrew Bible, which carefully catalogs the genealogies of its principal protagonists, Osteen hymns a God who blithely clears away the limiting impersonal forces of environment, history, and upbringing—the stuff of "the natural." And so it stands to reason that Osteen's own model patriarch—his father—exemplified his faith by his steadfast willingness "to go beyond the barriers of the past" and that this bold act proved the crucial step setting him on the path to prosperity.

The divine power counterposed to the natural is, of course, the realm of the *super*natural, and this is where, in Osteen's distinctly Gnostic account of divine mysteries, things get truly strange. The fundamental spiritual plight Osteen describes in his sermons and books is that of the defeatist soul, who has perversely denied him- or herself the saving vision of a true, and divinely sanctioned, life of personal abundance. This figure, not surprisingly, closely tracks the principal demographic and psychic profile of the 40,000-strong Lakewood congregation: an anxious member of the aspiring managerial class wrestling with domestic conflicts, professional challenges, and flagging self-esteem.

The good news Osteen preaches to this audience is that God is closely tending to their trials—and employing the mechanisms of consumer capitalism to engineer their just battery of worldly, yet supernaturally delivered, rewards. To hear Osteen preach or to read his genially confessional self-help books is to encounter in its purest form the American religion of the imperial, and materially resplendent, self. Across the many homilies and folksy anecdotes that Osteen retails, God's rather monotonously rendered mission is to awaken the laggard ranks of the faithful to their true conquering destinies in the capitalist marketplace. Indeed, a favorite biblical paraphrase of the Lakewood pastor has it that true Christian believers are "more than conquerors."[392]

A central Osteen homily—designed to illustrate the advantages of "a prosperous mind-set"—concerns an episode from the early phase of his father's preaching career. After John Osteen left his home denomination of Southern Baptism and launched his Word of Faith congregation at Lakewood, he was, as his son recalls, barely squeaking by financially. At a time when "our family barely had enough food to get along," the younger Osteen writes, his parents boarded a visiting minister in their house for a week. To help relieve the family's overstretched budget, one businessman in the congregation gave Osteen's father a check for $1,000—a significant sum back in the 1960s. But following the model of the humble shepherd in Christ, the Osteen patriarch turned the windfall over to the church, instead of his own struggling family. The moral of the story, for both the father and son, couldn't be plainer:

> Daddy later said, "With every step I took as I walked to front of the church to put that check in the offering, something inside was saying, *Don't do it. Receive God's blessings. Receive God's goodness.*"
>
> But he didn't listen. He reluctantly dropped the check into the offering. He later said, "When I did, I felt sick to my stomach."

God was trying to increase my dad. He was trying to prosper
him, but because of Daddy's deeply embedded poverty mentality, he
couldn't receive it . . . God was trying to get him to step up to the
banquet table, but because of Dad's limited mind-set, he couldn't see
himself having an extra thousand dollars.[393]

Several striking themes are concealed within this folksy yarn. It is, for
starters, a seamless leap for Osteen and other preachers of the prosperity
gospel to discern the divine will in a windfall of cash—though none of
these preachers are theologically driven to reckon with the implicit corollary of this casual claim: that God is deliberately *punishing* the less fortunate by virtue of his refusal to "prosper" them. No, the curious thing about
the Osteen conception of human agency in the Gnostic-capitalist scheme
of salvation is that, for all the careful attention He lavishes on mundane
financial and commercial transactions, God is almost entirely blameless
for hard times. Economic fortune, in this crudely oversimplified moral
economy, is a pure function of rousing believers to accept the supernatural gifts of grace: a bona fide Gnostic awakening into the unconditional,
abundant realm of what earlier prophets of America's Protestant money
faith called the higher self.

Then there is the unquestioned image of God seeking to elicit gratitude and reverence through a gift of money—an invitation to a banquet table perversely shunted away by a "poverty mentality." For all the
historic forces that have bound together Protestant faith and American
capitalism, few preachers of the success gospel have actually been bold
enough to cite the random fortunes allotted by the money culture as an
ironclad expression of God's will. Osteen's family parable, like most of
his other inspirational preaching, is crafted to refute the claim that God
moves in mysterious ways: In his version of the divine-human encounter, God moves in the ways clearly delineated by the market. The only
mystery is why depressive or dull-witted captives of the poverty mentality are so slow to grasp God's self-evident ambitions for their worldly
success.

The God of Small Things

Thanks to these enormous blind spots where a social ethic might otherwise be, it's tempting to see Osteen's brand of the prosperity faith as a crassly mundane—a contract for a pious life of improved health and wealth. In reality, though, it's pointedly metaphysical—indeed, almost animistic—in its determination to infuse the trappings of everyday life in the capitalist marketplace with divine significance. Osteen's vision of market deliverance is not *anti*-materialist, by any stretch of the imagination, but neither is it captive to the strictly calculating and morally nugatory image of the capitalist market famously bequeathed to us by Enlightenment rationalists such as Adam Smith. Indeed, so much of the commentary surrounding Osteen's ministry focuses obsessively on his superficial personal image—his 1,000-watt smile, his impeccably tailored power suits, his energetically acquisitive wife and Lakewood co-minister, Victoria—that it's easy to miss the underlying animistic thrust of the Osteen message, which resembles on closer inspection nothing so much as a Gnostic cargo cult.

Cargo cults were mid-twentieth-century religious movements, mainly centered around Melanesia, that regarded inbound shipments of goods from colonial manufacturing centers as divine blessings, and objects of worship in their own right. Despite several very sharp and nuanced anthropological studies of the phenomenon, cargo cults have always served, at least in the popular mind, as one of the vaguely reassuring indices of the psychic progress of industrial civilization. In pop-culture productions like the '80s movie *The Gods Must Be Crazy*, it flattered the vanity of the developed world to reflect that even the economic bounty that Western technocrats relegated to the colonial margins of their known world commanded the awed, and somewhat terrified, reverence of aboriginal holy figures.

But the animistic worship of the accoutrements of the good life is no monopoly of the less-developed world, as anyone who's waited in line at the Apple store for the latest iteration of the iPhone can readily attest. And Osteen, keenly attuned to the everyday anxieties and thwarted ambitions of his Sunbelt parishioners, takes pains to spell out in surprising detail just how the divine will should guide you in, say, keeping the interior of your car clean and orderly. As he exhorts readers to "start making more excel-

lent choices in every area of life, even the mundane," Osteen complains at
length about the spiritual toll involved in driving a car that looks, on the
inside, "like a storm hit it":

> I don't like driving a car like that. Not only does it represent God
> poorly, but it makes me feel unkempt, undisciplined, sloppy, and less
> than my best. Many times before I leave the house, I'll take a couple
> of minutes and clean out the car, not because I want to impress my
> friends, but because I feel better driving a clean car. You need to take
> pride in what God has given you.[394]

That's right: Joel Osteen believes that God—a power even greater
than Oprah Winfrey—has selected your car according to his will.

The same mysticism-of-small-things applies to Osteen's vision of
wardrobe upkeep: "You are made in the image of Almighty God, and how
you present yourself in your personal appearance is not only a reflection of
how you feel about yourself, it is a direct reflection on God."[395] To drive the
point home, Osteen delivers another car-related parable, about the time he
was dispatched on a last-minute grocery-shopping errand by his wife as
Victoria was preparing dinner for the family, while Joel was lying about in
his gym clothes after a workout:

> I thought, *Okay, I'll run up to the grocery store and try to get in and out
> of there quickly, so hopefully nobody will see me.* I drove to the store, still
> in my workout clothes. I pulled in the parking lot and was about to
> hop out of the car when God spoke to me. I mean, if God has ever
> spoken to me, He spoke to me right there! Right down inside, I'm
> sure He said, "Don't you dare go in there representing Me like that!"
> He said, "Don't you know that I'm the King of kings?"
>
> I turned around, went back home, took a shower, combed my
> hair, brushed my teeth, and put on some clean clothes. Then I went
> back to the grocery store . . . We need to remind ourselves that we
> represent Almighty God, and he does not appreciate laziness or slop-
> piness. When you go to the mall, and you accidentally knock those

clothes off the rack, don't act as though you don't see them and just leave them lying on the floor.[396]

He goes on to multiply several other didactic, small-bore life lessons, gleaned from the harried life of the exurban commuter: You shouldn't, if you aspire to represent God as a "person of excellence," lazily toss a discarded grocery-store item on a random shelf in the wrong section. Nor should you take a parking spot designated for handicapped drivers, or leave the lights on or air-conditioner running at a hotel room you're checking out of. Nor, especially, should model followers of Christ be obdurate, lazy, or inefficient workers. In yet another parable of the divinely ordered economy, Osteen describes the spiritual awakening of one company manager in the Lakewood congregation, who found himself blowing off many irksome features of the position he was preparing to leave for a better-paying managerial post at a rival firm. Here, too, the hand of God supervened, per the executive's testimony to Osteen:

> One day I went to work feeling kind of lazy, giving a half-hearted effort, and God spoke to me right down inside. He said, "Son, if you don't continue to honor this company by giving them your best effort, you're not going to excel at that new position." My friend realized who his real Boss is. He was not working for his company or his supervisor, he was working unto God, not unto men. God is the One keeping the records. He's the One who will reward us. He's the One who can promote you.[397]

Meanwhile, for office drones expressing discontent with the monotony and alienation of their lower-stakes perches in the corporate world, Osteen has some harsher counsel. Here he blithely takes up the self-improving, solidarity-averse maxims of Pealeism and the servant-leadership movement:

> You need to change your attitude. You should be grateful that you even have a job. You need to appreciate and stay excited about the

opportunities God has given you . . . If you work outside your home, don't give your employer a half-hearted effort. Don't dawdle on the telephone, wasting your employer's time and money. If you are digging a ditch, don't spend half the day leaning on your shovel; do your work with excellence and enthusiasm![398]

It's easy to make sport of such control-freak maxims, especially as they are attributed to the author of our Universe, who presumably should be preoccupied with more momentous questions than how his followers muster enthusiasm at their workplaces or choose to dress as they perform their household errands. But Osteen is quite serious. And on one level at least, why shouldn't he be? His immensely popular and influential version of the gospel speaks to the ordinary fears and anxieties of a class of ordinary strivers who feel themselves on the perpetual brink of socioeconomic pariah status. For Osteen's parishioners, viewers, and readers, a smartly turned-out appearance or diligently organized work station might mean the difference between a steady salary and an indefinite plunge into debt, unemployment, and depression—or, in the way that economic and personal misfortunes often intertwine, it might mark the dividing line between a divorce and a marital reconciliation. These are the realms where divine favor is often most desperately needed, and just as desperately felt to be absent.

There is, in short, a poignant quality to Osteen's efforts to benedict the workaday routines of family and office-park life with ultimate meaning, just as there'd been an unmistakable mood of epidemic economic uncertainty in the appeals that inundated Oral Roberts's seed-faith ministry of the seventies. Both messages expressed, just beneath their surface, an anxiety to appease an aggrieved and angry market God. Osteen's rage for personal order scarcely conceals the gnawing suspicion that the workings of the market, and the entire system of reward and punishment that they rationalize, are deeply *im*personal and, indeed, terrifyingly random. In this scheme of things, as in the fatalist world of the historical Gnostics, the only remedy at hand is the saving knowledge that the believer is actually in possession of a higher self, belonging to a realm beyond the flawed created order and destined for a redemption that far outstrips its present worldly bonds. The market can only be subdued by the more-than-conquering spirit if the hated limitations and weaknesses of the "natural" are dispelled, once and for all.

But of course, the abolition of the natural is the opposite of the message of a mature and morally responsible Christianity. Human limitation—suffering, illness, and death—are the immutable lot of humans under God's sovereignty ever since the fall of Adam, and religion's value lies largely in cultivating among believers a heightened awareness of these bracing facts of life. The chastened acknowledgment of human limitation likewise directly informs any viable religious social ethic. The universality of suffering, illness, and death constitutes the most potent possible reminder that one child of God can be elevated only so far over another— and that the storehouse of worldly splendors counts for precisely nothing when weighed in the balance of eternity. Releasing the self from its own stubborn penchant to cling to the relentless pursuit of its own favor is the great prelude to the winning of both personal and social wisdom.

But a money faith needs hysterically to deny or sublimate these core facts of a grown-up believing life. For Osteen, as for other preachers in the Word of Faith tradition, the believer's self is the only safeguard in a windswept landscape of otherwise senseless social forces and economic mandates. As a result, the self's core inner directives—to prevail against adversity, to achieve a divinely sanctioned excellence and above all, to prosper under God's blessing—have taken on talismanic powers of their own in an unpromising world of remote and irrational economic causation.

One key Word of Faith doctrine readily explains the movement's name: the notion that the words believers utter have the supernatural power to shape their destinies. If believers let themselves speak words of defeat, depression, or illness, they will typically—so the tradition teaches—succumb to failure, despair, or debilitating sickness. And if, on the other hand, they intone words of victory, success, and wealth, they will flourish, conquer, and prosper. "There is a miracle in your mouth," Osteen exhorts. ". . . When times get tough, don't give in to murmuring, disputing, and complaining. Speak to those problems. If you'll learn how to speak the right words and keep the right attitude, God will turn that situation around."[399] The name-it-and-claim-it brand of prosperity preaching represents, in short, the Gnostic repudiation of the social world in one of its most potent forms.

Unfortunately for the Osteen gospel, this tight identification of divine will and market prerogative hasn't aged especially well since 2008. In his books, the model success of Osteen's own ministry is rivaled by only one other thing: the success that he and Victoria have enjoyed in the Houston real-estate market. "God has blessed us abundantly," he writes. "He has prospered us through several real estate deals so we live in a lovely home and have all the material things we need."[400] In another revealing illustration of the arrangement of mundane financial transactions from on high, Osteen recounts how, in an overexuberant plunge into the housing market, he and Victoria had taken on the mortgage of a new home before they'd managed to sell their starter townhouse. As they carried two mortgages with no sign of a prospective townhouse buyer on the horizon, the couple elected to pursue a "seed-faith" strategy of actually increasing the payments on their first mortgage, so that the principal would be reduced ahead of its eventual sale. And sure enough, a buyer for the property surfaced shortly afterward—without the couple having to lower their asking price, as they'd feared. "We thought we'd have to discount [the townhouse] thousands of dollars. But I believe, because we sowed a seed in faith, God brought us not only a buyer, but He did more than we could ask or think. He gave us even more than we were hoping for!"[401] And in Osteen's follow-up book, *Become a Better You*, he offers the market-anointed epilogue to the tale. After reviewing the basics of the awkward and premature move—"In the natural, it didn't make a lot of sense," he writes—he records a wonderful premonition of blessings to come:

> The day we closed on [the new house], we were standing out in the front yard and a Realtor stopped by and offered us much more than we had paid. We thought, "What's going on?" We didn't understand it. Come to find out, they were in the process of changing the deed

restrictions in that neighborhood. And several years later, we sold the property for twice as much as we paid for it. That was God causing us to be at the right place at the right time.[402]

Of course, to endorse Osteen's logic here, one would have to believe that, post 2008, God has contrived to put many, many people—many of them people of great Christian faith—in the wrong place at the wrong time. One would also have to grant God's market-driven will absolute sovereignty over the enormous suffering, large-scale financial fraud, enormous bailouts of the purveyors of worldwide toxic debt—to say nothing, of course, of the crushing workaday disparities of housing markets in flusher times still brutally segmented by predatory preferences of class and race. Osteen's relentlessly upbeat sermons and anodyne advice for straightening out your work routines and grooming habits may not seem like the stuff of theodicy—a justification of the ways of God to man. But such is the brunt of prosperity preaching whenever an economic trend veers south: God always provides, and when the horn of plenty empties out, the punishment of all individual believers has to be just.

Nor, should we hasten to add, is this particular brand of magical economic thinking so very exotic or strange. Stripped of their religious language, Osteen's name-it-and-claim-it reveries of overnight fortune are no different in substance from the vast bubble-driven body of policymaking and economic thought that continues to dictate the terms of economic debate in this country. When Alan Greenspan famously proclaimed that the national housing market was, by definition, immune from a steep downturn, he was only offering a Randian variation on Osteen's confident surmise that God was directing him to flip his Houston townhouse and next home, in fairly rapid succession. When Lloyd Blankfein assured a British financial journalist that Goldman Sachs was "doing the Lord's work" by directing capital into the most productive sectors of the American economy, he was voicing a faith no more substantial in its concrete particulars than the assurances of material victory thundering down from the pulpits of the prosperity gospel. When Mitt Romney inveighed on the stump in 2012 against government handouts while championing the fanciful mandate to slash government spending in the troughs of a historic global recession, he was merely touting the conservative movement's pet variation of the name-it-and-claim-it faith. In this curious, irrational mode of policy prophecy, citizens are ultimately to be granted true and lasting good fortune via the spiritual war that the American right has been waging against the hateful idea of a functioning public sector—and the layabout beneficiaries of public spending would, in the grander scheme of things, be assailed with punitive austerity measures when the welfare state's marginal expansion was exposed as the dire moral folly that the initiates of our higher market wisdom knew it to be all along.

Just as Osteen's own Word of Faith doctrines no longer claim any clear provenance in denominational terms—like most major prosperity congregations, Lakewood comes out of the Pentecostal tradition, but now markets itself as a nondenominational concern—so has the magical thinking that animates the prosperity faith casually annexed ever greater stretches of our public life.

Incorruptible, Indestructible, Ever-Living

America's most popular preacher is a Gnostic figure in another sense, as well: He prophesies a vision of personal deliverance far above the plane of mere worldly conflict. Unlike other well-known preachers from his denomination and part of the country, Osteen disclaims any interest in politics or the full-throated prosecution of the culture wars. He's on record opposing abortion and gay marriage, but scarcely with the sort of fervor you'd call evangelical; in a 2013 TV interview, he counseled that believers should "be compassionate" in cases where same-sex couples are seeking equitable access to benefits such as hospital visitation rights, but that the practice didn't comport with his reading of the Bible.[403]

Unlike the recent kingmakers of the evangelical right, Osteen endorses no candidates for office or party platforms; the closest he appears to have come to political activism was to lobby the Houston City Council to approve Lakewood's plan to obtain a long-term lease on the stadium that now houses Osteen's church. (And even in this case, Osteen writes, the church won the decisive swing vote for the plan not through its exertions, but rather via the influential counsel of "an elderly Jewish lady" who leaned on the wavering council member at a critical moment to solicit his vote for Lakewood's long-term occupancy of the site. "As far as I know, I have never met this woman . . . To this day, I don't know who she is. All I know is that while were doing all that we could do, God was working behind the scenes in a way we never could have done on our own. What we couldn't do in our own ability and strength, God caused somebody else to do for us.")[404]

This studious shunning of the public square leaves Osteen with little else to talk about *other* than his own self-referenced parables of personal success. Osteen's placid recusal from the culture wars only reinforces the oddly claustral quality of a success gospel that hinges mainly on the miraculous appeal of its own messenger for its supporting evidence. In one sense, the creation story of the Osteen pastorate underlines the moral of all American success stories: Here was a classic entrepreneur of the spirit, wrestling a vision of future abundance from the unpromising conditions that the world has bequeathed him. But our earlier cohort of self-made men, however much they were incongruously mythologized and elevated into the status of quasi-deities in their own right, were at least makers of *things* as well as their own success stories. Success preachers of the Osteen stripe, by contrast, lean heavily on their own simple fame and fortune as the instructive parables of first resort—as though our society demanded a limitless supply of energetic pitchmen for the prosperity faith.

Cynics might observe in this regard that the private-sector analogue for Osteen isn't so much Countrywide's Angelo Mozilo or Enron's Ken Lay (to take a figure from Lakewood's backyard in Houston) as it would be the disgraced Ponzi-scheme investor Bernie Madoff. In Madoff's gospel, as with Osteen's, the principal product on offer isn't so much a proven investment plan or specific financial instrument as a kind of faith. In this view of things, Osteen, like Madoff, is a con man in the strictest and most literal sense of the term—an unscrupulous grifter offering no specific return in the real-world marketplace beyond the one he creates under his own illusion: i.e., his mark's own ability to believe in his pitch.

But this reading takes us back to the perceived personal trustworthiness of the Money Cult's messengers, rather than the substance of its gospel. It also doesn't account for the creed's curious longevity in hard times. In addition to dismissing figures such as Osteen as garden-variety hucksters, the tendency has been to shrug off the scattered outbursts of overt prosperity worship on the American religious scene as fleeting symptoms of a bubble—the religious equivalent of the investors' mania for tulip bulbs that famously convulsed Holland at the dawn of the capitalist age. But for that to be true, Osteen's ministry should have slowed down noticeably in the wake of the Great Recession of 2008. Here, after all, was ample and incontrovertible evidence that God was *not* arranging economic affairs to deliver believers into their best lives now, with millions of Americans evicted from underwater and/or foreclosed properties, and millions more relegated to the economic purgatory of long-term unemployment.

Instead, Osteen's brand of the prosperity faith has continued to flourish amid conditions of brutal and long-term economic distress—and no rival movement has taken root within the nation's vast Protestant mainstream either to question either the logic of sanctified capitalism or to draw attention to the predatory practices of the financial sector that have plunged so many Americans into such prolonged misery. As employment prospects stagnate or decline in regional job markets, as household debt continues, as more and more college graduates find themselves facing lifetimes of grinding debt obligations, the dominant message of our Protestant pulpits continues to be one long variation on Osteen's sunny individualist message of Gnostic retreat and redemption. If your bank is foreclosing on your house, believers are told, why, that's another trial that God has fashioned to sharpen your faith and work out his plan for an eventual life blessed with still greater abundance. Lost your job? Well, that just means that God has contrived to open an unexpected new window on your own foreordained vista of personal opportunity.

The distilled Gnostic message of the Osteen gospel is rendered quite vividly in the chant that opens every sermon he delivers before the 45,000 parishioners at Lakewood—and millions more TV viewers—each Sunday: "This is my Bible. I am what it says I am. I have what it says I have. I do what it says I can do. I am about to receive the incorruptible, indestructible, ever-living seed of God, and I will never be the same. Never, never, never. I will never be the same. In Jesus' name. Amen."

What's troubling in this ritual invocation isn't so much its blinkered vision of spiritual literature—whatever else the Bible may be, it most definitely isn't about the identity or aspirations of its individual readers. Nor is it the half-sexualized, half-infantilizing imagery of the chant. (However emphatically 45,000 believers may chant the words "Never, never, never" in unison, they can't help but come across like pouting toddlers.) No, what sets this oddly compelling refrain apart is its close cousinship to the consumer fantasies that populate the rest of American culture: the unshakeable conviction that whatever disappointments or calamities might overtake our common life, the integrity of the individual self is somehow forever unblemished, transcendent, and redeemed—transformed once and for all by anodyne life counsel that is "incorruptible, indestructible, ever-living."

The Gnostic genius of Joel Osteen is, in fact, the Gnostic genius of American capitalism. And the real mystery to unravel here isn't just how a huckster from the margins of the Protestant mainstream has come to captivate the spiritual imagination of a nation; it is, rather, just how America's once-austere and communal version of dissenting Protestantism developed into such a ripe recruiting ground for the sanctified capitalism of our financialized, upward-skewing, and uniquely destructive market order.

Acknowledgments

This is a work of synthesis, which is a polite euphemism for "magpie scholarship." Because this book covers a great span of time and tries to navigate many dramatic shifts in theological and social thought, it rests to a pronounced degree on the shoulders of giants. Among the departed outsize eminences are Alan Heimert, Charles Sellers, and Paul Boyer. The contemporary company includes Michael Kazin, Darren Dochuk, Matthew Avery Sutton, Joel Carpenter, William Leach, and Bethany Moreton. All have contributed immeasurably to my own understanding of the unique American spiritual sojourn into the pastures of plenty; each has produced work that richly rewards enterprising study.

As for more hands-on attention to my own errant word-smithery, I have a number of debts of gratitude to cheerfully acknowledge. Mark Krotov, my editor, expertly guided many wayward thoughts and sentences into stately repose on the printed page, and patiently endured a number of late-production freakouts from me. Deb Vanasse was an eagle-eyed line editor, and remains an even better sister. Thomas Frank, Jackson Lears, Jim Sleeper, and Sara Bershtel all gave me invaluable feedback and criticism, even when I wasn't all that happy to field it. James Marcus at Harper's helped to shape and prune an early version of what would become the chapter on Mormonism. Melissa Flashman marshaled this project through the all the many reversals and upsets that the publishing world always has to offer, and steadfastly believed in it, even when my own more meager faith was sorely tested. And yes, the usual author's disclaimer applies here, in spades: the improvements, interventions, and emotional rescues worked by friends and colleagues are exclusively their handiwork, while all errors, interpretive miscues, and solecisms are only, alas, my own.

Notes

Introduction: Pay to Pray

1. "LDS Church Reports 18 Percent Growth in the 2000s," by Joshua Bolding, Deseret News. May 30, 2012. www.deseretnews.com/article/865555185/LDS-Church-reports-18-percent-growth-in-2000s.html?pg=all.
2. Irvin G. Wyllie, *The Self-Made Man in America: The Myth of Rags to Riches* (New York: Free Press, 1954), pp. 58–59.

Chapter 1: A Founding Faith

3. For one representative such account among many, see Ralph Barton Perry, *Puritanism and Democracy* (New York: The Vanguard Press, 1944).
4. Francis J. Bremer, *Jonathan Winthrop: America's Forgotten Founding Father* (New York: Oxford University Press, 2005), p. 179.
5. Jonathan Winthrop, "A Modell of Christian Charity," in *The Journal of Jonathan Winthrop, 1630–1649*, edited by James Savage, Richard Dunn, and Laetitia Yaendle (Cambridge, MA: Harvard University Press, 1996), p. 2.
6. Ibid., p. 4.
7. Ibid., pp. 5–6.
8. Sacvan Bercovitch, *The American Jeremiad* (Madison: University of Wisconsin Press, 1978), p. 40.
9. Winthrop, op. cit., p. 6.
10. Ibid., pp. 6, 8.
11. Ibid., p. 9.
12. Ibid., pp. 9–10.
13. Bremer, op. cit., p. 180.
14. Quoted in Richard T. Hughes and C. Leonard Allen, *Illusions of Innocence: Protestant Primitivism in America, 1630–1875* (Chicago: University of Chicago Press, 1988), pp. 54–55.
15. Max Weber, *The Protestant Ethic and the Spirit of Capitalism*, translated by Talcott Parsons (New York: Charles Scribner's Sons, 1958), p. 55.

16. Ibid., p. 162.

17. Ibid., p. 170.

18. Ibid., p. 182.

19. Jon Butler, *Awash in a Sea of Faith: Christianizing the American People* (Cambridge, MA: Harvard University Press, 1990), p. 60.

20. Ibid., p. 61.

21. Ibid., p. 61.

22. Ibid., p. 50.

23. Ibid., p. 53.

24. Ibid., p. 70.

25. Quoted in Bercovitch, op. cit., p. 47.

26. See Paul Boyer and Stephen Nissenbaum, *Salem Possessed: The Social Origins of Witchcraft* (Cambridge, MA: Harvard University Press, 1974).

27. Brooke, op. cit., pp. 106–107.

28. Quoted in John Patrick Diggins, *The Lost Soul of American Politics: Virtue, Self-Interest, and the Foundations of Liberalism* (Chicago: University of Chicago Press, 1984), p. 21.

29. Edmund S. Morgan, *Benjamin Franklin* (New Haven: Yale University Press, 2002), pp. 307–308.

30. Richard T. Hughes, *Christian America and the Kingdom of God* (Urbana: University of Illinois Press, 2009), p. 24.

31. Patricia U. Bonomi, *Under the Cope of Heaven: Religion, Society, and Politics in Early America* (New York: Oxford University Press, 1986), p. 104.

32. Kerry S. Walters, *Benjamin Franklin and His Gods* (Urbana: University of Illinois Press, 1999), pp. 91–92.

33. Quoted in ibid., p. 91.

Chapter 2: Nation Building

34. Quoted in Gordon S. Wood, *The Americanization of Ben Franklin* (New York: Penguin, 2004), pp. 81–82.

35. Quoted in Harry S. Stout, *The Divine Dramatist: George Whitefield and the Rise of Modern Evangelism* (Grand Rapids, MI: Wm. B. Eerdmans, 1991), p. 232.

36. Quoted in ibid., p. 31.

37. Quoted in ibid., p. 32.

38. Quoted in ibid., p. 306.

39. Quoted in Frank Lambert, *"Pedlar in Divinity": George Whitefield and the Transatlantic Revivals* (Princeton, NJ: Princeton University Press, 1994), pp. 48–49.

40. Ibid., p. 18.

41. Quoted in ibid., p. 21.

42. Ibid., p. 33.

43. Quoted in ibid., p. 39.

44. Ibid., p. 104.

45. Quoted in ibid., p. 44.

46. Quoted in Heimert, op. cit., pp. 36–37.

47. Bonomi, op. cit., pp. 158–59.

48. Heimert, op. cit., p. 62.

49. Ibid., p. 36.

50. Quoted in ibid., pp. 46–47.

51. Quoted in ibid., p. 47.

52. Ibid., p. 154.

53. Ibid., p. 128.

54. Quoted in ibid., p. 50.

55. Ibid., p. 137.

56. Stout, op. cit., p. 93.

57. Stout, op. cit., p. 129.

58. Ibid., p. 130.

59. Michael Zuckerman, *Peaceable Kingdoms: New England Towns in the Eighteenth Century* (New York: Vintage Books, 1970), pp. 69–71.

60. Luke Tyerman, *The Life of Rev. George Whitefield, Vol. 2* (New York: Anson D. F. Randolph and Company, 1877), p. 251.

61. James P. Byrd, *Sacred Scripture, Sacred War: The Bible and the American Revolution* (New York: Oxford University Press, 2013), p. 17.

62. Quoted in Bonomi, op. cit., p. 159.

63. Quoted in ibid., p. 111.

64. Quoted in ibid., p. 56.

65. Quoted in ibid., p. 207.

66. Ibid., p. 122.

67. Lambert, op. cit., p. 182.

68. Quoted in George M. Marsden, *Jonathan Edwards: A Life* (New Haven: Yale University Press, 2003), p. 265.

69. Jonathan Edwards, *An Humble Attempt to Promote Explicit Agreement and Visible Union of God's People in Extraordinary Prayer for the Revival of Religion and Christ's Kingdom on Earth* (Boston: D. Henchman, 1747), p. 60.

70. Ibid., p. 64.

71. Ibid., pp. 76–77.

72. Ibid., pp. 80–81.

73. Ibid., pp. 81–82.

74. Mark A. Noll, *Christians in the American Revolution* (Grand Rapids, MI: Christian University Press, 1977), p. 63.

75. Jonathan Mayhew, *Two Discourses Delivered on October 25, 1759: Being the Day Appointed by Authority to Be Observed as a Day of Public Thanksgiving, for the Success of His Majesty's Arms, More Particularly in the Reduction of Quebec, the Capital of Canada* (Boston: Richard Draper, 1759), p. 60.

76. Ibid., p. 61.

Chapter 3: Free Will and Free Markets

77. William McNemar, *The Kentucky Revival* (Cincinnati, OH: John W. Browne, 1807; 2011, ebook edition, Michael D. Fortner), p. 20.

78. Ibid., p. 67.

79. Ibid., p. 30.

80. Ibid., p. 29; emphasis in original.

81. Harold Bloom, *The American Religion: The Emergence of the Post-Christian Nation* (New York: Touchstone Books, 1991), p. 63.

82. Charles Grandison Finney, *The Original Memoirs of Charles G. Finney*, ed. Garth M. Rosell and Richard A. G. Dupuis (Grand Rapids, MI: Zondervan, 1986), p. 9.

83. Ibid., p. 8.

84. Ibid., p. 11.

85. Ibid., p. 13.

86. Ibid., p. 16.

87. Ibid., p. 16.

88. Finney, op. cit., p. 20.

89. Ibid., pp. 25–26.

90. Ibid. pp. 26–27.

91. Ibid., p. 238.

92. Ibid., pp. 237–238.

93. See Paul W. Johnson, *A Shopkeeper's Millennium: Society and Revivals in Rochester, New York, 1815-1837* (New York: Hill & Wang, 2004 [25th anniversary edition]).

94. Paul K. Conklin, *Cane Ridge: America's Pentecost* (Madison: University of Wisconsin Press, 1990), p. 41.

95. Ibid., p. 103.

96. Ibid., pp. 152–53.

97. Charles Sellers, *The Market Revolution: Jacksonian America 1815–1846* (New York: Oxford University Press, 1991), p. 12.

98. Ibid., 18.

99. Ibid., p. 19.

100. Ibid., pp. 89–90.

101. See John Lauritz Larson, *The Market Revolution in America: Liberty, Ambition, and the Eclipse of the Common Good* (Cambridge: Cambridge University Press, 2009), pp. 102–103.

102. Charles Grandison Finney, *Lectures on Revivals of Religion* (New York: Leavitt, Lord & Co., 1835), pp. 19–20.

103. Quoted in Nathan O. Hatch, *The Democratization of American Christianity* (New Haven: Yale University Press, 1989), p. 138.

104. Ibid., p. 49.

105. Ibid., pp. 141–42.

106. Sellers, op. cit., p. 215.

107. John W. Compton, *The Evangelical Origins of the Living Constitution* (Cambridge: Harvard University Press, 2014), pp. 34–35.

108. Hatch, op. cit., p. 138.

109. See ibid., pp. 139–41.

110. Jackson Lears, *Something for Nothing: Luck in America* (New York: Viking Penguin, 2003), p. 130.

111. Quoted in ibid., p. 93.

112. Compton, op. cit., pp. 133–43.

113. Richard W. Carawardine, *Evangelical Politics in Antebellum America* (Knoxville: University of Tennessee Press, 1997), pp. 241–42.

114. Quoted in ibid., p. 110.

115. Quoted in George M. Fredericksen, *The Black Image in the White Mind: The Debate on Afro-American Character and Destiny, 1817–1914* (Middletown, CT: Wesleyan University Press, 1971), p. 34.

116. Quoted in ibid., p. 36.

117. Quoted in ibid., pp. 36–37.

118. Quoted in Daniel T. Rodgers, *The Work Ethic in Industrial America, 1850–1920* (Chicago: University of Chicago Press, 1974), p. 32.

119. Larson, op. cit., p. 139.

120. Charles G. Finney, *The Original Memoirs of Charles G. Finney*, Garth M. Rossell and Richard A. Dupuis, eds. (Grand Rapids, MI: Zondervan, 1989), pp. 330–31.

121. Ibid., p. 288.

122. Ibid., p. 332.

123. Ibid., p. 336.

124. Daniel Walker Howe, *The Making of the American Self: Jonathan Edwards to Abraham Lincoln* (Cambridge, MA: Harvard University Press, 1997), p. 135.

125. William E. Channing, *Self-Culture: An Address Introductory to The Franklin Lectures, Delivered at Boston, September, 1838* (Boston, Dutton and Wentworth Printers, 1838), pp. 34–36.

126. Ibid., pp. 13–14.

127. Ralph Waldo Emerson, "An Address," *The Writings of Ralph Waldo Emerson* (New York: Modern Library, 1940), pp. 72–73.

128. Ibid., p. 166.

129. Ibid., pp. 158–59.

130. Ibid., pp. 148–49.

Chapter 4: Of Lost Tribes and Latter Days

131. Richard Bushman, *Joseph Smith: Rough Stone Rolling* (New York: Vintage Books, 2005), p. 39.

132. Ibid., p. 26.

133. Ibid., p. 13.

134. John L. Brooke, *The Refiner's Fire: The Making of Mormon Cosmology, 1644–1844* (London: Cambridge University Press, 1996), pp. 66–67; pp. 73–78.

135. Ibid., p. 44.

136. Ibid., pp. 44–45.

137. *The Book of Mormon: Another Testament of Jesus Christ* (Salt Lake City, UT: Corporation of the President of the Church of Jesus Christ of Latter-Day Saints, 1981), Mormon, 8:35–37; Mormon, 8:39–40, pp. 483–84.

138. For the reading of Smith as a populist firebrand, see especially Hatch, op cit., pp. 113–21.

139. Doctrines and Covenants and the Pearl of Great Price (Salt Lake City, UT: Corporation of the President of the Church of Jesus Christ of Latter-Day Saints, 1981), 101:80: "And for this purpose, I have established the Constitution of this land, by the hands of wise men who I raised up unto this very purpose, and redeemed the land by the shedding of blood," p. 200.

140. Telephone interview with author, June 6, 2011.

141. Brooke, op. cit., p. 31.

142. Ibid., p. 31.

143. Brodie, op. cit. p. 192.

144. Quoted in ibid., p. 193.

145. Leonard J. Arrington, *Great Basin Kingdom: An Economic History of the Latter-Day Saints, 1830–1900* (Urbana, IL: University of Illinois Press, 2005), p. 34.

146. Brooke, op. cit., p. 195; on Young's Adamic theology, see John G. Turner, *Brigham Young: Pioneer Prophet* (Cambridge, MA: Belknap Press, 2012), pp. 232–33.

147. Ibid., pp. 12–13.

148. Quoted in Leonard J. Arrington and Davis Bitton, *The Mormon Experience: A History of the Latter-Day Saints* (New York: Alfred A. Knopf, 1979), p. 74.

149. Quoted in Robert Bruce Flanders, *Nauvoo: Kingdom on the Mississippi* (Urbana: University of Illinois Press, 1965), p. 80.

150. Quoted in ibid., pp. 186–87.

151. Quoted in ibid., p. 187.

152. Quoted in ibid., pp. 187–88.

153. Quoted in ibid., p. 189.

154. John G. Turner, *Brigham Young: Pioneer Prophet* (Cambridge, MA: Belknap Press, 2013), p. 112.

155. Ibid., p. 179.

156. Ibid., p. 352–53.

157. Ibid., p. 353.

158. Ibid., p. 358.

159. Ibid., pp. 397–98.

160. Ibid., p. 400.

161. Ibid., p. 401.

162. Ibid., p. 399.

Chapter 5: The Businessmen Awake

163. Talcott W. Chambers, *The New York City Noon Prayer Meeting* (Colorado Springs, CO: Wagner Publications, 2002 reprint of 1858 edition), p. 34.

164. Ibid., p. 36.

165. For a representative narrative of the Palmer revival, see Sandra King, "Through

the Lens of History," in Canada's Christian Library Online, www.evangelical-fellowship.ca/page.aspx?pid=5616.

166. John Corrigan, *Business of the Heart: Reason and Emotion in the Nineteenth Century* (Berkeley: University of California Press, 2002), p. 225.

167. Quoted in ibid., p, 217.

168. Quoted in ibid., p. 221.

169. Long, op. cit., pp. 111–12.

170. Quoted in Long, op. cit., p. 33.

171. Quoted in ibid., pp. 34–35.

172. Quoted in ibid., p. 38.

173. Quoted in ibid., p. 37.

174. Ibid., p. 83.

175. Quoted in Corrigan, op. cit., p. 214.

176. Ibid., pp. 207–208.

177. Quoted in ibid., p. 218.

178. Quoted in ibid., p. 219.

179. Ibid., p. 219.

180. William Leach, *Land of Desire: Merchants, Power and the Rise of a New American Consumer Culture* (New York: Pantheon Books, 1993), pp. 196–202. This discussion of Wanamaker's life and career is deeply indebted to Leach's authoritative account.

181. Quoted in ibid., p. 203.

182. Quoted in ibid., p. 213.

183. Ibid., pp. 213–15.

184. Quoted in ibid., p. 209.

185. Quoted in Donald Meyer, *The Positive Thinkers: Religion as Pop Psychology from Mary Baker Eddy to Oral Roberts* (New York: Pantheon Books, 1980), p. 199.

186. Quoted in Leach, op. cit., p. 229.

187. Quoted in ibid., p. 229.

188. Quoted in ibid., p. 259

189 This account of Eddy's early life is drawn largely from Donald Meyer's excellent study *The Positive Thinkers: Religion as Pop Psychology from Mary Baker Eddy to Oral Roberts* (New York: Pantheon Books, 1980), pp. 38–41.

190. Catherine Tumber, *American Feminism and the Birth of New Age Spirituality: Searching for the Higher Self, 1875–1915* (Lanham, MD: Rowman & Littlefield, 2002), p. 8.

191. Quoted in Meyer, op. cit., p. 79.

192. Edward Chase Kirkland, *Dream and Thought in the American Business Community, 1860–1900* (New York: Quadrangle Books, 1964), p. 14.

193. Russell Conwell, *Acres of Diamonds* (biographical afterword by Robert Shackleton) (New York: Harper Brothers, 1915), pp. 31–38.

194. Ibid., p. 8.

195. Ibid., p. 11.

196. Ibid., p. 12.

Chapter 6: Liberals at the End of History

197. Walter Rauschenbusch, *Christianity and the Social Crisis* (New York: Macmillan, 1907), p. 141.

198. Philip J. Lee, *Against the Protestant Gnostics* (New York: Oxford University Press, 1993), p. 149.

199. Josiah Strong, *Our Country: Its Possible Future and Present Crisis* (New York: American Missionary Society, 1885), p. 1.

200. Ibid., p. 173.

201. Ibid., pp. 173–74.

202. Ibid., pp. 213–15.

203. Ibid., p. 222.

204. Bruce Barton, *The Man Nobody Knows: A Discovery of the Real Jesus* (New York: Ivan R. Dee reprint of 1925, Bobbs-Merrill edition), p. 13 and p. 15.

205. Ibid., p. 52.

206. Ibid., p. 21.

207. Ibid., p. 84.

208. Quoted in Richard M. Fried, "Introduction," ibid., p. xii.

209. Fried, ibid., p. xiii.

210. Fried, ibid., p. xiv.

211. Barton, ibid., p. 47.

212. Fried, ibid., p. xxii.

213. Ibid., p. 4.

214. Ibid., p. 9.

215. Ibid., p. 37.

216. Ibid., pp. 64–65.

217. Ibid., pp. 44–45.

218. Ibid., p. 87.

219. Quoted in Michael Kazin, *A Godly Hero: The Life of William Jennings Bryan* (New York: Knopf, 2006), p. 60.

220. Ibid., pp. 60–61.

221. Ibid., p. 110.

222. Quoted in ibid., pp. 71, 105.

223. Ibid., p. 155.

224. Ibid., p. 137.

225. Quoted in ibid., p. 138.

226. Quoted in ibid., pp. 139–40.

227. William Jennings Bryan, *The First Battle: A Story of the Campaign of 1896* (Cincinnati, OH: W. B. Conkey Co., 1896), p. 629.

228. Quoted in Kazin, op cit., p. 172.

229. Quoted in ibid., p. 175.

230. Quoted in ibid., p. 275.

231. Quoted in ibid., p. 121.

232. Quoted in ibid., p. 277.

Chapter 7: Holy Abundance

233. Quoted in Molly Worthen, *Apostles of Reason: The Crisis of Authority in American Evangelicalism* (New York: Oxford University Press, 2014), p. 31.

234. Joel A. Carpenter, *Revive Us Again: The Reawakening of American Fundamentalism* (New York: Oxford University Press, 1997), p. 127.

235. Ibid., pp. 131, 139.

236. Ibid., p. 32.

237. Meyer, op. cit., p. 234.

238. Ibid., p. 221.

239. Ibid., pp. 313–14.

240. Darren Dochuk, *From Bible Belt to Sun-Belt: Plain-Folk Religion, Grass-Roots Politics, and the Rise of Evangelical Conservatism* (New York: W. W. Norton, 2011), p. 158

241. This summary of Pentecostal origins draws on the account in Grant Wacker's excellent study, *Heaven Below: Early Pentecostals and American Culture* (Cambridge, MA: Harvard University Press, 2001), p. 2.

242. Ibid., p. 14.

243. Quoted in ibid., p. 140; emphasis in original.

244. Quoted in ibid., p. 140.

245. Ibid., p. 136.

246. Ibid., p. 136.

247. Ibid., p. 254.

248. Quoted in ibid., pp. 254, 251.

249. Ibid., p. 219.

250. Ibid., p. 246.

251. George R. Marsden, *Fundamentalism and American Culture* (New York: Oxford University Press, revised edition, 2006), p. 227.

252. Carpenter, op. cit., p. 235.

253. Marsden, op. cit., p. 93.

254. Kate Bowler, *Blessed: A History of the American Prosperity Gospel* (New York: Oxford University Press, 2013), p. 17.

255. Ibid., p. 18.

256. Quoted in ibid., p. 23.

257. Ibid., p. 25.

258. Hans Jonas, *The Gnostic Religion* (Boston: Beacon Press, Second Edition Revised, 1991), p. 329.

259. Quoted in Matthew Avery Sutton, *Aimee Semple McPherson and the Resurrection of Christian America* (Cambridge, MA: Harvard University Press, 2007), p. 11.

260. Ibid., pp. 12–13.

261. Ibid., p. 61.

262. Ibid., p. 72.

263. Ibid., pp. 233–34.

264. Ibid., p. 244.

265. Ibid., p. 236.

266. Quoted in Dochuk, op. cit., p. 45.

267. Ibid., p. 158.

268. Ibid., p. 159.

269. Ibid., pp. 165–66.

270. Ibid., p. 188.

271. Ibid., p. 169.

Chapter 8: A New Spirit of Capitalism

272. William R. Martin, *A Prophet with Honor: The Billy Graham Story* (New York: William R. Morrow, 1986), p. 115.

273. Dochuk, op cit., pp. 142–43.

274. Martin, op. cit., p. 165.

275. Ibid., p. 177.

276. For one representative sample of this argument, written within the Protestant mainstream, see William S. McElvaine, *Grand Theft Jesus: The Hijacking of Religion in America* (New York: Crown Books, 2009).

277. Quoted in Lee, op. cit., p. 210.

278. Will Herberg, Protestant-Catholic-Jew (Garden City, NY: Doubleday Books, 1956), p. 370.

279. See Carol V.B. George, *God's Salesman: Norman Vincent Peale and the Power of Positive Thinking* (New York: Oxford University Press, 1993), pp. 117–18. A random survey of *Guidepost* readers in 1957 found that "women outnumbered men in the readership by two to one . . . The evidence was frustrating to Peale, who had been on the speakers circuit trying to attract industrial supporters, arguing in some cases that the magazine could be helpful in defusing industrial strife, only to discover that the majority of readers (or those engaged enough to respond to the survey) were married, middle-aged Protestant women. Some of the industries that had been taking the paper dropped it after running into union opposition or lack of reader interest."

280. Ibid., p. 32.

281. Ibid., p. 66.

282. Ibid., pp. 93–94.

283. Ibid., p. 167; p. 64.

284. Ibid., pp. 169–70.

285. Ibid., pp. 179–80.

286. Ibid., p. 179.

287. Ibid., p. 180.

288. Ibid., p. 108.

289. Ibid., pp. 108–109.

290. Ibid., p. 167; on Peale's ongoing friendship, and occasional collaboration with Graham, see ibid., pp. 147–49, 200, and 209.

291. Ibid., p. 174.

292. Quoted in Meyer, op. cit., p. 268.

293. Ibid., pp. 262–63.

294. Norman Vincent Peale, *The Power of Positive Thinking and the Amazing Results of Positive Thinking* (New York: Fireside Books edition, 2005), pp. 30–31.

295. The term originated with Sidney Ahlstrom, *A Religious History of the American People* (New Haven: Yale University Press, 1972), p. 1034.

296. Peale, op. cit., pp. 42–43.

297. Ibid., p. 108.

298. Ibid., p. 88.

299. Dochuk, op. cit., p. 405.

300. Ibid., p. 179.

Chapter 9: New Gospels of the Protean Self

301. Richard Nelson Bolles, *What Color Is Your Parachute? A Practical Manual for Job Hunters and Career Changers* (Berkeley, CA: Ten-Speed Press, Revised ed., 1974), pp. 83–84; emphasis in original.

302. Nikil Saval, *Cubed: A Secret History of the Workplace* (New York: Doubleday, 2014), pp. 205–14.

303. Bethany Moreton, *To Serve God and Wal-Mart: The Making of Christian Free Enterprise* (Cambridge, MA: Harvard University Press, 2009), pp. 107–11.

304. Ibid., p. 102.

305. Marabel Morgan, *The Total Woman* (Old Tappan, NJ: Fleming H. Revell, 1973), p. 31.

306. Ibid., p. 70.

307. Ibid., p. 58.

308. Ibid., p. 38.

309. Ibid., p. 87.

310. Jennifer Heller, "Marriage, Womanhood, and the Search for 'Something More': American Evangelical Women's Best-Selling Self-Help Books, 1972–1979," *Journal of Religion and Popular Culture 2* (Fall 2002), www.usask.ca/relst/jrpc/article-selfhelp.html.

311. Morgan, op. cit., p. 178.

312. Quoted in Heller, op, cit.

313. James Davison Hunter, *American Evangelicalism: Conservative Religion and the Quandary of Modernity* (New Brunswick, NJ: Rutgers University Press, 1983), pp. 98–99.

314. Cited in George, op. cit., p. 150.

315. Dochuk, op. cit., p. 180.

316. Oral Roberts, *A Daily Guide to Miracles and Successful Living through Seed-Faith* (Grand Rapids Michigan: F. H. Revell, 1980), pp. 228–31.

317. Bowler, op. cit., p. 59.

318. Ibid., p. 60.

319. Meyer, op. cit., p. 352.

320. David Edwin Harrell Jr., *All Things Are Possible: The Healing and Charismatic*

Revivals in Modern America (Bloomington: Indiana University Press, 1979), p. 147.

321. Bowler, op. cit., p. 73.

322. Ibid., p. 72.

323. Harrell, op. cit., p. 152.

324. See Worthen, op. cit., pp. 225–31.

325. Hal Lindsey, *The Late Great Planet Earth* (Grand Rapids, MI: Zondervan, 1970), p. 138.

326. See, for example, Bowler, op. cit., pp. 70–71.

327. Ibid., p. 96.

328. Ibid., p. 77.

329. Ibid., pp. 98–99.

330. Ibid., p. 100.

331. Quoted in James Hudnut-Beumler, *In Pursuit of the Almighty's Dollar: A History of Money and American Protestantism* (Chapel Hill, NC: University of North Carolina Press, 2007), p. 178.

332. Francis Schaeffer, *How Should We Then Live? L'Abri 50th Anniversary Edition* (Wheaton IL: Crossway Books, 2005), pp. 114, 205, and 210.

333. Jerry Falwell, *Listen America! A Conservative Blueprint for Moral Rebirth* (New York: Bantam Books, 1981), p. 7.

334. See D. G. Hart, *From Billy Graham to Sarah Palin: Evangelicals and the Betrayal of American Conservatism* (Grand Rapids, MI: W. B. Eerdmans, 2011), pp. 111–13.

335. Ibid., p. 1.

336. Moreton, op. cit., p. 35.

337. Ibid., p. 55.

338. Ibid., p. 89.

339. Ibid., p. 185.

340. Ibid., pp. 215–16.

341. Ibid., p. 228.

342. www.jameshunter.com/clients.htm.

343. James C. Hunter, *The Servant: A Simple Story About the True Essence of Leadership* (New York: Crown Business, 1998), pp. 5–6.

344. Ibid., p. 42.

345. Ibid., pp. 42–43.

346. Ibid., p. 44.

347. Renee Dudley, "Customers Flee Wal-Mart Empty Shelves for Target, Costco," Bloomberg News, March 26, 2013. www.bloomberg.com/news/2013-03-26/customers-flee-wal-mart-empty-shelves-for-target-costco.html.

Chapter 10: Secret Histories

348. www.people-press.org/2010/06/22/section-3-war-terrorism-and-global-trends/.

349. Lindsey, op. cit., p. 85.

350. See, for example, David S. Wells, *No Place for Truth: Whatever Happened to*

Evangelical Theology? (Grand Rapids: William Eerdmans, 1994); Mark A. Noll, *The Scandal of the Evangelical Mind* (Grand Rapids: William Eerdmans, 1995).

351. Paul Boyer, *When Time Shall Be No More: Prophecy Belief in Modern American Culture* (Cambridge, MA: Harvard University Press, 1992), p. 308.

352. Ibid., pp. 310–11.

353. Quoted in ibid., p. 299.

354. Joel C. Rosenberg, *Implosion: Can America Recover from Its Economic and Spiritual Challenges in Time?* (Carol Stream, IL: Tyndale House, 2012), p. 324.

355. Ibid., pp. 290–91.

356. Tim LaHaye and Jerry B. Jenkins, *Armageddon: The Cosmic Battle of the Ages* (Wheaton, IL: Tyndale House, 2003), pp. 249–50.

357. Tim LaHaye and Jerry B. Jenkins, *Nicolae: The Rise of the Antichrist* (Wheaton, IL: Tyndale House, 1997), p. 12.

358. Ibid., p. 18.

359. Ibid., pp. 24–25.

360. Tim LaHaye and Jerry B. Jenkins, *Tribulation Force: The Continuing Story of Those Left Behind* (Wheaton, IL: Tyndale House, 1996), pp. 90–91.

361. Tim LaHaye and Jerry B. Jenkins, *The Mark: The Beast Rules the World* (Wheaton, IL: Tyndale House, 2000), pp. 58–59.

362. Tim LaHaye and Jerry B. Jenkins, *Assassins: Assignment: Jerusalem, Target: Antichrist* (Wheaton, IL: Tyndale House, 1999), p. 311.

363. LaHaye and Jenkins, *Tribulation Force*, op. cit., p. 337.

364. Tim LaHaye and Jerry B. Jenkins, *Apollyon: The Destroyer Is Unleashed* (Wheaton, IL: Tyndale House, 1999), pp. 197–98.

365. Tim LaHaye and Jerry B. Jenkins, *Assassins*, op. cit., p. 131.

366. Ibid., p. 149.

367. Tim LaHaye and Jerry B. Jenkins, *Desecration: Antichrist Takes the Throne* (Wheaton, IL: Tyndale House, 2001), pp. 293, 290.

368. Ibid., p. 307.

369. Ibid., p. 290.

370. Tim LaHaye and Jerry B. Jenkins, *Soul Harvest: The World Takes Sides* (Wheaton, IL: Tyndale House, 1998), p. 307.

371. *The Mark*, op. cit., p. 292.

372. Tim LaHaye and Jerry B. Jenkins, *Glorious Appearing: The End of Days* (Wheaton, IL: Tyndale House, 2004), pp. 60–61.

373. Ibid., p. 61.

374. Ibid., p. 352.

375. *The Indwelling*, op. cit., pp. 77–78.

376. Ibid., p. 132.

377. Ibid., p. 149.

378. Ibid., p. 157.

379. Ibid., p. 230.

380. Ibid., p. 362.

381. Ibid., p. 235.

382. Ibid., p. 237.

383. Ibid., p. 190.

384. Ibid., p. 333.

385. Ibid., p. 134.

386. Ibid., p. 298.

387. Ibid., p. 340.

388. Ibid., p. 369.

389. Ibid., p. 339.

Conclusion

390. religion.blogs.cnn.com/2013/11/08/the-obamacare-question-pastors-shun/.

391. Joel Osteen, *Your Best Life Now: 7 Steps to Living at Your Full Potential* (New York: Faith Works, 2004), pp. 24–25.

392. Typical of many Osteen quotations from Scripture, this phrasing is completely sundered from its context. In Romans 8:35–37, Paul describes the afflictions that the martyrs of the early Church suffer at the hands of their persecutors: "Who shall separate us from the love of Christ? Shall trouble or hardship or persecution or famine or nakedness or the sword? As it is written: 'For your sake we face death all day long; we are considered as sheep to be slaughtered. No, in all these things we are more than conquerors through him who loved us.'" But in Osteen's usage, there's no remote suggestion that believers are expected to suffer any discomfort as a price of their faith—let alone that they "face death all day long" and stoically accept that fate like lambs bound for the slaughter. Rather, the image of conquest here is one of unalloyed spiritual transcendence—of a believer serenely recognizing his divine birthright in the material realm.

393. Ibid., p. 86.

394. Ibid., p. 283.

395. Ibid., p. 284.

396. Ibid., p. 285.

397. Ibid., p. 294.

398. Ibid., p. 298.

399. Ibid., p. 125.

400. Ibid., p. 169.

401. Ibid., p. 265.

402. Joel Osteen, *Become a Better You: 7 Keys to Improving Your Life Every Day* (New York: Free Press, 2007), p. 289.

403. www.christianpost.com/news/joel-osteen-im-for-everybody-but-same-sex-marriage-is-not-in-the-bible-92920/.

404. Osteen, *Become a Better You*, p. 292.

Index

Social Gospel (*cont.*)
Barton's *The Man Nobody Knows*, xiv, 202–206; Bryan, 207, 219; Primitive Church tradition, 196–97, 202, 205, 207; Rauschenbusch, 196–202; Strong, 196, 198–202
Soderquist, Don, 317–18
Southern Baptists, 229, 261, 301
Spencer, Herbert, 186
Spiritual Mobilization, 270, 273
Stanley, Charles, 358–59
Stiles, Ezra, 30
Stoddard, Samuel, 44
Stone, Barton W., 90
Stowe, Harriet Beecher, 164
Stringfellow, George E., 271
Strong, Josiah, 196, 198–202, 230
Students in Free Enterprise (SIFE), 318–19
Sunday, Billy, 225
Sunday school movement, 169, 172–74
Sutton, Hilton, 334
Sutton, Matthew Avery, 251–53
Swaggart, Jimmy, 307–308

Taft, William Howard, 214–15
televangelism, 248, 307–10
Tennent, Gilbert, 36, 55
Servant, The (Hunter), 320–24
therapeutic spirituality (self-improvement): Businessman's Revival, 154–55, 174, 178; evangelical, 264–69, 272, 273–83, 275, 284–87, 297–300; New Thought, 178–85, 216, 272, 275
Thomas, Norman, 205
Tocqueville, Alexis de, xxviii
Todd, John, xxiii
Total Woman, The (Morgan), 292–97
Towne, Elizabeth, 179
Transcendentalists, 117–23
Trine, Ralph Waldo, 185, 192, 206

Trinity Broadcasting Network, 308
Tumber, Catherine, 183, 191

Vanderbilt, Cornelius, 185
Wacker, Grant, 235, 236–37, 239–40
Wagner, C. Peter, 264
Wagner, Charles, 170–71
Wal-Mart, 314–20, 322, 324–25
Walton, Sam, 314–15, 318–19
Walton International Scholarship Program, 319
Wanamaker, John, 168–76, 185
Warren, Rick, xiv
Weber, Max, xvii–xx, 15–17, 28, 235
Welch, Bob, 258
Wells, Bob, 257–58
Wesley, John, 234, 241
What Color Is Your Parachute? (Bolles), 285–87
Whitefield, George, 32–62; First Great Awakening revival, 32–62, 64, 69, 83, 89–90, 93; New Birth theology, 37–38, 43, 45, 47–48, 57–58, 60; Primitive Church tradition, 52–60
Whitefield, James, 41, 46
Wigglesworth, Samuel, 36
Wilcox, Ella Wheeler, 216–17
Williams, David, 31
Williams, Roger, 13–14, 18, 21
Winthrop, John, 5–14, 18, 22, 39; the "City upon a Hill," 5–13, 68; "A Modell of Christian Charity," 5, 36
Winthrop, John, Jr., 25–26
Wise, John, 26
Wizard of Oz series (Baum), 180–82
women, evangelical, 291–97
Word of Faith tradition (Pentecostal), 245–49, 303, 308–10, 363–66, 371–72, 374; evangelical televangelists, 308–10; Hagin, 308–309; Osteen, 248, 363–66, 371–72
Worthen, Molly, 305

About the Author

CHRIS LEHMANN is the coeditor of *Bookforum*, senior editor and columnist for *The Baffler*, and columnist for *In These Times*. He has written for *Harper's Magazine*, *The Atlantic Monthly*, *The Washington Post*, *Slate*, *Salon*, *The Nation*, and many other publications. He is the author of *Rich People Things* and *Revolt of the Masscult*.